Oracle Press

Oracle Database 12*c*
Install, Configure & Maintain Like a Professional

Oracle Press™

Oracle Database 12*c*
Install, Configure & Maintain
Like a Professional

Ian Abramson
Michael Abbey
Michelle Malcher
Michael Corey

New York   Chicago   San Francisco   Athens
London   Madrid   Mexico City   Milan
New Delhi   Singapore   Sydney   Toronto

Cataloging-in-Publication Data is on file with the Library of Congress

Oracle Database 12c: Install, Configure & Maintain Like a Professional

1234567890   DOC DOC   109876543

ISBN   978-0-07-179933-1
MHID   0-07-179933-8

Sponsoring Editor	**Copy Editor**
Paul Carlstroem	Nancy Rapoport
Editorial Supervisor	**Proofreader**
Jody McKenzie	Lisa McCoy
Project Manager	**Indexer**
Nidhi Chopra, Cenveo® Publisher Services	Karin Arrigoni
Acquisitions Coordinator	**Production Supervisor**
Amanda Russell	George Anderson
Contributors	**Composition**
Fahd Mirza Chughtai, Marc Fielding, Michael McKee	Cenveo Publisher Services
	Art Director, Cover
Technical Editor	Jeff Weeks
Albert Hui	

We dedicate this book to all of our children who make us so proud each and every day—Ann Marie, Baila, Ben, Emily, Jillian, John, Jordan, Mandy, Michael Jr., Naomi, and Nathan.

About the Authors

Ian Abramson (@iabramson) lives in Toronto, Canada, where he works for EPAM Systems as the Canadian Director of Enterprise Data, a global leader in software engineering. Ian is a graduate in Mathematics from Concordia University in Montreal. His involvement with implementing solutions using Oracle technology and data warehouses reaches back over 25 years, as a developer of creative and innovative solutions for clients around the globe. He is the past president of the IOUG (Independent Oracle Users Group) and continues to share his knowledge through his lively presentations and published technical articles and blog. In his spare time, Ian spends his free time golfing in the summer and playing hockey in the winter.

Michael S. Abbey (@MichaelAbbeyCAN) has done nothing but Oracle since V3 in 1986. He has been a frequent presenter at tech shows on four continents since the early 1990s and started writing for Oracle Press in 1994. He is a well-known tech in the Oracle space and has a voracious appetite for the CORE Oracle technology. Michael has been actively involved in the user group programs for over two decades and is an Oracle ACE.

Michelle Malcher (@malcherm) is the current president of the Independent Oracle Users Group (IOUG). She is an Oracle ACE Director with more than 15 years' experience in database development, security, design, and administration. Michelle is based in Chicago, USA, where she leads a team of database developers and administrators. She has contributed articles to the *IOUG Select Journal*, has written the *Oracle Database Administration for Microsoft SQL Server DBAs*, and has contributed to other Oracle Press books. She enjoys presenting and sharing ideas about Oracle database topics at conferences and user group meetings.

Michael Corey (@Michael_Corey) is Founder and Chief Executive Officer of Ntirety. Michael is a frequent speaker at technology and business conferences throughout the world, from Australia to Brazil. Michael is a VMware vExpert and Oracle ACE, and is on the Talkin' Cloud 200 Computing Executives and Experts List.

Michael is a past president of the Independent Oracle Users Group; he helped found the Professional Association of SQL Server, is a current board member of the IOUG Virtualization SIG, and is actively involved in numerous professional associations and industry user groups. Michael is the original Oracle Press author and a frequent blogger for Database Trends and Applications, and has written numerous articles and books.

About the Contributing Authors

Fahd Mirza Chughtai (@fahdmirza) is all things Oracle. He is Oracle certified, and is an Oracle ACE, Oracle blogger, Oracle conference presenter, and a veteran Oracle expert. Starting from the wonders of Oracle 7, through the innovation of various Oracle technologies, Mirza is now immersed in Exadata. He lives in Australia with his wife, Yusra, and son, Ahnaf.

Marc Fielding (@mfild) is a passionate and creative problem solver, drawing on a deep understanding of the full enterprise application stack to identify the root cause of problems. He has extensive experience implementing Oracle's engineered system portfolio, including leading one of the first reference Oracle Exadata implementations. When not working, he can be found on the trail or ski slope, or indulging his latest passion, scuba diving.

Michael McKee has been working in the Oracle environment since 1994. He has multiple Oracle certifications and has been involved in all aspects of the Oracle database life cycle. He is currently living in Belfast, Northern Ireland, with his wife and three children.

About the Technical Editor

Albert Hui (@DataEconomist) is a BIDW, Big Data and Machine Learning, architect with over ten years of experience with Oracle products. Albert is a technology evangelist and researcher and has delivered a few multiterabyte data warehouses in Canada using Oracle. He frequently speaks at technology conferences around the world on topics of BIDW. He holds two master's degrees—one in engineering and one in business management.

Contents at a Glance

Contents

Acknowledgments

Ian Abramson

The process of writing a book is long and arduous, yet it provides such a rewarding conclusion.

There are many people who have helped me to achieve so much during my time as a data professional. My parents, Lily and Joe, encouraged a love of learning and logic. They provided the foundation for the person I have become and their memory lives on through me and my family. To my wife, Susan, and children, Baila and Jillian, you are my rock. Together we form a team that can't be beat. I am so lucky to have you on my side and appreciate all the support and help you've given me, and I hope I've done the same for you. My children have come so far in such a short time and I could not be prouder of them. They have both graduated with Honors from McMaster University; I am so gratified to see who they have become. Of course, a thanks to all the Astroffs, Wesikopfs, and Abramsons in my life. You guys all add to the fun.

I also have so many people to thank who have contributed to my life with Oracle databases and data in general. You have all taught me something along the way and in many ways helped me to write this book. Of course, my thanks to my coauthors Michael Abbey, Michelle Malcher, and Mike Corey who have helped me so much in getting this done and allowing me to be part of a dynamic and amazing writing team. Thanks to our contributors and editors, Albert Hui, Marc Fielding, Fahd Mirza, and Michael McKee—you have all helped to make this book the best ever. To all my friends at the IOUG and to the rest of the Oracle community, thank you. In particular, I would like to thank Ari Kaplan, Rich Neimeic, David Teplow, Todd Sheetz, Andy Flower, Carol McGury and everyone at SmithBucklin, Carl Dudley, John Matelski, Mike Gangler, and Judi Dolittle. I want to thank the many people who make EPAM (previously Thoughtcorp) a company that nurtures greatness: Kirk Robinson, David Bercovitch, Arkadiy Dobkin, Anatoliy Chudnovskiy, Ilya Cantor, Alex Lyashok, Victor Dvorkin, Howard Bigelow, Sam Rehman, Andrei Dzianisau, Predrag Stegnajic, Art Gray, Bob Paquin, Mark Rechsteiner, Jason Lee, Valentina Hedow, Nicole Devlin, Gino Marckx, Derek Mitchell, Tom Klimovski, Dino Chronopoulos, and so many others who have inspired me as part of these growing and thriving organizations. Finally, I want to thank my friends who impact me on a daily basis. You all are an important part of my life and make me strive to be a better person as well as a better golfer and hockey player. Thanks to Mark Kerzner and all the Kerzners (Arlene, Marissa, Amanda, Shane, and Dalia), Marc and Lydia Allaire, Gerry Belanger, Mike and Susie Brown, Jim Boutin, Terry and Sofie Butts, Chris Clarke and Noni Femby, Mark Davey, Ted Falcon, Moti Fishman, Pete Fortier, Judy and Roy Fricker, Ron and Ann Katz, Tim Haller, Rich and Ada Ljubecic, Marshall Lucatch, Ron and Jeff McIntosh, Doug Morgan, Al Murphy, Ken Sheppard, Lionel Silverman, Tom Tishler, and last but not least, Yak (Lawrie Yakabowsky). Thanks to everyone. In many ways it is because of all of you that I am here today and have this opportunity to help others. I thank you all for being part of my journey.

Michael Abbey
I would like to thank each and every one of you who has contributed to my lively career with the Oracle database software for the past 27 years. It has been a magic carpet ride from the beginning, way back in the 80s, to now. I've loved having you all along for the ride. Startup…

Michelle Malcher
It continues to be an awesome journey, and I want to thank all of you for being a part of it. Thank you to the coauthors of this book for your hard work and encouragement to make this a great project to be a part of. Thanks to my family, and especially my junior DBAs, Amanda and Emily, for their understanding and support. Thanks to all involved in the IOUG. Thank you for volunteering—keep sharing ideas and working with each other to sharpen each other's skills and grow careers.

Michael Corey
Thanks to a great group of authors who made this book possible. Thank you to the many people behind the scenes that supported everyone in this effort.

Introduction

This book provides the reader with an introduction to Oracle Database 12*c* and some of the state-of-the-art offerings of Oracle. It has been a long journey for technicians who have focused their careers on Oracle's technology all the way back to the late 1970s. Many skills acquired along the way are portable, and are upwardly compatible to the latest release. This is true for Database 12*c*. A large portion of what some readers may already know is applicable to this new release. What this book will do for the reader is

- Provide a foundation for people just getting started with the software

- Enhance existing skill sets with an idea of what is new with this latest release

- Pinpoint the highlights of what is important to get to know in the database, development, and engineered machine areas of 12*c*

- Introduce SQL*Plus and PL/SQL, the original and omni-powerful query languages with which one creates and manipulates data in the data repository

What's in This Book

The following chapter-by-chapter outline will guide you through the plethora of information presented in *Oracle Database 12c: Install, Configure & Maintain Like a Professional.*

Chapter 1: The Database: The Foundations of 12*c*

You are introduced to the volume of information and how it can be stored in the database. The chapter gives a brief introduction to data types and highlights concepts related to managing that data. It closes with an overview of some of the most important new features of the 12*c* offering.

Chapter 2: Installing Oracle

We show how the database software is installed and guide the reader through the network of screens and suggested answers to the many questions posed by the GUI installer. Many different types of configurations are available for the database, and this chapter follows one of the most common.

Chapter 3: SQL: Accessing and Retrieving Data

SQL*Plus is the heart of this chapter, which introduces fundamentals and covers syntax that will allow you to get started writing queries. We cover a number of ways to work with the data and familiarize the reader with how to go about creating, manipulating, and deleting data.

Chapter 4: Programming in the Database

Here we cover Oracle's procedural programming language called PL/SQL. Once you start programming with SQL*Plus, a more procedural approach is required to be able to process data sets in a sequential manner, similar to how aging developers may have used third-generation languages in the '80s and '90s.

Chapter 5: The Database Administrator

The database administrator plays the role of the technical gatekeeper of the database. The DBA manages the day-to-day operations of the database and serves the technology and end-user requirements to carry on a company's business. We cover some of the most common ongoing activities played by this all-important person, thereby giving the reader a taste of this role from the start.

Chapter 6: Backup and Recovery

We delve into the ever-popular and strong Recovery Manager (RMAN) tool and highlight its strengths and syntax. We include discussions on the types of backups you can write using RMAN and delve into the important topics of restore and recovery.

Chapter 7: High Availability: RAC, ASM, and Data Guard

This chapter is dedicated to the functionality embedded in Oracle Database 12c that keeps your applications running 24/7. One of the earliest questions new DBAs and managers ask is how one ensures that the database is always available. This chapter introduces the reader to a handful of the most important ways to bring that desire to fruition.

Chapter 8: Using and Managing Large Databases

One cannot listen to any form of media on the Internet or traditional airwaves without hearing about the ever-expanding size of data stores and the need to store larger and large volumes of data. Many new buzzwords have surfaced over the past few years, of which "big data" may be the most commonly heard. With the need to store and retrieve more and more unstructured data, the size of many databases has become overwhelming. This chapter dives into some of what Oracle has put together to manage this explosion of data.

Chapter 9: Oracle's Engineered Systems: From the Database Appliance to Exadata

Given the complexities of managing hardware and software, many corporations have thirsted for off-the-shelf solutions that can deliver an out-of-the-box solution for their business requirements. In this chapter, we discuss the heart of the solutions offered by Oracle in this very competitive arena.

Intended Audience

This book is suitable for the following readers:

- Database administrators and their managers who are just getting started with using the Oracle database product suite

- Developers who are looking for some knowledge of the database offering and how it could affect their day-to-day work

- Non-technical persons looking for a quick-start introduction to Oracle Database 12*c*

- Technical personnel looking for a broader understanding of state-of-the-art offerings from Oracle

No prior knowledge of the Oracle database, SQL, or PL/SQL is assumed. Everything you need to know to get started with Oracle database technology is covered in this book.

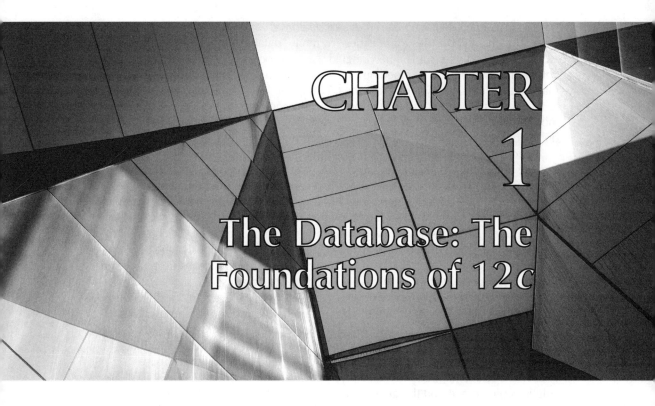

CHAPTER
1

The Database: The
Foundations of 12c

CRITICAL SKILLS

1.1 Define a Database

1.2 Become Familiar with the
Characteristics of a Database

1.3 Learn When to Use a Database

1.4 Learn the Oracle Database 12c
Architecture

1.5 Work with Objects in the Oracle
Database

1.6 Work with Data Types in an Oracle
Database

1.7 Pull It All Together: Objects and
Data Types

1.8 Interact with the Data

1.9 Learn the New Features of Oracle
Database 12c

Most people have heard the term *database*, which has been a buzzword in many industries for decades. To many, database processing is old hat, but to others it is a newfangled way to process information. Large corporations have been stampeding to the database market for decades. Is it really that special? Just ask anyone—from the CTOs of the large multinationals all the way to the local utility providers. The information storage and processing needs of industry and consumers over the past 30 years have blossomed into multibillions of dollars of expenses for every facet of the modern community.

Oracle has been developing corporate information storage solutions since its humble beginnings in the mid to late 1970s. After gargantuan growth through the 1990s and the first decade of the twenty-first century, Oracle is now positioned as *the* leader in the relational database technology space. This chapter is the beginning for the *beginner*. We will cover the following in the next few dozen pages, serving as the foundation to just about everything this monolithic company has brought to the market. Here comes that word again—*database*. A small fraction of the population has rubbed shoulders with database processing and rolled its sleeves up and gotten into the management engines that work directly with databases.

This chapter is the beginning of your descent into databaseland. Oddly enough, the deeper you get into databases, the more familiar words you run across. This time, rather than appearing at the end of a book and allowing the reader to quickly get to a topic of interest, the *index* is something in the database built to facilitate rapid access. Dr. E. F. Codd wrote about a newfangled concept for databases involving a relational model. In the early 1980s, vendors offering relational database solutions blossomed and the giants released early versions of some systems that are still commonplace today. The appearance of the World Wide Web highlighted a new need for information processing—the world. Never before had so much information been at consumers' fingertips. Some of the retail giants of yesteryear have withered away and fallen off the face of the earth. Over 120 years ago, R. W. Sears and A. C. Roebuck's brainchild was born. Now this behemoth is struggling; for whatever reason they must have been late embracing the electronic online shopping community. Where does that community hang out? In every corner of information technology, the community hangs out with a database—here a database, there a database, everywhere a database. Some web sites report over three billion email accounts around the world and over half a billion web sites. Where is all that data stored? You got that right … the database.

The capability to trap vast amounts of data and deliver it to a computer monitor in seconds has changed our lives. Picture the late 1800s. Lovers of chess used to play with opponents thousands of kilometers away. Moves would get sent back and forth by surface mail. Mordecai (white) would send a letter to Jacob … P-K4, a standard chess opening. If all went well, Jacob would receive this opening thrust and parry with P-K4. A year later, there was a grand total of thirteen moves by each player, with Mordecai's last move terminating with the exclamation *check MATE*.

Imagine, Jacob knew the game was over two to three weeks after his adversary. Fast-forward to 2012; google the words "online chess" to the tune of 141,000,000 results. After 82 pages of hits, Google exclaims, "In order to show you the most relevant results, we have omitted some entries very similar to the 820 already displayed. If you like, you can repeat the search with the omitted results included." We all know what made this possible—call it a database, *base de données, base de datos,* βάση δεδομένων, *adatbázis, cơ sở dữ liệu*—call it a miracle. Let's get started on the magic carpet ride we call *Oracle Database 12c: Install, Configure & Maintain Like a Professional.* Hold on tight; the going could get rough but it is worth the trip.

Define a Database

There are probably as many ways to define a database as there are administrators that care take these huge information repositories. In the very early days of studying information systems, we were told that a database is a set of *self-describing data;* that is a very good beginning. Someone else has defined a database as *a bunch of files.* What is meant by "self-describing"? Simply put, look nowhere else; it's right in front of you. Think of *onomatopoeia*—a figure of speech in many languages for a word that, when uttered out loud, sounds like what it means. One needs look no further upon hearing the word "boom" to figure out that it is more than likely a sudden and loud noise. Onomatopoetic words are self-describing. Were one to look under the covers at a database, one would find a similar phenomenon—data organized in a way that jumps out at you and describes itself. Let's translate that into elements of data that require no explanation. Lo and behold, an electronic collection of personnel information in a database is called *PERSON.* It almost jumps out at you. What would one expect to find in a collection entitled *PERSON?* It's obvious because it is *self-describing.*

A more familiar definition is as follows: *A database is an organized collection of data typically in digital format.* Once you become more familiar with databases in general and 12*c* in particular that definition still holds water. As you will see from reading the next few sections, what was once a very simple concept has blossomed into a network of electronic information repositories with billions of users in the global community.

Suppose you have a collection of information referred to as PERSON and dig a bit deeper into its contents and find more descriptive information about what it contains. What could be simpler? It seems that one can't walk any further than the corner store without stumbling into this well-used and somewhat familiar word "database." If you think of an information repository like a database, it seems so simple. You enter some information on a screen, click a button (or tab through different fields on the Amdahl mainframe using an IRMA board on your 8088!), and the characters are sent to a file and electronically stored for further retrieval at any time. That's where the fun begins. It's so simple to say "store data" and "retrieve data" but when put into practice, it is a great deal more complicated than it seems.

This is where modern relational database engines such as Oracle come into play. There's a new word—*relational*. Using this new word, let's expand on our original definition of a database, which now becomes *multiple sets of self-describing data, which are interrelated*. So in addition to PERSON, you then have a BUSINESS_UNIT collection of information, the composition of both items illustrating the relationship between data. Picture the following:

```
Each individual in PERSON works for one and only one BUSINESS_UNIT
As an individual is created in PERSON, a BUSINESS_UNIT is recorded
As people are recorded in person, only valid business units are
permitted
```

What more could there be? The relationships between collections of information in a database are the heart of the information storage tasks performed by database management software. Part of the job of database software is to enforce rules about the relationships between the information it manages. Here comes another twist to our definition of a database … *not only is it an electronically stored collection of data, but also a definer and enforcer on ways one item of information relates to other items.*

The characteristics of the modern database are too numerous to cover here; suffice it to say that a database must be capable of:

- Storing enormous amounts of information
- Providing mechanisms to get that information onto the user's screen
- Defining and providing an engine to enforce relationships between the data
- Permitting different views of the same data to satisfy a wide range of business needs
- Merging data sets that physically reside in different geographic locations
- Storing text data in every thinkable character set from the simplest (for example, English) to the most complex (for example, Chinese, Thai, and Arabic)

It's possible that a four-story library containing 4,000,000 books was the first database and no one knew it. Let's move on to further discussions of items crucial to the rest of the material presented throughout this book. You now know that a database is an organized set of self-describing information whose relationships between different bits of information are defined and enforced by the database's management software.

CRITICAL SKILL 1.2

Become Familiar with the Characteristics of a Database

As the information superhighway expands and as time marches on, the volume of data created by corporations grows exponentially. Not too many decades ago, many of us tingled in anticipation with excitement when we bought a PC with 40 rather than 20 megabytes of storage. We wondered how we could possibly ever think of using that much space on a hard drive. Realistically, compared to the overwhelming volume of data now traveling around corporate computer systems, the so-called *information superhighway* of the 1960s (when the expression was coined) was actually the *information dirt path*. When confronted with the task of storing more and more data, the speed of computer processing has expanded at a staggering pace. A book used in some information processing college courses in the 1970s explained that if there had been as many advances in the automobile industry in the past decade as there had been in computers, one would be able to buy a Rolls Royce for 25 cents that would last forever. Let's delve into three complexities of information processing that have brought the relational database technology onto the radar of all IT professionals—storage, data consistency, and data integrity.

Sharing

This is the mainstay of database management. In the past, companies often had many copies of the same data. Everyone is relieved that technology finally put an end to that. In days gone by, data anomalies were easily introduced into systems. In the days where clerks trapped the exact same data in multiple places, how did you handle updates? The change would have to be rippled through a variety of locations, and there was always a good possibility something would be left out of the updating exercise. Picture the surprise when the billing address spreadsheet said someone lived in a different place than that stored in human resources. Perhaps someone remembered to change only twelve of thirteen separate pieces of information, and thus the thirteenth became out of sync.

Why not store data in one and only one place and share it among organizations within the same company? Once that sharing is considered, experts begin to conjure up an assortment of problems that need to be addressed, including the following:

- **Security** Who is going to be allowed to work with what data?

- **Concurrent access** How will we be able to handle simultaneous access to exactly the same pieces of information?

■ **Filtering** How will the data be presented to different persons such that they see only what they are supposed to see?

■ **Auditing** How will anyone know who has done what with what data?

■ **Standards** Whose solution is going to be adopted for storage, retrieval, and manipulation of corporate data?

The previous five bullet points are just the tip of the iceberg … onward and upward.

Storage

Database management software vendors partner with purveyors of disk storage to enable quick reads from and writes to the files within which data is stored. By leaving the complexities of storage to the professionals, database management software is left alone to do what it does best. In the 1990s, we worked with databases in the many hundreds of megabytes arena, and now some professionals are tasked with managing databases that are thousands of gigabytes in size or more.

The volume of information modern processors, I/O systems, and disk technology are capable of working with grows in leaps and bounds daily. Table 1-1 presents some familiar (and some not-so-familiar) storage prefixes, the last few lines of which are intoxicating to the database management vendors. How long will it be until modern database and storage administrators will be confronted with supporting databases in excess of 10 exabytes?

As the size of databases increases, the challenge to the vendors is to ensure I/O operations are not a processing bottleneck. The size of many multinational corporate

Prefix	Bytes	Power of 2
Kilo	1,024	10
Mega	1,048,576	20
Giga	1,073,741,824	30
Tera	1,099,511,627,776	40
Peta	1,125,899,906,842,624	50
Exa	1,152,921,504,606,846,976	60
Zetta	1,180,591,620,717,411,303,424	70
Yotta	1,208,925,819,614,629,174,706,176	80

TABLE 1-1. *Storage Prefixes*

information repositories is staggering. As these databases grow and grow, the challenge is still three-fold:

- Getting the data into the database quickly

- Ensuring the data can be found after it has painstakingly been stored on high-speed disk

- Retrieving that data to satisfy processing requests by the applications with which it interacts

How the data is stored and where it is stored are best left to the database management suppliers as that is the mainstay of their business.

Data Consistency

This touches on the accuracy and usability of one's data. By nature, applications are used simultaneously by multiple users. As personnel interact with the database, they create, update, and delete data: INSERT, UPDATE, and DELETE are the buzzwords used in the relational database arena. The best way to illustrate the concept of data consistency is through the following sequence of events:

- An employee retrieves a personnel record on the screen and begins changing that person's benefits code from Y-22 to Y-27. The changed information sits on the screen until saved.

- Another person gets a copy of exactly the same personnel record and sees the benefits code of Y-22. Upon attempting to save the new value, an error message appears on the screen mentioning the fact that someone else has that row of information reserved for update.

- The operator saves her work, thereby making the new benefits code available to other sessions.

- The second user refetches that personnel record and sees the updated benefits code of Y-27.

Initially, you may think this is no big deal, but what is going on in the background is staggering. Oracle automatically provides read consistency at many levels:

- **To a query** All the data that a query sees comes from a single point-in-time; this is referred to as *statement-level read consistency*. Oracle guarantees that all data returned by a single query comes from a single point-in-time, the time the query began.

- **To a series of queries bundled together in a transaction** Oracle enforces the execution in serializable mode; all data accesses reflect the state of the database as of the time the transaction began.

Figure 1-1 illustrates the concept of read consistency. While Nick is performing an update to the row, Jenn's session reads the original state of the data that has been preserved using a special mechanism called the *undo segment.* This special entity is the approach Oracle has implemented to preserve read consistency.

Note the following about the views shown in Figure 1-2:

- At the outset, Nick and Jenn are looking at exactly the same data; they are both reading the row contents from Oracle's database files.

- Once Nick initiates his changes, Jenn's view stays exactly the same as before he started his update; Jenn is reading the row with its original column values partially from this undo segment. If Jenn were allowed to read the data as Nick was in the process of changing it, initially that would seem like a good idea. This undo segment and the read consistent model enable you to avoid a plague of the multiuser relational database management system called a *dirty read.*

- When Nick saves his work, Jenn's view changes to reflect the edits done by Nick; the image of the pre-update data maintained in the undo segment is released, as it is no longer used.

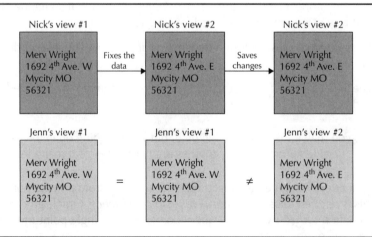

FIGURE 1-1. *Maintaining a read consistent view for all users*

Invoice # 2012-12-10-01

Jerry's Refuse Removal Services			Raleigh Apartments a
1901 St. Laurent			23 de Vendome
Montreal QC J3U 3T1			Montreal QC J8I 4T7
514-009-3521			514-002-9823

SKU		Unit price	Qty.	Owing
19002-P	b	110.11	8	880.88
19004-G	c	90.56	4	362.24
77001-L	d	301.80	12	3,621.60

| | | Kindly remit | 4,864.72 |

FIGURE 1-2.   *Invoice for refuse services*

NOTE
Data (or read) consistency has been a feature of the Oracle database since some of its earliest releases. The read consistent model is one of many characteristics of Oracle that has contributed to its phenomenal success.

Data Integrity

It sounds so simple at the outset. We have all heard of *dirty data*. Considering the money riding on some of the business decisions made by large corporations, imagine the havoc of allowing erroneous data to find its way into your database. Dirty data cannot be trusted, and the only way to ensure it is clean is by turning the definition of and enforcement of rules over to the database management tier. The following are characteristics of clean data:

■ *It is all valid.* Loading of data or manual data entry enforces a set of relationship-based rules. The simplest example is capturing addresses of employees. Each home address is located in a postal jurisdiction that must exist. A postal code in Liverpool that does not exist must not be used as an address during data capture. How is that enforced? A set of rules programmed into the database engine takes care of this requirement.

■ *Data type consistency is evident.* All the data representing identical elements is the same. Format masks and the position of different kinds of data in a string of characters must conform to a set of rules. In South Africa, postal codes are four digits—the two key components being length and data type.

Imagine the frustration at invoice time if an electrical utility company tried sending statements to clients in Cape Town whose addresses terminated in a postal code 80O—there are two issues here:

- The code is only three digits long and should be four.

- Only numbers (0 through 9) are allowed.

- *Information involved in a parent-child relationship is handled in the proper order.* The simplest example of this type of relationship is an invoice, as shown in Figure 1-2.

The information in the database for the invoice is stored in two separate locations:

- **INVOICE**   A number that uniquely identifies each bill

- **INVOICE_DET**   One or more line items that come together to define the money owed

The database management system must ensure the parent (invoice #) cannot be deleted when detail rows *b, c,* and *d* exist. Likewise, it must ensure the client information *a* cannot be deleted with an outstanding balance.

Oracle Database 12*c* uses a handful of mechanisms to ensure the integrity of data stored in its repository. These mechanisms are there to enforce rules on the data; you will run across the following items immediately once you become more familiar with database management:

- **NOT NULL**   Many fields are mandatory, and Oracle insists when a new row is created or an existing one updated that a value be supplied to fill these important columns.

- **UNIQUE KEY**   A combination of one or more columns that enforce uniqueness among all rows in the same table

- **PRIMARY KEY**   Like UNIQUE, this assures that each row is uniquely identified; with this constraint, one or more columns can be referenced by a foreign key constraint in another table.

- **FOREIGN KEY**   One or more column values in a table reference the primary key column values in another.

- **CHECK**   This enforces one or more values for a column in a table; this constraint is commonly used in a gender field that usually requires that a value of M or F is entered.

Ask the Expert

Q: Why are quantities of data such as kilobyte and megabyte all expressed as a power of 2?

A: All computers run on the binary numbering system, which is base 2. The binary numbering system has only two digits: 0 and 1.

Q: Because such large volumes of data are stored in a database, why do relational database companies not manufacture their own storage hardware?

A: As in all industries, it is best to concentrate on as few products as possible. Leave the database features to the relational database companies and storage to other companies expert in their field.

Q: What is read consistency and why is it so important in database management systems?

A: Read consistency ensures that all users of the database see rows in the database exactly the same as when their read requests were made. Even if other database users are in the midst of modifying some data, each session sees its own copy until other users either save or quit updating data.

Q: How can database vendors get so much data into the database and then retrieve it in seconds?

A: All vendors have their own proprietary methods of storing and retrieving data. They use compression and a sophisticated series of time savers (for example, indexes and other pointers) to make retrieval faster.

Q: Why is it important to ensure data entered into code fields conforms to rules set up at the application or database layer?

A: Strict enforcement of codes is mandatory if the data is going to be summarized and aggregated. Free-form fields are difficult to summarize.

CRITICAL SKILL 1.3

Learn When to Use a Database

In some circles that may be a trick question. Picture some 5-year-olds in front of a 27-inch monitor, devouring a video game based on characters from the Backyardigans, a television show that transforms a simple backyard into an adventure land for young people. These young people, unbeknownst to them, are the users of a database. The site they are on has hundreds of activities to occupy its visitors' time, and the data for those activities is stored in a database. So initially, the answer to the question of when we use a database is daily, even hourly.

In the corporate world, you use databases for information processing needs such as the following:

■ Storage of vast amounts of information that is expected to grow exponentially over short time periods. The 17GB database of today could be the 190GB database of tomorrow.

■ Processing speed cannot be compromised as the size of the database repository increases.

■ Rapid access to sets of data for reporting purposes.

■ Flexibility in the size of data sets retrieved and displayed on applications users' screens.

■ Electronic validation of data before posting new or changed data.

■ Sophisticated routines to ensure activities performed on data do not compromise related data in other locations.

■ Assistants to reduce and/or eliminate data anomalies—a situation where the validity of one's data could be compromised.

We have discussed what a database is and some of the reasons they are here to stay. In the next section, we look at the architecture of Oracle Database 12*c* and mention the roles played by the assortment of shared memory allocations, system support processes, and some of the players involved in a running database.

CRITICAL SKILL 1.4

Learn the Oracle Database 12*c* Architecture

This topic could fill an entire book, but for our purposes here, we'll focus on the most important aspects. This section highlights what makes most sense for this book—concepts and a general overview of the players that deliver this proprietary database management system. These players fall into three main categories:

- **Shared memory**   A section of the host server's memory through which all the data passes and the applications' code is stored and executed

- **System support infrastructure**   A mix of background and foreground processes that perform the tasks required to facilitate the application interaction with the 12*c* database

- **Operating system files**   A suite of no less than ten files that play individual roles as the database runs

The next three sections address these players and provide a bird's-eye view of what they do.

Shared Memory

Shared memory is nothing more than a newfangled name for what was and is sometimes still referred to as *RAM*—random access memory. As the 12*c* database is started, a handful of entries in its system parameter file contribute to the size of memory allocated to the *instance*. Many adopters of the Oracle technology use the words "database" and "instance" synonymously. There is a fundamental difference between the two:

- A *database* is an assortment of files that store data plus a handful of worker files that facilitate application access.

- An *instance* is a segment of shared memory and support processes that provide the capability for applications to work with the data stored in the database. Once the instance is started, the following areas of shared memory play a role in database management activities:

  - The system global area, or SGA, contains data and control information from a single database instance.

  - The program global area, or PGA, is part of the memory allocated to a 12*c* instance as it is started. Unlike the memory in the SGA, PGA memory is not shared. It contains data and control information specific to server processes, not the instance as a whole.

- The user global area, or UGA, is memory associated with each user session. Even though it is allocated from PGA memory, the UGA is discussed as one of the four main memory components.

- Software code areas are where SQL code is prepared for execution and sits in memory until used.

It would be impossible to get into the details of each of these components; as you encounter the memory structures that support a running Oracle instance, the terminology will not be brand new. Figure 1-3 is a graphical representation of the bullet points just discussed with minimal drill-down.

Oracle Database 12*c* offers two approaches for memory management—manual or auto:

- **Auto memory management**   A maximum amount of memory that can be used is defined, and the instance self-manages the size of the assortment of SGA components. This approach is recommended by Oracle and first appeared in Oracle9*i* around the turn of the century; it is referred to as automatic shared memory management (ASMM).

- **Manual memory management**   The administrator specifies fixed sizes for the components that make up the SGA; each component size is specified in the system parameter file as the 12*c* instance starts.

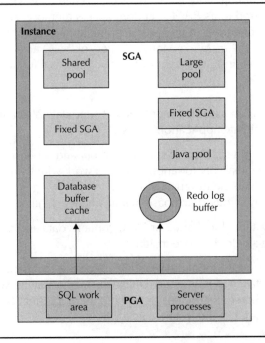

FIGURE 1-3.   *Overview of shared memory components for a 12c database*

Interaction with the database through the instance is brokered by system support processes introduced next.

System Support Processes

These processes are initiated automatically as an Oracle instance is started. Each one plays a role in the management of application interaction with the data. A full set of 12*c* processes from a running instance appears in Figure 1-4.

Table 1-2 presents some detail on the role played by each one of the highlighted processes.

The suite of background processes that you see on a running Oracle Database 12*c* may differ from what was discussed in this section. Some processes only appear when certain functionality of 12*c* is being used. The next section wraps up the architecture discussion by giving some insight into the system files that support the 12*c* database.

```
oracle@localhost:~
File  Edit  View  Terminal  Tabs  Help
/home/oracle> cat bgprocesses.txt
    ora_aqpc_obeg12c      ora_p000_obeg12c
    ora_cjq0_obeg12c      ora_p001_obeg12c
    ora_ckpt_obeg12c      ora_p002_obeg12c
    ora_d000_obeg12c      ora_p003_obeg12c
    ora_dbrm_obeg12c      ora_pmon_obeg12c
    ora_dbw0_obeg12c      ora_psp0_obeg12c
    ora_dia0_obeg12c      ora_q001_obeg12c
    ora_diag_obeg12c      ora_q003_obeg12c
    ora_fbda_obeg12c      ora_qm01_obeg12c
    ora_gen0_obeg12c      ora_reco_obeg12c
    ora_j000_obeg12c      ora_s000_obeg12c
    ora_j001_obeg12c      ora_smco_obeg12c
    ora_lgwr_obeg12c      ora_smon_obeg12c
    ora_lreg_obeg12c      ora_tmon_obeg12c
    ora_mman_obeg12c      ora_tt00_obeg12c
    ora_mmnl_obeg12c      ora_vktm_obeg12c
    ora_mmon_obeg12c      ora_w000_obeg12c
    ora_ofsd_obeg12c

oracle@localhost.localdomain-->(obeg12c)
/home/oracle> ▊
```

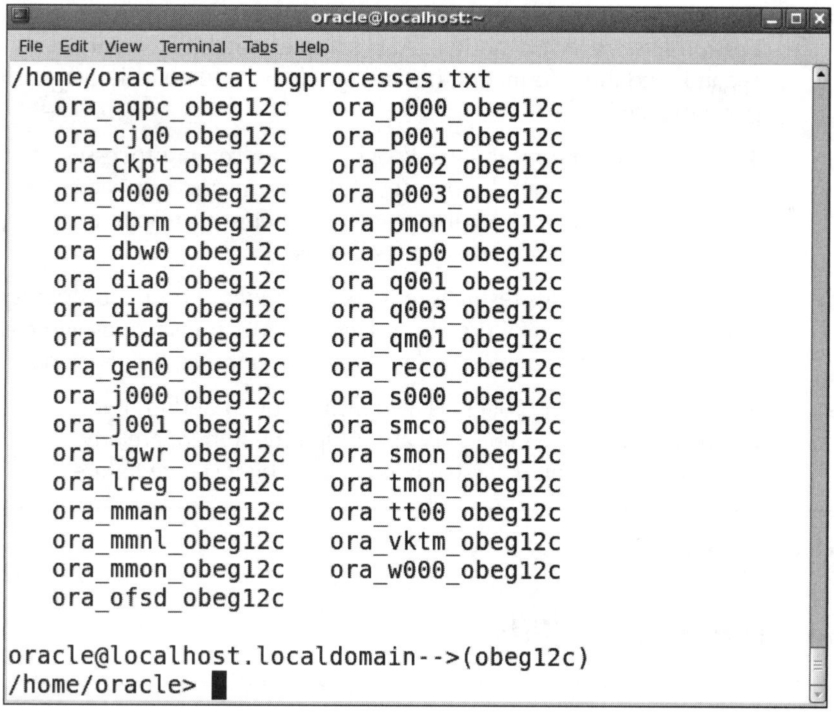

FIGURE 1-4. *Background processes that support the 12c database*

Process	Role
ckpt	The checkpoint process syncs the control file and data file headers with checkpoint information. At the same time, it signals the database writer process that it is time to perform its activities.
dbw0	The database writer process is responsible for copying the contents of database buffers in memory into their appropriate database files.
lreg	The listener registration process registers instance information for the Oracle Net listener process. If the listener process is not running at instance startup, *lreg* attempts to contact it from time to time to pass relevant information.
mmon	The manageability monitor process is associated with tasks related to Oracle's *Automatic Workload Repository* (AWR). AWR is delivered with the 12*c* database and stores workload and vital instance statistics for analysis and planning purposes.
mmnl	The manageability monitor lite process plays a role in the *Active Session History* (ASH) module. ASH samples database activity every second, and the information it traps can be used to assist in diagnosing performance issues.
pmon	The process monitor is the gatekeeper of other server processes. It monitors all background processes and performs recovery activities when other processes end abruptly. It also performs resource cleanup activities when required on client sessions.
reco	The recovery process resolves failures encountered during distributed database transaction failure. It resolves in-doubt transactions and cleans up the pending transaction table on all sites at the end of its work.
smon	The system monitor process is responsible for a handful of instance cleanup tasks such as recovery at startup time if there are any inconsistencies that may have been caused by instance failure.

TABLE 1-2. *Responsibilities of System Processes*

Operating System Files

A minimum of 11 files are created for the traditional Oracle instance. Table 1-3 lists the role of each.

Figure 1-5 illustrates the makeup of these operating system files, the barebones minimum as discussed in Table 1-3.

Category	Role	Notes
Control file	Metadata about the running instance	There must be a minimum of two control files.
System parameter (*spfile*)	A list of parameters and values to be used when the instance is started	This superseded the traditional initialization parameter file starting with Oracle9*i*.
Password file	Plays a role in determining who is allowed to initiate connections to the database to perform secure activities	The setting for the startup parameter *remote_login_password* file also plays a role in this functionality.
SYSTEM tablespace	The heart of the 12*c* database, containing the data dictionary as well as a host of tombstone information relevant to database activities	Part of a new database creation.
SYSAUX tablespace	Holds additional system-related information that used to be spread among a number of non-SYSTEM tablespaces	Part of a new database creation.
UNDO tablespace	A player in Oracle's read consistent model—containing the information required to roll back non-committed changes to data	Part of a new database creation.
TEMP tablespace	A work area used for intermediary result sets assembled during query processing and to support sort activities	Part of a new database creation.
Online redo	Transaction logs that contain a record/copy of all activities against the 12*c* database	There must be a minimum of two online redo groups, each containing one or more members.
TOOLS tablespace	The first user-defined tablespace to house non-SYSTEM-related data	The name of this tablespace need not be TOOLS; any name can be used.

TABLE 1-3.   *Operating System Files and Their Roles*

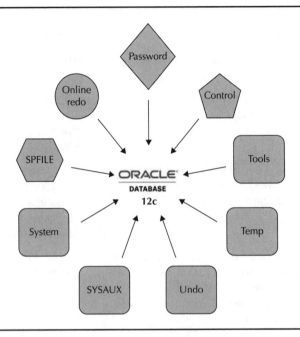

FIGURE 1-5. *Overview of system files that support the 12c database*

The next section discusses some of the commonly used objects when storing data in Oracle Database 12*c*.

CRITICAL SKILL 1.5

Work with Objects in the Oracle Database

In this section, we discuss the most common objects you will encounter from day one working with Oracle. Objects are used to perform a number of functions, including:

- Storing data to be used by applications—*tables*

- Presenting a subset of stored information to different users based on who they are—*views*

- Allowing users of the database to refer to objects that exist somewhere else in the database—*synonyms*

- Executing portions of code repetitively to initiate common tasks within the application—*stored objects*

Let's have a look at each one of these individually.

Tables

Tables are the most common object used in the database—no tables equates to no database. A table is represented in two dimensions somewhat like a matrix, forms of which we have all seen. Picture the PERSON table as mentioned a while back. The next listing shows some of the columns in this table:

```
COLUMN           NOTES
--------------   ------------------------------------
PID              A unique number from 1 to 8 digits
                 each person can be identified by this number
DID              A 3-digit number that specifies the location
                 of where each person works in the organization
PGIVEN           First name
PSURNAME         Last name
LID              Where the person's main place of work is located
...
...
SID              The salary bracket for each individual that
                 defines the range within which salary must fall
PHDATE           Date when the person first started work for the
                 company
```

Once created, data is stored in the table and it must conform to the rules laid out as the data types are specified for each column in each row. A *row* in this table belongs to one and only one individual. If you look at the salary bracket for each person, you are inspecting the series of values in each row's *column* of the table. In other words, rows are horizontal and columns vertical. A handful of records in the PERSON table could resemble those shown in Table 1-4.

Once we discuss data types in the next section, we will pull the preceding table and listing together and create the table in the Oracle database.

PID	DID	PGIVEN	PSURNAME	LID	SID	PHDATE
1990	12	Mel	Wood	02	14	12-NOV-2009
2099	19	Mary	Cross	02	10	01-FEB-2001
1299	17	Brittany	Cohen	09	10	12-MAR-1994

TABLE 1-4. *Three Records in PERSON*

Views

Suppose human resources wanted to share details of employees with another organization in the company, but only part of the information trapped in PERSON. This is where the view comes into play. This subset of the full table may look as follows:

```
V_PERSON
-----------
PID
DID
PGIVEN
PSURNAME
DID
LID
```

Notice there are a few columns missing—SID and PHDATE. We have just hit on two fundamental characteristics of a database:

- Views built on a subset of table columns can be used to enforce a flavor of security. Users outside personnel are not able to see anyone's salary bracket or hire date. Igor in shipping knows that boxes destined for Mel Wood are sent to procurement (department 12) in the Wichita office (location 02). Norma in human resources (HR) can put the final touches on a salary increase for Brittany Cohen, knowing the upper limit of allowable remuneration is $74,000 per annum as defined for salary bracket 10.

- Users inside and outside HR can use the same table for different applications. This conjures up a vast assortment of opportunities for consolidation as organizations move to mature database processing engines.

Synonyms

These handy objects are created and used as alternative names for objects, a pointer to the real table. Suppose as mentioned in the previous section, HR owned the PERSON table and shipping needed to reference their table using the name PERSLOC. Rather than duplicate the PERSON table for the purpose of shipping, a synonym would be created called PERSLOC pointing at the V_PERSON view. Once these pointers are set up, their uses are endless. In the non-database world, we have used synonyms all our lives—what North Americans call a delivery van, the British call a *lorry*. Figure 1-6 illustrates how tables/views/synonyms interact with one another.

In Figure 1-6, there is one and only one copy of the data:

- The <u>PART</u> table contains the data in capitals, underlined.

- The *Inventory* view looks at a subset of the columns in the table in mixed case, italics.

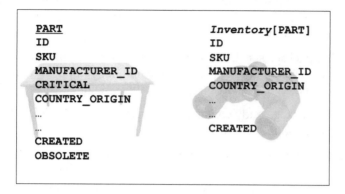

```
PART                    Inventory[PART]
ID                      ID
SKU                     SKU
MANUFACTURER_ID         MANUFACTURER_ID
CRITICAL                COUNTRY_ORIGIN
COUNTRY_ORIGIN          ...
...
...                     CREATED
CREATED
OBSOLETE
```

FIGURE 1-6.   *Table/view/synonym and how they relate to one another*

■   The applications that use the view use the synonym **PART** in capitals, bold to reference the *Inventory* view.

For decades, relational database vendors have been inventing ways to enhance the throughput of application code that works with data stored in their repositories. The next section discusses some ground-breaking inventions that first appeared more than 20 years ago.

Stored Objects

This involves encapsulating code segments in an assortment of database objects, which are then run implicitly or explicitly to perform pre-determined tasks. Code that is used over and over again in applications is often contained in stored objects and then called into action as required. This ensures consistent processing of data and can assist performance of applications at the same time. Stored objects first appeared with the release of Oracle7 in 1992. The most common stored objects fall into one of the following four categories:

■   *Procedures* can accept input parameters and perform processing based on the nature of the code they contain. They are invoked manually. Suppose some commodity needs replenishing in an inventory application. The procedure designed to perform this iterative task accepts a stock number and quantity to order and runs off and does its thing. Procedures can service a handful of applications as long as the expected results are the same.

■   *Functions* are invoked implicitly and return a single value. The returned value can be a wide assortment of data types.

- *Packages* group similar and connected processing units into a single object. They can contain an assortment of procedures and functions. They are made up of two parts:

  - The package specification defines how it interfaces with applications, specifying information such as the number of input and output parameters as well as sub-programs it contains.

  - The package body contains the programming units defined in the specification section.

- *Triggers* are program units aligned with one, and only one, table. The jargon used in database processing refers to how these code segments fire when certain activities are carried out—hence their name.

Stored objects are the backbone of Oracle's relational database technology implementation. They run on the database server, thereby

- Centralizing significant parts of your database applications for increased maintainability and security

- Enabling you to achieve a significant reduction of network overhead in client/server applications

- Contributing to the reusability of code since Oracle checks and compiles the codes when it is first executed and can be used over and over again

Procedures, packages, and functions can declare variables, constants, and cursors, as well as sophisticated exception handling. A *cursor* is simply a SELECT statement defined once in the stored object and then used repetitively. Packages can contain global variables and cursors that are available to all procedures and functions in the same package.

Progress Check

1. As tables are created, a unique name within the table is required for each column. What else needs to accompany the definition of each column?

2. What is the main use of views in a relational database?

3. What object in a relational database can be used as an alternate name for an object?

4. What is the one main reason for creating stored objects in a relational database?

CRITICAL SKILL 1.6

Work with Data Types in an Oracle Database

This is a big topic; for the purposes of this book, we will just scratch the surface with the basics without delving into the full suite of data types. We will cover those that you will run across from day one—variable length character, number, date, clob, and blob.

Variable Length Character—varchar2

This data type can be from 1 to 32,768 bytes. In multibyte character sets, it is possible that this 4,000 limit may not equate to the same number of characters. Oracle stores only relevant characters, and using proprietary compression, actually occupies significantly less database space than it appears to need when seen on the screen. Oracle has a few different ways to specify a variable length character field but the most common is VARCHAR2. As a table is created, one specifies the characteristics of variable length data as follows:

```
create table country
(country_code      varchar2(3),
 country_name      varchar2(30));
```

Oracle stores from 1 to 3 characters for the COUNTRY_CODE field and 1 to 30 for the COUNTRY_NAME. In the preceding simple statement used to create the COUNTRY table, column names can be as many as 30 characters. Though not as common as the VARCHAR2 data type, you may encounter and work with applications that use a few of the following:

- **VARCHAR**   Same as VARCHAR2, although its use is not recommended

- **CHAR**   Fixed length character data up to 2,000 bytes; there is a 1:1 relationship between characters and bytes with this data type. If a field

---

Progress Check Answers

1. The column names as well as each one's data type and length are specified. The definition must conform to limitations dictated by the Oracle database software.

2. Views are used to present a subset of columns in a table to some users who may not be in the same department of a corporation; this is a form of security.

3. Synonyms can be used to allow some users to refer to an object using a pointer that is not the same as the real name of that object.

4. Stored objects ensure certain processing performed by applications is done exactly the same each and every time.

value occupies less than the 2,000 byte maximum, trailing spaces are added at the end. In addition, if a field is null, 2,000 spaces are stored in this zero length field value up to this maximum.

- **NCHAR** Fixed length character data that takes into consideration the bytes required to represent a single character in some character sets is significantly stronger than the familiar US7ASCII. The storage of data in this field is treated exactly the same as CHAR if it is less than 2,000 bytes long or is null.

NOTE
All user-defined names used for just about anything in the Oracle database are limited to no more than 30 characters.

Number

Fields specified using this data type can store positive or negative numbers within a wide range that most applications do not even come close to reaching the upper and lower boundaries of. You can store integers with or without decimal digits included. The format for defining *number* fields is made up of two parts:

- The *precision,* which is the total length of the field; the decimal point, if present, does not occupy one of these positions. The highest precision that can be specified is 38.

- The *scale* is the number of decimal digits.

Column definitions for fields that will contain numeric data are summarized in Table 1-5.

Specification	Integer digits	Decimal digits
number	36	0
number (8,2)	6	2
number (8,3)	5	3

TABLE 1-5. *Integer and Decimal Storage for Number Data Types*

The next listing shows how some fields could be defined in a table and the range of numbers each one could store:

```
...
...
load_factor     number (2,1) - low -9.9 high 9.9
grade_factor    number (1,1) - low -.9 high .9
compensation    number (7,2) - low -99999.99 high 99999.99
```

NOTE
You need not specify the ability for a number field to also contain a sign; numbers can be stored in these fields whether they are positive or negative.

Datetime

Oracle provides a rich set of options for storing date and timestamp information. The following four offerings are available with Oracle Database 12*c* in the DATETIME data type:

- **DATE**   The most familiar data type that contains CENTURY, YEAR, MONTH, DAY, HOUR, MINUTE, and SECOND.

- **TIMESTAMP**   The same as DATE except fractions of seconds are stored if specified as the field is defined.

- **TIMESTAMP WITH TIME ZONE**   The same as TIMESTAMP except information of the locale where the data is created is stored in the field as well. In the multinational application, this is how a row created at 10:03:12.87 in New York City, USA can be equated to one created at 15:03:12.87 in London, England. It takes into consideration the five-hour time difference between the two cities.

- **TIMESTAMP WITH LOCAL TIME ZONE**   The same as TIMESTAMP except it does not store the time zone information internally. Hence, there would be no way of determining that information created at 10:03:12.87 in New York City, USA was indeed created in the eastern time zone.

A column defined using this data type is subject to a handful of rules to ensure its value is valid. The default display format for datetime fields is DD-MON-YY. It may seem odd that unless specified, Oracle displays a two-character year by default. The date December 15, 2014, is displayed as 15-DEC-14 by default; Oracle does store information to ensure the two century digits as well as timestamp are preserved.

Special output formatting has to be applied to date fields to get the century digits as well as the timestamp embedded in the database, as shown in the following listing:

```
SQL> select to_char(created,'DD-MON-YYYY HH24:MI:SS') created
  2> from pmaster
  3> where id = 2378871;
CREATED
--------------------
15-DEC-2014 17:00:52
```

CLOB/BLOB

This large object type can hold up to 128 terabytes of data, commonly used to store complex semi-structured and unstructured data. Oracle handled data of this type for many releases in the LONG data type; a few releases ago, administrators were told to wean themselves of the LONG data type in favor of these two large objects. In a nutshell

- CLOB is best suited for storing semi-structured data such as XML documents or files created by popular word processors. With semi-structured data, the database may not decompose the data into a format usable by applications; it simply stores the data and makes it available to application components for viewing and/or processing.

- BLOB is best suited for binary-based data such as photos or videos. The most common examples of unstructured data are photos and videos stored in the database as binary objects.

BLOB is used anywhere and everywhere when CLOB is not a solution.

Ask the Expert

Q: When a view is created on an existing table, do you need to name each column in the view and give it a data type?

A: If you want, columns in a view can have names different from the table. This is not required, and the columns in a view inherit the names and data types from the table.

Q: If you want, can the column name in a view differ from those in the table upon which it is built?

A: Yes, as the view is created, column names can be defined that are specific to the view. The following code snippet shows how that is done:

```
SQL> describe province
Name                              Null?      Type
-----------------------------     ---------  -----------
PROVINCE_CODE                     NOT NULL   VARCHAR2(2)
PROVINCE_NAME                     NOT NULL   VARCHAR2(40)

SQL> create view prov_cd (pcode, pname) as
  2> select province_code, province_name
  3> from province;
View created.
SQL> describe prov_cd
Name                              Null?      Type
-----------------------------     ---------  -----------
PCODE                             NOT NULL   VARCHAR2(2)
PNAME                             NOT NULL   VARCHAR2(40)
```

CRITICAL SKILL 1.7

Pull It All Together: Objects and Data Types

Before looking at what Oracle Database 12*c* is all about, let's wrap up the last few sections and look at how a table, view, and synonym are created, showing examples of the different data types we discussed.

```
create table employee (
  emp_id            number(6),
  emp_fname         varchar2(40),
  emp_sname         varchar2(40),
  hiredate          date,
  department        number(3),
  photo             blob,
  resume            clob,
  last_chkpt        date,
  job               varchar2(3),
```

```
   location        varchar2(2),
   manager         number(6)
   active          varchar2(1));

create view active_employee as
select emp_id, emp_fname, emp_sname, hiredate, last_chkpt,
       job, manager
  from employee
 where active = '1';
create synonym current_staff for active_employee;
```

Let's summarize exactly what was created in the preceding code snippet:

■ A traditional relational table was created to store employee information (table name is EMPLOYEE).

■ A view on that table was created (named ACTIVE_EMPLOYEE).

■ The view displays a subset of columns from the table (only rows whose ACTIVE column value is 1). As data is manipulated in the EMPLOYEE table, changes will be reflected in the view immediately.

■ A pointer (CURRENT_STAFF) was created to look at the data in the view, using a name different from the view to which it points.

Figure 1-7 illustrates what the code snippet and the previous bullet list accomplishes. The shading indicates the synonym points at the view that contains a subset of columns from the original table.

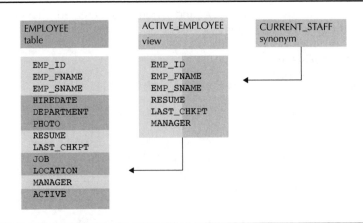

FIGURE 1-7. *Roadmap to the creation of the ACTIVE_EMPLOYEE view and CURRENT_STAFF synonym*

Ask the Expert

Q: What is the most common data type stored in the database?

A: Traditionally this was text-based alphanumeric data represented by *varchar2*. As the Internet world expands and the gamut of data-intensive video applications hits the desktops of today and tomorrow, if you were to use volume of data as a yardstick, probably the most common data type would be large binary objects.

Q: Besides consistent processing of application requests, what other advantages are there to using procedures, packages, and functions?

A: When Oracle receives a portion of code for execution, it tends to go through an exhaustive check on things such as syntax and object resolution. By using stored objects, that processing is performed once when the code is first executed. Then subsequent iterations of that code need not go through that check again.

Q: Often we see a description of a number field stored in a database that has an upper and lower limit on values it may contain. Why is the negative boundary often one value more than the positive counterpart (for example, from −1612 to 1611)?

A: That is because 0 is actually a positive number—in this example, 0–1611 is actually 1,612 values just like its negative counterpart.

Q: Since by default Oracle displays a two-character year in date fields, how did it deal with the millennium going from 1999 to 2000?

A: Even when Oracle displays a two-character year, internally the century component is stored as well.

Q: When thinking of sharing data between organizations in the same company, how does Oracle decide who "owns" the data and who gets to "use" the data?

A: This is actually a business decision rather than a relational database management task. Companies have to decide who owns what and what will be shared with others. Oracle provides mechanisms to implement the business rules agreed upon by different units in a corporation. Business rules can be implemented using Oracle privileges to control who owns what data and what portions of it can be shared with others.

Interact with the Data

Regardless of how one's code is delivered to the Oracle database engine for processing, it only understands one format—industry-standard SQL. This structured query language is native to all traditional relational database offerings although each vendor has its own proprietary implementation. Administrators, developers, and central application super users leverage the power of SQL*Developer, sqlplus, and PL/SQL as they interact with data. Let's have a look at these three engines.

NOTE
*At this point you may not have the 12c database installed yet. Chapter 2 covers installation after which you will have access to sqlplus, and PL/SQL. SQL*Developer can be downloaded from Oracle.*

SQL*Developer

Over the years there have been a number of offerings in the GUI environment with which users could interact with the Oracle data. Along came SQL*Developer a few years ago and users have never looked back. The installed product we are illustrating in this chapter is on an Oracle Linux x86-64 (VM Ware Fusion 5 on Mac Lion 10.7) server running Oracle Database 12*c*.

NOTE
*You may discover some configuration issues with your copy of SQL*Developer that may be unique to your environment.*

As you work with the Oracle software, the Oracle Technology Network site, shown in Figure 1-8, may be your best friend. There is a plethora of tech material there that can whet most appetites.

SQL* Developer is available for Windows, Mac, and Linux. The first time it is run, you will be asked what file types should be associated with the tools, as shown in Figure 1-9. Best to select all and click OK.

The main screen then appears, as shown in Figure 1-10. Before the main screen appears, you are shown the *Tip of the day*, which we have dismissed permanently.

The first thing you will do is define a database connection, the details of which are well beyond the scope of this discussion. Once you have your database installed

FIGURE 1-8. *Oracle Technology Network home page*

and accessible by Oracle's network transport called SQL*Net, you will fill in the fields shown in Figure 1-11. This is what we have done before capturing the screen:

- Specified a meaningful and unique connection name

- Specified login credentials to hook up to the target database

- Chosen the connection type of *TNS*

- Chosen the Connect identifier of *obeg12c,* which is a handle used from one of the SQL*Net configuration files to access this database

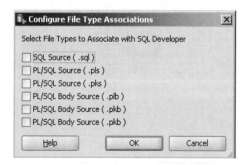

FIGURE 1-9. *Association of file types with SQL*Developer*

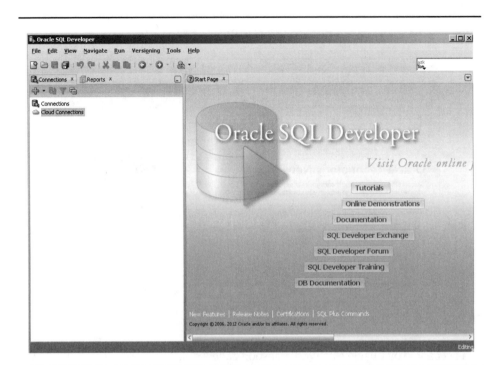

FIGURE 1-10. *Main screen of SQL*Developer*

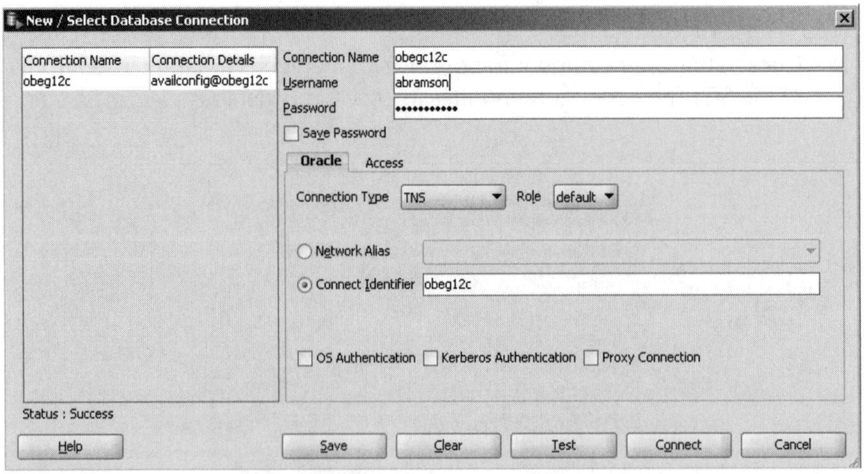

FIGURE 1-11. *Defining a database connection in SQL*Developer*

Notice the *Status: Success* in the bottom-left corner of Figure 1-11. This will come together easily once you have read more of this book and are familiar with more jargon and fundamentals. Once the connection is tested, click Connect to hook up to the database just defined. The work that can now be carried out is based on the two panes displayed as the connection is completed:

■   The left portion of the screen shows a list of object types, as shown in Figure 1-12; notice the object types. The list is much bigger than what we have discussed so far.

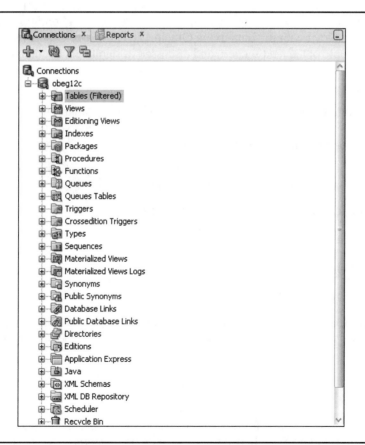

FIGURE 1-12.   *Pane showing available object types once database connection succeeds*

- The right portion of the screen is where the actual work is performed. Notice there are two tabs in this work area:

  - The worksheet where you formulate queries and pass them off to SQL*Developer for processing. Statements are processed once syntax checking and a handful of other tasks are executed successfully in the background.

  - The query builder where an assortment of buttons, checkboxes, and other familiar GUI interface items are used to formulate queries for processing by SQL*Developer.

These two portions of the main screen are shown in Figures 1-13 and 1-14. Enough said on SQL*Developer; we used version 3.2.09 Build MAIN-09.30 for the screenshots in this section of the chapter. Some readers may end up using a GUI front end to interact with the data in the Oracle 12*c* Database. Others may prefer *sqlplus,* the topic of the next section, and discussed in significant detail in Chapter 3.

sqlplus

The next listing shows how sqlplus is invoked from the command line where

- The text entered before the slash is the username

- The "/" character is a delimiter and must be entered if both username and password are placed on the command line

- The text entered after the slash is the password

```
oracleobg12c--> (obeg12c)

/home/oracle> sqlplus michael/******
SQL*Plus: Release 12.1.0.0.2 on Wed Aug 11 10:36:10 2014
Copyright (c) 1982, 2012, Oracle.  All rights reserved.
Connected to:
Oracle Database 12c Enterprise Edition Release 12.1.0.0.2 - 64bit
With the Partitioning, OLAP, Data Mining and Real Application Testing
options

SQL>
```

Once positioned at the SQL> prompt, there is a plethora of statements that you can pass off to the database for processing. There are some Oracle-specific extensions to standard SQL, hence the *plus* in the name *sqlplus.* After statements are passed to Oracle for processing, the next few sections provide an overview of the processing that takes place.

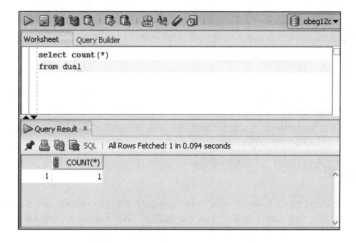

FIGURE 1-13.   *The worksheet panel on the SQL*Developer main screen*

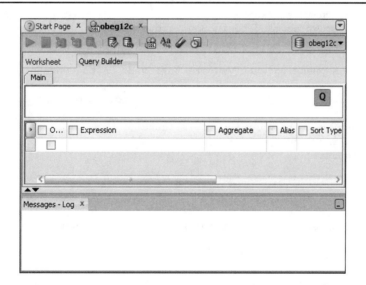

FIGURE 1-14.   *The Query Builder panel on the SQL*Developer main screen*

NOTE
There is a much lighter version of sqlplus called Instant Client, which is easy to install and uses significantly less disk space than the full Oracle Database 12c client.

Syntax Checking

The syntax of the statement is inspected, and an assortment of error messages are thrown based on what the interpreter finds. These errors depend on what the parser finds and how much it can see into what it receives to deduce the error message that is displayed.

```
-- sqlplus understands what you are saying it just cannot find
-- an object by the name EMPLOYEE_MASTER; the table created earlier
-- was simply called EMPLOYEE
SQL>  select name from employee_master;
ERROR at line 1:
ORA-00942: table or view does not exist

-- the first word in a SQL statement is a reserved word, usually a verb
-- the updte word is not recognized
SQL> updte employee set hiredate = sysdate
  2>  where emp_id = 372888;
SP2-0734: unknown command beginning "updte emplo..." - rest of line
ignored.

-- sqlplus is guessing what you are trying to do but encounters a

-- syntax error; the syntax of sqlplus does not support an opening

-- parenthesis in the position it is found
SQL> insert into employee (2);
insert into dual (2)
                *
ERROR at line 1:
ORA-00928: missing SELECT keyword

-- sqlplus has encountered a reference to a column name that is not

-- in the EMPLOYEE table
SQL> select count(*)
  2   from employee
  3   where id between 300000 and 310000;
```

```
where id between 300000 and 310000
       *
ERROR at line 3:
ORA-00904: ID": invalid identifier
```

Once sqlplus resolves the syntax, punctuation, and object references it encounters, the statement is processed and, we hope, does the work it was asked to do. Normal completion of statements usually receives feedback from Oracle along the lines of:

```
33 rows selected.
219 rows deleted.
no rows selected.
```

Before moving into a short discussion on PL/SQL, let's take apart a simple SQL statement, noting that the line numbers are not part of the statement:

```
1- select part_name
2- from part_master
3- where length(part_name) > 12
4- and owner <> 'INV'
5- /
```

Table 1-6 provides details on the lines of the statement presented.

Line #	Details
1	Starts with a recognized verb and then mentions a column from PART_MASTER; if PART_NAME does not exist in that table, an error will be thrown.
2	Defines the source table for the statement. Oracle must be able to resolve the name PART_MASTER or another error will be displayed.
3–4	The fancy name for this portion of a statement is the *predicate*. This section contains between one and an endless number of qualifying statements that control the criteria for data as it is retrieved for display as query results. Most statements contain only one *where* in this predicate and any number of *and* qualifiers.
5	This is the terminator for the SQL statement and instructs Oracle to start processing the text it has received. One can also use a semicolon in place of the slash at the end of the last line of code or on a new line by itself.

TABLE 1-6. *Dissection of the Lines of Text in a SELECT Statement*

Now let's move on and have a quick look at Oracle's procedural data manipulation engine called PL/SQL. Once users cut their teeth with sqlplus, many notice a lack of procedural processing capabilities. That changes once you become familiar with the subject material in the next section.

PL/SQL

This programming interface is always referred to as an extension to Oracle's implementation of the structured query language. You can use PL/SQL code segments in sqlplus, and it reads much like many programming languages people have encountered. Procedures, packages, functions, and triggers, as mentioned in the section "Objects in the Oracle Database" earlier in this chapter, all contain nothing but PL/SQL code. The feedback from sqlplus as a block of code completes successfully is always:

```
PL/SQL procedure successfully completed.
```

Many books have been written solely dedicated to PL/SQL, so let's look at a small code segment, pick it apart, and then move on.

```
SQL> begin
  2     declare
  3        v_number     number(3);
  4     begin
  5       select count(*)
  6          into v_number
  7          from dba_views
  8        where owner = 'INV';
  9     end;
 10   end;
 11   /
PL/SQL procedure successfully completed.
```

Table 1-7 examines this piece of code; this time, the line numbers were inserted by Oracle as the code was forced to spill into the next line.

Chapter 4 offers a great deal more detail, primarily discussing PL/SQL, the flagship resident programming environment since the release of Oracle7 in 1992—yet another offering from one of the most successful software giants of all time. So what's the big deal with 12*c*? Let's have a look at some of the new features embedded in 12*c*.

Line #	Details
1	This reserved word starts the PL/SQL block and is terminated by whitespace.
2	This begins the section of a PL/SQL block where local variables are commonly defined. As per many adopted best practices, the names used for local variables should be descriptive ... remember what was said about how a database is self-describing?
3	The local variable is defined and given a data type, in this case three integer digits.
4	The second *begin* is the start of the actual code that will be executed when the block is invoked.
5–8	The SQL statement that is embedded in the PL/SQL block. It reads like code outside of PL/SQL except the *into v_number* is included as a recipient of the count retrieved as the statement executes.
9–10	These reserved words are terminators to the previously issued *begin* keywords. Typically, there are exactly the same number of *begin* and *end* keywords.
11	This slash is the PL/SQL. In standard SQL statement processing, the terminator can also be a semicolon, but not with PL/SQL.

TABLE 1-7. *Dissection of the Lines of Text in a PL/SQL Statement*

CRITICAL SKILL 1.9

Learn the New Features of Oracle Database 12*c*

The first new feature we will a look at has been getting a great deal of attention since the 12*c* announcements started in October 2011. The *c* included in the name of release 12 of Oracle's flagship product stands for *cloud*. Previous releases used the characters *i* for *Internet* (versions 8 and 9) and then *g* for *grid* (versions 10 and 11). The new features discussed in this section were selected because they make the most sense for the audience for this book. More knowledge of the existing Oracle database offerings may be required for this section of Chapter 1 than what you have read so far.

Pluggable Databases

This is the new kid on the block, one of the newfangled features of 12*c*. According to the documentation, a pluggable database (PDB) is a portable collection of schemas, schema objects, and non-schema objects that appear to an Oracle Net client as a separate database. One or more PDBs together are called a container database (CDB). They are completely transparent to the users and applications and are 100 percent backwardly compatible with pre-12*c* databases.

The components of the CDB are as follows:

■   One or more PDBs

■   CDB$ROOT, the keeper of all the PDBs that are part of the collection

■   PDB$SEED, a template from which new PDBs can be created

12*c* refers to each of these components as a *container*. Each container is assigned a unique ID in the CDB. PDBs can be plugged into and unplugged from a CDB, and can only be associated with one CDB at a time. Administrators can be set up to manage the CDB as well as one or more PDBs.

Oracle encourages the install base to use PDB technology for a number of reasons, including reduction of cost, separation of data and code, ease of management and monitoring, and separation of administrative duties to name a few. Once you wrap up your planning, Oracle's database configuration assistant (DBCA) can be used to create the CDB. Once that is completed, the process of plugging and unplugging PDBs can begin. The following tasks are associated with pluggable databases:

■   **Planning**   Where you decide the number of PDBs that will be plugged into each CDB, the resources required to support the environment, and the configuration options that will be chosen.

■   **Creation**

   ■   Using the GUI database configuration assistant or sqlplus, create one or more CDBs.

   ■   Using sqlplus, create one or more PDBs and plug them into existing CDBs.

■   **Ongoing management**   Activities are performed on the CDB, the root, and one or more PDBs; Oracle Resource Manager can be used to allocate system resources among all players in the pluggable database environment.

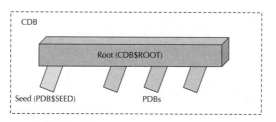

FIGURE 1-15.   *Newly created CDB with three PDBs plugged in*

Figure 1-15 shows a newly created CDB with a handful of PDBs plugged in. Familiar tools are used to execute common tasks associated with the management of CDBs and PDBs:

- sqlplus

- DBCA

- Oracle Enterprise Manager Cloud Control

- Oracle SQL Developer

- Server Control (aka srvctl)

Besides the fact that a CDB can contain one or more PDBs, the major difference between the two is that the former contains little or no user data; user data resides in the PDBs. PDBs can be created by

- Copying files from the seed and then associating the new files with the PDB being created

- Cloning an existing PDB

- Plugging a PDB that has been unplugged from an existing CDB into another CDB

- Creating a new PDB from a 12*c* non-PDB database and then plugging it into an existing CDB

NOTE
The data dictionary views that contain information about pluggable databases have the text CDB in their names rather than CONTAINER.

Application Development

New features in Oracle Application Express (Apex) include the following:

- An enriched look and feel of applications

- Movement of some of the menial management tasks associated with Apex into the engine itself

- Full Unicode support

- An increase in the maximum size of the VARCHAR2 data type to 32KB from 4,000 characters

- JDBC support for Sybase applications, which was added to assist you in migrating Sybase Java applications to Oracle if clients want to consolidate their database services

- A new engine that allows MySQL applications to interact seamlessly with Oracle

Availability

Data Guard has been one of the major components in Oracle high-availability offerings for many releases. It encapsulates tasks into a command-line or GUI interface making management tasks easier to master. Data Guard now supports global temporary tables on the standby site as well as the ability to manage a cascading standby. A cascading standby site is one that receives its archived redo from another standby rather than the master site.

Transaction Guard jumps out at developers and administrators. During an outage, the client receives an error message but no indication of the state (success or failure) of the commit activity that may have been at the end of any incomplete transaction. With Transaction Guard, applications use a newfangled logical transaction ID to decide what the outcome was of the last transaction issued prior to an outage.

Replication solutions leveraging Oracle GoldenGate, Streams, and the logical standby have been enhanced. XStream, part of the GoldenGate product, enables client applications to receive real-time changes to Oracle data. XStream contains a new suite of capture and apply parameters and has been optimized to handle large transactions more efficiently.

Automatic Storage Management (ASM) now contains a mechanism capable of detecting and fixing logical data corruption automatically. Since the release of Oracle Database 10*g*, ASM has been used as a manager for disk volumes and filesystems within which data is stored. A handful of operations not previously able to execute without interrupting the application can now be performed online.

Recovery Manager (RMAN) has been the backup tool of choice for administrators since the release of Oracle7 in 1992. Chapter 6 is dedicated to RMAN. The enhancements to this tool are copious, including:

- The active database duplication activity can perform native data compression on restore and the breaking up of activities into sections that can be parallelized.

- Administrators who use the command-line RMAN interface can now do the following at the RMAN prompt:

  - Issue SELECT statements at the RMAN prompt

  - Run most SQL commands without the SQL prefix

  - DESCRIBE database tables

- The ability to recover a table or set of tables, thereby reducing the time and complexity of performing this activity in earlier releases

Business Intelligence and Data Warehousing

Decision support has been one area of concentration as databases swell to ever increasing sizes. Oracle has improved the automatic degree of parallelism for the processing of SQL statements. Coupled with more flexibility utilizing flash devices, the Database Smart Cache Flash component eases the management of multiple devices that can benefit the throughput of queries and transactions. Scalability of large multinode clusters has been improved using enhanced in-memory parallel processing. Enhancements in this area have concentrated on features common in data warehousing, including cube query performance and cube statistics support. For clients with partitioned objects, there is a handful of enhancements in managing these large objects that will allow operations to be performed without making the tables temporarily unavailable. You can now instruct Oracle to perform concurrent statistics gathering, which could benefit all systems but especially the large repositories so common to a business intelligence (BI) or warehousing scenario.

Compression and Archiving

Database administrators can leverage a finer-grained support for compression at the row level. Auditing enhancements can be used to collect historical information on secure data dictionary tables. All LOB storage now defaults to Secure Files, a feature introduced with Oracle Database 11*g* to optimize the storage of and processing of these large objects. Archiving and compression in the database management arena have been hot topics for some time. They play a role in the areas of data retention as well as taming exponential growth in data volumes that tax existing disk space.

Overall Database Features

Enhancements in this area are copious and exciting. Here are the high-level highlights:

- **Database upgrades** More automation and ability to parallelize portions of the work.

- **Enterprise Grid Scheduler** With special attention to assist the management of RMAN, operating system scripts, and SQL scripts. New job types exist to streamline the introduction of canned scripts into enterprise data management tasks.

- **Data pump** Auditing capabilities, a mechanism to alter table compression on import, more compression options on export, and nologging capabilities on import will make an already highly configurable tool even more so.

- **SQL*Loader** The capability to audit direct path loads and command-line parameters to control loading operations will remove the drudgery of painstakingly creating the control file previously required.

- **Oracle Enterprise Manager Database Express** This tool replaces Enterprise Manager Database Control.

- **SQL Test Case Builder** Extracts relevant information to be able to reproduce an incident on another system; the builder can capture and replay all the actions to assist the process of diagnosing incidents.

Grid Features

Grid features primarily relate to ASM and RAC. Because ASM is used by many organizations for non-RAC installations, these features can benefit a wide assortment of clientele:

- **ACFS** Integration of Oracle Automatic Storage Management Cluster File System replication with ACFS compression and security

- **Cluster health** Multiple disks brought online and offline at one time, a Resync Power Limit to speed up these operations, the ability to resume (rather than restart) after instance failure, and more sophisticated and dependable RAC hang detection and node eviction failure to assist you in keeping clustered nodes online and operational more of the time

- **ASM**   More flexibility with operations that used to require the diskgroup to be offline as well as enhancements to the rebalance activity to improve its performance and reliability

Manageability

Oracle Database 12*c* has incorporated some features in this area that could simplify some menial tasks that had to be programmed and executed manually in the past. These include the following:

- Monitoring of long-running jobs by tracking SQL and PL/SQL activity as well as their timelines. Administrators can see exactly what is going on and establish a timeline for each step of the work being performed.

- The Automatic Database Monitor (ADDM) can be trained to wake up itself when the database is experiencing performance issues and trigger collection of information that could assist in isolating the culprit for the slowdown.

- Enterprise Manager Database Express has consolidated a handful of performance screens into one location called the Database Performance Hub.

- Database Replay permits multiple concurrent replays to track how one workload may interact with/affect another. The reporting enhancements are designed to help the administrator zero in on possible reasons for slow or fast replay.

- An engine to assist with masking confidential production data as it is copied into other environments for development, testing, or QA activities.

Performance

This is the final frontier for many application and database experts. 12*c* offers the following to reduce performance bottlenecks that can suddenly plague even the quietest and best-behaved databases:

- A new suite of SQL*Net parameters to allow compression of data on the network

- Support for network buffers larger than previous limits of between 8KB and 64KB

- A mechanism to control asynchronous I/O operations when using Direct NFS Client by limiting the number of requests that can be delivered simultaneously

■ New data dictionary view to assist in tracking the health of the I/O subsystem and in isolating possible culprits of slowdowns that degrade performance and lead to complaints about the speed of the applications

■ Threads, which allow concentration on sharing resources of emerging hardware solutions to take advantage of trends in hyper-threading and multicore processors

Progress Check

1. While there are many new features with Oracle Database 12c, which ones stand out as the most beneficial to adopters?

2. If a numeric field is defined as (5,3), what is the biggest number that it can possibly hold?

3. When coding in sqlplus, what character is used to terminate the code and instruct the processing engine to start its work?

4. Can one have a PDB plugged into more than one container database if more than one CDB could use that PDB's functionality?

Security

Ever since Sarbanes-Oxley reared its head in the 1990s, security has been a big issue in the industry. The following summarizes features in 12c in this important area:

■ Oracle Data Redaction enables sensitive information to be masked or scrambled at runtime or in the database storage locations.

■ Secure Hash Algorithm SHA-2 is now used for database password verification. SHA is a set of cryptographic hash functions designed to take meaningful data and scramble it into an encrypted format. SHA-2 can also be used by developers by calling a package stored as a database object.

Progress Check Answers

1. The suite of enhancements that address storage of ever-increasing volumes of data are the most exciting and compelling for early adopters.

2. The biggest value that can be stored in this field is 99.999.

3. The forward slash terminates a segment of SQL code and instructs Oracle to start processing.

4. A PDB can only be plugged into one CDB at a time.

- Association of database roles with privileges on stored code segments removes the need to explicitly grant these to database users.

- Oracle Data Guard allows non–super user (SYSDBA) personnel to be delegated the rights to perform administrative tasks.

- Database Entitlement Analytics allows one to assemble a list of privileges that are being *used* by database users. Once a list of what is being used is collected, one can deduce what of the privileges *given out* are actually required. This feature ensures that users of the database are not overly privilege-rich.

- The SYSBACKUP privilege can be used to give rights to users to perform backup-related activities without assigning the more powerful SYSDBA role. This contributes to a more secure environment.

- Real Application Security allows enforcement of application-level security in the database tier. This allows identical security policies to be used by multiple applications thereby establishing the consistency in enforcement that used to be an application-by-application code segment.

- Auditing is now the default at the database level and no longer requires downtime to enliven.

XML DB

As of Oracle Database 11*g* (circa 2008), XML DB has been embedded in the product thereby allowing for the power of the relational database technology coupled with the power and convenience of storing, navigating, and querying the XML data. The following summarizes some of the new features delivered with this already robust and popular XML engine in Oracle Database 12*c*:

- Efficiency improvements for a handful of access paths when executing XQuery operations

- Changes to the binary XML format and indexing to optimize the execution of XPath and XQuery operations

- More functionality in the W3C query language allowing fragment and node-level updates

- Added search operators such as MNOT and NEAR designed to add more flexibility in application development

- Full support for common physical partitioning approaches such as hash partitioning and sub-partitioning that administrators cut their teeth on with non-XML DB data

- Unification of best-of-breed query processing characteristics of Oracle and the previous BEA engine

- Support for domain indexes to use hash and interval partitioning

- Integration of support for debugging and viewing XQuery execution plans, aimed at optimizing access to data and throughput of processing

The documentation set for Oracle Database 12*c* should be consulted for further drill-down into the new features of Oracle XML DB.

This section has only scratched the surface of the new features of Oracle Database 12*c*. There will be/have been books on the market from Oracle Press completely dedicated to discussions of these features. As the product releases continue, new features will be added and existing features strengthened with an eye to performance and security as well as many other facets of database management.

☑ Chapter 1 Mastery Check

1. How many megabytes are there in a gigabyte?

2. Why are storage factors in the computer industry expressed as a factor of 2 and not the more common 10?

3. Which comes first—the table or the view?

4. What is the three-fold challenge presented to modern database management technologies?

5. If two users are looking at the same data and one session starts modifying the data, when does the other session see the changes, if ever?

6. What is the maximum number of characters that can be stored in a varchar2 field in the database?

7. What form of structured data is most common in full motion video—semi-structured or unstructured? Why?

8. What is a data anomaly? Give an example to illustrate your definition.

9. What is the biggest number that can be stored in a field defined as *number (6,3)*?

10. Can a view contain 13 columns when the table it is built on contains 23?

11. Can a PDB be plugged into more than one CDB?

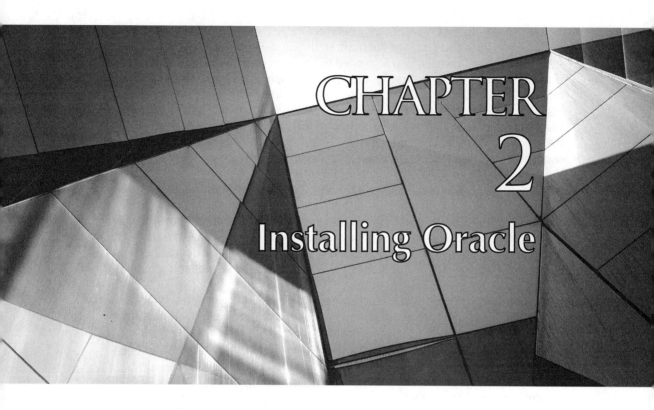

CHAPTER 2

Installing Oracle

CRITICAL SKILLS

Knowledge of the technology behind Oracle databases and understanding its tables and columns are basic skills you need when working with Oracle; however, you also need to know the available configuration options. From hardware to storage and operating system to high availability, the architecture and design of the database system are important when you begin installation. The installation of Oracle requires not just that you execute runInstaller but that you understand the install options of the software to take advantage of all of the functionality of the product. Oracle 12*c* also brings along additional choices at installation with a container database for pluggable databases or the non-container database, which is equivalent to database instances in previous releases. There are many product options and features that you will need to select during installation; for the purposes of this chapter, we suggest you consider installing options for your educational use of the product. Are you ready to install the Oracle software? You are probably not as ready as you think, unless you have already done some research and prepared the environment. Downloading or obtaining the media for the Oracle software is the easy part, but do you know which operating system you are using and have you set up the configurations for Oracle?

Oracle has a proven track record on a variety of operating systems. Oracle 12*c* was first released on the Linux platform, which has become the normal pattern in which Oracle develops and releases products. We suggest that you get the latest version of the software from the Oracle Technology Network (otn.oracle.com) for your chosen platform.

It is also critical to be able to configure the operating system or verify the operating system configuration for successful installs and, ultimately, well-running and well-performing systems. We recommend, therefore, that you have administrator access to the server that you plan to install the software on. Being able to tune or discuss the issues regarding the operating system comes in handy when you're looking at configurations for the system as a whole; deciding when the minimum is not enough and understanding where the dependencies are are valuable parts of successful implementations. This chapter will walk you through some basic steps for installing the Oracle software on Linux, including gathering the information needed for the system requirements and completing a checklist for a Linux installation.

CRITICAL SKILL 2.1

Research and Plan the Installation

Oracle provides some critical information needed for installing the Oracle software, both with the software itself and in the Oracle support site MyOracleSupport notes. These are important documents for successful installs that can help you with the planning and research (for example, the *Quick Installation Guide, Database Readme,* and *Database Release Notes*) and they contain hardware requirements, prerequisites, and the setup to be done before and after installation. Also, information on installation issues for Oracle software can be obtained from most recent release notes, which contain possible workarounds or updated steps for the installs.

Gathering information on what is required to install the software and running it effectively are very important first steps. Neglecting to do this by going straight to the install can mean a lot more work because it may mean that you'll need to uninstall and reinstall parts of the software. You'll want to watch for certain important information, such as what is needed for the operating system to be configured for Oracle to run and the fact that the initial settings are minimum values to be adjusted for larger systems.

With Linux and Unix environments, there are kernel parameters and settings that need to be adjusted when the system starts up. You can use these parameters in many ways, including to allocate shared memory for Oracle and to allocate the number of processes for Oracle. Failure to set parameters and verify the needed system requirements may allow the software to be installed, but it could prevent the database from starting up because the database is unable to get the needed system resources. Each operating system has a particular set of configurations that it needs. There are also patches that need to be in synch with the version of Oracle that is to be installed. So, knowing the requirements that are needed and gathering the needed patches and parameter values for application to the operating system are critical to the install.

Define System Requirements

Hardware minimum requirements are related to processors, memory, and the disk needed to install the OS and Oracle software. For Oracle 12*c*, at least 1GB of RAM is required, and the Oracle software requires 4.5 to 5GB of disk space. The processors themselves can be verified in preinstallation checks. Other hardware requirements, such as network adapters or additional disks, all depend on the environment that is being set up: for example, systems with Real Application Clusters or other additional features.

In taking a closer look at how to prepare the operating system for an Oracle install, let's use Linux as an example from installation to configuration. You'll start the Linux installation by obtaining the media and booting up the server with the Linux media. Oracle Enterprise Linux has included all the needed packages with the standard install. After a bootup of the server, the install screens will appear and will walk you through the simple process of setting up the operating system. The following section and related figures explain the Linux install screens and a basic configuration to get started with Linux.

Linux Installation

Most of the beginning screens simply step through the installation and enable you to configure the very basic server settings. The first install screen that might require additional information is *disk partition*, which has two options: to leave as is or customize. The options include partitions for swap, root, tmp, or other filesystem mount points. The filesystem mount points are the disk mounts for the directories where the software will be installed and the databases will eventually be created. Bare minimum partitions are swap and another device for the file mount points. Figure 2-1 shows the install screen with the standard disk partitions, which is definitely enough to get you started with the Oracle install on Linux.

In Figure 2-1, you can see one logical device for the swap space, which is the memory area on the disk that allows programs to swap to virtual memory when they need more memory than the physical memory contains. There is another device for the boot area, the initial partition of the disk, and then the rest of the disk under the root directory can be used for creating the directories for tmp, var, home, oracle, and so on. Even if it isn't defined on separate devices, the directories that Linux needs, such as the tmp and var directories, will be created during install. However, you will need to create a directory for the Oracle software before you install it.

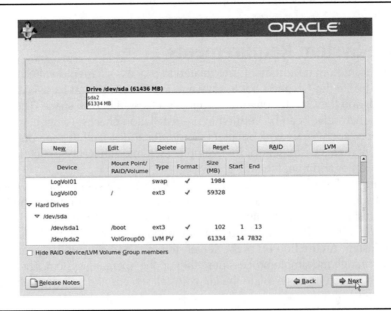

FIGURE 2-1. *Linux install disk partitions*

As shown in Figure 2-1, the devices are configured based on the disk available to the server, and the values and sizes can be adjusted at this point. The swap space can be adjusted later, but it is just as easy to configure here. Also, new mount points or filesystems can be created on the root directory, depending on your needs. After setting the values and mount points, click Next for the next configuration screen. After the *disk partitions* install screen, you need to make a choice about *boot loaders*. In Linux, a boot loader is the piece that loads the operating system into memory (there are usually a couple of them in use). The boot loaders in this case are LILO, Linux Loader, and Grand Unified Bootloader (GRUB). The GRUB boot loader is the default for RedHat and Oracle Linux and can be selected if needed.

The network configuration and devices are the next step. Plug in the IP address and edit the network device on the installation screen, shown in Figure 2-2. This can also be done after installation, using the network settings. This is where the hostname is defined as shown with the domain name; the miscellaneous settings are dependent on the network settings and configurations. Figure 2-2 also shows you where to manually enter the server name with the domain and the miscellaneous settings with the Gateway, Primary, and Secondary DNS.

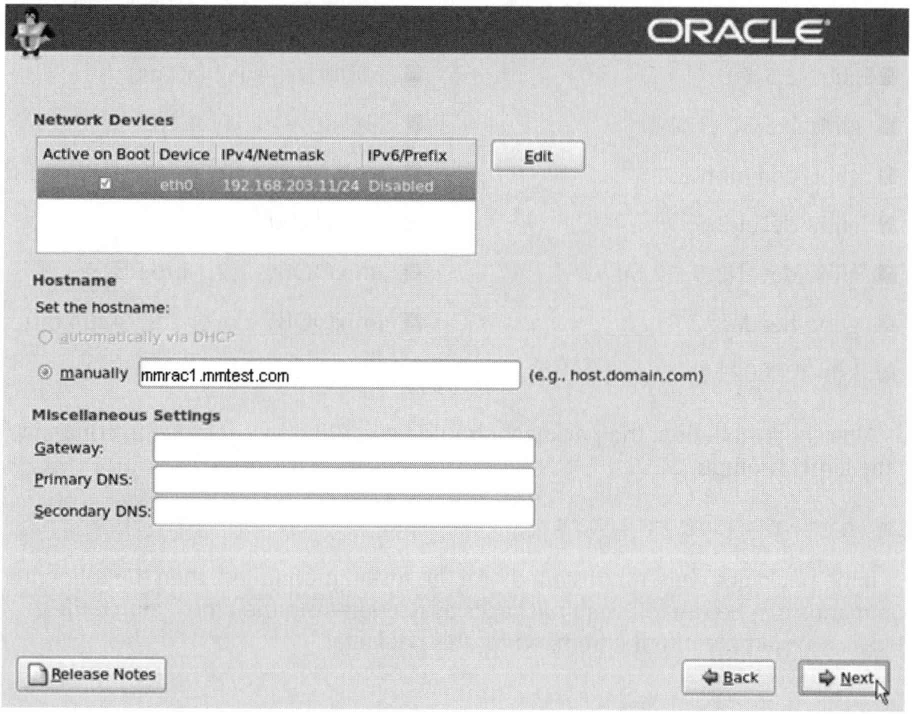

FIGURE 2-2. *Linux network*

The next couple of installation screens go through the root password and time zone information; the proper time zone for your location just needs to be chosen when going through the installation. Choose and remember the root password carefully. At this point, there is no other way to log in to the OS without the root password. The default install will include packages for generic use, but it should also be selected to support software development for this system. The option to customize can be done here, or the needed packages can also be installed afterward. During the install, the packages can just be selected and then verified after the install to ensure that they are completed. The required packages for Oracle Enterprise Linux 5.0 (based on the current installation guide) are as follows:

- binutils-2.17.50.0.6
- compat-libstdc++-33-3.2.3
- compat-libstdc++-33-3.2.3 (32 bit)
- elfutils-libelf-0.125
- elfutils-libelf-devel-0.125
- gcc-4.1.2
- gcc-c++-4.1.2
- glibc-2.5-58
- glibc-2.5-58 (32 bit)
- glibc-common-2.5
- glibc-devel-2.5
- glibc-devel-2.5 (32 bit)
- glibc-headers-2.5
- ksh-20060214

- libaio-0.3.106
- libaio-0.3.106 (32 bit)
- libaio-devel-0.3.106
- libaio-devel-0.3.106 (32 bit)
- libgcc-4.1.2
- libgcc-4.1.2 (32 bit)
- libstdc++-4.1.2
- libstdc++-4.1.2 (32 bit)
- libstdc++-devel-4.1.2
- make-3.81
- sysstat-7.0.2
- unixODBC-2.2.14 (64 bit)
- unixODBC-devel-2.2.14 (64 bit)

After the installation, the packages should be verified by running the command at the Linux prompt:

```
rpm -q unixODBC-devel-2.2.14
```

If the packages were not installed or if the installation failed, then the following commands can be run to install packages as needed from the Linux source files. Here is an example install command for this package:

```
rpm -ivh unixODBC-devel-2*rpm
```

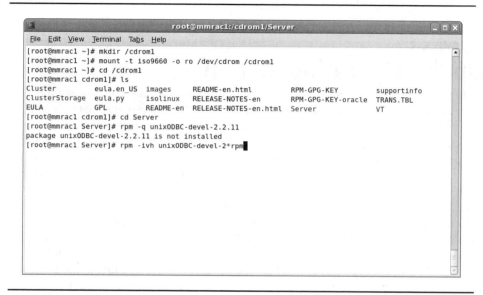

FIGURE 2-3. *Linux package install*

These steps are shown in Figure 2-3; the rpm –q used to verify the packages shows that the unixODBC package was not installed, so executing the command to install the package completes this step. This step is repeated for each of the required packages.

Progress Check

1. What documents are provided for system requirements and installation instructions by Oracle?

2. What is an important first step for installing Oracle software?

3. When installing Linux, which devices are needed when configuring the disk?

4. What is the command for verifying that a package is installed?

5. What is the memory requirement for 12*c*?

Set Up the Operating System

After Linux is installed and rebooted, information screens walk you through the license information and an option to create a user. We recommend that you take this opportunity to create another user besides root because the Oracle user is needed along with groups for the Oracle software inventory. The Oracle software should be installed under the Oracle user created here, but additional users can also be created now, as needed, for supporting different pieces of the software or for different options that may be installed. Oracle grid software can be installed under the software inventory user or a new user. The grid software piece supports an Automatic Storage Management instance, Clusterware, Oracle Restart, and grid control for the server. This is a separate install from the database software and creation, and we recommend that another user should own this software piece.

Figure 2-4 shows the creation of groups using the command line in the terminal window that is needed for Oracle installs. The groups are created using the groupadd command and then associated with a user ID using usermod with the listed parameters and options. Also shown in this figure are the ways that the passwords for the user can be easily changed with the passwd command. Adding another ID, such as osasm to manage the Automatic Storage Management instance, can be accomplished with the command useradd. Here are some examples of additional groups that can be used: OSDBA for the sysdba, OSBACKUPDBA for operating system users with the SYSBACKUP privilege, OSDGDBA for the Oracle Data Guard users with SYSDG, and OSKMDBA for the encryption key and Oracle Wallet Manager. Having the different users and groups will provide separation of duties to manage and administer the different areas of the environment.

The users and groups can be reviewed and managed using the User Manager in System Tools. This interface is also available for creating new users and for associating the groups to the user instead of using the command line in the terminal window. Any users created using this tool and even the users created by the command line, as in Figure 2-4, also have a home directory that is created for them at the same time they are created. The Add User and Add Group options in the User Management Tool do the same task as the useradd and groupadd commands; the tools in Linux make it

Progress Check Answers

1. *Quick Installation Guide, Database Readme, Database Release Notes*

2. Gathering information on system requirements

3. You need two disk devices: swap and / (root) for the file mount points.

4. rpm –q package_name

5. 1GB

```
┌─────────────────────────── root@mmrac1:~ ──────────────────┬───┬───┬───┐
│                                                             │ _ │ □ │ x │
├─────────────────────────────────────────────────────────────────────────┤
│ File  Edit  View  Terminal  Tabs  Help                                    │
├─────────────────────────────────────────────────────────────────────────┤
│ [root@mmrac1 ~]# groupadd oinstall                                        ▲
│ [root@mmrac1 ~]# groupadd oper                                            │
│ [root@mmrac1 ~]# usermod -g oinstall -G dba,oper,oracle oracle            │
│ [root@mmrac1 ~]# passwd oracle                                            │
│ Changing password for user oracle.                                        │
│ New UNIX password:                                                        │
│ Retype new UNIX password:                                                 │
│ passwd: all authentication tokens updated successfully.                   │
│ [root@mmrac1 ~]#                                                          │
│ [root@mmrac1 ~]#                                                          ═
│ [root@mmrac1 ~]# groupadd asmadmin                                        │
│ [root@mmrac1 ~]# useradd osasm                                            │
│ [root@mmrac1 ~]# usermod -g oinstall -G asmadmin,dba,oper osasm           │
│ [root@mmrac1 ~]# passwd osasm                                             │
│ Changing password for user osasm.                                        ▼
└───────────────────────────────────────────────────────────────────────────┘
```

FIGURE 2-4.   *Create groups and users.*

easy to perform these tasks in a way that is most familiar, with either the command lines or user interfaces. Here are the example commands to add a group:

```
#groupadd dba

#groupadd oper

#groupadd oinstall
```

Ask the Expert

Q: Are there security concerns with adding users? Do you really need any other users besides root and oracle?

A: Security for the operating system is important. Make sure that logins are created for users to install the Oracle software and that additional users are created for the purpose of allowing database administrators to log in and maintain Oracle and the database. Anyone logging into the system should have their own user ID; use of the Oracle login should be limited to installation and patching of the software. Different users should have permissions to access only areas that they should be allowed to access in order to perform tasks as needed. Filesystem permissions should be granted only to the groups and users that need the access, and should be limited where possible. Research best practices for security and don't share logins or root passwords. Keep the environment secure by limiting access to the Oracle software directories; make sure it is not open to just any user who is able to log into the server.

Because the Oracle user is the owner of the software binaries, the user needs certain other permissions along with resource permissions for the software to run well. This is done by adding the Oracle user to the /etc/security/limits.conf file and session information to the /etc/pam.d/login file. The file limits.conf, as listed next, shows that the Oracle user has been added with resources to nproc and nofile parameters at the end of the file. These files can be edited with Notepad, vi, or another text editor or a similar editing program when you open the files by using Explorer windows or a filesystem:

```
limits.conf file:
#<domain>   <type>   <item>   <value>
#
oracle       soft     nproc    2047
oracle       hard     nproc    16384
oracle       soft     nofile   1024
oracle       hard     nofile   65536
# End of file
```

These kernel settings are areas that can also be tuned for different environments and database usage. The following code illustrates how to set the minimum requirements; tuning would depend on usage and server resources. Along with limits.conf, the login file needs to be checked to pull in the configurations at login.

```
/etc/pam.d/login file:
#%PAM-1.0
auth [user_unknown=ignore success=ok ignore=ignore default=bad]
pam_security.so
auth        include    system-auth
account     required   pam_nologin.so
account     include    system-auth
password    include    system-auth

# pam_selinux.so close should be the first session rule
session     required   pam_selinux.so close
session     include    system-auth
session     required   pam_loginuid.so
session     optional   pam_console.so
# pam_selinux.so open should only be followed by sessions to be
executed in the  user context
session     required   pam_selinux.so open
session     optional   pam_keyinit.so force revoke
session     required   /lib/security/pam-limits.so
session     required   pam_limits.so
```

Now the operating system is installed and users and groups are created and configured with the needed permissions. You still need to verify (and possibly update) some configurations needed by the kernel parameters so that they match at least the minimum requirements for Oracle. The *Oracle Quick Installation Guide* is the reference for these requirements. We hope that you are starting to see the importance of these documents and why these pieces of information should be gathered before you start the installs.

Project 2-1 **Configure Kernel Parameters**

Oracle's Unbreakable Enterprise Kernel provides the kernel parameters based on the Oracle development kernel and the configuration being used. Use of the Oracle Kernel is optional, and if not being used there may be a need to adjust the kernel parameters. One should also verify the kernel version with uname –r to validate that the kernel is a supported version. There is a compatibility matrix on My Oracle Support, and the information is in the OS requirements documentation. This project walks you step by step through the process of changing the kernel parameters and shows the values of these settings.

Step by Step

1. Get the minimum values from the installation guide. Here is a quick list:

Semmsl	250
Semmns	32000
Semopm	100
Semmni	128
Shmall	2097152
Shmmax	The lesser of the two: either half the size of the physical memory or 4GB
Shmmni	4096
file-max	512*PROCESSES
ip_local_port_range	Min: 1024, max: 650000
rmem_default	4194304
rmem_max	4194304
wmem_default	262144
wmem_max	262144

2. Verify the parameters that are currently set. There may be values already set above the minimum value, so these would not need to be changed. At the command line, type the following:

```
# /sbin/sysctl -a | grep <param-name>
```

3. Substitute the parameter name for param-name. For example, shm will show the values for the semaphore parameters:

```
# /sbin/sysctl -a | grep shm
kernel.shmmni = 4096
kernel.shmall = 2097152
kernel.shmmax = 2147483648
```

4. Edit the /etc/sysctl.conf file to adjust the kernel parameter values. Use vi or another text editor to add the line as listed under #ORACLE 12cR1 kernel parameters at the end of the file. The other parameter that was changed was kernel.shmmax. Here is the example /etc/sysctl.conf file; the areas that need to change or be added are in bold:

```
sysctl.conf edits:
# Controls the maximum size of a message, in bytes
kernel.msgmnb = 65536
# Controls the default maximum size of a message queue
kernel.msgmax = 65536
# Controls for maximum shared segment size, in bytes
# CHANGED FOR ORACLE 12c # kernel.shmmax = 1073740324
kernel.shmmax = 2147483648
# Controls the maximum number of shared memory segments, in
pages
kernel.shmall = 2097152
#ORACLE 12c Kernel Parameters - add the following lines
fs.file-max = 6553600
kernel.shmmni = 4096
kernel.sem = 250 32000 100 128
net.ipv4.ip_local_port_range = 1024 65000
net.core.rmem_default = 4194304
net.core.rmem_max = 4194304
net.core.wmem_default = 262144
net.core.wmem_max = 262144
```

5. Reload the kernel parameters for the new values to take effect. This can be done by restarting the server or by using the following command to reload:

```
# /sbin/syctl -p
```

The execution of this command and its output are shown in Figure 2-5.

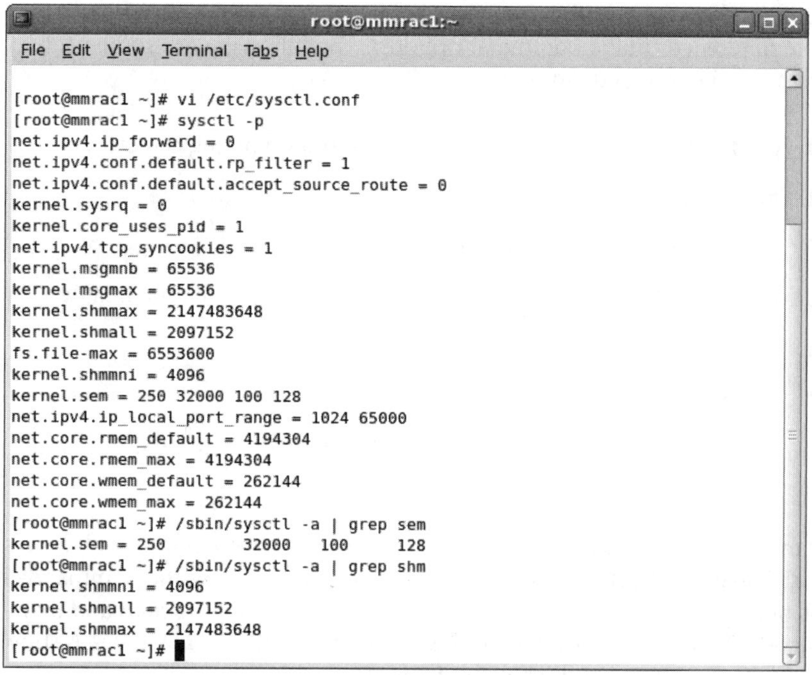

```
root@mmrac1:~
File  Edit  View  Terminal  Tabs  Help
[root@mmrac1 ~]# vi /etc/sysctl.conf
[root@mmrac1 ~]# sysctl -p
net.ipv4.ip_forward = 0
net.ipv4.conf.default.rp_filter = 1
net.ipv4.conf.default.accept_source_route = 0
kernel.sysrq = 0
kernel.core_uses_pid = 1
net.ipv4.tcp_syncookies = 1
kernel.msgmnb = 65536
kernel.msgmax = 65536
kernel.shmmax = 2147483648
kernel.shmall = 2097152
fs.file-max = 6553600
kernel.shmmni = 4096
kernel.sem = 250 32000 100 128
net.ipv4.ip_local_port_range = 1024 65000
net.core.rmem_default = 4194304
net.core.rmem_max = 4194304
net.core.wmem_default = 262144
net.core.wmem_max = 262144
[root@mmrac1 ~]# /sbin/sysctl -a | grep sem
kernel.sem = 250         32000    100      128
[root@mmrac1 ~]# /sbin/sysctl -a | grep shm
kernel.shmmni = 4096
kernel.shmall = 2097152
kernel.shmmax = 2147483648
[root@mmrac1 ~]#
```

FIGURE 2-5. *Verify the kernel parameters using sysctl –p.*

Project Summary

In walking through this project, you now know how to see the kernel parameters, make changes to the parameters, and verify those changes. In changing the kernel parameters, you are making the necessary optimizations for the Oracle software to run on the Linux platform.

CRITICAL SKILL 2.3

Get Familiar with Linux

Having the user interface and the terminal window for access to the command line means that there are a couple of ways to navigate through Linux and do what needs to be done. In previous examples of using the command line, files were edited, users were added, and parameters were set up. In managing some of the Oracle files and directories, it is useful to know some of the basic commands or how to look up the option for the commands. Changing directories, copying and moving files, editing, and looking at the content of the file are all basic actions in Linux (and the commands are almost the same as what is used in Unix, with a couple of possible differences in the parameter options). The following are some useful Linux commands, with a brief definition:

- **pwd**   This shows the current directory (print working directory).
- **more *filename***   Lists the file.
- **ls**   Lists the files in the directory.
- **echo $VAR**   Shows value of variables or echoes back the text.
- **mv *filename newfilename***   Renames a file.
- **cp *filename /newdirectory***   Copies a file.
- **rm *filename***   Removes (deletes) a file; wildcards can be used but are not recommended for a root directory.

Manual pages are available to provide details for commands as well as available options. The man pages also provide examples for how to use the commands in the details of the page. This information can be accessed by typing **man** and then the command. The following is an example of the command, and Figure 2-6 shows the results of this command and what can be found in the man pages.

 `$man grep`

Progress Check

1. How are kernel parameters verified on Linux?

2. What is the Linux command to view the manual pages for grep?

3. What is the command to create a Unix group?

Progress Check Answers

1. sysctl –p

2. man grep

3. groupadd oinstall

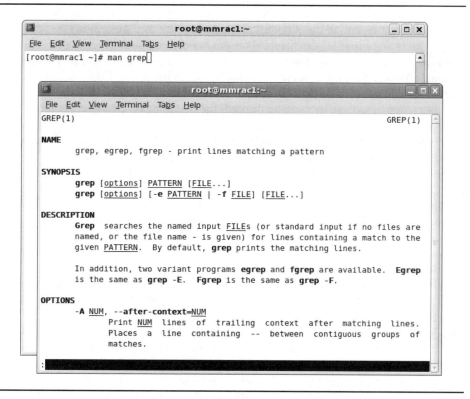

FIGURE 2-6. *OUTPUT of man commands*

CRITICAL SKILL 2.4

Choose Components to Install

Various components of the Oracle software are automatically installed; some are available as additional downloads. With Oracle 12*c*, the following products are installed by default with the database:

- Oracle Database Vault
- Oracle SQL Developer
- Oracle Configuration Manager
- Oracle Application Express
- Oracle Warehouse Builder

This section is not going to turn into a discussion of licensing for standard or enterprise editions and of the different products that are available; however, there are products that provide benefits for different needs. You should verify the licensing of the products and options once the needs have been identified. It's also helpful to review the products and versions to match them with business needs before installation of these products at the same time as the initial install. It is possible to add products by running through the install again and choosing the options that have not yet been installed.

High availability will be discussed more in Chapter 7, and Automatic Storage Management (ASM) is a part of Oracle Clusters but can also be installed on a non-clustered, standalone server. The reason for discussing this now is that ASM and Oracle Restart are actually a different install than the database. This is part of the Grid Infrastructure installation, which would need to be installed before the database install. The Grid Infrastructure should be installed in a separate home called the GRID_HOME. The Cluster Synchronization Services (CSS) and the ASM instance are the components that would be needed as part of this install. To use these components, refer to Chapter 7 for the Grid Infrastructure install.

The Oracle Universal Installer allows for the Basic install, which just installs the default options for Oracle. An advanced option is available for deselecting or selecting other available options. The installer will also step through different creation assistants after the install of the software, unless the option for only installing the software is chosen. With 12*c*, container databases can be installed after the software is installed and independently by stepping through the database creation assistant. Because this is the case, we recommended that you do the software-only install first, and then run through the different creation assistants individually.

Install the Oracle Software

To begin, run the Oracle Universal Installer as oracle from the downloaded software that has been unzipped on the filesystem:

```
[oracle@mmrac1 database]$ ./runInstaller
```

The first couple of steps are for setup of the configuration manager, which will help with patching information and getting updates from My Oracle Support. Providing an e-mail and Oracle support account should make updates and applying patches easier, as the databases will be connected to your support account. Under My Oracle Support, patches are listed based on the information from the database, thus saving you the trouble of searching for the appropriate patches and checking for compatibility.

Starting with Figure 2-7, let's walk through some of the screens of the Oracle Universal Installer. Each of the following illustrations provides some detail about what options to select and information to provide while installing the Oracle software.

As shown in Figure 2-7, the first choice is to install the software and to have the database creation assistant start right after the software install to allow for creation of the database. This is the default option, but it makes sense to do just a software install first for ease of troubleshooting any issues. Each of the assistants can be run independently afterward. The third choice is to perform an in-place upgrade of the database following the binaries install. This will upgrade in place any existing database chosen to be upgraded on the server.

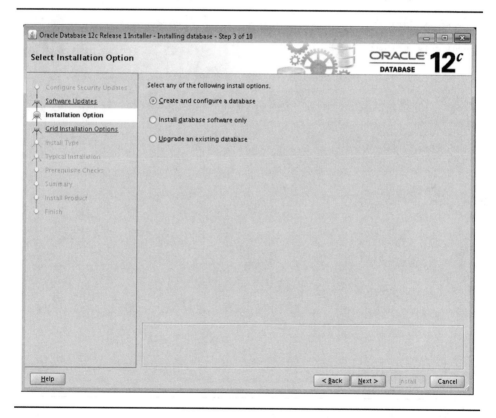

FIGURE 2-7. *Installation Options screen*

There are different classes of hardware that the software can be installed on. Most common when setting up a database server, the Server Class options should be selected for a server. However, in doing some testing or development work, it might make sense to choose the Desktop Class option to install on a laptop or desktop. Because a laptop has fewer resources than most servers, some of the options to configure database parameters and filesystems might be slightly different than the Server Class option, which is the option these steps are walking through.

Figure 2-8 shows the next choice, which is for a single instance install or installation of a Real Application Cluster. Real Application Clusters are discussed in greater detail in Chapter 7, including the steps needed for the software install.

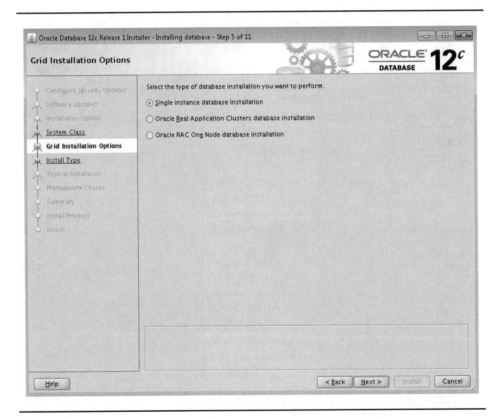

FIGURE 2-8. *Grid Installation Options screen*

There are some additional pre-installation tasks as well as a different installer for the Grid Infrastructure that will need to be installed first. For this walkthrough, we are going to do a single instance install.

As you can see in the next illustration, there are three types of installs: Enterprise, Standard, or Standard Edition One. Choosing Enterprise or Standard installs the default products for those versions. Obviously, the Enterprise and Standard versions have different licensing issues, and limitations are set on the Standard edition for CPUs and the options that can be added. Some may argue that you should install only what is needed, while others may suggest that for a development environment, you should install everything to allow developers to test and try out different options. The Select Options button is only available in the Enterprise Edition and allows for the selection of the following options: Oracle Partitioning, Oracle OLAP, Oracle Data Mining RDBMS Files, and Oracle Real Application Testing.

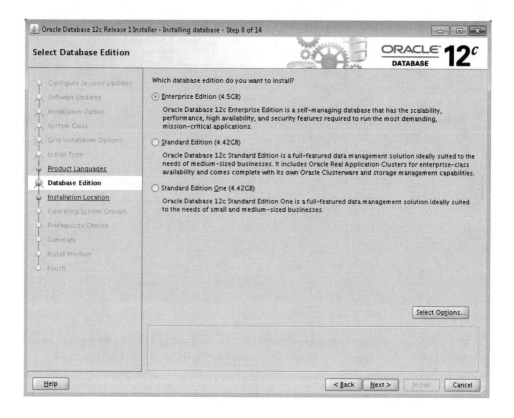

On a server, there can be several home directories with different versions, options, and patch sets installed. The following illustration shows an example of what the base directory and home directory should be set to. If doing a new install, this should be a new directory, and for additional components or patching existing ones, an existing Oracle home directory should be chosen. If a new directory is going to be created, the Oracle user will need to have permission on the base filesystem, or this can be set up before the install.

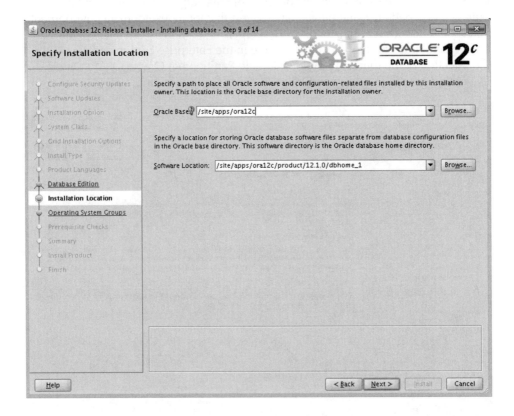

The users and groups that were created in the beginning of this chapter are now needed for the next screen, as shown in the following illustration. Each of these components can have its own OS user and group. That way, the owner of the encryption key can be different from the database or backup and recovery operator. The separation of duties for compliance reasons is the main goal of having these in different groups. You might also want to separate out the roles based on job tasks, and using the groups to own the software component will set up permissions for that.

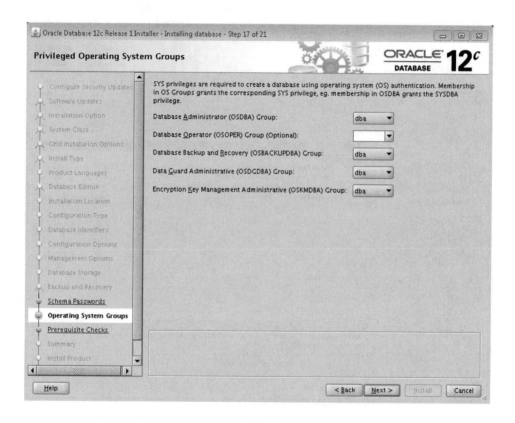

The prerequisite check validates the operating system and configuration. It has checks for filesystems, permissions, swap size, and several other requirements for successfully installing the Oracle software. You can attempt to address issues here directly as a script is created to make the needed changes. Other changes can be made outside of these scripts, and then there is a Check Again button to validate that these changes are successful. We don't recommend ignoring these issues. It is better to fix these issues here instead of waiting for failure during the install. If any issues or errors come up, this would be the first place to look for more information.

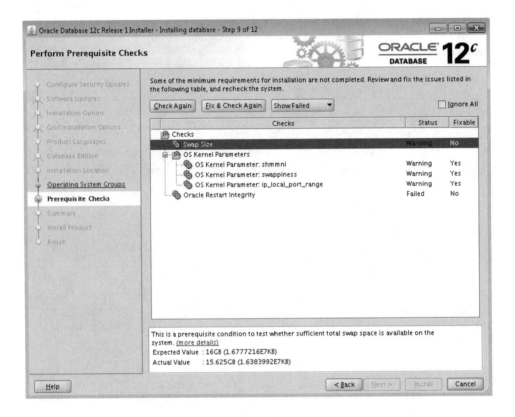

The next illustration provides the summary of the software installation. It will list the directories where the Oracle binaries are going to be installed. The space requirement and the options that were chosen as part of this install are also shown in this summary screen.

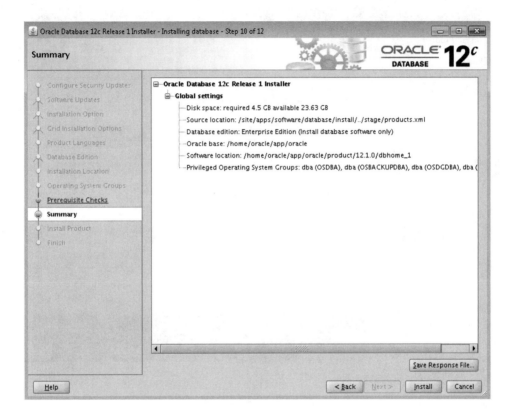

The following illustration shows the files are being copied and installed. Note the location of the log file. If any issues or errors come up, this would be the first place to look for more information.

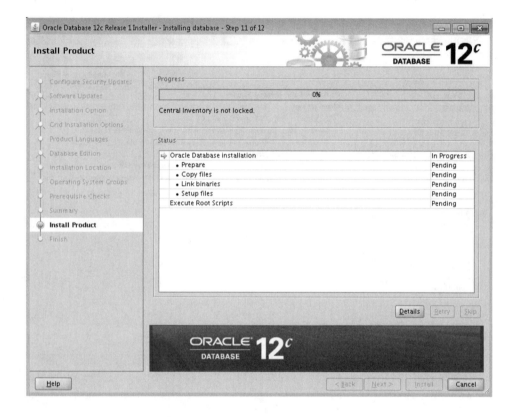

Your last steps are demonstrated in the following illustration. To complete the installation, you will need to make changes regarding permissions and directories that are owned by root. There are two scripts that need to be executed by the root owner to make these changes. Have the operating system administrator log in and run orainstRoot.sh and root.sh (as shown in the illustration).

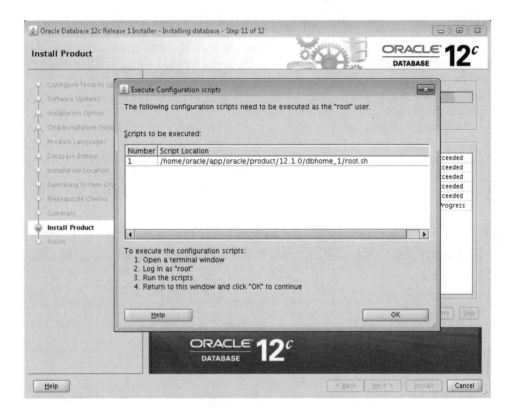

The final screen that states End of Installation is a good screen to see because it means that the installation of the Oracle software has completed successfully. The installation went through the basic install of the software. Now it is required to run through any creation assistance that is needed to complete the creation of the database.

Database Configuration Assistant

As part of the installation, the database configuration assistant (dbca) can be configured to start up after the initial software install. Otherwise, the assistant can be started any time to create a new database instance. The dbca has standard templates to be used for different types of databases; the templates have some parameter settings for memory and others based on the type of instance. The passwords and directories for the tablespaces can use the default values or be customized. As part of the planning process, you should decide these configurations based on the directory structures and templates to be used. The DBA needs to keep a checklist to determine which templates, parameter settings, and other choices are to be made within the assistant. The advantage is that even after the database instance is created, you can adjust parameters and file locations. However, some adjustments are easier than others, and there are even more dynamic parameters that can be changed while the database is up and available, instead of your having to restart the database instance to make the change in value for the parameter.

As shown in Figure 2-9, the database can be created or an existing database can be dropped. Until Oracle 11gR2, there was also the option to create an Automatic Storage Management (ASM) instance, which is described in more detail in Chapter 7, but now the ASM instance is part of the grid installation. The next option to Configure Database Options shows components of the database that can be selected to install

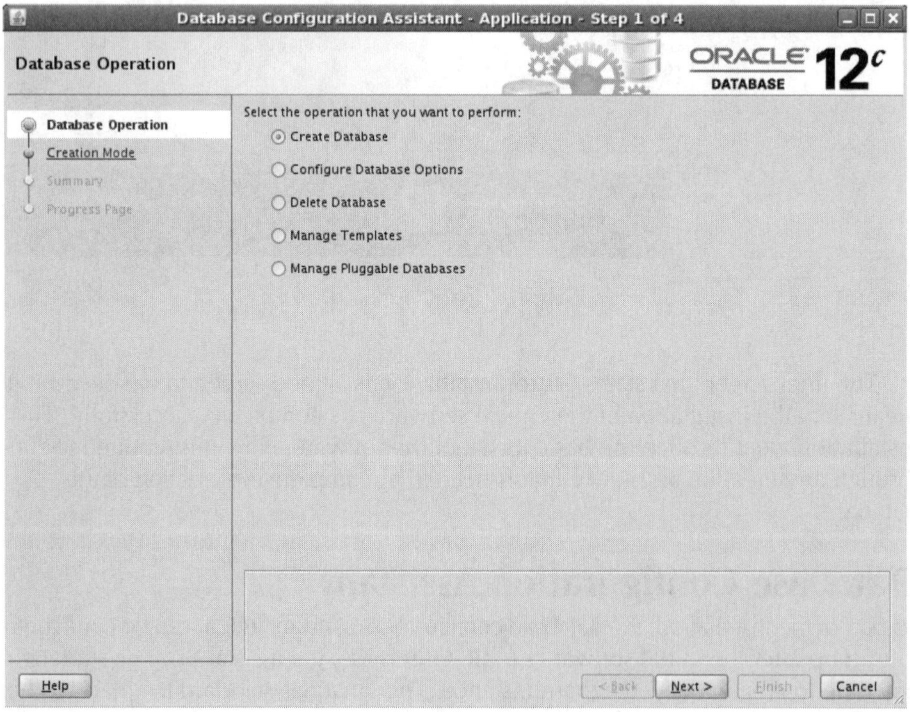

FIGURE 2-9. *Option for install of database*

on an existing database. There are now more default components that are installed with the database without previously selecting them. Managing Templates sets the default values for the different templates used to create the databases. Templates can be created from the Oracle templates or another existing database. The templates help with creating consistent databases across the environment.

Also seen in Figure 2-9, there is a new option in Oracle 12*c* to manage the pluggable databases. This will allow for new pluggable databases to be created, unplugged, or deleted. We discuss managing the pluggable databases in Chapter 5 because a container database must first be created to house the pluggable databases and manage them.

Seen in Figure 2-10, there are different modes for creation: Typical Mode or Advanced Mode. As with other screen options, there are additional customizations with advanced settings, or the basic components and setup with a typical install.

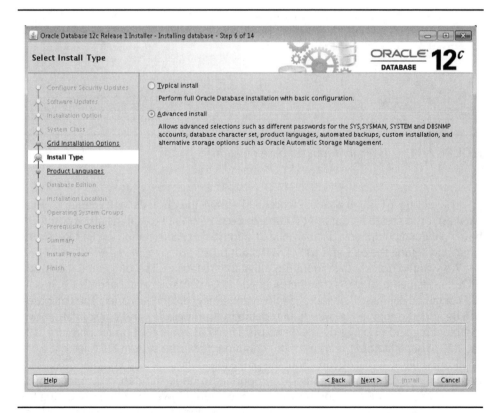

FIGURE 2-10. *Option for install of database*

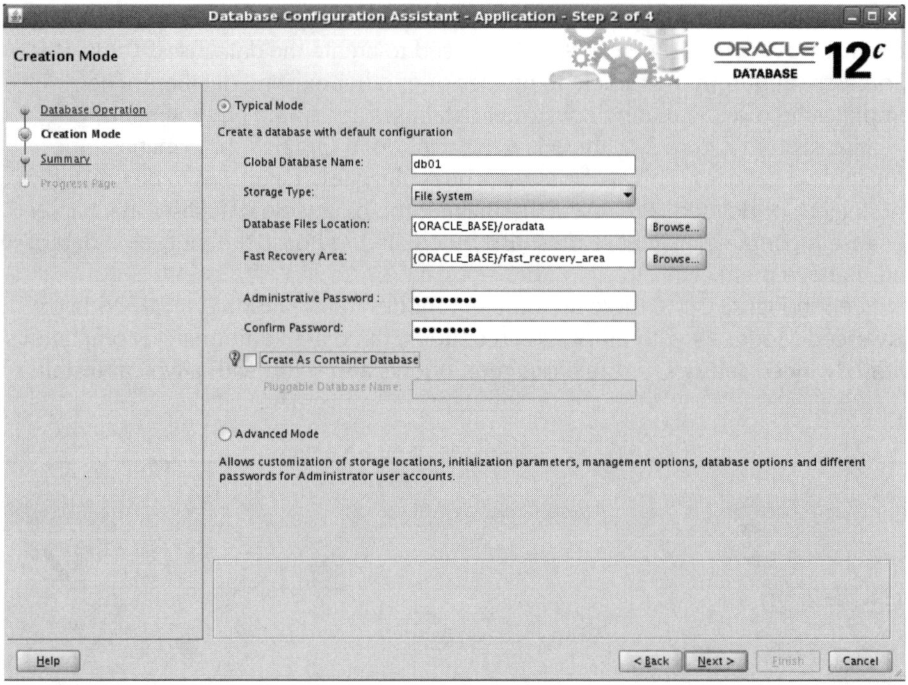

FIGURE 2-11. *Typical Mode database creation*

In selecting a Typical Mode, Figure 2-11 shows the choices for a regular, typical database or to create a container database. Even with the typical install, you still have configuration options: database file location, using ASM, setting the Fast Recovery Area, and setting the SYS and SYSTEM default password.

We want to quickly talk about the pluggable database. The pluggable database (PDB), as its name suggests, can be plugged into a container database (CDB). It is a self-contained database that makes deployment of new databases easier. The databases can be added or moved to a container database for upgrades and consolidation by just plugging and unplugging the database. The PDB can be set up for different security to separate out the roles of the container database system DBA from the application DBA. A discussion about the pluggable databases and container databases is continued in Chapter 5 because it is important to understand the advantages of using container databases and how to manage them. However, when discussing the installation, it is just a decision to be made for the dbca to create a general database or a container database. After the install, pluggable databases can be added by running through the database creation assistant.

If you're just running through the Typical Mode install, the information for database name, type of storage, and passwords needs to be entered, as Figure 2-11 illustrates.

In the Typical Mode, the next screen is just a summary confirming the database that is going to be created. Clicking Finish in the summary will create the database described. Even when selecting Create As Container Database, as Figure 2-12 shows, the next screen is the summary.

The Summary page shown in Figure 2-13 lists the information about the database to be created. This is the information that is used to create the database scripts and provide the detail for the template. It is a quick check before actually creating the database, and if there are options that were not expected or options that were needed, this is the opportunity to go back and run through an advanced database creation.

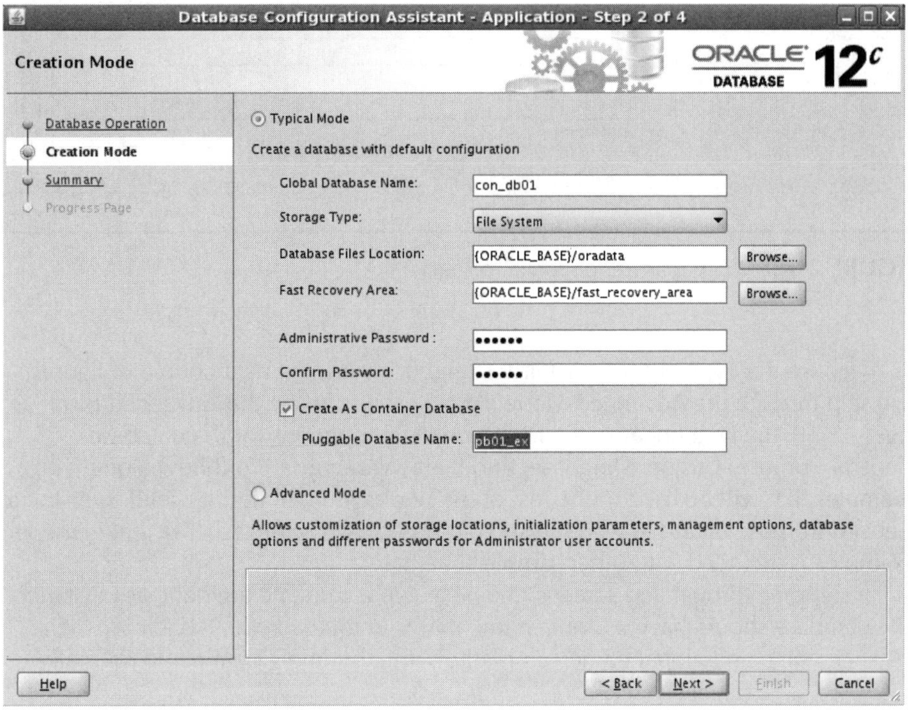

FIGURE 2-12.   *Create As Container Database*

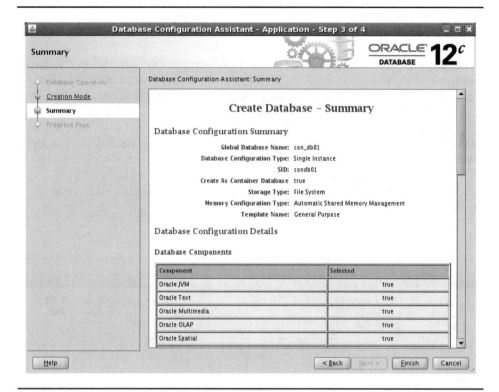

FIGURE 2-13. *Database Creation Summary*

Because the Typical Mode is fairly straightforward, the next couple of figures will step through the Advanced Mode. After you've chosen the Advanced Mode in Figure 2-10, the next dbca screen has three default options for the databases: General Purpose, Custom Database, and Data Warehouse. To follow along with examples that will be used in the rest of the book, you will find it useful to install a General Purpose database with the sample schemas. The SH schema that is used for examples is included with other sample schemas.

In stepping through the screens, the next step is to name the database instance. The database should have a global name that is unique across all databases. The instance name and global name can be the same, but the global name normally contains the full domain. Here again, you see the option to create a container database along with a number of pluggable databases. The pluggable databases can be added later, but for now, creating one pluggable database will get the container database with a database already plugged in ready to go.

Passwords should be set for SYS and SYSTEM. All of the system passwords can be the same, or they can all be different. The main thing is that these passwords should not be set with a default value as they have been in the past, and there will be a warning if the password chosen is not a strong password. Anyone who knows about installing Oracle and default passwords would be able to log into the database if the default were not changed. For now, you can limit the choices for the database install to defaults or basic choices. As you learn more about what the system is to be used for, you can make more adjustments with parameters and configurations.

The next step includes setting the storage type for the data files. This includes the option to use Automatic Storage Management (ASM) or filesystem location. Other storage decisions are the location and size for the Fast Recovery Area. The Fast Recovery Area will keep logs and possibly backups, depending on the size of the recovery area, for quicker recovery. The location for this space is set here along with the size. The size for this area can be changed dynamically, so a good estimate for size is all that is needed at the time of creation.

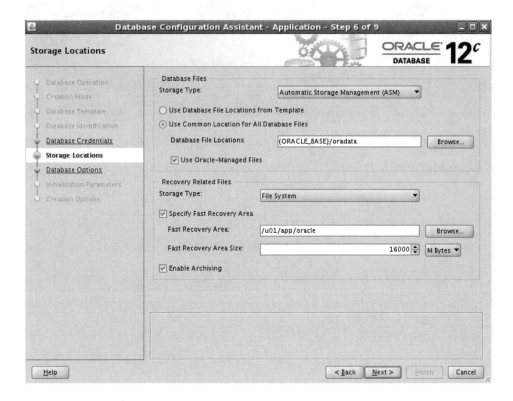

Sample schemas are available for testing some of the new functionality as well as learning Oracle. With that in mind, the sample schemas should be installed in a test database because there are examples in this book that use the sample schemas.

The next illustration shows the Sample Schemas checkbox, which needs to be selected to install the samples.

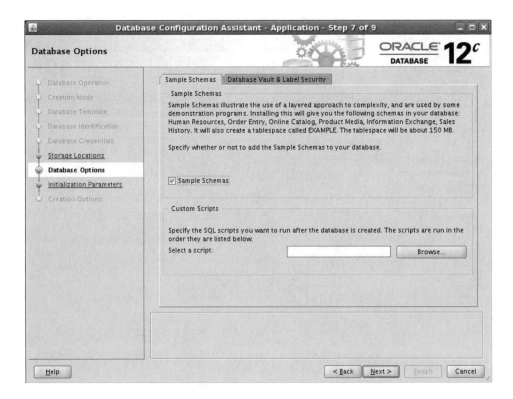

There is also an option to run custom scripts after the database's creation, which might be used for something like running a script to create user or tablespaces. The scripts can come from another database and serve as a way to keep the environments consistent. The next tab in this screen enables you to set up security options and configurations for Oracle Database Vault and Label Security.

The initialization parameters can be configured as you create the database. The following illustration shows Step 8 of the database configuration assistant, where these parameters can be configured. You can customize the memory or use default values based on a percentage of overall available memory. You should also set up the character set; it is more difficult to change, unlike the memory settings, so verifying the character set for the database is important. The character sets are important for databases with international characters and globalization of the characters. When dealing with international characters, we suggest that you use a character set that allows for these values. Unicode character sets support characters with different sizes and in multiple languages.

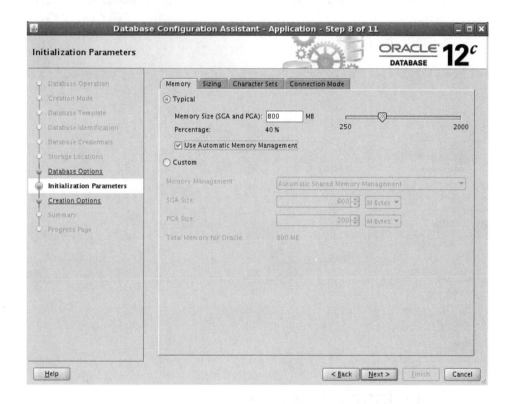

Creating the database, creating the scripts, and developing a template are the final steps before the database is actually created. The following illustration shows the option to save the database as a template and to generate database creation scripts. The database creation scripts are a valuable tool for creating another similar database, or when you need to create the database again without the assistant. Look through the script to see what the commands are for database creation. This is a good way to understand the pieces involved and may provide some tricks with the database administration. The templates will be added to the creation process of other databases in this Oracle home, again, making it easier to create another database that is similar in nature.

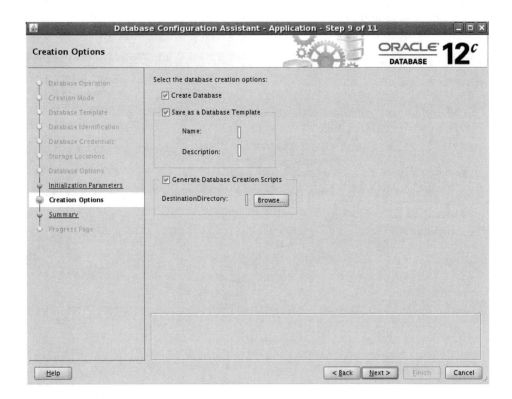

Verify the Installation

The operating system is now configured, the Oracle software is installed, and an initial database has been created. Now the system should be reviewed to confirm that everything is in the right place and that everything is working as expected. Looking through the directories and log directories of the database to verify the install is very useful. Check the install log file, which was the log file that was listed during the install of the software. See Figure 2-14 for example output of the log file.

Review the alert logs of the database and check the logs for any issues with the startup or parameters of the database. The default location for the log files is $ORACLE_BASE\admin\SID. This information can also be retrieved by queries to the database and selecting the value from v$parameter where the name = 'background_dump_dest'. Look at the filesystems to make sure that the data files are going to the directory that is expected. Again, a quick query against the database, such as select file_name from dba_data_files, will show all of the current data files.

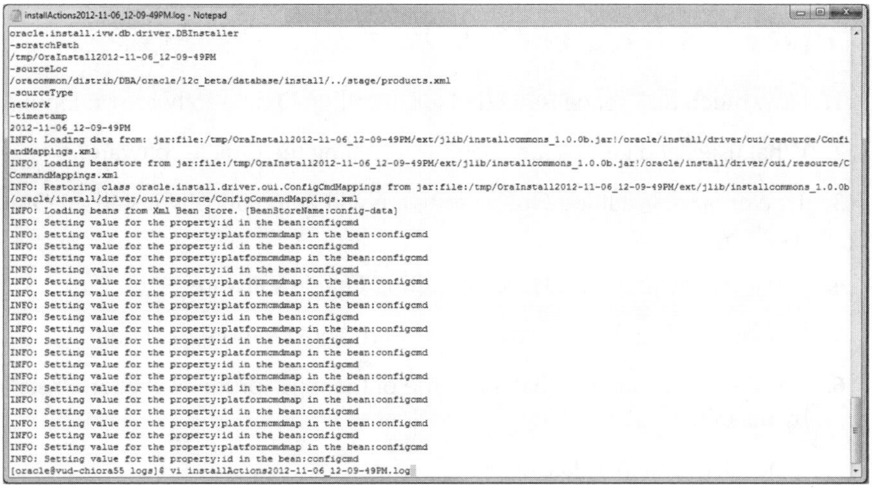

FIGURE 2-14. *Log file details*

Several of these checks are listed in greater detail in later chapters of the book and will show more details about the tools Oracle provides to manage the database. Check the memory usage on the operating system level to ensure that the right amount of memory was configured for Oracle and that there is space available for user processes, too. Use commands such as top to see what the top processes are and to view memory usage for the processes. The filesystems should also have enough space; you should verify this after installing Oracle and creating the database.

After these initial checks, the system should be ready to use, allowing you to install the front-end application, add users, and set up monitoring and backups. Setting up backups and monitoring also helps verify that the system is ready to go and might be a good step to complete before allowing other users to access the database.

Tie It All Together

When doing an Oracle install, the upfront planning and research are important. Gathering business requirements in order to match up database options and versions is also a critical first step to doing the installations. A basic understanding of an operating system is needed to work through the install and to ensure that the user permissions, required system, and hardware components are available. Oracle Enterprise Linux has a standard install, with packages that match up to the database requirements. Gathering documents that provide the latest information about issues and needed prerequisites will make the overall installation go smoothly and offer the added bonus of starting an install process that is repeatable in the production environment.

☑ Chapter 2 Mastery Check

1. How much disk space is needed for installing Oracle software on Linux?

2. What users and groups are used for installing the Oracle software?

3. True or false: Installing Oracle software will automatically install an Oracle database.

4. What are the prerequisites for installing Oracle software?

5. What is the Oracle home directory? Can there be more than one?

6. Besides the database, what are some of the other products that are installed by default?

7. What is a container database?

8. What is the tool for creating a database, after the Oracle software install?

9. What tool can be used for managing pluggable databases?

10. Which scripts need to be run by root (system administrator) after the install of the software?

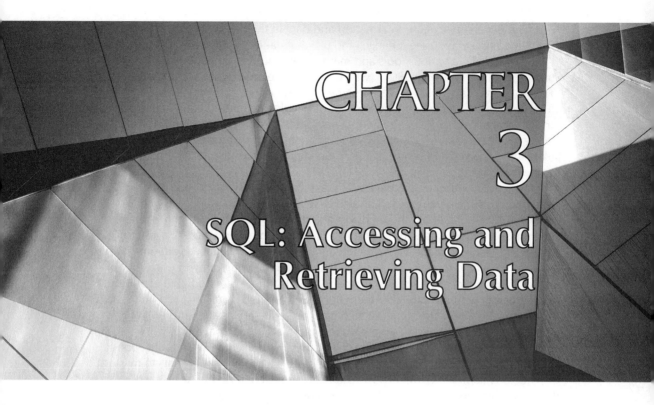

CHAPTER 3

SQL: Accessing and Retrieving Data

CRITICAL SKILLS

The capability to store information and data in the database is useful only if there is a way to see, change, and use that data. All databases can be accessed via various tools and methods, but at the foundation of all of this is Structured Query Language (SQL), which is the powerful language that allows you to do just that. With SQL, you can provide the insight into company information and data; it is the fundamental access tool of Oracle Database. In fact, it is the fundamental access tool of all relational databases. With SQL, or a form of it, you will be able to do everything you want to your data and database. This is how we talk to the database, and learning SQL is fundamental to your success with the Oracle database.

SQL is used to start up the database, make parameter changes, and monitor the performance of the database. SQL is also used to build database objects and to query and manipulate both these objects and the data they may contain. You cannot insert a row of data into an Oracle database unless you have first issued some basic SQL statements to create the underlying tables. Database administration requires being able to query the dictionary tables and issuing other queries to perform maintenance. While Oracle provides SQL*Plus, a SQL tool that enables you to interact with the database, there are also many GUI tools that can be used, such as Oracle's SQL Developer, which can then issue SQL statements on your behalf behind the scenes. However you decide to access the database, you will need to understand the fundamentals of SQL. SQL will become your connection to your data and it is an important starting point for all Oracle professionals to master.

Oracle Database 12c offers new features that make it easier to access sets of data and more functionality to allow more tables as part of outer joins, but at the basic level, SQL is a standard language to access databases, and you will need to understand how best to take advantage of the language to make your data manipulation as effective as possible. Examples of these will be discussed in this chapter. So let's get started and dive into the world of SQL.

CRITICAL SKILL 3.1

Learn the SQL Statement Components

Before you learn the many SQL commands that you will use frequently, you should take a look at the two different categories that SQL statements are classified into. They are DDL, or *data definition language,* and DML, or *data manipulation language.* The majority of this chapter will deal with the latter. There are two other types, which are more functional and administrative, but all are part of SQL as a whole. DCL, or *data control language,* provides users with the capability to grant and revoke privileges within the database, while TCL, or *transaction control language,* is used to control how data is posted to the database with commands such as commit and rollback. Together, all of these types of commands make up the SQL engine within the database.

DDL

DDL is the set of SQL statements that define or delete database objects such as tables or views. For the purposes of this chapter, you will concentrate on dealing with tables. Examples of DDL include any SQL statements that begin with create, alter, and drop: All of these commands act upon a database object, such as a table, view, or trigger, among many others. Table 3-1 provides a sample list of some DDL statements. It does not completely represent the many varied statements that all have a unique purpose and value.

The following SQL statements are examples of DDL create and drop statements in action:

```
SQL> create table answers
2 (response char(1));
Table created.

SQL> drop table answers;
Table dropped.

SQL> create table us_states
  2  (state_cd  char(2) not null,
  3  state_name varchar2(30));
Table created.
```

SQL Command	Purpose
CREATE TABLE	Creates a table
CREATE INDEX	Creates an index
ALTER TABLE	Adds a column, redefines an existing column, changes storage allocation
DROP TABLE	Drops a table
TRUNCATE TABLE	Removes all rows from the table
GRANT	Grants privileges or roles to a user or another role
REVOKE	Removes privileges from a user or a role
ANALYZE	Used to validate structure or list chained rows, also used for earlier releases for object statistics, but since the Oracle 10g DBMS_STATS package should be used to collect the object statistics

TABLE 3-1.   *Common Formats for Date Type Data*

After you have created your table, you should confirm that it was created as you expected. To display a description of a table, the describe command is used. Our experience suggests that you will find it very useful to be able to describe tables within the database after you create them or any time you need to know the exact nature of the table. You should take a closer look at the state table that you created in the previous example:

```
SQL> desc us_states;

Name                                          Null?      Type
--------------------------------------------- ---------- -------------------
STATE_CD                                       NOT NULL   CHAR(2)
STATE_NAME                                                VARCHAR2(30)
```

NOTE
The identity column is a new feature in Oracle 12c. In previous releases, an ID was incremented by a trigger and a sequence, but now a column can be created as an IDENTITY data type. Planning ahead to design the table with a unique identifier is the best way to create the table, but you can also use ALTER TABLE to add an identity column to the table after creation, but only if the table is empty.

```
SQL> CREATE TABLE customer
(customer_id number generated by default as identity(start with 1
increment by 1),
Customer_name    varchar2(50));
Table created.
SQL> ALTER TABLE us_states add state_id number generated by default as
identity (start with 1 increment by 1);
Table altered.
```

DML

DML refers to any SQL statement that begins with select, insert, update, delete, or merge. The remainder of this chapter will deal primarily with DML. Every DML SQL statement consists of a few basic components. The following three items form the basic foundation of most DML statements:

- Each DML statement begins with either a select, insert, update, delete, or merge command:

  - SELECT is used when you want to retrieve data from an Oracle database. It is the most common SQL statement you will see.

- ■ INSERT is used when you want to add rows into an Oracle table.

- ■ UPDATE commands are used to change one or more records in a table.

- ■ DELETE commands are issued when you want to remove one or more records from a table.

- ■ MERGE is a combination of an update statement with an insert if it doesn't exist. Deletes are also part of the merge to remove records meeting the criteria.

- ■ CALL is used to execute stored objects within the database created using PL/SQL.

- ■ All DML commands require reference to an object that will be manipulated. More often than not, the object being referenced is a table.

- ■ A conditional statement can be added to any select, update, or delete command. Absence of a conditional statement means that the command will be performed against every record in the object. A conditional statement is used when the DML command is intended to only act upon a group of records that meet a specific condition. The where clause will be discussed a little later in this chapter.

More optional DML statements will be described later in this chapter. For now, you should concentrate on understanding the fundamental structure of each DML statement, starting with the insert and select statements.

CRITICAL SKILL 3.2

Use Basic Insert and Select Statements

Getting data into a database and getting it out are two of the most important tasks of a database. Oracle provides two basic features that help you do just that. To get data into the database, use the insert command; to get it back out, use the select command. You must master these commands because they form the basics for most data access to your Oracle database. In this section, you first learn how to get data into your database and then how to get data out.

Insert

Let's return to the states table created in the DDL example. The following is an illustration of using the insert statement in its simplest form:

```
SQL> insert into us_states values ('AZ','Arizona');
1 row created.
```

Each time you execute an insert command, you receive the message "1 row created." Thus, you get immediate feedback that you are populating the given table with data. When you load data into a table, you should specify the column to load it into. This ensures that there is no mistaking where you want the data to be placed. In the next example, the columns are specified after the insert command:

```
SQL> insert into us_states (state_cd, state_name)
2> values ('NJ','New Jersey');
1 row created.

SQL> insert into us_states (state_cd, state_name)
2> values ('CA','California');
1 row created.

SQL> insert into us_states (state_cd, state_name)
2> values ('TX','Texas');
1 row created.

SQL> insert into us_states (state_cd, state_name)
2> values ('FL','Florida');
1 row created.

SQL> insert into us_states (state_cd, state_name)
2> values ('ME','Maine');
1 row created.
SQL> commit;
Commit complete.
```

The commit persists the change in the database. For the transaction, a commit or rollback is needed to complete the transaction. A rollback will do just that, roll back the transaction as if it didn't exist.

Select

As mentioned earlier, the select statement is used to retrieve data from the database. This is the most common SQL statement you will use. The five basic parts of the SQL statement are as follows:

- First is the keyword SELECT, followed by what you want to retrieve from the database. The names of the columns to be retrieved are listed here. The SELECT clause is mandatory.

- The word "from" is the next part of the SQL statement. Reference to the object that the data is being retrieved from is made here. This is usually a table name. The FROM clause is mandatory.

- As mentioned before, a conditional statement is optional for select statements. The word "WHERE," followed by the conditions, is the next part of the SQL statement. (See Critical Skill 3.3 for more details on the where clause.)

- A group by clause is another optional component of the select statement. This topic is covered in more detail in Critical Skill 3.9, once we have had the opportunity to discuss functions.

- The final component of a select statement is the order by clause. This will also be discussed in more detail later on in this chapter. This is an optional component, which will sort the results of the query before they are presented back to you.

You should now issue your first select statement against the state table you just populated in the insert statement examples:

```
SQL> select *
  2  from  us_states;

ST STATE_NAME
-- -----------------------------
AZ Arizona
NJ New Jersey
CA California
TX Texas
FL Florida
MN Maine

6 rows selected.
```

Notice the use of the asterisk in the select statement. The asterisk means "retrieve data from all the columns" of the state table. The command "select * from emp;" retrieves all columns from the EMP table.

Rather than using the asterisk as you did in the previous example, you can specify one or more columns after the select command in a comma-separated list. These examples have tables with only a couple of columns, but in the real world there are tables that are very wide and might have several columns. For performance, choosing only the columns that are needed is important, and can even allow for just index access to retrieve the data instead of going to the full table. You should rewrite the previous query and select only the state_name column this time:

```
SQL> select state_name
  2  from  us_states;

STATE_NAME
-----------------------------
```

```
Arizona
New Jersey
California
Texas
Florida
Maine

6 rows selected.
```

The semicolons in the two SQL examples force the immediate execution of the SQL statement within SQL*Plus. There are two ways to signify you have finished and that the SQL statement can be executed in SQL*Plus:

■ The semicolon at the end of a line

■ The slash on a separate line

Until SQL*Plus encounters either of these characters, it assumes you need an additional line. The following example highlights this point. Notice the use of the slash and semicolon.

```
SQL> select *
  2  from  a;

SQL> select *
  2  from  a
  3  /
```

The absence of the semicolon in the second example results in a new line. In these cases, the semicolon and slash on a separate line would force the execution of the statement.

CRITICAL SKILL 3.3

Use Simple WHERE Clauses

Up to now, you have seen how the select command can be used to retrieve records from a table. However, our basic examples have all retrieved every record from the table. If you want to see only certain rows, you must add a where clause.

Because the previous examples returned every record in the table, you created a simple table with a few rows in it for illustration purposes. Had you chosen to illustrate the select command against the large sample tables provided by Oracle, you would have returned thousands of rows—far too many for listing in this chapter. Now that you are introducing the where clause, you will be able to control the output. As a result, the remaining examples in this chapter will now use the customers, products, sales, and costs tables that are part of the Oracle sample database; they can be found in the SH schema that is included when you install the sample databases with a default installation. Let's describe each of these tables in the SH schema. This may be done in SQL*Plus or in a GUI that provides this type of table interface:

```
SQL> desc customers;
 Name                               Null?     Type
 ---------------------------------- --------- -------------------
 CUST_ID                            NOT NULL  NUMBER
 CUST_FIRST_NAME                    NOT NULL  VARCHAR2(20)
 CUST_LAST_NAME                     NOT NULL  VARCHAR2(40)
 CUST_GENDER                        NOT NULL  CHAR(1)
 CUST_YEAR_OF_BIRTH                 NOT NULL  NUMBER(4)
 CUST_MARITAL_STATUS                          VARCHAR2(20)
 CUST_STREET_ADDRESS                NOT NULL  VARCHAR2(40)
 CUST_POSTAL_CODE                   NOT NULL  VARCHAR2(10)
 CUST_CITY                          NOT NULL  VARCHAR2(30)
 CUST_CITY_ID                       NOT NULL  NUMBER
 CUST_STATE_PROVINCE                NOT NULL  VARCHAR2(40)
 CUST_STATE_PROVINCE_ID             NOT NULL  NUMBER
 COUNTRY_ID                         NOT NULL  NUMBER
 CUST_MAIN_PHONE_NUMBER             NOT NULL  VARCHAR2(25)
 CUST_INCOME_LEVEL                            VARCHAR2(30)
 CUST_CREDIT_LIMIT                            NUMBER
 CUST_EMAIL                                   VARCHAR2(30)
 CUST_TOTAL                         NOT NULL  VARCHAR2(14)
 CUST_TOTAL_ID                      NOT NULL  NUMBER
 CUST_SRC_ID                                  NUMBER
 CUST_EFF_FROM                                DATE
 CUST_EFF_TO                                  DATE
 CUST_VALID                                   VARCHAR2(1)

SQL> desc products;
 Name                               Null?     Type
 ---------------------------------- --------- -------------------
 PROD_ID                            NOT NULL  NUMBER(6)
 PROD_NAME                          NOT NULL  VARCHAR2(50)
 PROD_DESC                          NOT NULL  VARCHAR2(4000)
 PROD_SUBCATEGORY                   NOT NULL  VARCHAR2(50)
 PROD_SUBCATEGORY_ID                NOT NULL  NUMBER
 PROD_SUBCATEGORY_DESC              NOT NULL  VARCHAR2(2000)
 PROD_CATEGORY                      NOT NULL  VARCHAR2(50)
 PROD_CATEGORY_ID                   NOT NULL  NUMBER
 PROD_CATEGORY_DESC                 NOT NULL  VARCHAR2(2000)
 PROD_WEIGHT_CLASS                  NOT NULL  NUMBER(3)
 PROD_UNIT_OF_MEASURE                         VARCHAR2(20)
 PROD_PACK_SIZE                     NOT NULL  VARCHAR2(30)
```

```
SUPPLIER_ID                               NOT NULL NUMBER(6)
PROD_STATUS                               NOT NULL VARCHAR2(20)
PROD_LIST_PRICE                           NOT NULL NUMBER(8,2)
PROD_MIN_PRICE                            NOT NULL NUMBER(8,2)
PROD_TOTAL                                NOT NULL VARCHAR2(13)
PROD_TOTAL_ID                             NOT NULL NUMBER
PROD_SRC_ID                                        NUMBER
PROD_EFF_FROM                                      DATE
PROD_EFF_TO                                        DATE
PROD_VALID                                         VARCHAR2(1)

SQL> desc sales;
 Name                                      Null?    Type
 ----------------------------------------- -------- --------------------
 PROD_ID                                   NOT NULL NUMBER
 CUST_ID                                   NOT NULL NUMBER
 TIME_ID                                   NOT NULL DATE
 CHANNEL_ID                                NOT NULL NUMBER
 PROMO_ID                                  NOT NULL NUMBER
 QUANTITY_SOLD                             NOT NULL NUMBER(10,2)
 AMOUNT_SOLD                               NOT NULL NUMBER(10,2)
SQL> desc costs;
 Name                                      Null?    Type
 ----------------------------------------- -------- --------------------
 PROD_ID                                   NOT NULL NUMBER
 TIME_ID                                   NOT NULL DATE
 PROMO_ID                                  NOT NULL NUMBER
 CHANNEL_ID                                NOT NULL NUMBER
 UNIT_COST                                 NOT NULL NUMBER(10,2)
 UNIT_PRICE                                NOT NULL NUMBER(10,2)

SQL> desc promotions;
 Name                                      Null?    Type
 ----------------------------------------- -------- ----------------------
 PROMO_ID                                  NOT NULL NUMBER(6)
 PROMO_NAME                                NOT NULL VARCHAR2(30)
 PROMO_SUBCATEGORY                         NOT NULL VARCHAR2(30)
 PROMO_SUBCATEGORY_ID                      NOT NULL NUMBER
 PROMO_CATEGORY                            NOT NULL VARCHAR2(30)
 PROMO_CATEGORY_ID                         NOT NULL NUMBER
 PROMO_COST                                NOT NULL NUMBER(10,2)
 PROMO_BEGIN_DATE                          NOT NULL DATE
 PROMO_END_DATE                            NOT NULL DATE
 PROMO_TOTAL                               NOT NULL VARCHAR2(15)
 PROMO_TOTAL_ID                            NOT NULL NUMBER
```

The PRODUCTS table contains more than 70 products for sale. The following select statement will retrieve only one record for product ID (prod_id) 117, which is the use of the simplest of where clauses. In this case, you will perform an exact query to find product ID number 117, which is the product ID for a pack of CD-Rs:

```
SQL> select prod_id, prod_name, prod_category, prod_list_price
  2  from    products
  3  where   prod_id = 117;

   PROD_ID PROD_NAME                         PROD_CATEGORY
PROD_LIST_PRICE
---------- -------------------------------- -------------- ---------
       117 CD-R, Profess. Grade, Pack of 10 Software/Other      8.99
```

A WHERE Clause with AND/OR

A WHERE clause instructs Oracle to search the data in a table and then return only those rows that meet the criteria that you have defined. In the preceding example, you searched the products table for one specific record with a product ID equal to 117. This was accomplished with where prod_id = 117.

You will often be interested in retrieving rows that meet multiple criteria—for example, a list of customers from Utah who also have a credit limit greater than $10,000. The SQL statement would produce the following output:

```
SQL> select cust_id, cust_state_province, cust_credit_limit
  2  from    customers
  3  where   cust_state_province = 'UT'
  4  and     cust_credit_limit > 10000;

   CUST_ID CUST_STATE_PROVINCE                     CUST_CREDIT_LIMIT
---------- --------------------------------------- -----------------
     50601 UT                                                  11000
     24830 UT                                                  15000
     28983 UT                                                  15000
    100267 UT                                                  11000
    100207 UT                                                  11000
    103007 UT                                                  15000

6 rows selected.
```

In the previous example, you retrieved records that met all the criteria. You may be interested in retrieving records that meet one criterion or another. For example, if you wanted to find all the product IDs in the products table that are either in the

Hardware product category or have a weight class of 4, you would generate the following SQL statement and output:

```
SQL> select prod_id, prod_category, prod_weight_class WGT
  2  from    products
  3  where   prod_category = 'Hardware'
  4  or      prod_weight_class = 4;

   PROD_ID PROD_CATEGORY                                              WGT
---------- ------------------------------------------------- ---------
        15 Hardware                                                    1
        18 Hardware                                                    1
       139 Electronics                                                 4
```

The AND condition and the OR condition are known as logical operators. They are used to tell the query how the multiple criteria affect each other. Compound conditions connected by the AND keyword all have to evaluate to true for records to be retrieved. Records are returned by compound conditions connected by the OR keyword when either one of the conditions is true. If you mix your *AND* and *OR* conditions, you must carefully evaluate how these two types will interact.

The WHERE Clause with NOT

The capability also exists within Oracle to retrieve records with negative criteria. The "NOT EQUALS" operator is !=, or you can also use <>. For example, you might want to see all the products that are not in weight class 1. The following query and its output illustrate this example:

```
SQL> select prod_id, prod_category, prod_weight_class WGT
  2  from   products
  3  where  prod_weight_class != 1;
   PROD_ID PROD_CATEGORY                                              WGT
---------- ------------------------------------------------- ---------
       139 Electronics                                                 4
```

Ask the Expert

Q: Why is *Hardware* in quotes in the sample statement?

A: When a character column is used in a where clause, it is necessary to use the single quotes around the value to be compared.

The WHERE Clause with a Range Search

Oracle also supports range searches so you can query for records that are between two values. If you want to find all male customers in Connecticut who were born between 1936 and 1939, you would write a query with three conditions joined by the AND keyword (all three need to evaluate to true), and one of the conditions would use the range search BETWEEN keyword. The following example illustrates the query and resulting output:

```
SQL> select  cust_id, cust_gender, cust_year_of_birth
  2  from     customers
  3  where    cust_state_province = 'CT'
  4  and      cust_gender = 'M'
  5  and      cust_year_of_birth between 1936 and 1939;

   CUST_ID C CUST_YEAR_OF_BIRTH
---------- - ------------------
     20058 M               1937
     17139 M               1936
      1218 M               1938
      3985 M               1939
```

The WHERE Clause with a Search List

Oracle also supports searching for records that meet criteria within a list. If you want to find all customers in Utah and Connecticut with a credit limit of $15,000, you can do this with a search list. The following query represents a search list condition:

```
SQL> select  cust_id, cust_state_province, cust_credit_limit
  2  from     customers
  3  where    cust_credit_limit = 15000
  4  and      cust_state_province in ('UT','CT');

   CUST_ID CUST_STATE_PROVINCE                      CUST_CREDIT_LIMIT
---------- ------------------------------------     -----------------
     24830 UT                                                   15000
     28983 UT                                                   15000
    101798 CT                                                   15000
    103171 CT                                                   15000
    102579 CT                                                   15000
    102238 CT                                                   15000
    101515 CT                                                   15000
    103007 UT                                                   15000
    104381 CT                                                   15000

9 rows selected.
```

The WHERE Clause with a Pattern Search

The LIKE command exists within Oracle to search for records that match a pattern. The wildcard operator for pattern searches is the % sign. To search for all customers whose last name begins with the letter *Q*, the following query would produce these results:

```
SQL> select cust_last_name, cust_credit_limit
  2  from    customers
  3  where   cust_last_name like 'Q%';

CUST_LAST_NAME                          CUST_CREDIT_LIMIT
--------------------------------------- -----------------
Quinlan                                              9000
Quinn                                               11000
```

You can also ask Oracle to retrieve customers whose last names contain "inl" by using the wildcard at the beginning and end of the pattern search. The query and output would resemble the following:

```
SQL> select cust_last_name
  2  from    customers
  3  where   cust_last_name like '%inl%';

CUST_LAST_NAME
---------------------------------------
Quinlan
```

Ask the Expert

Q: Are character searches case-sensitive?

A: Yes. Character columns can contain upper- or lowercase alphas. If you searched the CUSTOMERS table for all instances of "INL" in the last names, you would not have retrieved any records. There are functions, lower and upper, that can be used to avoid issues with case sensitivity, but they will have an effect on performance. The good news is that there are function-based indexes that can be used for these types of functions in the where clause to help with performance.

Q: The percent (%) sign appears to be a multicharacter wildcard. Is there a single-character wildcard available for pattern searches?

A: Yes. The underscore (_) symbol serves as the single-character wildcard.

WHERE clauses filter out the data based on criteria, but sometimes it is useful just to return a handful of records, and it doesn't necessarily matter which records. This is good for testing, or possibly for sorting to return only the top 20. A simple way to return a specific number of rows is to use ROWNUM, and an Oracle 12*c* way is to use FETCH. FETCH is a new feature in Oracle 12*c* and will return by row or percent. Consider the following examples:

```
SQL> select cust_last_name
  2    from customers
  3    where rownum <= 10;
CUST_LAST_NAME
-------------------
Adjani
Adjani
Alexander
Alexander
Altman
Altman
Altman
Andrews
Andrews
Ashby
10 rows selected.
SQL> select cust_last_name
  2    from  customers
  3    FETCH first 10 rows only;
CUST_LAST_NAME
-------------------
Adjani
Adjani
Alexander
Alexander
Altman
Altman
Altman
Andrews
Andrews
Ashby
10 rows selected.
```

The first statement shown will return 10 random rows from the customer table. Using an order clause, as we have done in the next statement, will sort the data and then return the first 10 rows in the order that is needed. The random rows may be in the order expected, but without the ORDER command, you're not guaranteed to get the largest or smallest values in the proper order. In our next example we illustrate using other columns to manage how you return rows for your sample data set.

```
SQL> select cust_last_name, cust_credit_limit
  2  from   customers
  3  order by cust_credit_limit
  4  FETCH first 10 rows only;
CUST_LAST_NAME          CUST_CREDIT_LIMIT
-------------------- -----------------
Welles                        100
MacLaine                      100
Russell                       100
Pacino                        100
Taylor                        100
Sutherland                    100
MacGraw                       100
Hannah                        100
Cruise                        100
Mason                         100
10 rows selected.
SQL> select cust_last_name,cust_credit_limit
  2  from customers
  3  order by cust_credit_limit
  4  FETCH first 1 percent rows only;
CUST_LAST_NAME          CUST_CREDIT_LIMIT
-------------------- -----------------
Welles                        100
Pacino                        100
Taylor                        100
Sutherland                    100
SQL> select cust_last_name,cust_credit_limit
  2  from customers
  3  order by credit_limit
  4  FETCH first 10 rows WITH TIES;
CUST_LAST_NAME          CUST_CREDIT_LIMIT
-------------------- -----------------
Welles                        100
MacLaine                      100
Russell                       100
Pacino                        100
Taylor                        100
Sutherland                    100
MacGraw                       100
Hannah                        100
Cruise                        100
Mason                         100
Cage                          100
11 rows selected.
```

Using the WITH TIES clause you could return more than 10 rows depending on whether records have the same value in the grouped column. In the cust_credit_limit in the example earlier we select data from the customer table; it returned 11 rows because they all have the same 100 value as the credit limit. This clause allows us to bring back any records that have ties or the same number instead of *only* the 10 rows when not using the clause.

The WHERE clauses can filter on the different column values or pull back a set of data based on a percent or number of rows. Restricting the data returned is beneficial for performance, and ensures a reasonable set of data to work with. There might be reasons to pull back a million records from a table, but the filter allows for a manageable set of data to be returned from tables that might have millions or even billions of rows. The where clause can be combined with the fetch command.

```
SQL> select cust_last_name
  2   from   customers
  3   WHERE cust_last_name like 'M%'
  4   FETCH first 10 rows only;
CUST_LAST_NAME
--------------------

MacGraw
MacLaine
MacLaine
Mahoney
Malden
Martin
Martin
Mason
Mason
Mastroianni
10 rows selected.
```

Oracle 12*c* introduces a new feature to help with the FETCH function. The additional clause is named OFFSET. This clause allows you to skip rows at the beginning of the data set. For example, if you issue the following command, you will find that the result returns 10 rows but would skip the three lowest values:

```
SQL> select cust_last_name, cust_credit_limit
  2   from   customers
  3   order by cust_credit_limit
  4   OFFSET 3 rows
  4   FETCH next 10 rows only;
```

The WHERE Clause: Common Operators

As you can see from the preceding examples, Oracle has a very powerful set of operators when it comes to restricting the rows retrieved. Table 3-2 is a partial list of operators you can use in the where clause.

Operator	Purpose	Example
=	Tests for equality	select * from customers where cust_state_province = 'UT';
!=	Tests for inequality	select * from customers where cust_state_province != 'UT';
^=	Same as !=	select * from customers where cust_state_province ^= 'UT';
<>	Same as !=	select * from customers where cust_state_province <> 'UT';
<	Less than	select * from sales where amount_sold < 100;
>	Greater than	select * from sales where amount_sold > 100;
<=	Less than or equal to	select * from sales where amount_sold <= 500;
>=	Greater than or equal to	select * from sales where amount_sold >= 600;
IN	Equal to any member in parentheses	select * from customers where cust_state_ province is IN ('UT','CA','TX');
NOT IN	Not equal to any member in parentheses	select * from customers where cust_state_ province is NOT IN ('UT','CA','TX');
BETWEEN A and B	Greater than or equal to A and less than or equal to B	select * from sales where amount_sold is BETWEEN 100 and 500;
NOT BETWEEN A and B	Not greater than or equal to A, and not less than or equal to B	select * from sales where amount_sold is NOT BETWEEN 100 and 500;
LIKE '%tin%'	Contains given text (for example, 'tin')	select * from customer where cust_last_name is LIKE '%tin%';
IS NULL	Determines if a value is null or not	select * from customer where cust_phone_number IS NULL;
IS NOT NULL	Determines if a value is populated or not null	select * from customer where cust_last_name IS NOT NULL;

TABLE 3-2. *Common Comparison Operators*

NOTE
Performance of the select statement depends on the statistics of the tables and information needed and filtered in the where clauses. Indexes are very useful in optimizing statements, but operators such as NOT IN and LIKE will limit the use of indexes. When using the LIKE operator, you should try to put your wildcard at the end of the text such as like 'NICOLE D%'. This will allow the index to be used if one is available. However, when you place the wildcard at the beginning like '%BEN A%' then you lose the ability to leverage indexes for performance. The NOT IN statements will need to scan through a table and will not use an index, so take care when using these operators.

CRITICAL SKILL 3.4

Use Basic Update, Delete, and Merge Statements

While select will likely be the command you use the most, you'll use the update and delete commands regularly, too. As you will see in Chapter 5, your programs will have a mixture of DML statements. In this section, you take a closer look at the update and delete commands.

Update

It is often necessary to change data already stored within a table. This is done using the update command. There are three parts to this command:

- The word "update" followed by the table to which you want to apply the change. This part is mandatory.

- The word "set" followed by one or more columns in which you want to change the values. This part is also mandatory.

- A where clause followed by selection criteria. This is optional.

Imagine that one of your customers has requested an increase in their credit limit and your accounting department has approved it. An update statement will have to be executed to alter the credit limit. For the purpose of illustration, a customer record will be displayed before and after the update. The following example illustrates a simple update for one customer:

```
SQL> select cust_id, cust_credit_limit
  2  from    customers
  3  where   cust_id = 28983;

   CUST_ID CUST_CREDIT_LIMIT
---------- -----------------
     28983             15000

SQL> update customers
  2  set     cust_credit_limit = 20000
  3  where   cust_id = 28983;

1 row updated.

SQL> select cust_id, cust_credit_limit
  2  from    customers
  3  where cust_id = 28983;

   CUST_ID CUST_CREDIT_LIMIT
---------- -----------------
     28983             20000
```

This example reveals that customer 28983 had a $15,000 credit limit before the update statement was executed. The update statement is written against the CUSTOMERS table with a set clause issued against the column to be changed, cust_credit_limit, and a where clause to make the change only for customer 28983. After the command is executed, a select statement reveals that the customer now has a credit limit of $20,000. The update statement is a very powerful tool. It can be used against one record, multiple records meeting simple or complex criteria, or all records in a table.

Delete

Use the delete statement when you want to remove one or more rows of data from a table. The command has two parts:

- The keywords "delete from" followed by the table name you want to remove records from. This is mandatory.

- A where clause followed by the record selection CRITERIA. This is optional. As with the update, absence of a where clause will remove every record from the table.

If you want to remove all the customers from the CUSTOMERS table, you would issue the SQL statement DELETE FROM CUSTOMER;. As you become more familiar with Oracle, you will learn that the TRUNCATE CUSTOMER; command will also remove every record, but this doesn't allow you to roll back the changes if you make a mistake. It's very easy to accidentally drop all the records in a table. As with the update statement, be very careful when issuing the delete or truncate commands.

Insert

There have already been examples for the basic INSERT statement, but it makes sense to include a couple of examples that illustrate inserting into a table from a SELECT statement. A powerful tool is needed to take a query and insert the rows into another table—whether it is a temporary table for just holding information while processing or a permanent table that is providing a specific set of data for another purpose. We have seen the insert with values, and the select query just replaces the value clause. While an insert statement itself can't have a where clause, the select that is pulling the rows to insert can.

```
SQL> insert into customers_na ( cust_id,country_id,cust_credit_limit,cust_total)
  2   select cust_id,  country_id,cust_credit_limit,cust_total
  3   from customers
  4   where country_id in (52790,52772);
20530 rows inserted.
```

Use Basic Merge Statements

Looking at insert, update, and delete separately makes sense; however, you can combine all of these into a MERGE statement. The MERGE statement is useful for updating data, and if the data doesn't exist, then it will insert it. The other option is to delete a set of this data while merging other data.

- ■ The keywords MERGE INTO followed by the table name you want to update, insert, or delete records from. This is mandatory for the statement.

- ■ USING can be a table or query, but it is the source of the data that is to be used for the new values or the inserted values.

- ■ ON indicates that the join of the tables will be matching values for the rows to be updated or deleted.

- ■ WHEN MATCHED is actually optional if you want to insert the new values only; the update can be left off. This will perform the updates so a SET clause is needed. Deletes are also possible here.

- Use WHEN NOT MATCHED to know what values are not in the table based on the join matching. This will insert the new values.

- A where clause followed by the record selection criteria is optional. As with the other statements, absence of a where clause will update or remove every record from the table that matches on the matching criteria.

- An optional DELETE WHERE clause can be used to clean up after a merge operation. Only those rows that match both the ON clause and the DELETE WHERE clause are deleted.

```
SQL>  MERGE into customers2 c2
  2   USING (select customer_id,cust_last_name,cust_credit_limit
  3   from customers where cust_credit_limit > 1000) cl
  4    ON (c2.customer_id=cl.customer_id)
  5    WHEN MATCHED then UPDATE set c2.cust_credit_limit = cl.credit_limit*2
  6    DELETE where c2.cust_credit_limit > 10000
  7    WHEN NOT MATCHED then
  8    INSERT (c2.customer_id,c2.cust_last_name,c2.cust_credit_limit)
  9    values (cl.customer_id,cl.cust_last_name,cl.cust_credit_limit)
 10    where cl.cust_credit_limit < 10000;
209 rows merged.
```

Ask the Expert

Q: Can you use a where clause with every type of DML statement?

A: The where clause can be used only with select, update, and delete statements. The insert statement can never have a where clause.

Q: You mentioned that a where clause is optional for update statements. What would happen if one isn't used during an update?

A: If a where clause isn't used with an update statement, every record in the table will be updated.

Q: What statements can be used in a merge?

A: The update, delete, and insert statements can be used in a merge.

Let us now illustrate a deletion of all customers in the province of Delhi. The code listing first shows a count of customers in Delhi, so you see count(*) for the first time. This example is being used to illustrate the number of records you expect to delete when you issue the command. The second SQL statement issues the delete from command, which confirms the number of records deleted. The final SQL statement is a repeat of the first one to illustrate that there are no records remaining for the province of Delhi. In order to continue to use these records for later examples, you will roll back the changes so that they never get permanently committed to the database and re-run the first SQL statement one more time to confirm that the records have been restored:

```
SQL> select count(*)
  2  from    customers
  3  where   cust_state_province = 'Delhi';

  COUNT(*)
----------
        34

SQL> delete from customers
  2  where cust_state_province = 'Delhi';

34 rows deleted.

SQL> select count(*)
  2  from    customers
  3  where   cust_state_province = 'Delhi';

  COUNT(*)
----------
         0

SQL> rollback;

Rollback complete.

SQL> select count(*)
  2  from    customers
  3  where   cust_state_province = 'Delhi';

  COUNT(*)
----------
        34
```

Progress Check

1. Of the following four items, which one is not a DML keyword?

   A. select

   B. insert

   C. create

   D. update

2. How can the current column definitions of the CUSTOMERS table be displayed?

3. In order to retrieve data from the database, two keywords are mandatory. Name them.

4. Write a SQL statement to select the customer last name and city for all customers in Florida (FL) with a credit limit less than $5000.

CRITICAL SKILL 3.5

Order Data

So far, all of your select queries have returned records in random order. Earlier, you selected records from the customer table, where the customer was located in either Connecticut or Utah and had a credit limit of $15,000. The results came back in no apparent order. It is often desirable to order the result set on one or more of the

---

Progress Check Answers

1. C. The four DML keywords are select, insert, update, and delete.

2. The following code listing displays the defined columns for the CUSTOMERS table:

```
desc customers;
```

3. Every SQL statement that retrieves data from the database will have both the select and from keywords.

4. The following is an example of a SQL statement that selects the customer last name and city for all customers in Florida with a credit limit less than $5000:

```
SQL> select cust_last_name, cust_city
  2  from    customers
  3  where   cust_state_province = 'UT'
  4  and     cust_credit_limit < 5000;
```

selected columns. This ordering of data is known as *sorting*. Sorting will provide guidance to the reader on how they can direct and manage their data review and analysis. In this case, it probably would have been easier to interpret the results if they were sorted by state, and within that state were then sorted by customer ID. Take a look at the query syntax and resulting output:

```
SQL> select cust_id, cust_state_province, cust_credit_limit
  2  from    customers
  3  where   cust_credit_limit = 15000
  4  and     cust_state_province in ('UT','CT')
  5  order by cust_state_province, cust_id;

    CUST_ID CUST_STATE_PROVINCE                            CUST_CREDIT_LIMIT
---------- -------------------------------------------    -----------------
     101515 CT                                                        15000
     101798 CT                                                        15000
     102238 CT                                                        15000
     102579 CT                                                        15000
     103171 CT                                                        15000
     104381 CT                                                        15000
      24830 UT                                                        15000
     103007 UT                                                        15000

8 rows selected.
```

Any column specified in the order by statement could be sorted either in ascending or descending order. By default, Oracle will sort each column in ascending order. In order to sort a column in descending order, the use of desc following the order by column will accomplish this. You should look at the previous example one more time with the customer IDs sorted in descending order:

```
SQL> select cust_id, cust_state_province, cust_credit_limit
  2  from    customers
  3  where   cust_credit_limit = 15000
  4  and     cust_state_province in ('UT','CT')
  5  order by cust_state_province, cust_id desc;

    CUST_ID CUST_STATE_PROVINCE                            CUST_CREDIT_LIMIT
---------- -------------------------------------------    -----------------
     104381 CT                                                        15000
     103171 CT                                                        15000
     102579 CT                                                        15000
     102238 CT                                                        15000
     101798 CT                                                        15000
```

```
101515 CT                                              15000
103007 UT                                              15000
24830  UT                                              15000
```

```
8 rows selected.
```

CRITICAL SKILL 3.6

Employ Functions: String, Numeric, Aggregate (No Grouping)

So far, you have created a number of fairly simplistic DML statements. You've selected some records from different tables using criteria, you've updated existing rows, and you've even inserted and deleted some records.

Oracle provides us with many functions that allow us to analyze and aggregate the data, returning results that differ greatly from the result sets you've seen so far. A function manipulates the contents of a column in a SQL statement. You can find what the largest credit limit is in the CUSTOMERS table, and you can round numbers or pad results with characters. In fact, when you ran a count of customers that were in the province of Delhi before and after deleting these records, you took a sneak peek ahead at functions.

This section introduces you to three different types of functions: string (or character), numeric, and aggregate.

String Functions

String functions, also known as character functions, can be categorized into two types: those that return character values and those that return numeric values.

Table 3-3 represents the most common functions you will perform with the character data type; it's only a partial list. The examples that follow all use the *dual* table, which is an internal Oracle table that is useful in SQL and PL/SQL for performing functions that return a single row. It can be used to return the current system date and time, to perform arithmetic functions, or to obtain a generated sequential number (more on this later in the chapter).

Function	Action	Example	Displays
LOWER(*char*)	Converts the entire string to lowercase.	select LOWER('DAliA') from dual;	dalia
REPLACE(*char*, *str1*,*str2*)	Replaces every occurrence of *str1* in *char* with *str2*.	select REPLACE('Scott', 'S', 'Boy') from dual;	Boycott
SUBSTR(*char*, *m,n*)	Extracts the characters from *char* starting in position *m* for *n* characters.	select SUBSTR('ABCDEF',4,2) from dual;	DE
TRIM(*char*)	Removes spaces before and after *char*.	Select TRIM(' testing ') from dual;	testing
LENGTH(*char*)	Returns the length of *char*.	select LENGTH('Marissa') from dual;	7
RPAD(*expr1*, *n,expr2*)	Pads *expr1* with *expr2* to the right for *n* characters. Often used for space padding in the creation of a fixed-length record.	select RPAD('Amanda', 10, '1') from dual;	Amanda1111
INITCAP(*char*)	Changes the first character of each element in *char* to uppercase.	select INITCAP('shane k.') from dual;	Shane K.

TABLE 3-3. *Common String Functions*

Numeric Functions

Table 3-4 illustrates some common numeric functions, their syntax, and the results they produce. These are only a few of the many functions available.

Function	Action	Example	Displays
CEIL(*n*)	Returns nearest whole number greater than or equal to *n*.	select CEIL(12.3) from dual;	13
FLOOR(*n*)	Returns nearest whole number less than or equal to *n*.	select FLOOR(127.6) from dual;	127
ROUND(*n,m*)	Rounds *n* to *m* places to the right of the decimal point.	select ROUND(579.34886,3) from dual;	579.349
POWER(*m,n*)	Multiplies *m* to the power *n*.	select POWER(5,3) from dual;	125
MOD(*m,n*)	Returns the remainder of the division of *m* by *n*. If *n* = 0, then 0 is returned. If *n* > *m*, then *m* is returned.	select MOD(9,5) from dual; select mod(10,5) from dual; select mod(6,7) from dual;	4 0 6
SQRT(*n*)	Returns the square root of *n*.	select SQRT(9) from dual;	3
ABS(n)	Returns the absolute value of *n*.	select ABS(-29) from dual;	29
TRUNC (n1, n2)	Returns a value with the required number of decimal places while a negative *n2* rounds to the left of the decimal.	select TRUNC(29.16, 1), trunc(31.2,-1) from dual;	29.1 30

TABLE 3-4. *Common Numeric Functions*

Aggregate Functions

Unlike the character or numeric functions, which act on a single row, aggregate functions act on an entire column of data. Aggregate functions save the developer from having to write a lot of code to determine the maximum column value in a set of records or an average, for example. A single result row is returned by aggregate functions based on the group of rows. Table 3-5 illustrates the more commonly used aggregate functions but is only a partial list. As simple as these are, we're sure you'll agree that they are indeed quite powerful.

Function	Action	Example	Displays
COUNT(*expr*)	Returns a count of non-null column values for each row retrieved	select COUNT(cust_id) from customers where cust_state_ province = 'NY';	694
AVG(*expr*)	Returns the average for the column values and rows selected	select AVG(amount_sold) from sales where prod_id = 117;	9.92712978
SUM(*expr*)	Returns the sum of the column values for all the retrieved rows	select SUM(amount_sold) from sales where prod_id = 117;	170270.13
MIN(*expr*)	Returns the minimum value for the column and rows retrieved	select MIN(prod_list_price) from products;	6.99
MAX(*expr*)	Returns the maximum value for the column and rows retrieved	select MAX(prod_list_price) from products;	1299.99

TABLE 3-5. *Common Aggregate Functions*

CRITICAL SKILL 3.7

Use Dates and Data Functions (Formatting and Chronological)

Date is the next most common type of data you'll find in an Oracle database after character and numeric data. The date data type consists of two principal elements: date and time. It's important to keep in mind that the date data type includes time when comparing two dates with each other for equality.

The default date format in many Oracle databases is DD-MON-YY, where DD represents the day, MON is the month, and YY is the two-digit year. The date format is set up with database creation and can be changed as needed. Different tools might also have different defaults for the dates, so these date functions for queries are important to get proper results when looking at the date fields. Also, a date can be inserted into a table without specifying either the four-digit year or a value for the time element. Oracle will default the century to 20 for years 00–49 and 19 for years 50–99. Without a time being specified during an insert, the time will default to midnight, which is represented as 00:00:00.

Date Functions

As with the numeric and character data types, Oracle has provided many date functions to help with the manipulation of date data. If you were to routinely print customized letters to your best customers, offering them a special deal that expires on the last day of the month, the last_day function could be used to automatically generate the expiration date for the offer. Table 3-6 shows the most common date functions.

Special Formats with the Date Data Type

Date formats are used to change the display format of a date. This is done using the to_char conversion function along with the date and format mask. Table 3-7 shows a sample of the more common date formats and their output.

Nested Functions

It is also common to nest functions within functions. Using the months_between example from Table 3-7, it would be possible to round the number of months between the two dates. The following statement and output illustrates this example:

```
SQL> select round(months_between('17-MAR-61','21-APR-62'))
  2  from dual;

ROUND(MONTHS_BETWEEN('17-MAR-61','21-APR-62'))
---------------------------------------------
                                          -13
```

The inner function is evaluated first, and then the outer function is evaluated second. This is true for all nested functions and, as this example illustrates, different function types can be combined. Pay special notice to the parentheses for the outer and inner functions. For the purpose of illustration, this example nests only one function within another. However, it is possible to nest many functions within each other. Just be careful; the order of the functions is important, and the complexity of debugging nested functions increases with each additional nested function.

Function	Action	Example	Displays
SYSDATE	Returns current system date. Time can also be retrieved using the to_char function, which is discussed in the next section.	select sysdate from dual;	17-MAR-08 on March 17, 2008
LAST_DAY(*date*)	Returns last day of the month for *date*.	select last_day('17-MAR-08') from dual;	31-MAR-08
ADD_MONTHS(*d,n*)	Adds *n* or subtracts −*n* months from date d.	select add_months('21-APR-08', 2) from dual;	21-JUN-08
MONTHS_BETWEEN(*d1,d2*)	Returns difference in months between date *d1* and date *d2*.	select months_between('17-MAR-61', '21-APR-62') from dual;	-13.129032
NEXT_DAY(*d,day*)	Returns the date that corresponds with the day of the week after date *d*.	select next_day('01-FEB-08', 'Saturday') from dual;	07-FEB-08
CURRENT_TIMESTAMP	Returns the current timestamp along with the time zone offset.	select sessiontimezone, current_timestamp from dual;	01-NOV-08 01.17.56.917550 PM -05:00
TRUNC(date,format)	Returns a truncated date based on the date part in the format. If it is the year, it will truncate the date to be the first of the year, or for month to be the first of the month.	select trunc('23-DEC-12', 'MON') from dual;	01-DEC-12

TABLE 3-6. *Common Date Functions*

Format Mask	Returns	Example	Displays
Y or YY or YYY	Last one, two, or three digits of year	select to_char(sysdate,'YYY') from dual;	014 for all dates in 2014
YEAR	Year spelled out	select to_char(sysdate,'YEAR') from dual;	TWO THOUSAND FOURTEEN in 2014
Q	Quarter of year	select to_char(sysdate,'Q') from dual;	3 for all dates in August
MM	Month	select to_char(sysdate,'MM') from dual;	12 for all dates in December
Month	Name of month as a nine-character name	select to_char(sysdate,'Month') from dual;	March followed by four spaces for all dates in March
WW	Week of year	select to_char(sysdate,'WW') from dual;	29 on July 15, 2014
W	Week of the month	select to_char(sysdate,'W') from dual;	3 on May 15, 2014
DDD	Day of the year	select to_char(sysdate,'DDD') from dual;	359 on December 25 in non-leap years
ROUND(months_ between DD	Day of the month	select to_char(sysdate,'DD') from dual;	09 on September 9 in any year
D Day of the week	(1 through 7)	select to_char(sysdate,'D') from dual;	5 on January 29, 2004

TABLE 3-7. *Common Formats of Date Type Data*

CRITICAL SKILL 3.8
Employ Joins (ANSI vs. Oracle): Inner, Outer, Self, Apply

Up until now, all of the examples in this chapter have selected data from only one table. In actual fact, much of the data that you need is in two or more tables. The true power of a relational database (and the source of its name) comes from the ability to easily relate different data together in a meaningful and useful way. Understanding this concept is critical to harvesting the information held within the database. This is more commonly known as *joining* two or more tables.

With Oracle Database 12*c*, queries can be written using either Oracle's SQL syntax or ANSI syntax. Oracle made ANSI syntax available in Oracle 9i, and continues to provide ANSI standards, such as APPLY for joins, as well as their platform syntax. Many third-party tools accept ANSI SQL but, as you'll see shortly, the joins are quite different.

Inner Joins

An inner join, also known simply as a join, occurs when records are selected from two tables and the values in one column from the first table are also found in a similar column in the second table. In effect, two or more tables are joined together based on common fields. These common fields are known as *keys*. There are two types of keys:

- A *primary key* is what makes a row of data unique within a table. In the CUSTOMERS table, CUST_ID is the primary key.

- A *foreign key* is the primary key of one table that is stored inside another table. The foreign key connects the two tables together. The SALES table also contains CUST_ID, which, in the case of the SALES table, is a foreign key back to the CUSTOMERS table.

Oracle Inner Joins

The tables to be joined are listed in the from clause and then related together in the where clause. Whenever two or more tables are found in the from clause, a join happens. Additional conditions can still be specified in the where clause to limit which rows will be returned by the join. For example, when you queried the SALES table on its own, the only customer information available was the CUST_ID. However, if you join each record, you retrieve from the SALES table by the CUST_ID to the same column in the CUSTOMERS table, and all the customer information becomes available to you instantly.

This first join example displays both the city and state details for each customer who has purchased a particular product under a specific promotion. The product ID and quantity sold are also displayed:

```
SQL> select prod_id, quantity_sold, cust_city, cust_state_province
  2  from    sales, customers
  3  where   sales.cust_id = customers.cust_id
  4  and     prod_id = 117;

   PROD_ID QUANTITY_SOLD CUST_CITY        CUST_STATE_PROVINCE
---------- ------------- ---------------- --------------------
       117             1 Fort Klamath     OR

       117             1 San Mateo        CA

       117             1 Frederick        CO
```

. . .

The from clause identified two tables and the where clause joins them with table_name.column_name syntax. Later in this chapter, you'll take a brief look at the report formatting capabilities of SQL*Plus, which will allow you to control the look of the output.

NOTE
You must adopt the table_name.column_ name construct to tell Oracle exactly which tables and columns to join. This is to avoid any ambiguity when different tables have columns that are named the same.

SQL statements can become quite confusing once you start joining tables, especially when you're joining more than two. Oracle also allows you to give the tables an alternative name known as a table alias. You should present this query again using "s" as the table alias for the SALES table and "c" as the table alias for the CUSTOMERS table:

```
select prod_id, quantity_sold, cust_city, cust_state_province
from    sales s, customers c
where   s.cust_id = c.cust_id
and     prod_id = 117
```

You should take this join example one step further. cust_id is the column you are using to join the two tables, and therefore it is found in both the SALES and CUSTOMERS tables. If you want to display cust_id as part of the select list, you would need to prefix it with the table alias:

```
select  s.prod_id, s.quantity_sold, c.cust_id, c.cust_city,
        c.cust_state_province
from    sales s, customers c
where   s.cust_id = c.cust_id
and     s.prod_id = 117
```

All the column names in this example were prefixed with the table alias qualifier. While it's only necessary for columns that appear in more than one table, it enhances the readability of the SQL statement as the statements become more complex and include more than one table join.

This leads you into the final example, which presents the concept of joining more than two tables. In addition to joining the CUSTOMERS table to the SALES table as you have in all of the preceding examples, you are also joining the CUSTOMERS table to the PRODUCTS and PROMOTIONS tables so you can pull in columns from those tables as well:

```
select  c.country_id, p1.promo_name, p2.prod_category, s.quantity_sold,
from    sales s,
        customers c,
        promotions p1,
        products p2
where   s.cust_id = c.cust_id
and     s.promo_id = p1.promo_id
and     s.prod_id = p2.prod_id
and     s.prod_id = 117
```

It's that simple to join a bunch of tables. Name each of the tables in the from clause, alias them, and then join them to each other in your where clause using the foreign key relationships.

ANSI Inner Joins

With ANSI joins, the join criteria is found in the from portion of the SQL statement. The where clause only lists the selection criteria for the rows. There are a couple of different ways to join the tables with ANSI syntax.

ANSI on/using   A simple join can be specified with an on or using statement. The columns to be joined on will be listed, while the where clause can list additional selection criteria. The following two examples illustrate the on syntax followed by the using syntax:

```
select c.cust_id, c.cust_state_province,
       s.quantity_sold, s.prod_category
from sales s join customers c
  on s.cust_id = c.cust_id
where prod_id = 117;

select cust_id, c.cust_state_province,
       s.quantity_sold, s.prod_category
from sales s join customers c
  using (cust_id)
where prod_id = 117;
```

The ANSI syntax also allows for two or more tables to be joined. This can be accomplished with multiple *join on* or multiple *join using* statements in the from section of the SQL statement. You should also note the USING clause, which is used if several columns share the same name only and the columns listed in the USING clause can't have any qualifiers in the statement, including the WHERE clause.

The following statement shows how to do this by using joins in place of the USING clause:

```
select c.cust_id, c.cust_state_province,
       s.quantity_sold, p.prod_name
from    sales s
  join customers c
    on s.cust_id = c.cust_id
  join products
    on s.prod_id = p.prod_id
where p.prod_id = 117
and c.country_id = 52790;

select cust_id, c.cust_state_province,
       s.quantity_sold, p.prod_name
from    sales s
  join customers c using (cust_id)
join products p using (prod_id)
where p.prod_id = 117
and c.country_id = 52790;
```

Ask the Expert

Q: Why does the cust_id column in the ANSI on join have a table prefix qualifier while the cust_id column in the ANSI using join does not?

A: The on join syntax tells Oracle which columns to use in the table join. Like the Oracle inner join examples, the table prefix is required for cust_id within both the select list of columns and the table join. The using syntax declares only the column name and allows Oracle to resolve the join. The table qualifiers for the cust_id column are absent from the join portion of the SQL statement and need to be kept out of the select list as well. If you forget, don't worry—Oracle will return an "ORA-25154: column part of USING clause cannot have a qualifier" error message.

ANSI Natural Join   ANSI SQL also gives you a third join alternative: the natural join. In this case, the columns to be joined are not specified but rather are resolved by Oracle. They must be similarly named in the tables to be joined. As always, additional selection criteria can be specified in the where clause:

```
select cust_id, c.cust_state_province,
       s.quantity_sold, p.prod_name
from sales s
     natural join customers c
     natural join products p
where prod_id = 117;
```

As you found out with the using syntax, you couldn't use the table alias qualifier on the cust_id column. If you did, you would get an "ORA-25155: column used in NATURAL join cannot have qualifier" error message.

Although it would be very poor database design, it's entirely possible that similarly named columns could exist in different tables but have no relationship to each other. Be careful while naturally joining tables to make sure that it makes sense to join them. While this could just as easily happen with a regular Oracle join, the simple act of having to specify which columns to join could force you to go through this thought process. It's an important fact to know your tables and what you want to accomplish with the joins.

Outer Joins

Unlike an inner join, which only returned records that had matching values for a specific column in both tables, an outer join can return results from one table where the corresponding table did not have a matching value.

In our sample set of data, a number of customers haven't recorded any sales. There are also a number of products that haven't been sold either. These examples will be used in the following explanation of Oracle and ANSI outer joins.

Oracle Outer Joins

In order to find rows from one table that don't match rows in another, known as an outer join, Oracle presents you with the "(+)" notation. The "(+)" is used in the where clause on either of the tables where nonmatching rows are to be returned.

You have found that cust_id = 1 does not have any sales, while cust_id = 80 has exactly two. Now take a look at what happens when you select these two customers from the CUSTOMERS table and request some SALES table details if they exist:

```
SQL> select c.cust_id, c.cust_last_name, s.prod_id, s.quantity_sold
  2  from    customers c, sales s
  3  where   c.cust_id = s.cust_id(+)
  4  and     c.cust_id in (1,80);

   CUST_ID CUST_LAST_NAME                         PROD_ID QUANTITY_SOLD
---------- ------------------------------- ---------- -------------
         1 Kessel
        80 Carpenter                            127             1
        80 Carpenter                             36             1
```

The *outer join* allows you to display the CUSTOMERS columns alongside the nulls for the nonmatched rows' SALES records. A simple join would have only returned the two records for cust_id 80.

Project 3-1 Join Data Using Inner and Outer Joins

With the sample tables Oracle has provided, there are no *outer join* examples. When you learn about referential integrity and constraints later in this chapter, this will become a little clearer. Suffice it to say that the customers, products, and promotions in the sales table all exist in their respective tables. In this project, you're going to create your own simple tables where you can better demonstrate *outer joins*. Once you discuss the ANSI version of joins, you'll revisit this project and introduce a new concept available only with the ANSI syntax.

Step by Step

You should start by creating and populating two very simple tables that will join on a common column. Open up a SQL*Plus session and issue the following commands:

1. create table temp1 (id number(3), desc1 char(5));

2. create table temp2 (id number(3), desc2 char(5));

3. insert into temp1 values (123, 'ABCDE');

4. insert into temp1 values (456, 'FGHIJ');

5. insert into temp2 values (456, 'ZZZZZ');

6. insert into temp2 values (789, 'MMMMM');

7. commit;

Tables temp1 and temp2 each have two records. The two tables join with each other on the "ID" column, and they have one ID in common: 456. You should continue now by displaying all the records from temp1 and temp2 followed by writing an *inner, right outer,* and *left outer join.* In SQL*Plus, enter the code from the following code listing and check that you get the same output.

1. Display the records from temp1 (remember to use select * when doing so):

   ```
           ID DESC1
   ---------- -----
          123 ABCDE
          456 FGHIJ
   ```

2. Display the records from temp2:

   ```
           ID DESC2
   ---------- -----
          456 ZZZZZ
          789 MMMMM
   ```

3. Use an inner join to join the two:

   ```
   SQL> select a.id, a.desc1, b.desc2
     2  from    temp1 a, temp2 b
     3  where   a.id = b.id;

           ID DESC1 DESC2
   ---------- ----- -----
          456 FGHIJ ZZZZZ
   ```

(continued)

4. Create an outer join table called temp2, as in the following:

```
SQL> select a.id, a.desc1, b.id, b.desc2
  2  from    temp1 a, temp2  b
  3  where   a.id = b.id(+);

        ID DESC1          ID DESC2
---------- ----- ---------- -----
       123 ABCDE
       456 FGHIJ          456 ZZZZZ
```

5. Generate the outer join table temp1:

```
SQL> select a.id, a.desc1, b.id, b.desc2
  2  from    temp1 a, temp2  b
  3  where   a.id(+) = b.id;

        ID DESC1          ID DESC2
---------- ----- ---------- -----
       456 FGHIJ          456 ZZZZZ
                          789 MMMMM
```

6. Now generate the outer join on both sides, as in the following:

```
SQL> select a.id, a.desc1, b.id, b.desc2
  2  from    temp1 a, temp2  b
  3  where   a.id(+) = b.id(+);
where   a.id(+) = b.id(+)
                        *
ERROR at line 3:
ORA-01468: a predicate may reference only one outer-joined table
```

Apply is supported in Oracle 12c. The cross apply will act like an inner join, and outer apply will look at the rows in the left side like an outer join. The same example can be walked through with the apply syntax, as you can see in the following examples:

```
SQL> select * from oe.temp1 a cross apply
  2  (select * from oe.temp2 b
  3  where a.id=b.id);

        ID DESC1          ID DESC2
---------- ----- ---------- -----
       456 FGHIJ          456 ZZZZZ
SQL> select * from oe.temp1 a outer apply
  2  (select * from oe.temp2 b
  3  where a.id <= b.id);
```

```
      ID DESC1        ID DESC2
---------- ----- ---------- -----
       123 ABCDE        456 ZZZZZ
       123 ABCDE        789 MMMMM
       456 FGHIJ        456 ZZZZZ
       456 FGHIJ        789 MMMMM
```

Project Summary

The *outer join* of table temp2 returned all records from temp1 even if they had nonmatching rows in temp2. The *outer join* of table temp1 returned all records from temp2 whether or not they had matching rows in temp1. Last, you tried an outer join on both sides to see what would happen. This syntax did not work, and Oracle gave you a helpful error message (that's not always the case!). When you learn the union critical point later on in this chapter, you'll see that there's a way to do this with Oracle's syntax. However, you should move on to the ANSI outer join examples now, where you'll see that it is possible without writing a lot of code (that's a good thing!).

ANSI Outer Joins

With Oracle9*i*, Oracle began the journey to fully support ANSI SQL standards. To meet this goal, Oracle started the support of ANSI joins as discussed previously. Let's now turn our attention to ANSI outer joins. As we alluded to in Project 3-1, the ANSI outer join syntax allows you to perform right outer joins, left outer joins, and full outer joins.

ANSI Right Outer Joins   As with the ANSI inner joins, the ANSI outer joins have moved the join to the from clause. A right outer join can be written with keywords "right outer join" or "right join" because "outer" is redundant. Rewriting the SALES and CUSTOMERS example, discussed earlier in the chapter, with the ANSI syntax produces the following:

```
SQL> select c.cust_id, c.cust_last_name, s.prod_id, s.quantity_sold
  2  from sales s right join customers c
3       on c.cust_id = s.cust_id
4  where c.cust_id in (1,80);

   CUST_ID CUST_LAST_NAME                                    PROD_ID QUANTITY_SOLD
---------- ------------------------------------------- ---------- -------------
         1 Kessel
        80 Carpenter                                         127             1
        80 Carpenter                                          36             1
```

As with the Oracle example, the SALES table nonmatched rows are returned. The main difference is that s.cust_id had the (+) notation before; now you state that SALES will be right joined to CUSTOMERS. The join syntax is in the from clause, while the where clause contains only the selection criteria (in this case, only customer 1's and 80's records). This query can also be written with using or natural right join ANSI syntax. Go ahead and try that on your own. Make sure you get the exact same results as you did with the on example from the preceding example.

ANSI Left Outer Joins   The ANSI left outer join works exactly the same as the right outer join and can be written using either left outer join or left join. As with the right outer join, the join on, join using, or natural left join styles are all available. Any of the combinations will produce exactly the same results. Hold off on the left outer join example until you revisit the outer join idea later in Project 3-4.

ANSI Full Outer Joins   A full outer join is possible when using the ANSI syntax without having to write too much code. With a full outer join, you will be able to return both the right outer join and left outer join results from the same query.

The full outer join queries can be written as full outer join or full join and once again, the on, using, or natural joins are all possible. You should revisit Project 3-1: Join Data Using Inner and Outer Joins and try the ANSI syntax out.

Project 3-2   Join Data Using ANSI SQL Joins

Using the temp1 and temp2 tables you created and populated, try out the ANSI right, left, and full outer joins.

Step by Step

You've just learned that you can write the ANSI outer joins with or without the outer keyword in each of the ANSI right, left, and full outer joins. You also learned that the ANSI on, using, and natural join syntax is available as well. The following step-by-step instructions use a combination of these for illustration purposes. Feel free to try alternative syntax, but we encourage you to adopt a consistent style to allow your code to be self-documenting and traceable by other developers.

1. Use the ANSI right outer join:

```
SQL> select id, desc1, desc2
  2  from    temp2 right outer join temp1
  3          using  (id);
```

```
        ID DESC1 DESC2
---------- ----- -----
       456 EFGH  ZZZZ
       123 ABCD
```

2. Use the ANSI left outer join, shown in the following:

```
SQL> select id, desc1, desc2
  2  from  temp2 b natural left join temp1 a;


        ID DESC1 DESC2
---------- ----- -----
       456 EFGH  ZZZZ
       789 MMMM
```

3. Use the ANSI full outer join to complete the syntax:

```
SQL> select a.id, a.desc1, b.id, b.desc2
  2  from   temp1 a full join temp2 b
  3            on a.id = b.id;


        ID DESC1         ID DESC2
---------- ----- ---------- -----
       456 FGHIJ        456 ZZZZZ
       123 ABCDE        789 MMMMM
```

Project Summary

The three examples in this project show an alternative way of performing outer joins using ANSI SQL. The first join, the right outer join, returns all of the rows from the table listed on the right side of the from clause, temp1, regardless of whether or not they match to a row from the other table, temp2.

The second example switches the logic. The table on the left, temp2, returns all rows with a left outer join specified as a natural left join.

The final example introduces the full outer join concept available with ANSI SQL. In this case, all rows are returned from each table, regardless of whether or not a match was made.

Self-Joins

A self-join is used for a relationship within a single table. Rows are joined back to the same table instead of joining them to a related second table as you have seen with the many CUSTOMERS and SALES tables examples throughout this chapter.

A common example involves hierarchical relationships where all of the records and related records are stored within the same table. A family tree is one such hierarchy that best illustrates the self-join. You should take a look at the FAMILY table that you have defined for this concept:

```
SQL> desc family
 Name                                      Null?    Type
 ----------------------------------------- -------- --------------
 NAME                                      NOT NULL CHAR(10)
 BIRTH_YEAR                                NOT NULL NUMBER(4)
 FATHER                                             CHAR(10)
```

The table contains columns for a person's name and birth year as well as their father's name. The fathers each have their own row in the table with their respective birth years and names. This table could be filled out with every known relationship in the family tree. For this example, Moishe, born in 1894, has a son, Joseph, who was born in 1930. Joseph has three children: Michael, born in 1957; David, born in 1959; and Ian, born in 1963. You can see that Ian then had two children. The example first takes a look at all of the records in the table followed by your hierarchical self-join example. In the first record, we show you all of the data we created. You can simulate this example by adding your own insert statements to the family table:

```
SQL> select * from family;

NAME         BIRTH_YEAR FATHER
---------- ----------- ----------
Moishe           1894
Joseph           1930 Moishe
Michael          1957 Joseph
Davi             1959 Joseph
Ian              1963 Joseph
Baila            1989 Ian
Jillian          1991 Ian

SQL> select a.name, a.birth_year,
  2            a.father, b.birth_year
  3    from    family a, family b
  4    where   a.father = b.name;

NAME         BIRTH_YEAR FATHER       BIRTH_YEAR
---------- ----------- ----------   ----------
Joseph           1930 Moishe             1894
Michael          1957 Joseph             1930
David            1959 Joseph             1930
Ian              1963 Joseph             1930
Baila            1989 Ian                1963
Jillian          1991 Ian                1963
```

The FAMILY table is found in the from clause twice, with table aliases of a and b. The table is joined back to itself to retrieve the father's details. In order to accomplish this, the value found in the father column for each retrieved record (a.father) is joined back to the table to obtain a match on the name column (b.name), which will return the father's details—in this case, his year of birth (b.birth_year). Although this appears complex on the surface, you will find that connecting information together, whether from multiple tables or one table back to itself, is a regular way for you to view your data in a more meaningful manner.

CRITICAL SKILL 3.9

Learn the Group By and Having Clauses

Earlier, you learned about functions that can work on sets of rows. You can also group sets of rows to lump similar types of information together and return summary information, also referred to as aggregated information. A large number of queries you write will perform group functions as the data is retrieved from the database. Mastering the use of functions and grouping is fundamental to understanding the full power of SQL.

Group By

You can use many of the functions you were presented with earlier with or without the group by clause, but when you use them without it, Oracle treats all of the selected rows as one group. For example, the following query, when written without a group by clause, returns the average amount sold for products within the Electronics category:

```
SQL> select  avg(amount_sold)
  2  from    sales s, products p
  3  where   s.prod_id = p.prod_id
  4  and     prod_category = 'Electronics';

AVG(AMOUNT_SOLD)
----------------
      125.551667
```

The entire Electronics category was treated as one group. If you wanted to see the average amount sold for each subcategory within the Electronics category, you will need to use a group by clause in your query, lumping each of the Electronics subcategories together before calculating the average. Each group by clause is accomplished by putting the column or columns to group by in the select list, followed by one or more functions. A group by statement follows the where clause, and it must include each of the select list columns that are not acted upon by a group function. Consider the following example:

```
SQL> select prod_subcategory, avg(amount_sold)
  2  from    sales s, products p
  3  where   s.prod_id = p.prod_id
  4  and     prod_category = 'Electronics'
  5  group by prod_subcategory;

PROD_SUBCATEGORY                                        AVG(AMOUNT_SOLD)
-------------------------------------------------- ----------------
Game Consoles                                                 300.523928
Y Box Accessories                                             18.7803303
Home Audio                                                    582.175922

Y Box Games                                                   22.640670
```

This group by example illustrates a column and function in the select list and the repetition of the column again in the group by clause.

Having

Just as you have used selection criteria to reduce the result set, you can apply the having clause to summarized data from a group by operation to restrict the groups returned. Consider the previous example, and suppose you want to see only the Product Subcategory groups that have an average amount sold greater than 300. The following is a having clause executed against the avg(amount_sold) aggregation example:

```
SQL> select prod_subcategory, avg(amount_sold)
  2  from    sales s, products p
  3  where   s.prod_id = p.prod_id
  4  and     prod_category = 'Electronics'
  5  group by prod_subcategory
  6  having avg(amount_sold) > 300;

PROD_SUBCATEGORY                                        AVG(AMOUNT_SOLD)
-------------------------------------------------- ----------------
Game Consoles                                                 300.523928
Home Audio                                                    582.175922
```

Project 3-3 Group Data in Your Select Statements

One final example will demonstrate the grouping of multiple columns and more than one function being performed for each group. As you build on this example, you will be introduced to column aliases, the round function combined with an avg function, and the use of a substr function, which enables you to select only a specified number of characters for the product subcategories and names results.

Step by Step

Start with the preceding group by example and build on it as you introduce some formatting and intermediate concepts. Look at the output each time and see how you are transforming it along the way. A final output listing has been provided at the end for you to compare against.

1. Start SQL*Plus and re-execute the preceding group by example:

```
select prod_subcategory, avg(amount_sold)
from    sales s, products p
where   s.prod_id = p.prod_id
and     prod_category = 'Electronics'
group by prod_subcategory;
```

2. Add the product name to the select list. Don't forget to add it to the group by also:

```
select prod_subcategory, prod_name, avg(amount_sold)
from    sales s, products p
where   s.prod_id = p.prod_id
and     prod_category = 'Electronics'
group by prod_subcategory, prod_name;
```

3. Rewrite the query to use a natural join, remove the table aliases, and exclude the 'Home Audio' subcategory from the selection:

```
select prod_subcategory, prod_name, avg(amount_sold)
from    sales natural join products
where   prod_category = 'Electronics'
and     prod_subcategory != 'Home Audio'
group by prod_subcategory, prod_name;
```

4. Add a max function calculation on the amount_sold to the query:

```
select prod_subcategory, prod_name, max(amount_sold),
avg(amount_sold)
from    sales natural join products
where   prod_category = 'Electronics'
and     prod_subcategory != 'Home Audio'
group by prod_subcategory, prod_name;
```

(continued)

5. Add a substr function to both the prod_subcategory and prod_name, selecting the first 18 and 25 characters, respectively, to shorten the displayed results. Don't forget to change the group by at the same time:

```
select substr(prod_subcategory,1,18),
       substr(prod_name,1,25),
       max(amount_sold),
       avg(amount_sold)
from   sales natural join products
where  prod_category = 'Electronics'
and    prod_subcategory != 'Home Audio'
group by substr(prod_subcategory,1,18),
         substr(prod_name,1,25);
```

6. Add a round function to the avg(amount_sold) function. In this step, you should also give the column names aliases to make the results more readable:

```
select substr(prod_subcategory,1,18) Subcategory,
       substr(prod_name,1,25) Product_Name,
       max(amount_sold) Max_Amt_Sold,
       round(avg(amount_sold),2) AvgAmt
from   sales natural join products
where  prod_category = 'Electronics'
and    prod_subcategory != 'Home Audio'
group by substr(prod_subcategory,1,18),
         substr(prod_name,1,25);
```

7. Add a having clause to return aggregated rows that have both a maximum amount sold and an average amount sold greater than 10. As one final measure, you should also add an order by:

```
select substr(prod_subcategory,1,18) Subcategory,
       substr(prod_name,1,25) Product_Name,
       max(amount_sold) Max_Amt_Sold,
       round(avg(amount_sold),2) AvgAmt
from   sales natural join products
where  prod_category = 'Electronics'
and    prod_subcategory != 'Home Audio'
group by substr(prod_subcategory,1,18),
         substr(prod_name,1,25)
having max(amount_sold) > 10
and    avg(amount_sold) > 10
order by substr(prod_subcategory,1,18),
         substr(prod_name,1,25);
```

8. Your final output should look like this:

```
SUBCATEGORY          PRODUCT_NAME              MAX_AMT_SOLD AVGAMT
-----------------    ------------------------  ------------ ------
Game Consoles        Y Box                           326.39 300.52
Y Box Accessories    Xtend Memory                      29.8  24.15
Y Box Games          Adventures with Numbers          17.03  13.78
Y Box Games          Bounce                           25.55  21.13
Y Box Games          Comic Book Heroes                25.76  22.14
Y Box Games          Endurance Racing                 42.58  34.29
Y Box Games          Finding Fido                      16.6  12.79
Y Box Games          Martial Arts Champions           25.76  22.14
Y Box Games          Smash up Boxing                  38.64  33.2

9 rows selected.
```

Project Summary

While the final example, and a few transformations along the way, are more in keeping with what you see in intermediate SQL, take some time to study each of the steps and the resulting changes to the output. Once you understand the different components of the SQL statement that evolved in this project, you'll be well on your way to unleashing the power of SQL.

Progress Check

1. Retrieve a list of all product categories, subcategories, names, and list prices where the list price is greater than $100. Order this query by product category, subcategory, and name.

2. List the aggregate total sales for every product category and subcategory group using the ANSI natural join syntax.

3. Retrieve a list of all customer IDs and last names where the customer has only one entry in the SALES table.

Learn Subqueries: Simple and Correlated Comparison with Joins

Within SQL, functionality exists to create subqueries, which are essentially queries within queries. This powerful capability makes it possible to produce results based on another result or set of results. Let's explore this concept a little further.

Simple Subquery

Without the functionality of subqueries, it would take a couple of SQL queries to retrieve product information for the product with the maximum list price. The first query would have to find the value of max(prod_list_price). A subsequent query would have to use the value resolved for max(prod_list_price) to find the product details. Take a look at how you can resolve this with a subquery embedded in the where clause of the main query:

```
select prod_id, prod_name, prod_category
from    products
where   prod_list_price = (select max(prod_list_price)
                             from    products);
```

Progress Check Answers

1. An ordered list of all product categories, subcategories, names, and list prices greater than $100 is returned by the following query:

```
SQL> select prod_category, prod_subcategory, prod_name, prod_list_price
  2  from    products
  3  where   prod_list_price > 100
  3  order by prod_category, prod_subcategory, prod_name;
```

2. The SQL statement that will return the aggregate amount sold for every product category and subcategory using the ANSI SQL natural join is shown here:

```
SQL> select prod_category, prod_subcategory, sum(amount_sold)
  2  from    products natural join sales
  3  group by prod_category, prod_subcategory;
```

3. The list of all customer IDs and last names for customers that had only one sale is returned by the following SQL statement:

```
SQL> select c.cust_id, cust_last_name, count(*)
  2  from    customers c, sales s
  3  where   c.cust_id = s.cust_id
  4  group by c.cust_id, cust_last_name
  5  having count(*) = 1;
```

The subquery is enclosed in parentheses and is part of the where clause. The main query is resolved based on the results of the subquery: in this case, the maximum product list price. As you can see, the ability to have a query within a query is very powerful.

Running SQL queries with embedded subqueries can affect performance. As your experience with subqueries increases, you will find that you will need to work closely with your database administrator, more commonly referred to as a DBA, to optimize statements with subquery processing.

Correlated Subqueries with Joins

A *correlated subquery* is a query that references a column from the main query. In the example that follows, you are able to first retrieve the average list price for each product category and then join it back (correlate it) to the product category in the outer query. Take a look at the example and its output:

```
SQL> select  substr(prod_category,1,22) Category,
  2          substr(prod_name,1,39) Product,
  3          prod_list_price List
  4   from    products p
  5   where   prod_list_price > (select avg(prod_list_price)
  6                              from    products
  7                              where   p.prod_category = prod_category)
  8   order by substr(prod_category,1,22), prod_list_price desc;

CATEGORY                 PRODUCT                                    LIST
-------------------- ----------------------------------------- --------
Electronics          Home Theatre Package with DVD-Audio/Vid    599.99
Electronics          8.3 Minitower Speaker                      499.99
```

Ask the Expert

Q: What would happen if the subquery returned multiple values?

A: Because the subquery in the example can return only a single value, it is acceptable for it to be written with the equals (=) operand. If multiple values are expected from the subquery, the *in* list operand should be used.

```
Electronics              Y Box                                    299.99
Hardware                 Envoy Ambassador                        1299.99
Peripherals and Access   17" LCD w/built-in HDTV Tuner            999.99
Peripherals and Access   18" Flat Panel Graphics Monitor          899.99
Peripherals and Access   Model NM500X High Yield Toner Cartridge  192.99
Peripherals and Access   SIMM- 16MB PCMCIAII card                 149.99
Photo                    Mini DV Camcorder with 3.5" Swivel LCD  1099.99
Photo                    5MP Telephoto Digital Camera             899.99
Software/Other           Unix/Windows 1-user pack                 199.99
Software/Other           Laptop carrying case                      55.99
Software/Other           DVD-R Discs, 4.7GB, Pack of 5             49.99
Software/Other           O/S Documentation Set - English          44.99
Software/Other           O/S Documentation Set - German           44.99
Software/Other           O/S Documentation Set - French           44.99
Software/Other           O/S Documentation Set - Spanish          44.99
Software/Other           O/S Documentation Set - Italian          44.99
Software/Other           O/S Documentation Set - Kanji            44.99

19 rows selected.
```

The main query retrieves the Category, Product, and List Price details for each product that is greater than the average list price of all products within its category. This wouldn't be possible without the subquery. Data from the subquery's product category is joined with the main query's product category and referenced by the main query's table alias.

Notice as well that the order by exists on the outer query. If it were placed in the subquery, it wouldn't work. The displayed results are what you want to order, not the subquery results.

CRITICAL SKILL 3.11

Use Set Operators: Union, Intersect, Minus

One of the nice things about a relational database is that SQL queries act upon sets of data versus a single row of data. Oracle provides you with a series of set functions that can be used to bring data sets together. The set functions will be discussed in the next few sections by referencing two single-column tables: Table x and Table y. Before proceeding to the discussion on the set functions, you should first take a look at the contents of these tables.

Table x:

```
SQL> select * from x;

COL
---
1
2
3
4
5
6

6 rows selected.
```

Table y:

```
SQL> select * from y;

COL
---
5
6
7

3 rows selected.
```

Union

When you use the UNION operator in SQL*Plus, it returns all the rows in both tables without any duplicates. Oracle accomplishes this with a sort operation. In the preceding table listings, both tables have columns with values of 5 and 6. The union query and resulting output are shown here:

```
SQL> select * from x
  2  union
  3  select * from y;
COL
---
1
2
3
4
5
6
7

7 rows selected.
```

Union All

The UNION ALL set function is similar to the union query with the exception that it returns all rows from both tables with duplicates. The advantage here, if the rows are not duplicated or if duplicates are expected, is that a union all will be the faster query because you don't need to spend time doing the comparison. The following example is a rewrite of the preceding union example using UNION ALL:

```
SQL> select * from x
2   union all
3   select * from y;

COL
---
1
2
3
4
5
6
5
6
7

9 rows selected.
```

Intersect

The INTERSECT operator will return all the rows in one table that also reside in the other. Column values 5 and 6 exist in both the tables. The following example demonstrates the INTERSECT set function:

```
SQL> select * from x
2   intersect
3   select * from y;

COL
---
5
6
```

NOTE
Please be aware that the intersect set operator can introduce major performance problems. If you are venturing down this path, weigh the alternatives first.

Minus

The MINUS set function returns all the rows in the first table minus the rows in the first table that are also in the second table. The order of the tables is important. Pay close attention to the order of the tables and the different results in these two query examples:

```
SQL> select * from x
  2  minus
  3  select * from y;

COL
---
1
2
3
4

SQL> select * from y
  2  minus
  3  select * from x;

COL
---
7
```

Project 3-4 Use the Union Function in Your SQL

During the discussion of Oracle outer joins and the associated Project 3-1, you learned that a full outer join wasn't readily available using the Oracle syntax. You also learned about the union set function, and you took a moment to revisit the creation of an outer join without using ANSI SQL syntax.

Step by Step

You should first recall the Oracle right outer join and left outer join examples you were working on in Project 3-1.

1. Start by using the right outer join example from Project 3-1:

```
SQL> select a.id, a.desc1, b.id, b.desc2
  2  from   temp1 a, temp2  b
  3  where  a.id = b.id(+);
```

(continued)

```
        ID DESC1          ID DESC2
---------- ----- ---------- -----
       123 ABCDE
       456 FGHIJ          456 ZZZZZ
```

2. Use the left outer join example from Project 3-1:

```
SQL> select a.id, a.desc1, b.id, b.desc2
  2  from    temp1 a, temp2  b
  3  where   a.id(+) = b.id;


        ID DESC1          ID DESC2
---------- ----- ---------- -----
       456 FGHIJ          456 ZZZZZ
                          789 MMMMM
```

3. Put the two together with a full outer join using union. ANSI SQL outer join syntax provided you with a full outer join option that wasn't available with Oracle's standard SQL. With the union set function in your Oracle tool belt, you have another way to solve this problem. So now, take the two queries from the recalled examples and union them together:

```
SQL> select a.id, a.desc1, b.id, b.desc2
  2  from temp1 a, temp2 b
  3  where a.id = b.id(+)
  3  union
  5  select a.id, a.desc1, b.id, b.desc2
  6  from temp1 a, temp2 b
  7  where a.id(+) = b.id;

        ID DESC1          ID DESC2
---------- ----- ---------- -----
       123 ABCDE
       456 FGHIJ          456 ZZZZZ
                          789 MMMMM
```

Project Summary

In this project, by combining the right and left outer join Oracle statements together with a union set operator, you were able to mimic the ANSI SQL full outer join functionality.

CRITICAL SKILL 3.12

Use Views

Views are database objects that are based on one or more tables. They allow the user to create a pseudo-table that has no data. The view consists solely of a SQL query that retrieves specific columns and rows. The data that is retrieved by a view is presented like a table.

Views can provide a level of security, making only certain rows and columns from one or more tables available to the end user. You can hide the underlying tables, CUSTOMERS and SALES, from all the users in your organization and only make available the data for states they are entitled to see. In the following example, you are creating a view to show only specific details about Utah-based customer sales:

```
SQL> create view utah_sales
  2  as
  3  select c.cust_id ID,
  4         substr(cust_last_name,1,20) Name,
  5         substr(cust_city,1,20) City,
  6         substr(cust_state_province,1,5) State,
  7         sum(amount_sold) Total
  8  from   customers c, sales s
  9  where  c.cust_id = s.cust_id
 10  and    cust_state_province = 'UT'
 11  group by c.cust_id,
 12         substr(cust_last_name,1,20),
 13         substr(cust_city,1,20),
 14         substr(cust_state_province,1,5);

View created.
```

The create view statement names the view and then uses keywords such as select to define the select list, tables, and selection criteria that the view will be based upon. The following code listing issues a DESC statement to demonstrate that the view looks just like a table. Notice that the column names have been changed from their original names and were instead created using the column aliases from the select statement in the preceding view creation DDL:

```
SQL> desc utah_sales
 Name                                      Null?    Type
 ----------------------------------------- -------- -------------------
 ID                                        NOT NULL NUMBER
 NAME                                               VARCHAR2(20)
 CITY                                               VARCHAR2(20)
 STATE                                              VARCHAR2(5)
 TOTAL                                              NUMBER
```

The view looks like a table, as demonstrated by the preceding code listing, so you should now issue a couple of queries against it. The first query that follows selects all rows and columns from this view. The second example selects only the name and total columns for customers whose sales are greater than 20,000. Keep in mind that this is still only for Utah customers:

```
SQL> select *
  2  from  utah_sales;
        ID NAME                  CITY                  STATE     TOTAL
---------- --------------------  --------------------  -----  ----------
       118 Kuehler               Farmington            UT       23258.4
       392 Eubank                Farmington            UT      21297.49
       411 Vankirk               Farmington            UT      19279.94
       462 Nielley               Farmington            UT      64509.91
       599 Robbinette            Farmington            UT      11167.65
      7003 Bane                  Farmington            UT      62605.42
    100207 Campbell              Farmington            UT         11.99
    100267 Desai                 Farmington            UT        240.95
    100308 Wilbur                Farmington            UT        190.96

9 rows selected.

SQL> select name, total
  2  from  utah_sales
  3  where  total > 20000;

NAME                      TOTAL
--------------------  ----------
Kuehler                 23258.4
Eubank                 21297.49
Nielley                64509.91
Bane                   62605.42
```

It's easy to see how you can keep certain users in your company from accessing sales information from more than the states they are granted access to. If this sample database has sale representatives with assigned territories, one can imagine how the use of territory-based views can keep one salesperson from viewing the sales and commissions of another territory representative.

You have demonstrated here that views contain no data. All the data for the view example in this section resides in the underlying tables. In Chapter 9, we introduce you to *materialized views*: physical implementations of views that are used to improve performance when you have a significant amount of data.

CRITICAL SKILL 3.13

Learn Sequences: Just Simple Stuff

Before Oracle 12c and the identify column, primary keys in tables were simply generated numeric values that are sequential. In the sample database that you've used throughout this chapter, cust_id and prod_id in the CUSTOMERS and PRODUCTS tables are likely candidates for creation using a sequence.

Sequences are objects in the database that can be used to provide sequentially generated integers. Without these valuable objects available to users, generating values sequentially is possible only through the use of programs.

Sequences are generally created and named by a DBA. Among the attributes that can be defined when creating a sequence are a minimum value, a maximum value, a number to increment by, and a number to start with. They are then made available to the system's applications and users that would need to generate them.

For the following example, you will have established a cust_id_seq sequence, which increments by one each time it's called. When you created the sequence, you specified that 104501 should be the number to start with. For demonstration purposes, you'll use the DUAL table to select the next two sequence numbers. More often than not, an application will retrieve and assign the sequence numbers as records are inserted into the associated table:

```
SQL> create sequence cust_id_seq
  2  start with 104501;

  Sequence created
SQL> select cust_id_seq.nextval
  2  from dual;

   NEXTVAL
----------
    104501

SQL> select cust_id_seq.nextval
  2  from dual;

   NEXTVAL
----------
    104502
```

CRITICAL SKILL 3.14

Employ Constraints: Linkage to Entity Models, Types, Deferred, Enforced, Gathering Exceptions

When we discussed database joins you were introduced to the concept of primary and foreign keys. These were, in fact, constraints on the tables. Constraints preserve the integrity of the database by enforcing business rules.

The primary key for the PROMOTIONS table in the sample schema is an integrity constraint. It requires that each value in promo_id be unique. You should see what would happen if you tried to insert a row in this table with a promo_id value that already exists:

```
SQL> insert into promotions
  2     (promo_id,
  3      promo_name,
  4      promo_subcategory,
  5      promo_subcategory_id,
  6      promo_category,
  7      promo_category_id,
  8      promo_cost,
  9      promo_begin_date,
 10      promo_end_date,
 11      promo_total,
 12      promo_total_id)
 13  values
 14     (36,
 15      'Thanksgiving Sale',
 16      'Newspaper',
 17      28,
 18      'ad news',
 19      4,
 20      250,
 21      '23-NOV-03',
 22      '27-NOV-03',
 23      'Promotion Total',
 24      5);
insert into promotions
*
ERROR at line 1:
ORA-00001: unique constraint (SH.PROMO_PK) violated
```

Because the value 36 already existed for promo_id, the unique constraint was violated when you tried to insert another row in the table with the same value. This constraint preserved the integrity of the data by enforcing the business rule that every promotion must be identified uniquely.

Linkage to Entity Models

Many organizations have complex databases and, as a result, they use entity models to document each system's database objects and constraints. These models of the organizations' database schemas graphically represent the relationships between objects.

The function of database design could be the responsibility of the developer, DBA, or a database designer. Among other uses, entity-modeling software allows the database designer to graphically define and link tables to each other. The result is a data model with tables, columns, primary keys, and foreign keys. Throughout this chapter, you have issued DDL to create tables. Typically, entity-modeling software will generate the DDL in a script that can be executed against the database. This makes the job of defining and maintaining database objects (and their associated constraints and relationships with each other) a lot easier.

Types

There are a number of different types of integrity constraints. The following is a list of the integrity constraints that are available in Oracle Database:

- NULL constraints are defined on a single column and dictate whether or not the column must contain a value. If a column is defined as NOT NULL, it must contain values in each and every record.

- UNIQUE constraints allow a value in a column to be inserted or updated providing it contains a unique value.

- PRIMARY KEY constraints require that the key uniquely identifies each row in the table. The key may consist of one column or a combination of columns.

- FOREIGN KEY constraints define the relationships between tables. This is commonly referred to as referential integrity. These are rules that are based on a key in one table that assures that the values exist in the key of the referenced table.

- CHECK constraints enable users to define and enforce rules on columns.

■ Acceptable values are defined for a column and insert, update, and delete commands are interrogated and are then accepted or rejected based on whether or not the values are specifically allowed. A separate check constraint definition is necessary if the requirement exists to perform either similar or different checks on more than one column. The following example illustrates the creation of a table with a single check constraint, followed by an insert with an acceptable value and an attempted insert with a disallowed value:

```
SQL> create table check_constraint_example
  2      (col1 char(1)
  3          constraint check_col1
  4          check (col1 in ('B','G','N')));

Table created.

SQL> insert into check_constraint_example values ('B');

1 row created.

SQL> insert into check_constraint_example values ('C');
insert into check_constraint_example values ('C')
*
ERROR at line 1:
ORA-02290: check constraint (SH.CHECK_COL1) violated
```

Ask the Expert

Q: Is a single space an acceptable entry into a NOT NULL constrained column?

A: Yes. Oracle will allow you to enter a space as the sole character in a NOT NULL constrained column. Be careful, however. The single space will look like a NULL value when a select statement retrieves and displays this row. The space is very different from a NULL.

Deferred

When constraints are created, they can be created either as deferrable or not deferrable. A constraint that is not deferred is checked immediately upon execution of each statement and, if the constraint is violated, it is immediately rolled back. A constraint that is deferred will not be checked until a commit statement is issued. This is useful when inserting rows or updating values that reference other values that do not exist but are part of the overall batch of statements. By deferring the constraint checking until the commit is issued, you can complete the entire batch of entries before determining if there are any constraint violations.

CRITICAL SKILL 3.15

Format Your Output with SQL*Plus

Throughout this chapter, you've seen the results of many SQL queries. In some, you added functions such as substr to reduce the size of the columns and keep the results confined within one line. In SQL*Plus, there are many parameters that can be set to control how the output is displayed. A list of all of the available settings is easily obtained by issuing the show all command within SQL*Plus. Alternatively, if you know the parameter and want to see its current value, the command show parameter_name will give you the answer. Before we close out this chapter, you should visit a number of the more useful SQL*Plus parameters.

Page and Line Size

The set linesize command tells Oracle how wide the line output is before wrapping the results to the next line. To set the line size to 100, enter the command set linesize 100. There is no semicolon required to end set commands.

Ask the Expert

Q: Once I set parameters, do I ever have to set them again?

A: Yes. Parameters are good only for the current setting. The parameters always reset to their default settings when you start up a new SQL*Plus session. However, the parameter defaults can be overwritten at the start of each SQL*Plus session by entering and saving them in the login.sql file.

The set pagesize command determines the length of the page. The default page size is 14 lines. If you don't want to repeat the result headings every 14 lines, use this command. If you want your page to be 50 lines long, issue the command set pagesize 50.

Page Titles

The ttitle (for top title) command includes a number of options. The default settings return the date and page number on every page followed by the title text centered on the next line. Multiple headings can also be produced by separating the text with the vertical bar character. The command ttitle 'Customer List | Utah' centers the text "Customer List" on the first line, followed by "Utah" on the second line.

Page Footers

The btitle command will center text at the bottom of the page. The command btitle 'sample.sql' places the text "sample.sql" at the bottom center of the output listing. The command btitle left 'sample.sql' results in the footer text "sample.sql" being placed at the left edge of the footer.

Formatting Columns

Quite often, you'll need to format the actual column data. The column command is used to accomplish this. Suppose you are going to select the last name from the CUSTOMERS table along with a number of other columns. You know that, by default, the last name data will take up more space than it needs. The command "COLUMN CUST_LAST_NAME FORMAT A12 WRAP HEADING 'LAST | NAME'" tells SQL*Plus that there should be only 12 characters of the last name displayed and that the column title "Last Name" should be displayed on two separate lines.

Project 3-5 Format Your SQL Output

Now put these SQL*Plus concepts together and format the output of a SQL query. The following step-by-step instructions will lead you through a few of these basic formatting commands.

Step by Step

In this project, you're going to select some customer and sales information for the customers from Utah. First take a look at our sample SQL query and output before any formatting kicks in:

```
SQL> select cust_last_name, cust_city, sum(amount_sold)
  2  from    customers natural join sales
```

```
 3  where  cust_state_province = 'UT'
 4  group by cust_last_name, cust_city;

CUST_LAST_NAME      CUST_CITY        SUM(AMOUNT_SOLD)
----------------    ---------------  ----------------
Bane                Farmington               62605.42
Desai               Farmington                 240.95
Eubank              Farmington               21297.49
Wilbur              Farmington                 190.96
Kuehler             Farmington               23258.40
Nielley              Farmington               64509.91
Vankirk              Farmington               19279.94
Campbell             Farmington                  11.99
Robbinette           Farmington               11167.65
9 rows selected.
```

The following steps correspond to the set commands in the code listing that follows and formats the text into a more useful and consumable result. The original SQL query will also be executed a second time with much nicer formatting results.

1. Set the page size to 15. (You'll probably never have such a small page size, but you're doing this to illustrate multiple pages with this small result set.)

2. Set the line size to 70.

3. Add a title at the top of the page with "Customer Sales Report" and "Utah Region" in the first and second lines, respectively.

4. Add a footer with "CONFIDENTIAL REPORT" displayed.

5. Format the last name to be exactly 12 characters long and with a title "Last Name" listed on two separate lines.

6. Format the city with "City" as the title and the data fixed at 15 characters long.

7. Format the summed amount sold with a two-line title "Total Sales." Format the data to include a dollar sign, two digits following the decimal point, and a comma to denote thousands.

```
SQL> set pagesize 15
SQL> set linesize 64
SQL> ttitle 'Customer Sales Report | Utah Region'
SQL> btitle 'CONFIDENTIAL REPORT'
SQL> column cust_last_name format a12 wrap heading 'Last | Name'
SQL> column cust_city format a15 heading 'City'
```

(continued)

```
SQL> column sum(amount_sold) format $999,999.99 wrap
SQL> column sum(amount_sold) heading 'Total | Sales'
SQL> select cust_last_name, cust_city, sum(amount_sold)
  2  from    customers natural join sales
  3  where   cust_state_province = 'UT'
  4  group by cust_last_name, cust_city;
```

```
Mon Jan 12                                              page  1
                        Customer Sales Report
                            Utah Region


Last                            Total
   Name        City             Sales
------------ --------------- ------------
Bane         Farmington      $62,605.42
Desai        Farmington         $240.95
Eubank       Farmington      $21,297.49
Wilbur       Farmington         $190.96
Kuehler      Farmington      $23,258.40
Nielley      Farmington      $64,509.91
                     CONFIDENTIAL REPORT


Mon Jan 12                                              page  2
                        Customer Sales Report
                            Utah Region


Last                            Total
   Name        City             Sales
------------ --------------- ------------
Vankirk      Farmington      $19,279.94
Campbell     Farmington          $11.99
Robbinette   Farmington      $11,167.65



                     CONFIDENTIAL REPORT


  9 rows selected.
```

Project Summary

With some simple formatting commands available within SQL*Plus, you were able to transform the unformatted, difficult-to-read output into a simple and effective report. SQL*Plus has many more formatting options available than you have seen demonstrated here. As you become more familiar with SQL and SQL*Plus, take the time to research and try more of the available formatting options. We think you'll agree that SQL*Plus is an effective query tool and report formatter.

Writing SQL*Plus Output to a File

The spool command will save the output to a data file. If your database is on a Windows operating system, the command spool c:\reports\output.dat would capture the output of the query execution in the output.dat file.

☑ Chapter 3 Mastery Check

1. DDL and DML translate to _____ and _____, respectively.

2. Which of the following descriptions is true about insert statements?

   A. Insert statements must always have a WHERE clause.

   B. Insert statements can never have a WHERE clause.

   C. Insert statements can optionally include a WHERE clause.

3. In addition to the two mandatory keywords required to retrieve data from the database, there are three optional keywords. Name them.

4. Write a SQL statement to select the customer last name, city, state, and amount sold for the customer represented by customer ID 100895.

5. Retrieve a list of all product categories, subcategories, names, and list prices where the list price is greater than $100 while displaying the results for the product category all in uppercase.

6. Rewrite the query from the previous question and round the amount sold so that there are no cents in the display of the list prices.

7. Retrieve a list of all customer IDs and last names where the customer has more than 200 entries in the SALES table in SH schema.

8. Display the product name of all products that have the lowest list price.

9. Create a view that contains all products in the Electronics category.

10. Sequences provide _____ generated integers.

11. This referential integrity constraint defines the relationship between two tables. Name it.

12. Check constraints enable users to define and enforce rules for:

    A. One or more tables

    B. No more than one column

    C. One or more columns

    D. Only one table

13. Deferred constraints are not checked until the _____ statement is executed.

CHAPTER

4

Programming in the
Database

CRITICAL SKILLS

We know that the Structured Query Language (SQL) is the language to manage your database, to get data into and out of the database, and to make any change that the data within the database needs. It is how we talk at the most basic level to the database. Databases are designed to hold a very large amount of data, and it is natural to perform actions on that massive amount of data to manipulate it in a way that brings value to the organization. For instance, if there is a requirement of performing some changes to thousands of rows in a database table, would it be easier to write thousands of SQL statements or would it be easier to write one SQL statement, put it in some kind of loop, and run that loop thousands times to do that change? Or if you need to read through a series of records and process each one which specific business logic? Therefore, you need to go beyond the single commands of SQL and take it to a different level. You need to have the ability to process information in a logical and dynamic way so that you can truly bring value to your information, and this is where Oracle's programming language PL/SQL comes to support this need.

PL/SQL, or Procedural Language/Structured Query Language, provides some very simple yet powerful tools to handle any amount of data so that it can be processed through a logical set of commands and loops. PL/SQL provides you with the ability to loop through data to go through a series of rows of tables to perform operations such as deletions or updates based on logical choices. It gives you the capability to create shared database objects for frequently used functions of instructions and store them in procedures, functions, and packages within the database. PL/SQL allows you to manipulate your data in a database on the basis of conditions that can meet any level of complexity. The data in the Oracle Database can be accessed through various other programming languages, but PL/SQL is way ahead when it comes to integration with Oracle SQL and Oracle Database and should be part of your Oracle toolkit. PL/SQL is a powerful programming environment that you need to learn and master.

As the user or manager of a database system, PL/SQL is one skill that you must have in your bag. From implementing and managing security to resource management, and from scheduling to performance optimization and much more, you need to know PL/SQL.

Oracle took inspiration from the Ada computer language to create PL/SQL. The beauty of Ada is that it is easier to learn as it is closer to the English language than other programming languages, and it has all the components of a modern computer language with Oracle adding new and powerful features to it with every release.

In this chapter, we discuss the basic concepts and constructs of PL/SQL so that you understand how to create your own PL/SQL programs. There is a lot to cover, but as important as it is to learn SQL, you will need to know PL/SQL as well; if you're looking to become a DBA or an Oracle Database developer, you must have knowledge of PL/SQL in your database toolkit.

CRITICAL SKILL 4.1

Define PL/SQL and Learn Why We Use It

Oracle Database 12c is more than just a database management system—it's also an engine for many programming languages. Not only does it serve as a Java engine with the built-in Java Virtual Machine (JVM), it's a PL/SQL engine as well. This means that the code you write can be stored in a database and then run as required when it is needed.

The PL/SQL engine is bundled together with the database and is an integral part of the Oracle server, providing you with a powerful language to empower your logic and data. Let's look at how PL/SQL fits into the Oracle server. Figure 4-1 shows you how PL/SQL works from both within and outside the database.

At the center of the Oracle Database 12c server in Figure 4-1 is the primary engine for the database, which serves as the coordinator for all calls to and from the database. This means that when a call is made from a program to the server to run a PL/SQL program, the Oracle server loads the compiled program into memory and then the PL/SQL engine and SQL engine execute the program. The PL/SQL engine will handle the program's memory structures and logical program flow and then the SQL engine issues data requests to the database. It is a closed system and one that allows for very efficient programming.

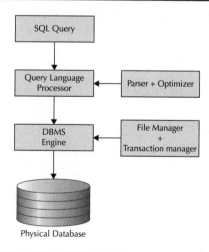

FIGURE 4-1. *PL/SQL architecture*

PL/SQL is used in numerous Oracle products, including the following:

- Oracle Database Server
- Application Express
- Oracle Data Miner
- Oracle Warehouse Builder
- Oracle Data Integrator
- Oracle eBusiness Suite
- Oracle Portal

All of these programs use PL/SQL to some extent. If you look at the internals of Oracle applications, you'll see that there can be as many as five million lines of PL/SQL code contained within it. PL/SQL interfaces can be developed and utilized from these Oracle development environments:

- SQL*Plus
- SQL*Developer
- Oracle Grid Control/Oracle Enterprise Manager
- Oracle Pre-compilers (such as Pro*C, Pro*COBOL, and so on)
- Oracle Call Interface (OCI)
- Server Manager
- Oracle Application Server 12*c*
- jDeveloper

As you can see, PL/SQL is well established within Oracle's line of products. The reasons for using PL/SQL are primarily its tight integration with the database server and its ease of use. You will find that there are few tasks that PL/SQL cannot handle.

TIP
Use PL/SQL to program complex tasks or for program elements that may be used over and over again.

CRITICAL SKILL 4.2

Describe the Basic PL/SQL Program Structure

The structure you use in PL/SQL is the foundation for the language as a whole. Once you've mastered it, you will then be able to move forward; however, if you do not take the time to get this first step right, your journey will be difficult. Thankfully, it's quite simple.

The structure is quite basic. You will have areas for your program parameters (these are used to pass values from outside a program to the program itself), your internal variables, the main program code and logic, and various ways to deal with problem situations. Let's look at the basic form of a PL/SQL block:

```
[DECLARE]
    -- Put Variables Here
BEGIN
    -- Put Program Here
[EXCEPTION]
    -- Put exception handlers here
END;
/
```

That's it: the basic structure of every PL/SQL program. When we talk about PL/SQL programs, they are referred to as PL/SQL blocks. *PL/SQL blocks* are simply programs that are complete and that are programmed to run successfully. A PL/SQL program comprises one or more of these blocks, which you can think of as *routines*. So at the basic level, you only need one block for a valid PL/SQL program, but as you consider writing a more complex program, you will find it easiest if each block addresses a particular task or subtask; it is these structures that you will use in all of your PL/SQL programs to create the most robust code possible. The PL/SQL block structures form the basis for any program you write in PL/SQL. This chapter builds upon that fundamental form, each section helping you move toward more complex programs.

In its basic form, you will usually need to declare variables in your PL/SQL program. It is these variables used in the PL/SQL that hold the declarative or working storage area (including constants, local program variables, select statements, data arrays, and such) within your program. These variables are then available for use in your program. So if you need a counter, a data array, data variables, or even Boolean variables, you will declare them here.

Next is the program body or executable section. It is the only section you really need to include in your PL/SQL block because you could write a program without variables or exception handling. It is in this section that you build your program logic and database access. That is why you must always remember BEGIN and END; these are your PL/SQL bookends. It is between these two lines that your program logic is contained.

Ask the Expert

Q: What are the only lines of the PL/SQL block that are required to create a functional program?

A: The only lines of the basic PL/SQL block that are required to create a functional program are BEGIN and END.

The final section is the exception section. It is within this section that you will find all the error handling needed for your program. This section is an optional portion of the PL/SQL block. However, we recommend that all programs include the use of exception handling to ensure a controlled run of your programs.

CRITICAL SKILL 4.3

Define PL/SQL Data Types

The use of local variables within a PL/SQL program is important for everyone using the language to understand. It is a basic component of each program, and as such, it is invaluable for understanding what is available and how best to use it. You can now look at how you use and define variables and working storage within your PL/SQL programs.

As with all programming languages, there are characters that you use to write your programs. Each language has its own rules and restrictions when it comes to the valid characters. In the following sections, we will show you

- Valid characters when programming in PL/SQL
- Arithmetic operators
- Relational operators

Valid Characters

When programming in PL/SQL, you can use only characters as defined here:

- Characters can be typed in either upper- or lowercase. PL/SQL is case insensitive.
- All whole numbers between 0 and 9.
- The following symbols: ( ) + - * / < > = ! ~ ; : . @ % , " ' # ^ & _ | { } ? [ ]

Some of these characters are for program commands; others serve as relational or arithmetic operators. Together they form a program.

Arithmetic Operators

Table 4-1 shows the common arithmetic operators used in PL/SQL. They are listed in the order of precedence in which they are executed (that is, by priority). When the functions appear in the same line, it means that they are executed with the same level of precedence, so the position of the expression determines which goes first in the operational execution.

Table 4-2 shows the common relational operators used in PL/SQL. These are the logical variables that are used to compare data. As with any comparison, they need to conform to logic hierarchies, especially when using multiple operators in your conditional clauses.

The use of variables in a PL/SQL program is usually required to truly leverage the power of the language. It is here that you define how your data is to be held while you work it through your program. These variables can be the same types you have already learned about in the SQL language. However, in addition to these standard data types, there are some special ones that have been created specifically for the PL/SQL language.

NOTE
All SQL within Oracle is supported directly with PL/SQL.

One of the important features of Oracle Database 11*g* is the tight integration of the SQL and PL/SQL engines into one system. This means that from Oracle9*i* forward you can run the same commands in PL/SQL that you use in SQL. This was not true in earlier versions of PL/SQL, so take care if using these versions (it may be time to consider an upgrade). That would also qualify you as more than a beginner.

Operator	Meaning
**	Exponent
*,/	Multiplication, Division
+,-, ||	Addition, Subtraction, Concatenation

TABLE 4-1. *Arithmetic Operators*

Operator	Meaning
=	Equal
<> or !=	Not equal
>	Greater than
<	Less than
>=	Greater than or equal to
<=	Less than or equal to

TABLE 4-2. *Relational Operators*

Now you can move on to the most common data types that you will use when writing PL/SQL programs:

- varchar2
- number
- date
- Boolean

You'll use these variables in PL/SQL the same way that you would use them in SQL. Assigning values to variables is very important when programming in PL/SQL or any other programming language. You can assign values to variables in any section of your program code, and you can also assign values to variables in the DECLARE section. Defining your variable in the DECLARE section is done to initialize values in advance of their use in the program or to define values that will be used as constants in your program. To assign a value to a variable in the declaration section, you would use the following format:

```
Variable_name    variable_type    := value;
```

> **NOTE**
> *The important item to notice here is that you use the*
> *:= to assign a value. This is the standard used in PL/SQL.*

You can also define variable values in the execution and exception sections of your PL/SQL program. Within the program, you would use the following format to assign a value to a variable:

```
Variable_name    := value;
```

To assign values to variables you use, let's look at a small program that assigns values in each section of a program:

```
-- Declaration section of the program
declare
        l_counter    number := 0;      -- initiate value to 0
        l_today      date := sysdate; -- assign system date to variable
        l_name       varchar2(50);      -- variable is defined but has no value
        l_seq_val    number := ian_seq.nextval; -- assigns the next sequence
value to the variable
---
--- Execution section of the program
begin
      l_counter := l_counter + 1; -- add one to current value of counter
      l_name := 'DIZZY THE CAT';    -- set a value to character variable
-- Error (EXCEPTION) handling section of the program
exception

        -- Generic error handling to handle any type of error
        when others then
-- print out an error message
raise_application_error (-20100, 'error#' || sqlcode || ' desc: ' sqlerrm)
end;
```

NOTE
Oracle has some special variables that can be used in a PL/SQL program. In the example, we used the SQLCODE and SQLERRM variables. These variables represent the Oracle error number and the Oracle error message, respectively. You can use these variables to capture Oracle errors in your program.

The VARCHAR2 Data Type

VARCHAR2 is a variable-length alphanumeric data type. In PL/SQL, it may have a length up to 32,767 bytes. When you define the VARCHAR2 variable in the DECLARE section, remember to terminate the line with a semicolon (;). The following is the form of VARCHAR2 variable declarations:

```
Variable_name    varchar2(max_length);
```

where MAX_LENGTH is a positive integer, as in

```
l_name  varchar2(30);
```

You can also set an initial or default value for the variable. This is done on the same line as the variable declaration in the DECLARE section of your program. You can do this by using the following syntax:

```
l_name  varchar2(30) := 'ABRAMSON';
```

The preceding statement will set that value of the variable l_name to the value of ABRAMSON.

The NUMBER Data Type

The NUMBER data type is used to represent all numeric data. The format of the declaration is

```
Number_field number(length, decimal_places);
```

where the length can be from 1 to 38 numerical positions, and decimal_places represents the positions for numerical precision of the decimal place for the variable. Keep this in mind when you define your numerical variable, as in

```
l_average_amount  number(12,2);
```

This describes a variable that can hold up to ten digits [Length(12) – decimal_places(2)] and up to two decimal places. This means the variable can hold a number up to a value of 9,999,999,999.99. The NUMBER data type has a number of supported subtypes. These include DECIMAL, FLOAT, REAL, and others. These are quite familiar to people who use other languages to program for their business needs.

The DATE Data Type

The DATE data type variable is used to store DATE and DATETIME values. The following is the format of the date declaration:

```
Date_variable  date;
```

By default, Oracle displays values using the format *DD-MON-YY*. So a value of 14-JAN-08 would be the equivalent of saying January 14, 2008. When programming in PL/SQL, you should always use this data type when performing date manipulation. It is possible when combining this data type with some built-in Oracle functions to extend the flexibility of your date manipulations. For example, let's say that you create a variable for a start date and you want to place values into this variable. Let's see how this can be done:

```
Declare
      L_start_date  date;
Begin
    L_start_date := '29-SEP-89';  -- Sets variable
                                  -- to September 29, 1989.
    L_start_date := to_date('29-SEP-2083 ', 'DD-MON-YYYY');
                                  -- Sets variable to September 29, 2083
   L_start_date := to_date('09-JUN-91:13:01 ', 'DD-MON-YY:HH24:MI');
                                  -- Sets variable to June 9, 1991, 1:01
p.m.
End;
```

So here you have set the date variable in three different forms. The first is the simplest, while the second is more complex (because it uses the TO_DATE function), although it does allow for more flexible data declarations because you can use a four-digit year definition. The final example shows you how to put a DATETIME into the variable. Again, you'll use the TO_DATE function, but you'll include the time in the value and then define it with the date mask definition.

NOTE
For more information on other Oracle built-in functions, see "Oracle Database SQL Reference," in the Oracle Database 11g documentation.

You should also familiarize yourself with the variations of the DATE data type. This includes the TIMESTAMP data type, which provides additional date support that may not be available with the simple date data type.

The BOOLEAN Data Type

The final basic data type we will discuss is the BOOLEAN data type. Simply put, this variable will hold a value of either true or false. When you use this data type, you must test its status and then do one thing if it is true and another if it is false. You can use a Boolean expression to compare arithmetic expressions or character expressions. So, if you have the following arithmetic values, you'll get

```
L_record_goals := 91;
L_season_goals := 77;
-- Therefore the following expression will be true
L_record_goals > l_season_goals
-- However the next is false
l_record_goals <= l_season_goals
```

If you wish to compare character strings, the same can be done. Here's an example:

```
V_compare_names Boolean;

l_web_developer := 'MOTI FISHMAN;
l_Oracle_dba := 'PETER FORTIER';
-- The following expression will be true in a true Boolean value
v_compare_names := l_Cognos_developer <> l_oracle_dba;
```

It is important to understand that these comparisons provide Boolean results that can then be used during conditional program control, so you should take the time to know the difference between true and false. There are numerous other data types, but by mastering these simple ones, you can already build some complex programs. In C++ and other languages, Booleans can be represented as either true/false or 1/0. In PL/SQL, the value is assigned only true or false.

The VARRAY Data Type

The VARRAY is another type that is quite commonly used in PL/SQL. PL/SQL provides a data structure called the VARRAY, which can store a fixed-size sequential collection of elements of the same type. A VARRAY is used to store an ordered collection of data, but it is often more useful to think of an array as a collection of variables of the same type. A VARRAY is similar to a nested table except an upper bound must be specified in the declaration. Like nested tables, they can be stored in the database. But unlike nested tables, individual elements cannot be deleted so they remain dense.

The following code shows how a simple example can be rewritten to use a VARRAY:

```
SET SERVEROUTPUT ON SIZE 1000000
DECLARE
    type namesarray IS VARRAY(5) OF VARCHAR2(10);
    type grades IS VARRAY(5) OF INTEGER;
    names namesarray;
    marks grades;
    total integer;
BEGIN
    names := namesarray('Ian', 'Michelle', 'Mike', 'Clarke', 'Albert');
    marks:= grades(95, 94, 99, 85, 90);

    total := names.count;
    dbms_output.put_line('Total '|| total || ' Students');
```

```
   FOR i in 1 .. total LOOP
      dbms_output.put_line('Student: ' || names(i) || '
      Marks: ' || marks(i));
   END LOOP;
END;
/
Student: Ian  Marks: 95
Student: Michelle  Marks: 94
Student: Mike  Marks: 99
Student: Clarke  Marks: 85
Student: Albert  Marks: 90
PL/SQL procedure successfully completed.
```

There are a variety of methods that can be applied on the collections to help for more advanced calculations and processing:

- **EXISTS(n)**   Returns TRUE if the specified element exists

- **COUNT**   Returns the number of elements in the collection

- **LIMIT**   Returns the maximum number of elements for a VARRAY, or NULL for nested tables

- **FIRST**   Returns the index of the first element in the collection

- **LAST**   Returns the index of the last element in the collection

- **PRIOR(n)**   Returns the index of the element prior to the specified element

- **NEXT(n)**   Returns the index of the next element after the specified element

- **EXTEND**   Appends a single NULL element to the collection

- **EXTEND(n)**   Appends n NULL elements to the collection

- **EXTEND(n1,n2)**   Appends n1 copies of the n2th element to the collection

- **TRIM**   Removes a single element from the end of the collection

- **TRIM(n)**   Removes n elements from the end of the collection

- **DELETE**   Removes all elements from the collection

- **DELETE(n)**   Removes element n from the collection

- **DELETE(n1,n2)**   Removes all elements from n1 to n2 from the collection

The collections can help you process information in sets and provide higher performance for your PL/SQL processing.

Ask the Expert

Q: How do you let Oracle set the definition of a variable within PL/SQL programs based on a table's column definition?

A: Dynamic variable definitions based on column definitions are very important, and you should always utilize them within PL/SQL. This ties the variable definition to a table within the database. When defining your variable, use the name of the table, the column, and the special string %TYPE. The following is an example of using the product table's prod_id as a variable data definition:

```
v_product_id   products.prod_id%TYPE
```

By using the %TYPE variable type, you have freed your program of the need to ever redefine this field. If the column's definition changes, so will the variable within your program.

Progress Check

1. Name four programs or facilities where you can use PL/SQL.

2. Name three sections that can be contained in a PL/SQL block.

3. What is the only required section in a PL/SQL block?

4. What data type would you use to store each of the following?

   A. 12344.50

   B. True

   C. April 11, 1963

   D. "PINK FLOYD"

   E. 42

CRITICAL SKILL 4.4

Write PL/SQL Programs in SQL*Plus

When you write PL/SQL programs, you have a couple of options for how to run a program. A program can be run directly in SQL*Plus (or some other SQL environment such as SQL Developer), or it can be stored in the database and then run from a SQL environment or a program. When you store a program in the database, it's called a *stored program* or *stored object*. (We cover this later in the chapter.) For now, let's discuss how to write a program using SQL*Plus. While we illustrate this example from within the SQL*Plus environment, these programs can also be run using other SQL interfaces such as SQL Developer, TOAD, or any other product that you prefer.

When first writing a program, you can create and modify it using the command line in SQL*Plus. To do this:

1. Log into SQL*Plus. Depending on your environment you may need to issue a sqlplus command on the command line. You should note that with Oracle Database 11*g*, the Windows version of SQL*Plus has been deprecated, so if you wish, you can also perform this exercise using SQL Developer.

2. Type in your program via the command line.

3. For each line you write, press ENTER to get to the next line.

Progress Check Answers

1. Any four from among the following would be acceptable answers: Oracle Forms, Reports, Warehouse Builder, Oracle Applications, Oracle Portal, SQL*Plus, Oracle Grid Control, Oracle Pre-compilers, and Oracle Application Server.

2. The three sections that can be contained in a PL/SQL block are Declaration, Execution, and Exception.

3. The Execution section is the only required section in a PL/SQL block.

4. The data types used to store each of the variables would be

A. NUMBER or NUMBER(8,2). The storage of a number should always be done in a number data type. You can specify the precision or simply define it as a number with no precision when you do not know the exact nature of your data.

B. BOOLEAN. The BOOLEAN data type is used to store true and false information.

C. DATE. The DATE data type stores date and time information.

D. VARCHAR2(10). Character values should be stored in the VARCHAR2 data type. This is more effective for storing the data, yet it has a limit of 32,767 bytes. If you need more than 32KB bytes, you should then use the LONG data type, which allows you to store up to 2GB of data.

E. NUMBER or NUMBER(2). These are the preferred data types for numbers when no decimal places are required (integers).

4. When you finish typing in your program, remember to terminate it with a "/" character. This tells Oracle to run the program that you just finished entering.

5. Monitor Oracle to see if your program ran successfully. If your program does run without errors (syntax errors), you will see the message "PL/SQL procedure successfully completed." If you see anything else, this is an indication that an error occurred.

6. To see the errors created by your program (if you have created a stored object as we discuss later in this chapter), type **Show errors**. SQL*Plus will display the errors it encountered during the current run of your program.

7. Should you receive an error, you will need to edit your program. If your SQL*Plus and Oracle environment is set up correctly, you should be able to simply enter **edit** on the command line and your program will be loaded into an editor where you can then fix it. Once you exit the editor, the program will be reloaded into the SQL buffer and can be run again.

Now let's move on to an illustration for how to construct a PL/SQL program and get some output of our results.

Ask the Expert

Q: How can I get feedback/output from my PL/SQL programs?

A: Oracle provides a built-in package named DBMS_OUTPUT for this purpose. Oracle supplies many of these packages that provide users with additional functionality, such as outputting data to the screen. By placing the DBMS_OUTPUT.PUT_LINE command into your programs, Oracle PL/SQL can then provide information to the user, as shown in this chapter's examples.

To actually see this information, you must enable screen output by entering **SET SERVEROUTPUT ON** at the SQL> prompt before executing your PL/SQL routine.

Project 4-1   Create a PL/SQL Program

This is the first PL/SQL program that you will create. The concept is straightforward; you will first declare some variables, place some values into them, and then output the data to the screen with SQL*Plus.

Step by Step

1. Log in to SQL*Plus.

2. At the SQL> prompt, enter the SERVEROUTPUT command: **SET SERVEROUTPUT ON;**

3. Enter the following PL/SQL program:

```
Declare
        L_start_date   date;
Begin
        L_start_date := '29-SEP-2005';
        dbms_output.putline (l_start_date); --show date
End;
/
```

4. You should now see the following output on your screen:

```
SQL> /
29-SEP-05
PL/SQL procedure successfully completed.
```

5. You have now completed your first PL/SQL program.

6. Take the time to add to the program and add lines that use other date formats or perform some date addition. For example, you may wish to add the following code and see the results that it provides:

```
L_start_date := to_date('14-JAN-2063', 'DD-MON-YYYY');
dbms_output.put_line (l_start_date);
L_start_date := to_date('09-JUN-91:13:01', 'DD-MON-YY:HH24:MI');
dbms_output.put_line (l_start_date);
```

Next, we need to discuss how to include database data within your PL/SQL programs.

Project Summary

This project enables you to see how to construct a PL/SQL program. You now have seen how to create, run, and then re-run it, which allows you to see the output. This is a simple example, presented to show you the basis of all PL/SQL programs.

SQL in Your PL/SQL Programs

You have looked at a lot of structures up until now. You should know that a PL/SQL program will always have a BEGIN and END statement. It may have variables, loops, or logic control, but now you need to get real database data into your programs. What gives PL/SQL its power is its tight integration with SQL. You may want the information so that you can create a report, update data, create new data, delete old data, or perform just about any other function you can think of. It is very important for you to see how you can integrate data into PL/SQL code. Without data, PL/SQL is just PL.

PL/SQL Cursors

How do you get data into your programs? Simple—select it from the database. This is the easiest way to use SQL in your program. Thus, inserting a line like the following will provide you with the capability to access data in the database:

```
select prod_name
into  v_prod_name
from products
```

Let's break down the statement and look at what it means to the program. As you look at the SELECT statement, you can see that it looks very similar to a standard SELECT statement. However, you should also have noticed the word "INTO" in the statement. You may be wondering what it's for. This is how you put a value into a variable using a SELECT statement.

The following example illustrates how you include a SQL statement in your PL/SQL program:

```
1  declare
2     v_prod_name varchar2(80);
3  begin
4       select prod_name
5       into  v_prod_name
6       from products
7       where rownum = 1;
8    dbms_output.put_line(v_prod_name);
9* end;
10  /
```

In addition to selecting one value from the database, you have the ability to select more than one value and add conditions that you want to include. To do this, use the following cursor format:

```
select prod_name, prod_list_price, prod_min_price from products
where rownum < 10
```

You can use any SQL statement you want within your program. It can be a SELECT, INSERT, UPDATE, or DELETE statement. All of these will be supported. When you use a SELECT statement as you did in the preceding example, it is called an *implicit cursor*. An implicit cursor is a SQL statement that is contained within the executable section of the program and has an INTO statement (as in the case of a SELECT statement). With an implicit cursor, Oracle will handle everything for you, but there is a cost to doing this: The program will run slower. You need to understand what you're doing because although it may not be the best way to perform a SELECT statement, you must use an implicit cursor when you want to run a INSERT, UPDATE, or DELETE statement. So, let's move on to see a better way of doing the same thing. We will revisit your previous example so that you can compare the two.

The better way is to create an explicit cursor. An *explicit cursor* is a SELECT statement that is declared in the DECLARE section of a program. You do this so that Oracle will then prepare your SQL statement before running your program.

At times, you may not know the exact SQL statement you want to run. To help you with a more dynamic solution that allows you to define the SQL statement at runtime, PL/SQL supports both dynamic and static processing within a program. Dynamic SQL enables you to build SQL statements dynamically at runtime, while static SQL statements are known in advance. You can create more general-purpose, flexible applications by using dynamic SQL because the full text of a SQL statement may be unknown at compilation time.

To process most dynamic SQL statements, you use the EXECUTE IMMEDIATE statement. Dynamic SQL is especially useful for executing SQL statements. The following example shows you how to use dynamic SQL to make your programs more flexible and responsive to change:

```
DECLARE
    sql_stmt            VARCHAR2(200); -- variable to hold SQL statement
    column_name         VARCHAR2(30);  -- variable for column name
    dept_id             NUMBER(4);
    dept_name           VARCHAR2(30);
    mgr_id              NUMBER(6);
    loc_id              NUMBER(4);
BEGIN
-- create a SQL statement (sql_stmt) to execute with EXECUTE IMMEDIATE
-- the statement INSERTs a row into the departments table using bind
variables
-- note that there is no semi-colon (;) inside the quotation marks
'...'
    sql_stmt := 'INSERT INTO departments VALUES (:dptid, :dptname,
:mgrid, :locid)';
    dept_id := 46;
    dept_name := 'Special Projects';
    mgr_id := 200;
    loc_id := 1700;
-- execute the sql_stmt using the values of the variables in the USING
clause
```

```
-- for the bind variables
      EXECUTE IMMEDIATE sql_stmt USING dept_id, dept_name, mgr_id,
loc_id;
-- use EXECUTE IMMEDIATE to delete the row that was previously
inserted,
-- substituting for the column name and using a bind variable
  column_name := 'DEPARTMENT_ID';
  EXECUTE IMMEDIATE 'DELETE FROM departments WHERE ' || column_name  ||
' = :num'
      USING dept_id;
END;
```

In Oracle 12*c*, the types that can be used as bind variables have been extended: BOOLEAN variables and nested tables can now be used as bind variables in Dynamic SQL. Ultimately this further extends the flexibility and functionality that can be supported by Dynamic SQL.

This makes for very efficient use of memory by the program. Let's look at what the program would look like with an explicit cursor:

```
1   declare
2     v_prod_name varchar2(80);
3     cursor get_data is
4       select prod_name
5       from products;
6   begin
7       open get_data;
8       fetch get_data into v_prod_name;
9       dbms_output.put_line(v_prod_name);
10      close get_data;
11*  end;
```

In the previous code, we converted the initial example into one that uses an explicit cursor. Notice that the SELECT statement is now contained in the declaration section. There is also no longer an INTO clause. This functionality is moved into the execution section, where it is used in the FETCH command.

Ask the Expert

Q: Why did we include rownum = 1 in our SELECT statement?

A: We include rownum = 1 when using an implicit cursor because, in this particular case, the SELECT statement will return more than one row. This will result in an Oracle error that terminates the processing of this PL/SQL block. To avoid this situation, we include the rownum = 1 condition.

Also note that we introduced three new PL/SQL commands: OPEN, FETCH, and CLOSE. With these three simple commands, you can get data from your database using SQL cursors. The OPEN command tells Oracle to reserve memory that will need to be used by the SELECT statement. Meanwhile, the FETCH command pulls the data from the first row of the result set, and the CLOSE command closes the cursor you just opened and returns the memory back to Oracle for other uses.

NOTE
Always remember to explicitly close your cursors when you are done with them. If you don't, you can start getting memory problems, or you could get results that you don't expect.

The Cursor FOR Loop

You get a better sense of the power of the cursor by combining it with a loop. The cursor FOR loop is the result of combining the select cursor with a FOR loop (we go into additional detail about this loop in the next section). This allows you to retrieve multiple rows from the database if your result set should do this. It also is simpler to program, and you don't have to worry about opening or closing your cursor; Oracle handles all that within the loop. Let's look at an example of the cursor FOR loop. The important lines have been set in boldface for you:

```
SQL> set serveroutput on
SQL>  declare
   2     v_prod_name varchar2(80);
   3     cursor cur_get_data is
   4     select prod_name
   5     from products;
6  begin
   7     for i in cur_get_data
   8     LOOP
   9             dbms_output.put_line(i.prod_name);
  10     END LOOP;
  11 end;
  12 /
5MP Telephoto Digital Camera
17" LCD w/built-in HDTV Tuner
Envoy 256MB - 40GB
Y Box
Mini DV Camcorder with 3.5" Swivel LCD
Envoy Ambassador
Laptop carrying case
Home Theatre Package with DVD-Audio/Video Play ...
```

NOTE
To reference columns during a FOR loop, use the name of the loop and concatenate it with the name of the column as defined within the cursor declaration. Thus, your result will be a variable named cursor_name.fieldname (in our example, we did this using the variable i.prod_name).

The cursor FOR loop is truly PL/SQL power in action. It provides you with the ability to easily move through the result set of a SELECT statement and perform the logic and manipulations you need to be successful.

We have just touched the surface of getting information from PL/SQL. You will need to get comfortable with debugging PL/SQL programs, which can be a very complex task. Experience has taught us that finding your errors can never be taken lightly or ignored. Using a simple facility such as DBMS_OUTPUT, you have a way of tracking the progress of your program.

NOTE
Oracle provides a couple of packages to analyze your PL/SQL programs. The first is DBMS_PROFILER. This package analyzes how your program is running and collects statistics on how long each line takes to execute. This helps you find code that runs slowly or inefficiently. When you need to access more advanced statistics about your programs, take the time to investigate this package and how to integrate it into your PL/SQL code. Because this is a beginner's guide, we'll only direct you to an important feature when you need its functionality. With the release of Oracle 12c, Oracle also introduced another function, UTL_CALL_STACK. This package provides an interface for PL/SQL programmers to obtain information about currently executing programs, including the subprogram name from dynamic and lexical stacks and the depths of those stacks. Individual functions return subprogram names, unit names, owner names, edition names, and line numbers for given dynamic depths. More functions return error stack information. Such information can be used to create more revealing error logs and application execution traces.

Having seen how to write and debug programs, you can now make those programs more complex.

Handle Error Conditions in PL/SQL

As you have seen in the previous section, bad things happen to good programs. However, you also have to deal with bad or problematic data as well. To deal with problems during the processing of data, PL/SQL provides you with the robust ability to handle these types of errors. We call this type of program code *exception handling*.

To raise an error from within a PL/SQL program, use the built-in procedure named RAISE_APPLICATION_ERROR. The procedure requires two arguments: One is for the error number and must be between –20,000 and –20,999, whereas the second argument is the error that you want the user to see.

As with all exception handling, this program code is placed into the EXCEPTION section of your PL/SQL program. Thus, your program structure will now be

```
BEGIN
     -- Put Program Here
EXCEPTION
-- Put exception handlers here
END;
/
```

Table 4-3 provides some examples of the most common errors that Oracle can help you handle.

NOTE
You must always make the OTHERS error handle the last one in your program because Oracle will not process any exception handles after this one. In addition, the WHEN OTHERS exception should be a last resort and should not be used as a catch-all, error-handling mechanism.

The following is the line that your program may contain to provide feedback to the user:

```
raise_application_error (-20123, 'This is an error, you have done a bad
thing');
```

ExceptionName	Explanation	Oracle Error
NO_DATA_FOUND	When a SELECT statement returns no rows, this error may be raised. It usually occurs when you use an implicit cursor and perform a SELECT INTO.	ORA-01403
TOO_MANY_ROWS	When a case that should only return a single row returns multiple rows, this exception is raised.	ORA-01422
DUP_VAL_ON_INDEX	This exception is raised when you try to insert a record into a table that has a primary key on it and the record that you are inserting is a duplicate of one that already exists in the table.	ORA-00001
VALUE_ERROR	This error occurs when you attempt to put a value into a variable, but the value is incompatible (for example, inserting a value of "LAWRIE YAKABOWSKY" into a numerical field). It also occurs when you input a value that is too large to be held in the defined field (for instance, inputting "JILLIAN ABRAMSON" into a character variable that is only ten characters long).	ORA-06502
ZERO_DIVIDE	This error is encountered when you attempt to divide by zero.	ORA-01476
OTHERS	This exception is used to catch any errors not handled by specific error handles.	Non-specific

TABLE 4-3.   *Built-in PL/SQL Exceptions*

So let's see how these all come together in a single program:

```
SQL> run
  1  declare
  2          l_emp_count number;
  3          i  number;  -- We will use this as our counter
  4          l_row  employee%rowtype;
  5      begin
  6          select *
  7          into l_row
  8          from  employee
  9          order by emp_name;
 10   EXCEPTION
 11   WHEN no_data_found then
 12    raise_application_error (-20052,'Sorry no data in this table.
TRY AGAIN!');
 13   WHEN others then
 14    raise_application_error (-20999,'Something has gone really
wrong...you better guess');
 15*  end;
declare
*
ERROR at line 1:
ORA-20052: Sorry no data in this table. TRY AGAIN!
ORA-06512: at line 12
```

This program will handle instances where no data is found, as well as anything else that happens that is not a result of lack of data. So with these simple techniques, you can now handle problems that might occur in your programs.

You can also extend the functionality of the Oracle exception handling facility with your own *user-defined exceptions.*

User-defined exceptions are defined within your program code. There are three components to defining and using this exception type. They include

■ Declaring the exception

■ Raising the exception during program execution

■ The exception handle itself

These three items must all be in place for an exception to be valid and to be used within the program. This differs from the Oracle-defined exceptions, which can be used within a program without declaring them or even raising an error condition. So let's see how this all comes together in a program:

```
Declare
        L_counter   number := 0;
        L_name employee.employee_name%type;
        Cursor get_employee_name is
        Select employee_name
        From employee;
excep_old_friend      Exception;
never_met_them        Exception;
Begin
        Open  get_employee_name;
        Fetch  get_employee_name into l_name;
        If l_name = 'CARL DUDLEY' then
                Raise excep_old_friend;
Else
        Raise excep_never_met_them;
        End if;
        Close get_employee_name;
Exception
        When excep_old_friend then
                Dbms_output.put_line('I know this person');
When      excep_old_friend then
                Dbms_output.put_line('I do not know this person');
End;
```

As you can see in this program, the definition and use of a user-defined exception is really driven by your needs. In this case, you select data from the employee table. Should the name of the person you retrieve be *Carl Dudley,* then you raise the exception that you defined called excep_old_friend. In any other case, you would raise excep_never_met_them. Based on this decision, you *raise* the exception that you want to handle for the situation.

So let's look at the three components you need to use to create this exception. First, there is that you will need to declare the exceptions. These go into the DECLARE section of you PL/SQL program. You simply name the exception and tell Oracle that they are of the type EXCEPTION, just as we have done in the following lines of program code:

```
excep_old_friend  Exception;
never_met_them  Exception;
```

Next, you need to call the appropriate exception within the program code. You'll want to call the exception when something occurs—in this case, when you obtain the name of a friend or the name of a stranger.

NOTE
User-defined exceptions can be raised to handle an error or to handle a condition that may not be seen by Oracle as an error.

In your case, you are not concerned with an error; you just want to deal with a situation. Therefore, in your program code, all that is needed to call a user-defined exception is to simply use the RAISE command followed by the name of the exception, as in the following code snippet:

```
Raise excep_old_friend;
```

You have taken the first two steps toward defining and calling your own exception (Declaration and Execution sections); all that's left is to define what the exception is going to do. This is done in the EXCEPTION section of your program. To do this, simply include the exception in the EXCEPTION section:

```
EXCEPTION
      When excep_old_friend then
            Dbms_output.put_line('I know this person');
```

In your case, you simply will output that you know this person.

This example has shown you how to set up user-defined exceptions and how to use them. The ways in which you can implement exceptions are limited only by your imagination.

Error Handling Using Oracle-Supplied Variables

In addition to being able to define your own exceptions within your PL/SQL program, Oracle also provides some standard variables that can be used in your PL/SQL programs. These variables are available to you in many different forms depending on where you use them in your program. These variables are known as *pseudo-columns*. A pseudo-column is a column that can be used in a SELECT statement or during the processing of data. We use the term "pseudo-column" so that you can consider their use similar to how you would use a column. They include

- Current system date (SYSDATE)
- Row number (ROWNUM)
- Oracle error number (SQLCODE)
- Oracle error message (SQLERRM)

In this section, you will look at the last two, which in exception handling are the two that are often used. They provide you with access to the Oracle error number and message and will therefore allow you to write programs that always end successfully. Even though the program may still encounter an error, it's handled in a manner that is quite robust and manageable. Let's look at the same program, except this time you will add another exception handle for when any error occurs. You do this by adding the generic catch-all WHEN OTHERS exception:

```
Declare
      L_counter  number := 0;
      L_name employee.employee_name%type;
      Cursor get_employee_name is
      Select employee_name
      From employee;
excep_old_friend     Exception;
never_met_them        Exception;
Begin
      Open  get_employee_name;
      Fetch  get_employee_name into l_name;
      If l_name = 'CHRISTINE LECKMAN' then
              Raise excep_old_friend;
Else
      Raise excep_never_met_them;
End if;
      Close get_employee_name;
Exception
      When excep_old_friend then
              Dbms_output.put_line('I know this person');
When excep_never_met_them then
              Dbms_output.put_line('I do not know this person');
      When others then
                  Dbms_output.put_line('Oracle Error: ' || sqlcode);
                  Dbms_output.put_line('Oracle error message is: '||
sqlerrm);
End;
```

As you can see, you have now added an extra error-handling condition—the infamous WHEN OTHERS exception. As previously discussed, this exception can be used to handle any error that occurs for which no other exception has been defined. Most important, it must also be the last exception in your EXCEPTION section because Oracle stops processing when it encounters an exception that meets the criteria. Therefore, if this exception is first, Oracle will stop once it hits the WHEN OTHERS condition. As we mentioned before, this is a dangerous practice;

you need to handle this error carefully and you should even consider *not* utilizing the WHEN OTHERS condition because it could mask the real issues with your program.

In our example, we have now used the functions SQLCODE and SQLERRM. You should always consider using these variables in your program code to ensure your PL/SQL program completes in a manageable manner and provides the necessary feedback for diagnosing potential problems and errors. In addition, you can use the new Oracle 12*c* function UTL_CALL_STACK, which has been added to provide better feedback of errors with functions such as DYNAMIC_DEPTH(), UNIT_LINE(), SUBPROGRAM(), CONCATENATE_SUBPROGRAM(), OWNER(), CURRENT_EDITION(), and LEXICAL_DEPTH(). These functions now provide the developer with more powerful functionality to support debugging and performance tuning.

Progress Check

1. What facility do you use to get output from within a PL/SQL program?

2. What is wrong with the following cursor declaration?

```
Cursor get_data is;
Select cust_id, cust_last_name
From customers;
```

3. What are the two basic types of exception handlers within PL/SQL?

4. To call an exception, what PL/SQL command should you use?

5. Name two pseudo-columns that help with exception feedback.

Progress Check Answers

1. The dbms_output package can be used to get output from within a PL/SQL program.

2. The extra semicolon (;) on line 1 of the cursor should not be there.

3. Built-in exceptions such as WHEN OTHERS and WHEN NO_DATA_FOUND are the two basic types of exception handlers within PL/SQL.

4. The RAISE command is used.

5. Two pseudo-columns that help with exception feedback are SQLCODE and SQLERRM.

CRITICAL SKILL **4.6**

Include Conditions in Your Programs

The inclusion of conditions in your programs is the heart of all advanced programming languages. In the previous section, you actually included some statements for performing these types of tasks and you may have noticed IF statements and loops. It is in this section that we now illustrate how to construct a PL/SQL program with these types of features by providing you with a step-by-step guide. Because programs are written to handle a number of different situations, the manner in which different conditions are detected and dealt with is the biggest part of program control. This section provides you with details on the following topics:

- Program control

- Various types of IF logic structures

- CASE expressions

- Various types of looping structures

Program Control

Program control is governed by the status of the variables that it uses and the data it reads and writes from the database. As an example, picture yourself going to the Department of Motor Vehicles to renew your driver's license. Upon entering the office, you are presented with a number of directional signs. One sign is "Drivers Testing"; for this you go to the second floor. Another sign tells you that "License Renewals" are on the third floor. So, because you are here for a renewal, you proceed to the third floor. Once you arrive in the renewal office, you are once again faced with some new choices—after all, this is a government office; it's not going to be a simple exercise. So, now you have to decide if you are going to pay by cash or credit card. Cash payments are being accepted to the right and credit cards are to the left. Noting that you have enough cash, you head to the payment wicket on the right. Let's look at Table 4-4 and see how the program control influenced your choices.

IF Logic Structures

When you are writing computer programs, situations present themselves in which you must test a condition. So, when you ask a question in your program, you are usually presented with one of two answers. First, it may be true or it may be false; computer programs are black and white. In computer logic there can be only true or false answers to our questions, no maybes here. PL/SQL provides you with three distinctive IF logic structures that allow you to test for true and false conditions. In everyday life, you are presented with decisions that you need to make. The following sections show you how to do this using PL/SQL.

Step #	Process or Decision to Make	Next Steps
1	Here for a driver's license transaction	Yes = 2; No = 4
2	Here for a driving test	Yes = 5; No = 3
3	Here for a license renewal	Yes = 6; No = 4
4	Ask for help	Right place = 1; Wrong place = 13
5	Go to second floor	7
6	Go to third floor	9
7	Line up for driver's test	8
8	Pass test (we hope)	6
9	Payment method	Cash = 10; Credit = 11
10	Cash payment wicket	12
11	Credit-card payment wicket	12
12	Receive new license	13
13	Leave building, head home	

TABLE 4-4. *Logical Flow*

IF/THEN   The IF/THEN construct tests the simplest type of condition. If the condition evaluates to TRUE, then one or more lines of program code will be executed. If the condition evaluates as FALSE, then no action is taken. The following code snippet illustrates how this is performed with a PL/SQL program:

```
IF l_date > '11-APR-63' then
      l_salary :=  l_salary * 1.15; -- Increase salary by 15%
END IF;
```

In this case, you are asking that if the value of the variable l_date is greater than (>) April 11, 1963, the salary should increase by 15 percent. This statement can also be restated using the following:

```
IF not(l_date <= '11-APR-63') then
     l_salary :=  l_salary * 1.15; -- Increase salary by 15%
END IF;
```

You can nest IF/THEN statements to increase the power of your statements. So let's add a condition to limit who gets the raise:

```
IF l_date > '11-APR-63' then
IF l_last_name = 'PAKMAN' then
                    l_salary :=  l_salary * 1.15; -- Increase salary by 15%
END IF;
END IF;
```

Not only must the date be greater than April 11, 1963, but your last name must be equal to "PAKMAN" in order to get the raise. This is a method we use to make sure that human resource programs ensure that programmers get a raise every year.

What you should also notice in this code is that there are now two END IF statements. This is a required construct because you must always pair up an IF statement with an END IF. So, if you are going to have nested IF statements, you must ensure that each is paired with a matching END IF.

> **NOTE**
> *Each IF statement block must have at least one line of program code. If you wish to do nothing within your program code, then simply use the NULL; command.*

IF/THEN/ELSE   The IF/THEN/ELSE construct is similar to the simple IF/THEN construct. The difference here is that if the condition executes as FALSE, you perform the program statements that follow the ELSE statement. The following code illustrates this logic within PL/SQL:

```
IF l_date > '11-APR-63' then
            l_salary :=  l_salary * 1.15; -- Increase salary by 15%
ELSE
l_salary := l_salary * 1.05;  -- Increase salary by 5%
END IF;
```

In this code listing, you see the condition that if the date is greater than April 11, 1963, you will get a 15 percent salary increase. However, when the date is less than or equal to this date, you receive only a 5 percent increase.

As with the simple form of the IF/THEN construct, you can nest the IF/THEN/ELSE construct. Let's look at how this might appear in your PL/SQL program:

```
IF l_date > '11-APR-63' then
If l_last_name = 'PAKMAN' then
            l_salary :=  l_salary * 1.15; -- Increase salary by 15%
ELSE
```

```
                        l_salary :=  l_salary * 1.10; -- Increase salary by 10%
END IF;
ELSE
                        l_salary := l_salary * 1.05;  -- Increase salary by 5%
END IF;
```

It's important to note the following when using the IF statement within PL/SQL:

■ There can be only one ELSE statement within every IF statement construct.

■ There is no semicolon (;) on the line starting with ELSE.

IF/THEN/ELSIF   The final IF construct that we will show you is IF/THEN/ELSIF. In this case, you have the option to test additional conditions where the first IF condition is evaluated as FALSE. So, should you want to test for more than one condition without using nested IF statements, this is the type of statement you might use:

```
IF l_last_name = 'PAKMAN' then
                        l_salary :=  l_salary * 1.15; -- Increase salary by 15%
ELSIF l_last_name = 'ASTROFF' then
                        l_salary :=  l_salary * 1.10; -- Increase salary by 10%
ELSE
                        l_salary :=  l_salary * 1.05; -- Increase salary by 5%
END IF;
```

In this statement, if your last name is Pakman, you get a 15 percent raise. If it is Astroff, you get 10 percent, and the rest of us get only a 5 percent raise.

Note that there is no limit to the number of ELSIF conditions you can use within this construct. The following shows an example of using multiple ELSIF statements within the construct:

```
IF l_city = 'OTTAWA' then
      L_team_name := 'SENATORS';
ELSIF l_city = 'BOSTON' then
      L_team_name := 'BRUINS';
ELSIF l_city = 'MONTREAL' then
      L_team_name := 'CANADIENS'
ELSIF l_city = 'TORONTO' then
      L_team_name := 'MAPLE LEAFS';
END IF;
```

NOTE
There is no matching END IF statement for each ELSIF. Only a single END IF is required within this construct.

When writing your PL/SQL program, you should use indentation to simplify the reading of the program. Notice in our code segments that we use indentation to make it easier for you to read the code statements. As a rule, you should line up each IF/THEN/ELSE statement and indent the program code that lies between each of these words.

CASE Statements

The next logical step from the IF statement is the CASE statement. The CASE statement was introduced with Oracle9i and is an evolution in logical control. It differs from the IF/THEN/ELSE constructs in that we now can use a simple structure to logically select from a list of values. More important, it can be used to set the value of a variable. Let's explore how this is done.

First, let's look at the format you will need to follow:

```
CASE variable
      WHEN expression1 then value1
      WHEN expression2 then value2
      WHEN expression3 then value3
      WHEN expression4 then value4
      ELSE value5
END;
```

There is no limit to the number of expressions that can be defined in a CASE statement. The following is an example of the use of the CASE expression:

```
SQL> run
  1  declare
  2     val    varchar2(100);
  3     city   varchar2(20) := 'TORONTO';
  4  begin
  5     val := CASE city
  6        WHEN 'TORONTO' then 'RAPTORS'
  7        WHEN 'LOS ANGELES' then 'LAKERS'
  8        WHEN 'BOSTON' then 'CELTICS'
  9        WHEN 'CHICAGO' then 'BULLS'
 10        ELSE 'NO TEAM'
 11  END;
 12
 13     dbms_output.put_line(val); -- output to the screen
 14* end;
RAPTORS
PL/SQL procedure successfully completed.
```

Ask the Expert

Q: How do I add comments to my PL/SQL programs?

A: To add comments to your code, simply start a comment with /* and end it with */ or use -- (as we have done previously). If you use -- you need to make sure you put it on its own line, or after your program code if you place it on the same line. The following are examples of valid comments:

```
/* This is a comment */
-- This is also a comment
```

Although you may have been able to use the IF/ELSIF/THEN/ELSE construct to achieve the same purpose, the CASE statement is easier to read and is more efficient with the database.

Loops

When was the last time you visited an amusement park? Well, if you have been to one in recent years, you will surely have seen a roller coaster. That roller coaster, if it's a really good roller coaster, probably had one or more loops. PL/SQL is that kind of ride—one that includes loops. Loops are control structures that allow you to repeat a set of commands until you decide that it is time to stop the looping.

Generally, all loops have the following format:

```
LOOP
      Executable statements;
END LOOP;
```

Each time the loop is executed, the statements within the loop are executed, and the program returns to the top of the LOOP structure to do it all over again. However, if you ever want this processing to stop, you need to learn about the EXIT statement.

The EXIT statement allows you to stop executing within a loop without a condition. It then passes control back to the program and continues on after the LOOP statements.

The following is how to get out of a tight LOOP:

```
LOOP
      IF l_bank_balance >= 0 then EXIT;
      ELSE
            L_decision := 'ACCOUNT OVERDRAWN';
      END IF;
END LOOP;
```

NOTE
Without an EXIT statement in a simple LOOP, the loop will be infinite.

There are many other kinds of loops, some of which enable you to have more control over your looping. Each type of loop has its use in PL/SQL programming and each should be learned in order to give your programming the greatest flexibility.

The WHILE Loop

The WHILE loop will continue to execute as long as the condition that you have defined continues to be true. When and if the condition becomes false, then you exit your loop. If your condition is never satisfied, you will end up in a loop that will never exit. Let's look at an example:

```
WHILE l_sales_total < 100000 LOOP
        Select sales_amount into l_sale_amount from daily_sales;
        l_sales_total := l_sales_total + l_sale_amount;

END LOOP;
```

Although you may have used the EXIT command to do the same thing, it is better form to use the WHILE expression.

The FOR Loop

The FOR loop is one of the most common loops you will encounter in your PL/SQL programming, and it allows you to control the number of times a loop executes. In the case of the WHILE loop, you are never quite sure how many times a loop is executed because it will continue to loop until a condition is met. However, in the case of the FOR loop, this isn't true.

The FOR loop allows you to define the number of times to loop when you program the loop itself. You will define the value that starts your loop, as well as the value that terminates it. Let's look at its syntax:

```
FOR l_counter IN 1 .. 10
LOOP
        Statements;
END LOOP;
```

So, what is important to note in the preceding statement? First, you need to know that the variable l_counter will hold the value between 1 and 10. How do you know it will be between 1 and 10? Well, after the IN word, you place the counter's range. In this case, you want the counter to start at 1 (the lowest boundary) and then continue to 10. You should also note that between the two integer values (1 and 10) you place two dots (..). You do this to tell Oracle that you would like it to count between these two numbers. You should also notice that we have not shown you any type of Declaration section, as they are not explicitly defined because LOOP counters are defined when they are used. You also have the ability to count backwards using the REVERSE clause. This listing shows you how the REVERSE clause can be used:

```
declare
  l_counter number;
begin
  FOR l_counter IN REVERSE 1..5
  LOOP
        dbms_output.put_line(l_counter);
  END LOOP;
end;
/
5
4
3
2
1
PL/SQL procedure successfully completed.
```

Now you can see how simple it is to use simple loops. But don't be fooled—loops have a lot of power, some of which you will see later. When you use loops such as the WHILE loop or the FOR loop, you have the ability to use variables instead of hard-coded values. This allows you to have the greatest possible flexibility because you can have the database or external data provide you with the limits within your loop. Let's look at how this might work. The following example illustrates the simplest form of the FOR loop. In this case, you select the number of employees you have in your employee table and then simply show how the counter counts from 1 to the number of employees in your small company:

```
SQL> run
  1  declare
  2    l_emp_count number;
  3    i  number;   -- We will use this as our counter
  4  begin
  5  -- Select the number of employees in the l_emp_count variable
  6    select count(*) into l_emp_count from employee;
  7
```

```
 8     FOR i IN 1 .. l_emp_count  LOOP
 9            dbms_output.put_line('Employee ' || i);
10     END LOOP;
11* end;
Employee 1
Employee 2
Employee 3
Employee 4
Employee 5
Employee 6
PL/SQL procedure successfully completed.
```

So, as you might have guessed, you have six employees in your company. It may be small, but it's very good. However, the important thing to know is that you can use variables in your loops. The other line you may have noticed is the SELECT statement contained in the PL/SQL block.

Project 4-2   Use Conditions and Loops in PL/SQL

In this project, you create a PL/SQL program that will read the data in the products table and then print out the products that are priced above $50.

Step by Step

1. Log in to SQL*Plus.

2. At the SQL> prompt, enter the SERVEROUTPUT command: **SET SERVEROUTPUT ON;**.

3. Enter the following PL/SQL program:

```
declare
  cursor get_data is
  select prod_name, prod_list_price
  from products;
  begin
  for i in get_data
  LOOP
  if i.prod_list_price > 50 then
  dbms_output.put_line(i.prod_name||' Price: '||
i.prod_list_price);
end if;
END LOOP;
end;
```

4. You should now see the following output on your screen:

```
SQL> /
5MP Telephoto Digital Camera Price: 899.99
17" LCD w/built-in HDTV Tuner Price: 999.99
Envoy 256MB - 40GB Price: 999.99
Y Box Price: 299.99
Mini DV Camcorder with 3.5" Swivel LCD Price: 1099.99
Envoy Ambassador Price: 1299.99
Laptop carrying case Price: 55.99
Home Theatre Package with DVD-Audio/Video Play Price: 599.99
18" Flat Panel Graphics Monitor Price: 899.99
SIMM- 8MB PCMCIAII card Price: 112.99
SIMM- 16MB PCMCIAII card Price: 149.99
Unix/Windows 1-user pack Price: 199.99
8.3 Minitower Speaker Price: 499.99
Multimedia speakers- 5" cones Price: 67.99
Envoy External 8X CD-ROM Price: 54.99
Model NM500X High Yield Toner Cartridge Price: 192.99
Model A3827H Black Image Cartridge Price: 89.99
128MB Memory Card Price: 52.99
256MB Memory Card Price: 69.99

PL/SQL procedure successfully completed.
```

5. You may now change the criteria we have used so that you print out messages for products under $50. This is done by adding the following text in the right place in the code:

```
else
    dbms_output.put_line(i.prod_name || ' Product under 50');
```

6. More output will appear, including that of all the products.

Project Summary

This project illustrates how to use loops and conditional clauses and how you can easily select data and use it within a PL/SQL program.

CRITICAL SKILL 4.7

Create Stored Procedures—How and Why

PL/SQL is a very powerful language; one of its most important features is the ability to store programs in the database and share them with others. We generally refer to these as *stored objects* or *stored subprograms*. There are four distinct types: procedures, functions, triggers, and packages. Up until now in this chapter, you have looked at anonymous PL/SQL blocks. Stored PL/SQL programs differ from these because they are named objects that are stored inside the database. Anonymous blocks are not stored in the database and must be loaded each time you want to run them.

You create stored programs for a number of reasons. The most important reason to create programs that are stored and named instead of anonymous is that it provides you with the ability to share programs and optimize performance. By storing programs, you can grant many different users the privilege of running your program. You can also simplify your programs and have different programs perform specific functions. These programs can then be called from a central program, which can optimize performance and programming time. This concept is very familiar to object-oriented programmers and is known as *modularity*.

If you are to truly take advantage of PL/SQL within the confines of your Oracle Database, you will need to understand how to create and maintain PL/SQL stored objects. Let's look at the various types of PL/SQL stored programs.

The first stored object is called a *stored procedure*. A stored procedure is a PL/SQL program-adding construct that tells the database you want to store an object. Just as you do when you create a table, a procedure is created or updated with the CREATE PROCEDURE command. By adding this at the beginning of a PL/SQL block, you create an object in the database known as a procedure. Another feature of stored procedures, provided to you at no extra cost, is the ability to pass values in and out of a procedure.

NOTE
You should put CREATE OR REPLACE PROCEDURE in your CREATE PROCEDURE commands. If you do not use the REPLACE portion of the command, you will need to drop your procedure before trying to re-create it. By including REPLACE, the procedure will be created if it does not exist or will be replaced if it does.

Let's look at one of the programs you have already created and convert it to a stored procedure:

```
 1   create or replace procedure print_products
 2   as
 3   declare
 4     cursor get_data is
 5       select prod_name, prod_list_price
 6       from products;
 7   begin
 8   for i in get_data
 9    LOOP
10     if i.prod_list_price > 50 then
11       dbms_output.put_line(i.prod_name || ' Price: ' ||
i.prod_MIN_price);
12     else
13       dbms_output.put_line(i.prod_name || ' Product under 50');
14     end if;
15    END LOOP;
16*  end;
Warning: Procedure created with compilation errors.
```

Now it looks like we have a couple of errors. Even authors get errors when writing PL/SQL. To see what errors you have received from your program, simply enter **SHOW ERRORS** after you tried to run your program. Oracle will then show you the errors that have occurred during the compiling of your program. Let's see what we did wrong:

```
SQL> show errors

Errors for PROCEDURE PRINT_PRODUCTS:
LINE/COL ERROR
-------- ------------------------------------------------------------------
3/1      PLS-00103: Encountered the symbol "DECLARE" when expecting one of
         the following:
         begin function package pragma procedure subtype type use
         <an identifier> <a double-quoted delimited-identifier> form
         current cursor external language
         The symbol "begin" was substituted for "DECLARE" to continue.
16/4     PLS-00103: Encountered the symbol "end-of-file" when expecting
         one of the following:
          begin case declare end exception exit for goto if loop mod
          null pragma raise return select update while with
```

```
<an identifier> <a double-quoted delimited-identifier>
<a bind variable> << close current delete fetch lock insert
open rollback savepoint set sql execute commit forall merge
<a single-quoted SQL string> pipe
<an alternatively-quoted SQL string>
```

It looks like we have errors on lines 3 and 16. When creating a stored object, you do not always need to include the DECLARE statement since PL/SQL understands that, based on the way the program is structured, after a CREATE statement it expects to see the reserved word AS, which will be followed by the Declaration section. So you can think of it this way: AS replaces DECLARE when creating a stored object. Let's now look at the repaired PL/SQL code. The lines we changed are highlighted in bold:

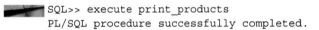

```
 1   create or replace procedure print_products
 2   as
 3     cursor get_data is
 4       select prod_name, prod_list_price
 5       from products;
 6   begin
 7       for i in get_data
 8       LOOP
 9       if i.prod_list_price > 50 then
10         dbms_output.put_line(i.prod_name ||' Price: '|| i.prod_LIST_price);
11       else
12          dbms_output.put_line(i.prod_name || ' Product under 50');
13        end if;
14       END LOOP;
15*  end;
SQL> /

Procedure created.
```

That's good news. The program has compiled and will now run when we call it. Let's look at how to call a procedure from SQL*Plus. Using the EXECUTE command, you can run a stored program:

```
SQL>> execute print_products
PL/SQL procedure successfully completed.
```

Ask the Expert

Q: I get an error "ORA-20000: ORU-10027: buffer overflow, limit of 2000 bytes" when running my PL/SQL programs that use DBMS_OUTPUT. How can I fix this problem?

A: The default buffer size for the DBMS_OUTPUT package is 2,000 bytes. This is usually sufficient for most testing purposes. However, if you need to increase this, you can do it through the SERVEROUTPUT command. One parameter it has is size, whose value may be set to between 2,000 and 1,000,000 bytes. You perform this by issuing the following command and defining the limit of the output:

```
SQL> set serveroutput on size 100000
```

You have added a parameter to your program to show you how to get information into it. You use parameters within the program when you supply data to the procedure, and you can then return a value to the program that calls it through another output parameter. It is also possible to define parameters as both input and output. This example will input a character that will be used to find only products that begin with the input string:

```
 1  create or replace procedure print_products
 2  (FIRST_CHARACTER IN VARCHAR)
 3  as
 4    cursor get_data is
 5     select prod_name, prod_list_price
 6     from products
 7     where prod_name like FIRST_CHARACTER || '%';
 8  begin
 9  for i in get_data
10   LOOP
11    if i.prod_list_price > 50 then
12    dbms_output.put_line(i.prod_name ||' Price: '|| i.prod_LiST_price);
13    else
14    dbms_output.put_line(i.prod_name || ' Product under 50');
15    end if;
16   END LOOP;
17* end print_products;
```

Now, let's see how to describe your procedure, as indicated by the bold text in the next listing. Here, you learn the name of the program and get a list of any parameters you may need to pass:

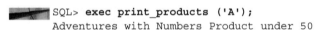

```
SQL> describe print_products
PROCEDURE print_products
Argument Name                   Type                    In/Out Default?
------------------------------  ----------------------  ------ --------
FIRST_CHARACTER                 VARCHAR2                IN
```

Next, you need to run the procedure. In this case, you are running it in SQL*Plus. When in this facility, if you want to receive data from a program, you need to declare a variable. This is done in the first line of the following listing. You will then run the program with the EXECUTE command:

```
SQL> exec print_products ('A');
Adventures with Numbers Product under 50

PL/SQL procedure successfully completed.
```

As you can tell, the program was named print_products. You want to print the products that begin with an "A." The results show you that you have only one product that begins with the character "A." As you may have gleaned from the results, the program has functioned as expected.

Now that you have learned to create stored objects in Oracle Database 11*g*, let's look at a specialized program, called a function, which can extend the functionality of the database.

Progress Check ⟲

1. What type of IF structure should be used if you had a single test and only one alternate choice?

2. What is wrong with the following IF structure? What other way can this type of logic be implemented with Oracle Database 11*g*?

   ```
   IF surname = 'ABRAMSON' then
        Salary = salary * 1.12;
   IF surname = 'ABBEY' then
        Salary = salary * 1.22;
   IF surname = 'SHEETZ' then
        Salary = salary * 2.5;
   END IF;
   ```

3. True or False: When naming your stored programs, you must follow the same rules as naming a table.

4. What are the three types of procedure parameters you can have?

5. What SQL*Plus command do you use to run your stored programs?

CRITICAL SKILL 4.8

Create and Use Functions

You can also create stored objects that can be used within a SELECT command. Oracle provides you with functions. There are functions to trim spaces from a field, or replace one character with another. All of these provide you with the ability to extend the capabilities of Oracle itself.

Functions are very much like stored procedures. The main difference is that functions can be used within a SELECT statement in the column list or can also be used in the WHERE clause.

When creating a function, you perform a CREATE OR REPLACE FUNCTION command. You can have variables input to the function and return a value to the calling statement. A function must return a value. The data type of the returned value must be defined when creating the function. This is how a function differs from a procedure. The function will then perform its task during regular processing, allowing you to utilize the results along with your regular data, thus extending the value of your data and your database.

Project 4-3   Create and Use a Function

The following project will walk you through the process of defining a function. Then, you use the function in two SELECT statements. The first will use the function in the returned columns and the next will use it as a data constraint. The function that you create will perform the simple task of adding a 15 percent tax to the list price, giving the price with taxes included.

(continued)

Progress Check Answers

1. You would use the IF/THEN/ELSE structure.

2. You should not use chained IF statements, but instead use ELSIF in the secondary IF statements. The best way to implement this type of logic is to employ a CASE statement.

3. True. When naming your stored programs you must follow the same rules as naming a table.

4. You can have any or all of the following: INPUT, OUTPUT, or INPUT&OUTPUT.

5. Use the EXECUTE command to run your stored programs.

Step by Step

1. Log in to SQL*Plus.

2. At the SQL> prompt, type in the following command:

```
create or replace function GetProductTaxIn
(in_product_id number)
return number
is
    v_price number;
    cursor get_price_tax  is
    select nvl(round(prod_list_price * 1.15,2),0)
    from   products
    where  prod_id = in_product_id;
begin
      open get_price_tax;
      fetch get_price_tax into v_price;
      return v_price;
exception
    when others then v_price := 0;
    return v_price;
end;
Function created.
```

3. If you receive any errors, you will need to fix them before you move on.

4. Create a SELECT statement that uses the function in the columns specification. The following is an example:

```
select prod_id, prod_list_price, GetProductTaxIn(Prod_id)
from products
```

5. Your results may look similar to this:

```
PROD_ID PROD_LIST_PRICE GETPRODUCTTAXIN(PROD_ID)
---------- --------------- ------------------------
        13          899.99                  1034.99
        14          999.99                  1149.99
        15          999.99                  1149.99
        16          299.99                   344.99
        17         1099.99                  1264.99
        18         1299.99                  1494.99
        19           55.99                    64.39
        20          599.99                   689.99
        21          899.99                  1034.99
        22           24.99                    28.74
        23           21.99                    25.29
```

6. Now use the function in the WHERE clause of a SQL statement. The following is an example of using the function within a WHERE clause:

```
select prod_id, prod_list_price, GetProductTaxIn(Prod_id)
   from products
   where GetProductTaxIn(Prod_id)>= 500
```

Project Summary

This project illustrates how you can extend the functionality of your database as well as add value to your organization by building standard rules that can be utilized by everyone using your database.

Functions provide you with the ability to define standard rules and derivations for your user community and ensure that programs perform predictably and optimally.

Call PL/SQL Programs

Up to this point in the chapter, you have done the following:

- Defined a PL/SQL block

- Defined a PL/SQL program

- Created a stored program

- Debugged your code

This is fine if you want to write every program and have it run as a simple standalone program. However, as with many programming languages, it is important to write a number of separate programs that perform specific tasks rather than a single program that performs all of your tasks. So, when writing PL/SQL programs, you should think the same way. Have programs that perform table maintenance, perform complex logic, or simply read data from tables or files. This leads to calling programs from other programs, a process similar to calling subroutines within C programs. Procedures may be called from programs ranging from Oracle Forms to Perl scripts, but for this section we will simply show you how to call procedures from each other.

To call a procedure from another, you can use your previous procedure, named print_products. Let's create another procedure that calls this procedure:

```
create or replace procedure call_print_prods
as
begin
for l_alpha IN 65 .. 90
LOOP
print_products(chr(l_alpha));
END LOOP;
end;
/
```

You have created a new procedure. It loops through the values of 65 to 90, the ASCII values for A to Z. Using the CHR function, you can convert the value to an ASCII character. You need to do this because you cannot loop through character values. So the procedure will loop through the values calling the print_products procedure each time. This calling of programs can be looped extensively and can be organized into efficient and simple program units. This is similar to modularization seen in an object-oriented programming language.

As you can tell, Oracle's PL/SQL is a powerful and deep language. In this chapter, we've helped provide you with the ability to start writing programs and to incorporate some complex logic using the basic features of the language. As with any language, you can achieve a significant amount of productivity with only a limited number of commands. We encourage you to use this as a starting point and build upon it to ultimately create the programs you and your organization will need.

☑ Chapter 4 Mastery Check

1. Where is PL/SQL executed?

2. Which types of PL/SQL statements would you use to increase the price values by 15 percent for items with more than 1,500 in stock and by 20 percent for items with fewer than 500 in stock?

    A. A cursor FOR loop

    B. An IF/THEN/ELSE command

    C. An INSERT statement

    D. An UPDATE statement

3. What is the FETCH command used for?

4. What will the following command do?

```
V_PRICE_TOLERANCE := 500;
```

5. What is wrong with this function definition?

```
CREATE OR REPLACE FUNCTION raise_price
(original_price IN NUMBER)
RETURN number
IS
BEGIN
RETURN (original_price * 1.25);
END lower_price;
```

6. What is the advantage of using the %TYPE attribute when defining PL/SQL variables?

7. What values are returned from the SQLCODE and SQLERRM functions?

8. A COMMIT command that is issued in a PL/SQL program will commit what?

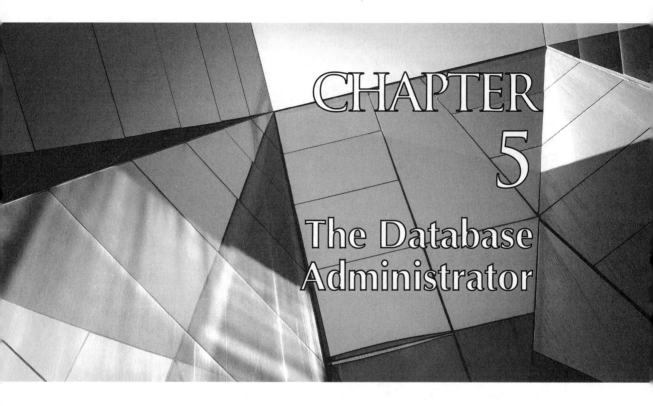

CHAPTER
5

The Database
Administrator

CRITICAL SKILLS

S
o, you've decided to be a database administrator (DBA). Great choice! On top of that, you've chosen Oracle as the Database Management System (DBMS) that you want to work with. Even better! All you need to figure out now is what to learn in order to do the job. Reading this book is a great start. However, a DBA's job cannot be learned entirely in a few short months. It is a work in progress and it can take several years to become really good at it. Don't get us wrong—you can learn the basics that will make you a productive DBA in a few short months. However, there is a great deal to learn, and you won't become really good at this job until you've actually run the utility, executed the SQL, or performed the task. In other words, don't just read this book—try out the examples and don't be afraid to make mistakes.

<h2>CRITICAL SKILL 5.1</h2>

Learn What a DBA Does

The role of a DBA is more of a career than just a job. Those of us who have been doing this for many years are always learning new things and are just trying to keep up! That's the exciting thing about being a DBA: The job keeps changing. Databases are growing at a phenomenal pace, the number of users is increasing, availability requirements are striving for that magical 24/7 mark, and security has become a much greater concern. As you will see in this book, databases now include more than just data. Knowledge of databases also encompasses the Internet, grid computing, XML, storage management, clustering, Java, and server hardware. With Oracle's complete stack offerings, Exadata, and other Exa-machines, there are opportunities to administer more than just the database. There might even be a shift in DBA roles to include more server management, or there might be a growth in a new role of database machine administrator (DMA). The last chapter of this book explores Exadata, but when considering the role of the DMA, there are different tasks than just looking at the database. These tasks include understanding the server, storage, and how to best utilize the engineered system. These types of roles are no longer just architecting the system, but also active roles in implementation and administration. Oracle 12*c* also provides additional options with consolidation and virtualization, and demonstrates how the DBA is changing and is always providing new challenges.

So, how long will it take you to learn how to be a DBA? The answer is: for as long as you're planning to practice this career. There are some concrete steps that you can take to jumpstart your learning process. Undertaking an Oracle Certification will provide you with a structured program that offers clear steps for learning the details of the job. Instructor-led courses and Internet-based classes can help you through the process. We highly recommend getting involved in user groups in order to learn from other DBA experiences. Also, read as much as you can and then get your hands on a test database and practice what you've learned.

Applications come and go, but data stays around. All of the information that makes your company valuable is (or should be) stored in a database. Customer, vendor, employee, and financial data, as well as every other kind of corporate data, is stored in a database; your company would have great difficulty surviving if any of that data was lost. Learn your job well. People are depending on you.

There is good news for DBAs: Oracle has tools to help you do your job and manage your databases. These tools have existed for many versions of Oracle and have improved with each release to the point where the Oracle Database 12c offerings are extensive. You will have the option of doing your job using either a graphical user interface (GUI) or a command-line interface. We recommend learning both. In many cases, you will need to use the command-line interface to schedule work through scripts. Tools such as SQL Developer and Oracle Enterprise Manager, on the other hand, can be used for performing day-to-day operations and can also be used as a great learning tool the first time you perform an operation. Often you will be able to generate the low-level commands from these tools and then copy them to a file to be used later on.

DBAs will need to perform many tasks, from managing users to backing up the database. Performing some tasks might have gotten easier with the improved management tools; however, architecture areas such as high availability, data security, and manageability of the database options have gotten more complex. Oracle 12c also provides different options for consolidation and organizing the schemas or pluggable databases. The pluggable databases will change how to look at resources for the database instance, and managing these resources based on CPU, memory, and I/O will be a part of managing the 12c database instance because the resource management can be done at the pluggable database level in a container database. The ability to move the pluggable databases to be able to patch a system changes how to apply patches. A DBA's skill set now must include understanding these areas and how to design the architecture of the database environment to meet requirements coming from the business.

As we've mentioned previously, there is a great deal that you will need to know in order to be able to provide well-rounded coverage of your Oracle environment. Because of this, we have categorized the specialized areas of database management so that you will be aware of the whole picture and can break your work into well-defined groupings.

Perform Day-to-Day Operations

In order to properly perform the role of database administrator, you will need to develop and implement solutions that cover all areas of this discipline. The amazing part of this job is that you may be asked to do many, or perhaps all, of the different aspects of your job on any given day. Your daily tasks will vary from doing high-level architecture and design to performing low-level tasks. Let's take a look at the things that you will be getting involved in.

Architecture and Design

DBAs should be involved with the architecture and design of new applications, databases, and even technical infrastructure changes. Decisions made here will have a large impact on database performance and scalability, while database knowledge will help you choose a better technical implementation. Data modeling tools such as SQL Developer Data Modeler can assist the DBA.

Capacity Planning

Short- and long-range planning needs to be performed on your databases and applications. You should focus on performance and sizing characteristics of your systems that will help to determine upcoming storage, CPU, memory, and network needs. This is an area that is often neglected and can lead to big problems if it is not done properly. There is a shift in planning environments to be able to add resources easily as systems grow, either with virtualization or cloud environments. With virtualized database environments, these resource concerns and planning for capacity might be less on the DBA side, but those who are now planning out the virtualized environment capacity will be concerned with overall usage. These environments tend to scale better because there are ways to add resources as needed. Still, being able to communicate database growth and how it will be using the different resources will assist in managing the overall environment.

Backup and Recovery

A backup and recovery plan is, of course, critical for protecting your corporate data. You need to ensure that the data can be recovered quickly to the nearest point in time as possible. There is also a performance aspect to this because backups must be performed using minimal resources while the database is up and running, and recoveries need to be performed within a time limit predefined by Service Level Agreements (SLAs) developed to meet customers' requirements. A complete backup and recovery implementation should include local recovery and remote recovery that is also referred to as disaster recovery planning (DRP). Oracle 12*c* offers backup and recovery at a pluggable database level, and this will need to be factored into recovery plans. You will see more on backup and recovery in Chapter 6.

Security

Security is an area that has become extremely important because of the number of users that can access your databases and the amount of external, web-based access. Database users need to be authenticated so that you know with certainty who is accessing your database. Users must then be given authorization to use the objects in Oracle that they need to do their job. However, despite this need for permissions and access in order to do their jobs, a best practice is to grant only the minimum amount of permissions and access for the role or user. This can be managed with Oracle Enterprise Manager, as you'll see in some examples of this later in this chapter. External users require extra web-based security that is beyond the scope of this book.

Managing user permissions is just part of the security in the database environment. Encryption of data, auditing of access and permissions, and looking at the data access of system users in development environments are a few other areas that need attention in order to provide a secured database environment.

Performance and Tuning

Performance and tuning is arguably the most exciting area of database management. Changes here are noticed almost immediately, and every experienced DBA has stories about small changes they've made that resulted in large performance gains. On the other hand, every performance glitch in the environment will be blamed on the database and you will need to learn how to deal with this. Automatic Workload Repository (AWR) Reports, Statspack, OEM Performance Management, and third-party tools will assist you in this area. There is a lot to learn here, but the proper tools will simplify this considerably.

Managing Database Objects

You need to manage all schema objects, such as tables, indexes, views, synonyms, sequences, and clusters, as well as source types, such as packages, procedures, functions, and triggers, to ensure they are valid and organized in a fashion that will deliver adequate performance and have adequate space. The space requirements of schema objects are directly related to the tablespaces and data files that are growing at incredible rates. SQL Developer or OEM can simplify this, something you'll see examples of later in this chapter.

Storage Management

Databases are growing at incredible rates. You need to carefully manage space and pay particular attention to the space used by data files and archive logs. Also, with Fast Recovery Area (FRA) there are backup areas that need to be managed for their space usage. With Automatic Segment Space Management (ASSM), the need for reorganization of database objects has decreased. Reorgs also use considerable resources so there should be some evaluation of whether an object needs to be reorganized or not. There are online utilities that are supposed to help with reorganization of indexes and tables while they remain online, but do not perform these operations unless it is necessary. See the section "Manage Space," later in the chapter, for more on this.

Change Management

Being able to upgrade or change the database is a skill that requires knowledge of many areas. Upgrades to the database schema, the procedural logic in the database, and the database software must all be performed in a controlled manner. Change control procedures and tools such as Oracle's Change Management Pack and third-party offerings will assist you.

Schedule Jobs

Since Oracle Database 10g, DBMS_SCHEDULER was introduced with the existing DBMS_JOBS. It allows for jobs to be scheduled for a specific date and time, and to categorize jobs into job classes that can then be prioritized. This means that resources can be controlled by job class. Of course, other native scheduling systems such as crontab in Linux and Unix can be used, as well as other third-party offerings.

Jobs can include any of the database maintenance tasks such as backups and monitoring scripts. Grouping the monitoring and maintenance jobs into a job class can give them a lower priority than an application batch job that needs to finish in a short batch window.

Network Management

Oracle Networking is a fundamental component of the database that you will need to become comfortable with. Troubleshooting connections to the database is similar to troubleshooting performance issues, because even though the database is up and available, if your applications can't reach it, it's the same as if it's down and unavailable. Database connectivity options such as tnsnames, the Oracle Internet Directory (OID), and the Oracle Listener require planning to ensure that performance and security requirements are met in a way that is simple to manage. Details of this are discussed in the "Understand Database Connections" section of this chapter.

High Availability

With information and data being available 24/7, architecting highly available systems has fallen into the hands of the database administrator. Options on the database side include Real Application Clusters, Data Guard, replication, and fast recovery options. There are also hardware and virtualization options to provide redundant and available systems. Chapter 7 looks at some of these options on the database side.

Troubleshooting

Although troubleshooting may not be what you'd consider a classic area of database management, it is one area that you will encounter daily. You will need tools to help you with this. My Oracle Support provides technical support and is an invaluable resource. Oracle alert logs and dump files will also help you greatly. Experience will be your biggest ally here and the sooner you dive into database support, the faster you will progress.

You've seen the areas of database management that need to be handled; now it's time to look at the Oracle schema and storage infrastructure.

CRITICAL SKILL 5.3

Understand the Oracle Database 12*c* Architecture

Oracle's memory and process architecture have already been discussed in Chapter 1. In this section, you take a look at the Oracle schema and storage infrastructure because these are a large part of what you will be required to manage.

Schemas

An Oracle database can have many schemas contained in it. The schema is a logical structure that contains objects such as segments, views, procedures, functions, packages, triggers, user-defined objects, collection types, sequences, synonyms, and database links. A *segment* is a data structure that can be a table, index, or temporary or undo segment. The *schema name* is the user that controls the schema. SYSTEM, SYS, SCOTT, and SH are examples of schemas. Figure 5-1 shows the relationship between these schema objects.

Segments, Extents, and Blocks

Oracle database allocates logical database space for the objects and data in the database. As you can see in Figure 5-1, a schema can have many segments and many segment types. Each segment is a single instance of a table, partition, cluster,

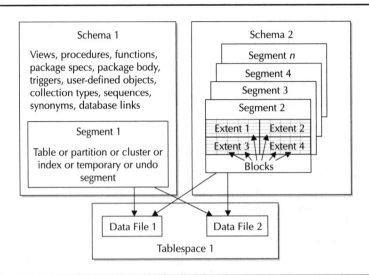

FIGURE 5-1. *The database and user schemas*

index, or temporary or undo segment. So, for example, a table with two indexes is implemented as three segments in the schema. A segment is broken down further into *extents,* which are a collection of contiguous data blocks. As data is added to Oracle, it will first fill the blocks in the allocated extents and once those extents are full, new extents can be added to the segment as long as space allows. Oracle automatically allocates extents and can manage the sizing of the extents, or a uniform size can be defined. Oracle segment types are listed here:

- **Tables**   The data is kept in rows and columns. This is the heart of your database with tables implemented in one schema and one tablespace. The exception to this is a special type of table called a partitioned table, where the table can be split into different ranges or sets of values called a *partition,* with each partition implemented in a different tablespace. Remember, however, that each partition is itself a segment and each segment can only reside in one tablespace. Clustered tables are another special case where two tables with a close link between them can have their data stored together in a single block to improve join operations.

- **Indexes**   These are optionally built on tables for performance reasons and to help implement integrity constraints such as primary keys and uniqueness. In previous releases, indexes and tables were kept in separate tablespaces to keep the segments in different areas, but with Automatic Segment Space Management and disk systems, this type of separation is no longer needed. Index segments are like table segments.

- **Temporary segments** Oracle uses these as a temporary storage area to run a SQL statement. For example, they may be used for sorting data and then discarded once a query or transaction is complete.

- **Undo segments** These are used to manage the before image of changes, which allows data to roll back if needed and helps provide data consistency for users querying data that is being changed. You learn more about this in Chapter 6.

Segments can be thought of as physical structures since they actually are used to store data that is kept in a tablespace (although some of this is temporary in nature). There are other structures stored in the schema that are more logical in nature.

Pluggable Databases

The pluggable database is a new feature in Oracle 12*c* and is another way to organize the storage and objects of the database. The pluggable database (PDB) is a collection of schemas and schema objects that is portable from one container database (CDB) to another. The pluggable database is created in a container database, and has its own storage and the data files that are allocated to the pluggable database (see Figure 5-2). The storage for the PDB is used for the tablespaces and the objects that are in the PDB.

The PDB can be created with the database creation assistant or in sqlplus with or without the storage clause.

```
SQLPLUS> CREATE PLUGGABLE DATABASE peopledb ADMIN USER peopleadm
IDENTIFIED BY password;
SQLPLUS> CREATE PLUGGABLE DATABASE appsdb ADMIN USER appadm IDENTIFIED
BY password STORAGE (MAXSIZE 500M MAX_SHARED_TEMP_SIZE 100M) DEFAULT
TABLESPACE appsdata DATAFILE
'/u01/oracle/oradata/appsdb/appsdata01.dbf' SIZE 250M AUTOEXTEND ON;
```

The PDB is a way to organize the schemas and objects together; similar to objects in a schema, the objects still have segments, extents, and blocks (refer back to Figure 5-1 for the segments).

Logical Schema Structures

Not everything stored in a database and schema is data. Oracle also manages source modules and supporting structures (such as sequences) that are used to populate new unique and primary key values when inserting data into the database.

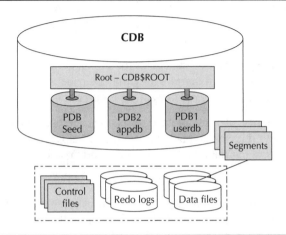

FIGURE 5-2. *The pluggable databases*

These objects belong to a schema and are stored in the Oracle Catalog. These, as well as view properties of the objects, can all be easily managed through SQL Developer, as shown in Figure 5-3. Take a look at the following for a brief description of these logical structures:

■ **Views** Views give you the capability of subsetting a table and combining multiple tables through a single named object. You can think of them as a *stored query*. With the exception of a special type of view called a materialized view, which is used for data warehousing, data is not stored in views. Views are simply a new way of defining access to the underlying tables, which can be used for security, performance, and ease-of-use.

■ **Synonyms** Synonyms are used to create a new name or alias for another database object such as a table, view, or another synonym, and sources such as a procedure, package, function, java class, and so on. They can be used to simplify access. As with views, data is not stored in a synonym.

■ **Sequences** Sequences are used to generate new unique numbers that can be used by applications when inserting data into tables. Selecting the NEXTVAL from the sequence provides a unique identifier. Also available with 12*c* is the identity data type that will automatically increment for an ID column.

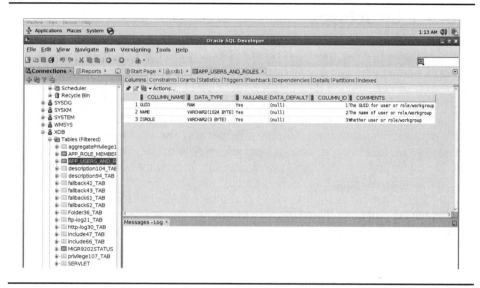

FIGURE 5-3.   *SQL Developer table definition view*

- **Source programs**   These can be stored in the catalog and written either in Oracle's proprietary PL/SQL or in Java. PL/SQL source types include business logic that can be written as packages, procedures, and functions. Triggers can also be used to implement business logic, but are often used to implement data integrity because they are not executed directly by a user or source program, but rather are automatically executed when an action is performed on the database. Java sources and Java classes are also implemented directly in Oracle. This server-side support of application logic improves performance because the logic resides with the data, and the source code and data is backed up together.

- **User types**   These can be created by you to support object-oriented development. Array types, object types, and table types can all be created by you. Also, the Oracle XML Schema Processor supports XML processing by adding data types to XML documents that can be used to ensure the integrity of data in XML documents.

So now that you have seen all of the schema objects, it's time to tie these together to your storage architecture.

Storage Structures

As shown earlier in Figure 5-1, the physical schema objects are stored as segments in the database. Each segment can be stored in only a single tablespace, with a tablespace being made up of one or more data files. If a tablespace is running out of space, you can expand the data files it is made up of, or you can also add a new data file to the tablespace. A data file can only store data for a single tablespace.

A single tablespace can store data for multiple segments and, in fact, for several segment types. Segments from multiple schemas can also exist in the same tablespace. So, for example, table_a from schema1 and index_b from schema2 can both be implemented in the same tablespace. Oh, and by the way, a tablespace can store data for a single database only.

The logical structures such as views and source code are stored in the Oracle Catalog but are part of a schema. So, this means that the Oracle-supplied SH schema can contain all of the objects that it needs to run the entire application under its own schema name. This provides strong security and management benefits.

Progress Check

1. Name five areas that you will need to address as a DBA.

2. What is a schema and what does it contain?

3. What is a PDB and what does it contain?

4. Can a tablespace store more than one segment type?

5. List an example of nondata structures or logical structures in a database.

Progress Check Answers

1. As a DBA, you will need to address architecture, capacity planning, backup and recovery, security, and performance, among other things.

2. A schema is a logical structure that contains objects such as segments, views, procedures, functions, packages, triggers, user-defined objects, collection types, sequences, synonyms, and database links.

3. A PDB is a pluggable database and is a portable database that contains schemas and schema objects.

4. A single tablespace can store data for multiple segments and different segment types. Segments from multiple schemas can also exist in the same tablespace. So, for example, table_a from schema1 and index_b from schema2 can be implemented as two segments in the same tablespace.

5. Source programs such as triggers, stored procedures, functions, and packages are logical structures. Other examples include views, synonyms, sequences, and types.

CRITICAL SKILL 5.4

Operate Modes for an Oracle Database 12*c*

Oracle is a software package like many others that you may have used. However, when you run most programs, they run one and only one way. So, when a user opens the accounting software, it will run it the same way all the time. However, you have options with Oracle. This section discusses the many ways that you can run Oracle. Some of these methods will be important to administrators, while others will allow for full use. This feature is important when you need to perform both critical and noncritical activities and not interfere with your users or your data.

Modes of Operation

Oracle has several modes of operation. In most cases, when you start Oracle, you will simply issue the command:

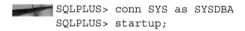

```
SQLPLUS> conn SYS as SYSDBA
SQLPLUS> startup;
```

This command actually takes Oracle through three distinct startup phases automatically, although you can also choose to explicitly step through these phases:

- **nomount phase**   In this phase, the database reads the SPFILE or the init.ora parameter file and starts up the Oracle memory structures as well as the background processes. The instance is started, but the database is not yet associated with the newly started instance. This is usually used in cases where you need to re-create the control file. The command to perform this is

  ```
  SQLPLUS> startup nomount;
  ```

- **mount phase**   You use this phase in order to associate a database with the instance; the instance "mounts" the database. The previously read parameter file is used to find those control files that contain the name of the data files and redo logs. The database is then mounted to allow some maintenance activities to be performed. Data files and redo logs are not opened when the database is in mount mode, so the database is not yet accessible by end users for normal tasks. Commands to mount a database are

  ```
  SQLPLUS> startup mount;
  SQLPLUS> -- Database already started in nomount can be mounted
  with the alter database

  SQLPLUS> alter database mount;
  ```

■ **open phase**   In this phase, Oracle opens the data files and redo logs, making the database available for normal operations. Again, if the database is just started up in mount mode, the ALTER DATABASE command is needed to open the database. Your redo logs must exist in order for the database to open. If they do not, the RESETLOGS command must be used to create new redo logs in the location specified in the control files:

```
SQLPLUS> startup {open} {resetlogs};
SQLPLUS> alter database open;
```

Container Database STARTUP

A container database is started in the same manner with STARTUP and the other modes of STARTUP. The pluggable databases are mounted when the container database is started up. The pluggable databases will need to be opened using the ALTER DATABASE OPEN statement. The difference here is that one, many, or all can be opened with the command. PDBs can be excluded from being opened when using the ALL command.

```
SQLPLUS> alter pluggable database ALL open;
SQLPLUS> alter pluggable database ALL EXCEPT appdb1;
```

Other Ways to Open the Database

There are other options for opening a database. For example, you may want to open it in read-only mode so that no database changes (inserts, updates, or deletes) can be performed. There are also the upgrade/downgrade options that allow a database to be opened to perform a downgrade or upgrade to another version of Oracle:

```
SQLPLUS> alter database open read only;
```

A common option you will use to perform maintenance will be to open the database in *restricted mode*. When you issue the command STARTUP RESTRICT, only users with both the create session and restricted session privileges will be able to use the database. So, as a DBA, this is a helpful way to open the database that only you can use:

```
SQLPLUS> startup restrict;
```

The database can be placed in a state where only the SYS and SYSTEM users can query the database without stopping the database and performing a subsequent STARTUP RESTRICT. The activities of other users continue until they become inactive.

This can be performed using the QUIESCE option of ALTER SYSTEM when the Database Resource Manager option has been set up:

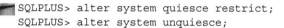

```
SQLPLUS> alter system quiesce restrict;
SQLPLUS> alter system unquiesce;
```

Forcing a Startup

Over time, you will run into situations where Oracle has not shut down properly and you are unable to restart it. In these rare instances, you will need to use the FORCE option of the STARTUP command. This will first perform a "shutdown abort," which forces the database to shut down (see the next section for more information on this) followed by a database startup:

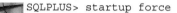

```
SQLPLUS> startup force
```

Database and Instance Shutdown

When shutting down an instance, perform these steps, which are the reverse from those you just saw when opening a database:

1. Close the database (including the data files and redo logs) so that it is no longer usable for normal tasks.

2. Unmount the database from the instance so that only the instance memory structures and background tasks are left running without a database associated with them.

3. Shut down the instance to close the control files.

In order to shut down a database, four different approaches can be used: shutdown NORMAL, IMMEDIATE, TRANSACTIONAL, and ABORT.

- **NORMAL** is, in a sense, the perfect way to shut down because this approach will wait for all users to disconnect from the database and all transactions to complete before the shutdown occurs. Once this command has been issued, new users are not allowed into the system. This can be impractical in cases where users remain on the system for long periods of time:

  ```
  SQLPLUS> shutdown normal;
  ```

- **IMMEDIATE** is a practical shutdown approach that also leaves the database in a consistent state. When the database is put through a "shutdown immediate," all current transactions are rolled back and users are disconnected. No new transactions are allowed into the system. This will be relatively quick if the rollback operations are small and it's an excellent way to shut down the database before performing a database backup:

```
SQLPLUS> shutdown immediate;
```

■ **TRANSACTIONAL** is similar to the immediate variety except that running transactions are allowed to complete. So, once transactions have been committed, the user running it is disconnected. This is useful in cases where you do not want to shut down until currently running transactions have finished or in cases where it will be quicker to complete existing transactions than it will be to roll them back:

```
SQLPLUS> shutdown transactional;
```

■ **ABORT** is the least graceful shutdown option of the four. When this is used, all transactions are ended immediately without waiting for a rollback or commit and all users are instantly disconnected while the database is brought down. Use this only if you are experiencing problems shutting down the database using one of the three options described previously or in cases where you need to shut down the database immediately. The database needs to go through recovery procedures the next time it is restarted. After a shutdown abort has been performed, you should try to immediately start up the database so that you can then perform a shutdown (normal, immediate, or transactional) to bring the database down in the proper manner:

```
SQLPLUS> shutdown abort;
```

When connected to a pluggable database with an alter session, the shutdown will just close the pluggable database and not the container database. When logged into the container database, the same shutdown commands apply and the pluggable databases will be closed if a shutdown was issued.

```
SQLPLUS> alter session set container=appdb1;
SQLPLUS> shutdown;
Oracle instance shutdown (Meaning that the pluggable database was
closed)
SQLPLUS> alter pluggable database close ALL immediate;
Pluggable database altered.
```

Oracle Enterprise Manager (OEM) can help with instance and database startup and shutdown, including container and pluggable databases, as shown in Figure 5-4. First, open OEM in a web browser. Then, on the Oracle Databases tab under the Control section, choose Shutdown (or Startup, depending on if the database is currently running). The advanced options allow for the different types of shutdown.

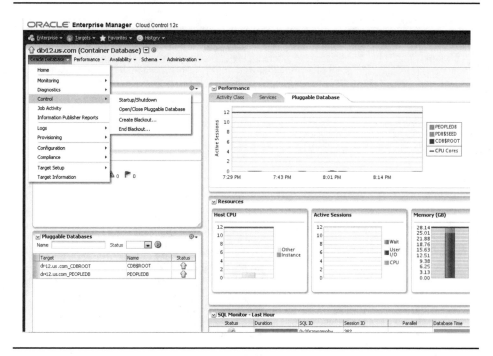

FIGURE 5-4.   *Enterprise Manager Control page view*

Get Started with Oracle Enterprise Manager

Oracle Enterprise Manager (OEM) is a great tool for assisting the beginner DBA to become an experienced one. In previous versions of Oracle, DBControl was a way to manage an individual Oracle database as an individual install of Oracle Enterprise Manager. The DBControl has been replaced with Oracle Enterprise Manager Express in Oracle 12c, which allows for basic database configuration and monitoring of the database instances, as shown in Figure 5-5. Oracle Enterprise Manager Express is created as a final step of the database creation assistant. The URL is given as the database creation is finished, and it is normally something along the lines of http://hostname:5501/em.

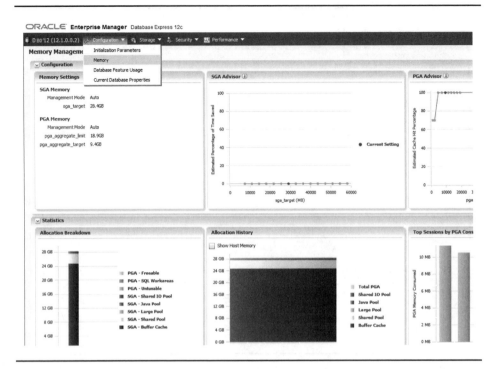

FIGURE 5-5. *Oracle Enterprise Manager Express*

Oracle Enterprise Manager Express can be a place to configure parameters and tablespaces, and to look at performance for the database server, as shown in Figures 5-6 and 5-7. The express version is a quick way to look at the database instance and verify the parameters in a GUI format. It offers a look at a single database, and not multiple databases. If there are many databases in an environment, it becomes difficult to manage each of these single OEM Express versions, and Oracle Enterprise Manager Cloud Control should be used.

Oracle Enterprise Manager 12*c* Cloud Control (OEM12*c*) can manage multiple targets and databases. It is a separate install from the database, and agents can be installed on the target machines that are monitored and administered. Figure 5-8 shows the assignment of the URL for OEM12*c* after the installation is complete. This provides a way to manage the database and all of the components of the database

FIGURE 5-6. *Oracle Enterprise Manager Express – Performance*

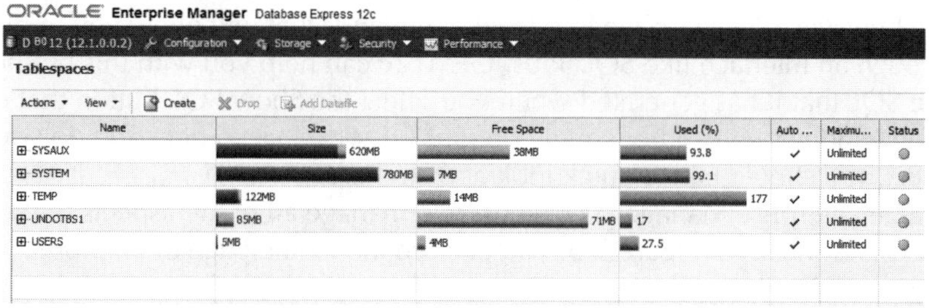

FIGURE 5-7. *Oracle Enterprise Manager Express – Tablespaces*

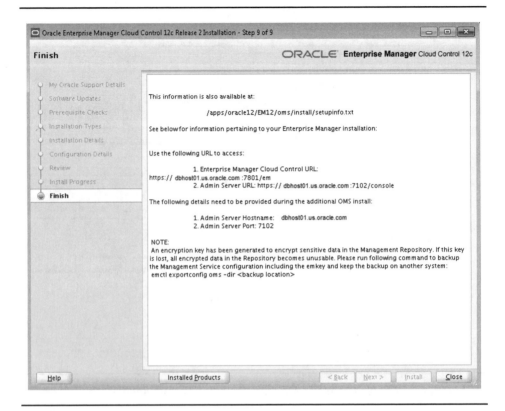

FIGURE 5-8. *OEM12c Installation Finish*

that are installed. Configurations can also be done from the OEM12*c* tool. You should, however, also learn the low-level commands that will allow you to do your job through an interface like SQL*Plus. OEM12*c* can help you with this by showing you the SQL that it has generated when you select the Show SQL button that exists on many windows. Given how many options OEM12*c* has to help you do your job as a DBA, you should take a quick look at them here.

Oracle Enterprise Manager can be used to manage all of the aspects of the databases. As shown in Figure 5-9, you can see the Home page of Enterprise Manager and details about the current state of the database. The menus show the different areas of databases that can be managed: Oracle Databases, Performance, Availability, Schemas, and Administration.

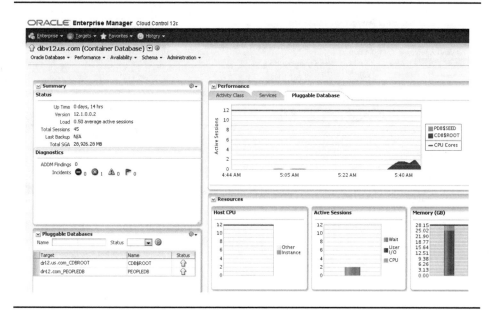

FIGURE 5-9. *Oracle Enterprise Manager Cloud Control 12c*

Instance Configuration

Also shown in Figure 5-9 is the state of an instance and server. By selecting one of the menus from the Home page, such as Oracle Database, you can see different areas to configure and do monitoring and diagnostics. The configuration submenu has options to manage the parameters and memory settings. Figure 5-10 shows the submenus for monitoring that will configure what metrics are being collected, view history, and set up alerts and blackouts for maintenance work.

User Sessions

Now that you have seen some ways to manage instances and databases, through the Performance menu you can look at the SQL activity and then drill down to your user sessions to see exactly what is going on inside the database. By choosing a session, you can see some general information such as the user session ID, when the user logged in, and what the OS username and terminal name are for this user. In Figure 5-11, you can see the SQL that is currently running, along with the explain plan being used. You can follow the order that each explain step is being performed

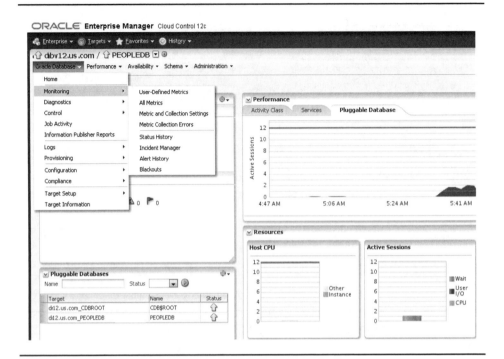

FIGURE 5-10. *OEM 12c – Oracle Database menu*

in by the Step # column and can step through the plan or see it in a graphical layout. You can also manage sessions and disconnect users by right-clicking the username and issuing the KILL SESSION command. The command name may sound a bit harsh, but it does get the idea across.

Resource Consumer Groups

When consolidating databases into a container database, or just planning schemas and pluggable databases, it is useful to be able to manage resources that are available. The Resource Manager provides a way to manage resources by group. A resource consumer group provides a way to group together users so that they can share similar processing requirements. The DATABASE_RESOURCE_MANAGER package is used to allocate the maximum amount of CPU that a session can use or to set a limit for parallel execution for a session or the number of sessions that can be active

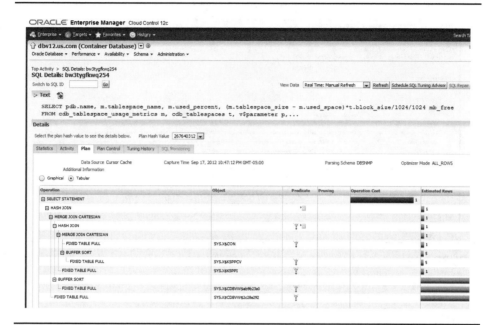

FIGURE 5-11.   *SQL explain plan*

for a consumer group. OEM can assist in managing these groups by giving you an easy way to add new groups and edit those that exist. This panel allows you to enter a description of the group and attach users and database roles to a group. If you look at Figure 5-12, you will see a list of resource consumer groups. From here you can edit groups or create new groups. If you select one of these consumer groups, you will be presented with the capabilities to manage users, roles, and general information about the group.

A resource plan builds on the resource consumer groups by providing a way to define how system resources will be allocated to the resource consumer groups that we just discussed. The resource plan can set thresholds on amount of CPU, parallelism, execution time, and amount of I/O for the group. Group switching allows for a session to change groups after a predefined amount of execution time has been reached. Presumably, you would move the user to a lower priority group to free resources to other sessions. The resource plan schedule can be used to set daily schedules to enable and disable resource plans.

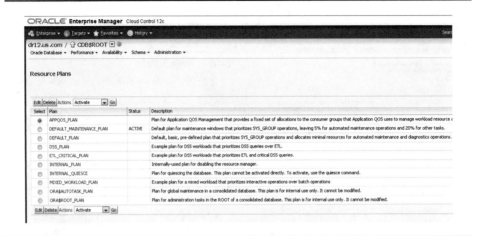

FIGURE 5-12. *Enterprise Manager, Resource Manager view*

Other Tools

Other menus offer ways to manage the database, as shown in Figure 5-13, which provides a view of the security tools and options. These tools are useful when looking at other areas of the database, and they make the job a little easier.

- Database tools enable you to analyze data and performance, and manage tablespaces and parameters. The backup and recovery tools are available under the Availability tab. Statistics management is also an important area for running statistics and getting information about the workload repository.

- Oracle Scheduler provides tools to set up jobs and manage schedules. Job classes can be set up here, as well as standard maintenance jobs to be automated.

- Tuning facilities such as performance manager, outline management, and tablespace maps are provided through Query Optimizer.

- Pluggable database creation is under the Administration menu with Storage, Scheduler, and Security. As shown in Figure 5-14, the pluggable databases can be created, migrated, and unplugged from here.

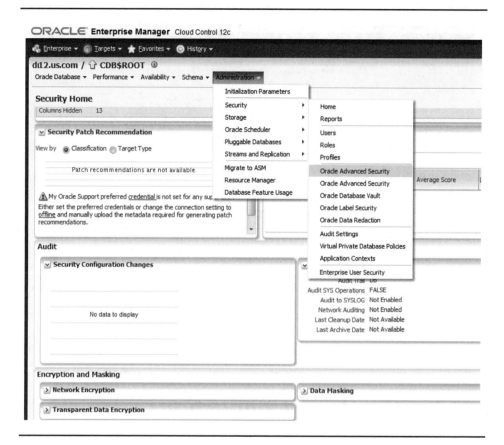

FIGURE 5-13. *Enterprise Manager, Security home page*

As you can see from this overview of OEM console capabilities, many of the tools that you need to perform your day-to-day tasks can be found in this one console. Now that you have confidence that there's a toolset to support you, let's take a quick look at what you need to think about when managing database objects.

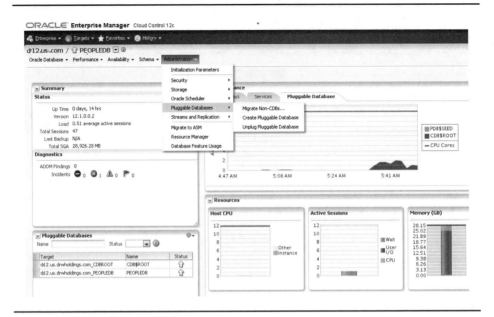

FIGURE 5-14.   *OEM 12c, Create Pluggable Database*

Understand Database Connections

Connections to the database are just as important as the database being up and available. If users cannot connect and get information, all of the database management to keep the database running will not help. The client/application needs information about the database to connect, and the database needs to listen for the client connections. These are part of the Oracle Net Services.

Oracle Net Services

Oracle Net is the part of Oracle Net Services that manages data communication between a remote application and the Oracle database; it runs on top of a network protocol such as TCP/IP. The software used by Oracle Net resides on the remote system and the Oracle database platform.

A listener process must be running on the database server to receive the network request. (A *listener* is a program that listens on a port for incoming network requests and then hands the request to another program for processing.) The listener then determines the appropriate type of process to handle the request.

The listener is created with installation of the Oracle software, and as a database is created with the database creation assistant the information is added to the listener. The default listener is LISTENER, and there can be multiple listeners created on the server. A listener.ora file is created, much like the following sample listener.ora file:

```
LISTENER =
     (DESCRIPTION_LIST =
         (DESCRIPTION =
           (ADDRESS_LIST =
             (ADDRESS = (PROTOCOL = IPC)(KEY = EXTPROC0))
           )
             (ADDRESS_LIST =
             (ADDRESS = (PROTOCOL = TCP)(HOST = eclipse)(PORT = 1521))
           )
         )
       )
SID_LIST_LISTENER =
  (SID_LIST =
       (SID_DESC=
               (GLOBAL_DBNAME=ora12c.customer.com)
               (ORACLE_HOME=/u01/oracle/12.1.0/dbhome_1)
               (SID_NAME=ora12c)          )
 )
```

Command-Line Utilities

The Listener Control utility can be used to start and stop listeners, check their status, and perform tracing and other management operations. The syntax is as follows:

```
lsnrctl  command [listener_name]
```

Listener commands can also be executed from within the Listener Control utility. The listener name is the one defined in the listener.ora file, but a default listener named LISTENER can be used instead. If LISTENER is used, a listener name does not need to be specified.

The following shows how to stop the listener. Here, executing the lsnrctl command generates an LSNRCTL prompt:

```
$ lsnrctl
LSNRCTL> stop
Connecting to (DESCRIPTION=(ADDRESS=(PROTOCOL=IPC)(KEY=EXTPROC0)))
The command completed successfully
```

The next example shows a sample of the type of information displayed when starting the listener:

```
LSNRCTL> start

LSNRCTL for Linux: Version 12.1.0.0.2 - Beta on 18-SEP-2012 23:06:13

Copyright (c) 1991, 2012, Oracle.  All rights reserved.

Starting /u01/oracle12/dbhome_1/bin/tnslsnr: please wait...

TNSLSNR for Linux: Version 12.1.0.0.2 - Beta
System parameter file is /u01/oracle12/dbhome_1/network/admin/listener.ora
Log messages written to /u01/oracle/diag/tnslsnr/listener/alert/log.xml
Listening on: (DESCRIPTION=(ADDRESS=(PROTOCOL=tcp)(HOST=
eclipse)(PORT=1521)))
Listening on: (DESCRIPTION=(ADDRESS=(PROTOCOL=ipc)(KEY=EXTPROC1521)))

Connecting to (DESCRIPTION=(ADDRESS=(PROTOCOL=TCP)(HOST=
eclipse)(PORT=1521)))
STATUS of the LISTENER
-----------------------
Alias                     LISTENER
Version                   TNSLSNR for Linux: Version 12.1.0.0.2 - Beta
Start Date                18-SEP-2012 23:06:13
Uptime                    0 days 0 hr. 0 min. 0 sec
Trace Level               off
Security                  ON: Local OS Authentication
SNMP                      OFF
Listener Parameter File   /u01/oracle12/dbhome_1/network/admin/listener.ora
Listener Log File         /u01/oracle/diag/tnslsnr/listener/alert/log.xml
Listening Endpoints Summary...
   (DESCRIPTION=(ADDRESS=(PROTOCOL=tcp)(HOST= eclipse)(PORT=1521)))
   (DESCRIPTION=(ADDRESS=(PROTOCOL=ipc)(KEY=EXTPROC1521)))
Service "ora12c" has 1 instance(s).
   Instance "ora12c", status UNKNOWN, has 1 handler(s) for this service...
The command completed successfully
```

The STATUS command displays detailed information on the status of the listener. Information includes the start time of the listener, the location of log and configuration files, and so on.

```
LSNRCTL> status
```

The SERVICES command lists dispatchers in a shared server environment and dedicated servers in a dedicated server environment:

```
LSNRCTL> services
```

Connections

A connection is an Oracle communication path between a user process and the Oracle database server. If this communication path is dropped, a user must establish a new session. The current transaction is rolled back if the connection for its session is lost. A session is a specific connection for a user between the user process and the Oracle database server.

If a connection cannot be made, it is important to be able to troubleshoot these issues and problems. The repository holds trace files and other errors collected into a standard place. This troubleshooting facility for diagnosing network problems is the same as the one you will use to analyze and diagnose database problems. With tools like this, it is easier to find connection issues and avoid problems.

Maintain Connections

The Oracle Net Foundation Layer establishes and maintains connections with the database server. Transparent Network Substrate (TNS) is the common interface between all the industry-standard protocols. Oracle Protocol Support maps the industry-standard protocols (TCP/IP, TCP/IP with SSL, SDP, and Named Pipes) used in the connection.

Figure 5-15 shows you how Oracle Net works. Oracle Net software will reside on the database server platform and the platform that is running the Oracle applications. With an application server, HTTP runs on top of a network protocol between the browser platform and the application server platform. Oracle Net then runs on top of a network protocol between the application server and the database server. For a client/server configuration, Oracle Net will reside on the client platform and the database server platform, and will run on top of a network protocol between the client and the database server platforms.

If Java programs are running, a Java Database Connectivity (JDBC) OCI, or Thin driver, will communicate with Oracle Net to process the database request. A JDBC OCI driver requires Oracle Net on the remote platform and the database server. A Thin driver doesn't require a full Oracle Client to be installed and uses network calls to connect to a database. So, a JDBC Thin driver written entirely in Java uses JavaNet to communicate, and requires Oracle Net only on the server platform.

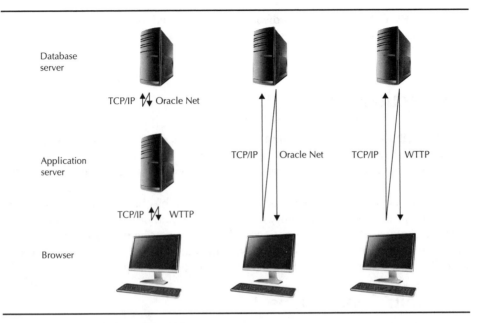

FIGURE 5-15. *An Oracle network overview*

Define a Location

Locations need to be defined so a remote application can find the correct Oracle database server on the network. A service name, such as customer.us.beginner.com, is used to define the unique location of each database server. In the preceding example, customer is the database name and us.beginner.com is the domain name. On the plus side, if the physical location of the database is changed, the service name can stay the same while the definition or settings of the name can change underneath.

A database can support multiple services. The service name, defined with the initialization parameter SERVICE_NAMES, makes the physical location of the database transparent and will default to the global database name (the name of your database), which uses the format database_name.database_domain, as in customer.us.beginner.com.

The database domain name is the domain where the database is located, and is made up of the initialization parameters DB_NAME and DB_DOMAIN. The combination of the DB_NAME and DB_DOMAIN (customer.us.beginner.com) name distinguishes one database from another, as shown in the following examples:

```
DB_NAME=customer
DB_DOMAIN=us.beginner.com
```

Ask the Expert

Q: Why is it important for DBAs to understand the networking setup and configuration for Oracle Database 12c?

A: Often as systems interact with the database, networking bottlenecks surface that require attention from DBA personnel in addition to those who manage the applications. Familiarity, if not fluency, with setting up Oracle Net services and its configuration files arms the DBA with the skills required to intervene.

A Connect Descriptor

A connect descriptor is used to define the service name and the location of the database. The address component of a connect descriptor defines the protocol, hostname, and port number. Although port numbers can be between 1 and 65535, those from 1 to 1024 are usually reserved for special processes. The default port for Oracle Listener is 1521. The connect data component of the description describes the service to which you want to connect. If you do not include the instance_name in your descriptor, it will default to the Oracle SID.

A sample connect descriptor for customer.us.beginner.com looks like the following:

```
(DESCRIPTION =
  (ADDRESS=(PROTOCOL=tcp)(HOST=eclipse)(PORT=1521))
  (CONNECT_DATA=
    (SERVICE_NAME=customer.us.beginner.com)))
```

A specific connect descriptor can be defined for a specific service handler. For example, in a shared server architecture, a dedicated service handler can be chosen, which can be set to dedicated (SERVER=dedicated) or shared (SERVER=shared). If no dispatchers are available, a dedicated server will be used and the default service handler is shared:

```
(DESCRIPTION =
  (ADDRESS=(PROTOCOL=tcp)(HOST=eclipse)(PORT=1521))
  (CONNECT_DATA=
    (SERVICE_NAME=customer.us.beginner.com)
    (SERVER=dedicated)))
```

Define a Connect Descriptor

When establishing a connection, you have two choices: A detailed connect descriptor can be defined or a manual name that maps to a connect descriptor can be used. The following example shows you how to define a manual connect descriptor or name a connection descriptor name:

```
-- Manual definition of a connection descriptor
CONNECT
username/password@(DESCRIPTION = (ADDRESS=(PROTOCOL=tcp) (HOST=eclipse)
 (PORT=1521))  (CONNECT_DATA= (SERVICE_NAME=customer.us.beginner.com)))
-- Connect using a pre-defined descriptor
CONNECT username/password@cust
```

Oracle networking plays a critical role in performance and availability. Each new version of Oracle is designed to support more data and users than the previous release. This increased amount of database activity and network traffic needs to be addressed from an availability and performance perspective and should be managed by the DBA. The material provided here was just beginning information to provide a basic understanding about the listener and connections to the database.

CRITICAL SKILL 5.7

Manage Database Objects

A large part of your job as a DBA will be to manage the objects that exist in a database. Let's look at the objects that you need to concern yourself with and discuss the main management issues that you will have in each of these areas.

Control Files

It is critical to the database that you have at least one valid control file for your database. These are small binary files that contain the records of the physical structure of the database and are important for database recovery. They can be multiplexed by the Oracle instance. Ensuring that you have at least three copies of the control files (remember, they are small), as well as text and binary backups whenever a data file, log file, or tablespace is changed and on a regularly scheduled basis (at least daily), will go a long way toward ensuring that your control files are in good shape. Control files are discussed in more detail in Chapter 6.

Redo Logs

Redo logs are necessary to ensure database integrity and should be duplexed in Oracle. More than one group of logs are needed, and duplexing them will keep another mirrored copy of the logs. Oracle mirroring helps even if your redo logs are mirrored by your storage subsystem because Oracle will use the alternative redo log if one should become corrupt. You will need to ensure that you have enough redo logs and that they are sized properly to support database performance. How large should your redo logs be? They should be large enough that a log switch does not typically occur more than once every 15 minutes due to the checkpointing that occurs during a log switch and the overhead that is incurred during this operation. Checkpointing writes information out to the data files from the logs and is important for data consistency. Checkpoints need to happen on a regular basis so that all of the buffers get written out to data files. How many redo logs should you have? You should have enough redo logs that the system will not wrap around to a log that has not yet completed a checkpoint or completed archiving (for systems in archivelog mode). Redo logs can be added, deleted, and switched through Oracle Enterprise Manager.

Undo Management

The before images of changed rows are stored in the Undo segment. Oracle will manage your undo segments for you, but you need to determine how large to make the tablespace that the Undo segment is stored in. The size that you make this depends on the length of time that you want the undo information to be available to you. There are parameters to manage the retention in the Undo tablespace and the size of the Undo. UNDO_MANAGEMENT set to AUTO turns on automatic undo management, UNDO_TABLESPACE sets the tablespace, and UNDO_RETENTION sets the time retention for keeping the information in the Undo tablespace.

Schema Objects

As discussed earlier in this chapter, you can manage schema objects through SQL Developer. There are also some things that you may want to do with your own SQL scripts that run as scheduled jobs. When managing schemas, you need to ensure that those physical objects that take up a great deal of space do, in fact, have enough space to grow. These include tables, indexes, clusters, and partitioned tables. Manage these objects through sizing of the tablespaces where they are implemented. Just because an object may have hundreds of extents doesn't mean that a reorganization of the object is not necessary. You need to reorg only if there are a large number of chained or migrated rows. It is also possible for the reorgs to gain back unused space. Indexes, on the other hand, will need to be rebuilt more frequently and do provide some performance benefits. These rebuilds and reorganizations of indexes can typically be done online and are easy to take care of at a time when there is not much going on in the database. You find out more about managing space in the next section.

It is important to keep up-to-date statistics on your tables and indexes. This will assist the optimizer in making better decisions when choosing access paths for your queries and can be used to validate the structures. Besides statistics about the object, there are also system statistics that help determine the resources available. The DBMS_STATS package will gather statistics for the overall system (DBMS_STATS.GATHER_SYSTEM_STATS) and for the database-level statistics (DBMS_STATS.GATHER_DATABASE_STATS). In Oracle Database 12c, a scheduler job called gather_stats_job will run during a maintenance window between 10:00 p.m. and 6:00 a.m., by default, and will run statistics for those objects in cases where they have not been collected yet or are stale (statistics that are old due to recent changes in data). There is a table, DBA_AUTOTASK_TASK, to check what maintenance jobs have been scheduled. Setting the Oracle Database 12c initialization parameter STATISTIC_LEVEL to TYPICAL (the default) will allow Oracle to automatically update statistics as a background task on a regular basis and is the recommended approach for gathering statistics. In pre–Oracle Database 11g releases, the DBMS_STATS package should be run manually. Especially after upgrade of a database, it is important to manually run object, database, and system statistics.

Triggers, views, synonyms, procedures, functions, and packages are logical schema objects that do not take up a lot of space in the tablespace; however, these objects need to be watched to ensure they are not invalid. They can become invalid with an ALTER table statement or changes in structure to any dependent objects. These objects should be valid, and you can check this with the SQL statement that follows:

```
SQLPLUS> select owner, object_name, object_type
from dba_objects where status <> 'VALID';
```

You've looked at many of the database objects that will require your attention. Let's now explore one area that requires special attention due to the size of today's databases.

Ask the Expert

Q: Why is it important for DBAs to get involved with the architecture and design of a new system?

A: Decisions made on the technical infrastructure as well as data and application designs will have a significant impact on database performance and scalability. Database knowledge will enable you to choose a better technical implementation. Once chosen, these can be difficult to change.

Q: Which method do you normally use to shut down a database?

A: Although the shutdown normal operation is a recommended approach, it is often impractical because you need users to disconnect themselves. The approach that we prefer is to perform a checkpoint using the command alter system checkpoint, which will write data out to data files and speed up the restart. The preferred method is a SHUTDOWN IMMEDIATE. A SHUTDOWN ABORT should be used as a last resort. If doing a SHUTDOWN ABORT, it should be immediately followed by a STARTUP RESTRICT and SHUTDOWN IMMEDIATE. This is a fast, guaranteed shutdown that leaves the database in a consistent state once all of the steps have been completed.

Q: What is the best way to become a good Oracle DBA quickly and then to keep improving?

A: There are many things that you will need to do and many skills that you'll need to develop to do this job. First, learning the basic DBA skills, which you can get from books such as this, as well as from courses, will give you a head start. Practicing what you see is probably the quickest and most practical way to learn. Getting involved in supporting some databases in development and production will force you to learn very quickly. Then, working on development systems for different types of applications will help to round out your skills. If you keep reading and learning and never assume that you know it all, you will do very well.

CRITICAL SKILL 5.8

Manage Space

The challenge of managing data in Oracle Database 12*c* is one that provides you with options. In this section, you will look at the methods that have been used in the many versions of the database to manage your information. Today's version of the database provides you with options. The first that we will discuss is managing your data and the files in which they reside in a manual way. Another option, Automatic Storage Management, is discussed in Chapter 7.

Archive Logs

When you put the database in archive logging mode, the redo logs are written out to a directory that is named in the SPFILE. If that directory becomes full and the database attempts to write another archive log, database activity will be suspended until sufficient space is made available for the new file. Create a large directory and schedule jobs to move the archive log files from online storage to tape before you encounter a space issue. Recovery Manager (RMAN), a utility used for backup and recovery, does a nice job of helping you manage this. Please see Chapter 6 for more information on backing up the archive log files to tape and managing these files.

Tablespaces and Data Files

Space should be managed at the data file and tablespace level rather than at an object level like a table or index. Using locally managed tablespaces with uniform extent sizes will simplify your management. Do not worry that you have multiple extents in a tablespace or for an object. This does not create a performance issue because the extents contain a number of blocks that must be contiguous, and the extents will be reused and created as needed. You can see the amount of space available in your data files or tablespaces in OEM, as shown in Figure 5-7. The figure shows the amount of free space available in the currently allocated space. Using the segment management will also reduce the need to set PCTFREE and PCTUSED when creating tables. If you have used the autoextend feature to allow a data file to extend in size when more space is needed, the extra space is not shown in this graph.

TIP
Be careful if autoextend is set for temporary and undo tablespaces because they will quickly grow to use all of the space. We recommended that you set a limit for these tablespaces to which they can autoextend.

What do you do if you run out of space in a data file? Just enter OEM Express: From the storage menu, you can drill down into the tablespace and data file. Once there, you can change the autoextend feature and enter the size of the extensions that you would like. Do not forget to limit the size of the data file so that it doesn't grow until it uses all of your space. After you've completed this, click Apply and you're done. If you select the Show SQL button, you can see the alter database syntax, which is also shown here:

```
SQLPLUS> alter database datafile '/u01/oradata/ora11g/example01.dbf'
autoextend on next 50M maxsize 5000M;
```

You can write your own scripts to compare the amount of allocated space for a data file in DBA_DATA_FILES view to the amount of free space in DBA_FREE_SPACE view.

OEM also provides you with a more detailed map of how space is used. In OEM, select a tablespace and then navigate from Tools to Tuning Features, finally choosing Tablespace Map. This opens a graphical layout showing each segment in the tablespace. From the tablespace map, you can choose the Tablespace Analysis Report tab for a written report on the space being used.

Managing the database objects discussed earlier will be a large part of your role as a DBA. In the next section, you'll take a look at setting up and managing users. After all, without database users, there is no point in doing any of this!

Progress Check

1. What's better: shutdown transactional or shutdown immediate?

2. Do you only need to worry about logical schema objects that take up a large amount of space?

3. What happens if your archive log directory becomes full?

4. Why would you want to use a command-line interface rather than a GUI to perform your tasks as a DBA?

5. Under what circumstances would you bother to start up the database in nomount mode?

CRITICAL SKILL 5.9

Manage Users

Before you can do anything in Oracle, you need to have a user ID created to enable you to log into Oracle. As a DBA, you will begin with the SYS or SYSTEM accounts because these accounts both have the DBA role and exist in all Oracle databases. They are often used to perform database administration tasks. The SYS account is also granted the SYSDBA privilege and is the schema that the Oracle catalog is stored in. You should only use the SYS account when you need to perform a task as SYS or need the sysdba privilege. If your database was created using the database configuration assistant (DBCA), you will also automatically get the SYSMAN and DBSNMP accounts. SYSMAN is used to administer Oracle Enterprise Manager (OEM), and DBSNMP is used by the agent that OEM employs to monitor Oracle databases. Several other accounts will also be set up for the "example" schemas, such as the Sales History (SH) user that you will see utilized throughout this book. The OUTLN schema will be created to allow you to use query plan stability through the stored outline feature.

Depending on the options you choose when creating your database, other accounts may be set up for you. For example, if you install the OLAP option, the OLAPSYS account will be created.

TIP

We recommend that you create your own user account and just grant minimal privileges to that account, possibly the DBA role, so that you don't have to use the SYS and SYSTEM login.

Progress Check Answers

1. Both leave your database in a consistent state. It depends on how long your transactions will take to complete or roll back. If all things are equal, and you think that it will take as long to commit the transactions that are already running, then you should use "shutdown transactional" because commits will be allowed to complete and no data will be lost.

2. No, logical schema objects also need to be watched to ensure they are in a valid state.

3. If the database attempts to write an archive log after the directory has become full, the database activity will be suspended until sufficient space is made available for the new file.

4. You may want to place the command in a script that is scheduled or run as a repetitive task.

5. When started in nomount mode, the parameter file is read, and memory structures and processes are started for the instance. The database is not yet associated with the instance. You would use this in circumstances when you need to re-create the control file.

Securing the database is valuable for protecting the company's data assets, so granting permissions and using appropriate privileges is part of that secure configuration. Oracle 12c provides new security features, a topic that is beyond the scope of this book but something you can investigate on your own. When it comes to users and permissions, new roles have been created in Oracle 12c to assist in the separation of duties and granting only the privileges that needed for that user. New roles include SYSBACKUP for use with RMAN backups and recovery, and SYSKM for key management.

Create a User

When you create a user, you can use either the create user syntax or the OEM Express Wizard, which is an easier approach. In order to create a user, you will need to decide the following:

- The default tablespace where segments created by this user will be placed unless a tablespace name is used in the DDL to override this.

- Whether to expire the password so that the user needs to change it the first time they log into Oracle.

- A temporary tablespace to store internal data used by Oracle while queries are running. Sort operations make use of the temporary tablespace if there is not enough room in the SGA to perform the sort operation.

- Whether to employ user quotas on tablespaces, which put a limit on the amount of space that a user's objects can take up in that tablespace.

- The authentication type, which allows you to specify whether you want Oracle to force users to specify a password when they log in, or you can trust the operating system to do this for you.

- The initial password that the user will log in with. The user must change this during the first logon if you chose to expire the password in advance of the user's first logon.

- Privileges to grant to the user. These can be direct privileges or roles. You'll see these discussed in the next section.

- A profile for the user, which can be employed to manage the user's session by limiting resources that sessions can use and that help implement corporate password policies. You will also see this in the next section.

- The account status of the user (*lock* or *unlock*) as it is created.

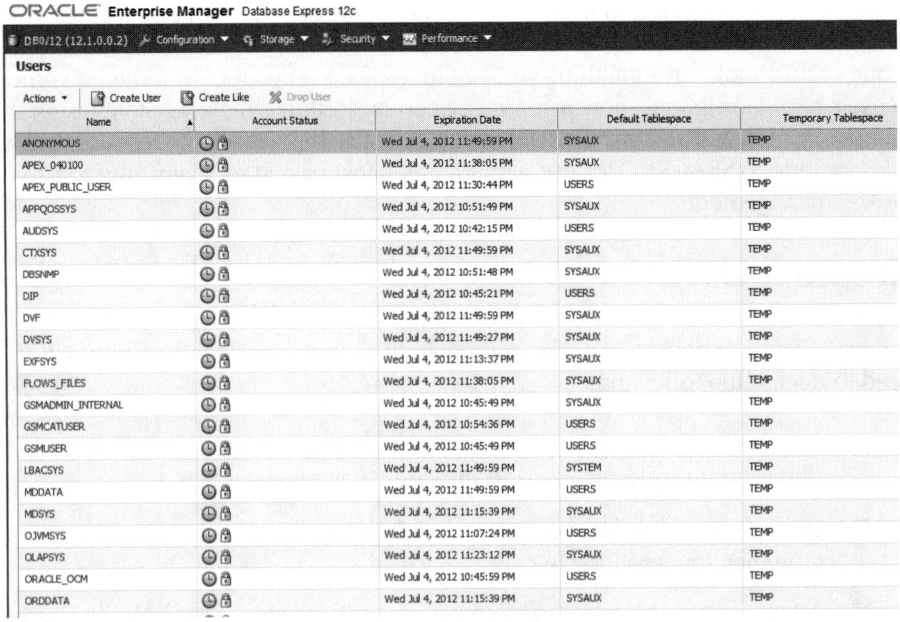

Name	Account Status	Expiration Date	Default Tablespace	Temporary Tablespace
ANONYMOUS		Wed Jul 4, 2012 11:49:59 PM	SYSAUX	TEMP
APEX_040100		Wed Jul 4, 2012 11:38:05 PM	SYSAUX	TEMP
APEX_PUBLIC_USER		Wed Jul 4, 2012 11:30:44 PM	USERS	TEMP
APPQOSSYS		Wed Jul 4, 2012 10:51:49 PM	SYSAUX	TEMP
AUDSYS		Wed Jul 4, 2012 10:42:15 PM	USERS	TEMP
CTXSYS		Wed Jul 4, 2012 11:49:59 PM	SYSAUX	TEMP
DBSNMP		Wed Jul 4, 2012 10:51:48 PM	SYSAUX	TEMP
DIP		Wed Jul 4, 2012 10:45:21 PM	USERS	TEMP
DVF		Wed Jul 4, 2012 11:49:59 PM	SYSAUX	TEMP
DVSYS		Wed Jul 4, 2012 11:49:27 PM	SYSAUX	TEMP
EXFSYS		Wed Jul 4, 2012 11:13:37 PM	SYSAUX	TEMP
FLOWS_FILES		Wed Jul 4, 2012 11:38:05 PM	SYSAUX	TEMP
GSMADMIN_INTERNAL		Wed Jul 4, 2012 10:45:49 PM	SYSAUX	TEMP
GSMCATUSER		Wed Jul 4, 2012 10:54:36 PM	USERS	TEMP
GSMUSER		Wed Jul 4, 2012 10:45:49 PM	USERS	TEMP
LBACSYS		Wed Jul 4, 2012 11:49:59 PM	SYSTEM	TEMP
MDDATA		Wed Jul 4, 2012 11:49:59 PM	USERS	TEMP
MDSYS		Wed Jul 4, 2012 11:15:39 PM	SYSAUX	TEMP
OJVMSYS		Wed Jul 4, 2012 11:07:24 PM	USERS	TEMP
OLAPSYS		Wed Jul 4, 2012 11:23:12 PM	SYSAUX	TEMP
ORACLE_OCM		Wed Jul 4, 2012 10:45:59 PM	USERS	TEMP
ORDDATA		Wed Jul 4, 2012 11:15:39 PM	SYSAUX	TEMP

FIGURE 5-16. *User Management view*

The OEM Express in Figure 5-16 shows the options available to you to create and edit a user. When creating a user, a wizard walks you through the process of setting the permissions and tablespaces, as discussed previously. You can see the SQL that will be generated by selecting the Show SQL button at the bottom of the panel. Another great option allows you to model a user and create another user like one that already exists. To do this, click the user that you want to model, select Object from the top of the panel, and then select the Create Like option.

The following is a sample CREATE USER statement:

```
SQLPLUS> CREATE USER "NEWUSER" PROFILE "DEFAULT" IDENTIFIED BY
"newpassword"
PASSWORD EXPIRE DEFAULT TABLESPACE "USERS" TEMPORARY TABLESPACE "TEMP"
QUOTA UNLIMITED ON TEMP QUOTA UNLIMITED ON USERS
ACCOUNT UNLOCK;
SQLPLUS> GRANT "CONNECT" TO "NEWUSER";
```

Edit Users

Once a user has been created, you will be asked at different times to alter it in order to change quotas, reset passwords, or unlock an account. This can be easily performed through OEM Express by selecting the user, choosing the option you want to change through the GUI, and then applying the change.

Editing users can also be performed using the ALTER USER statement, as shown next, where a user account is unlocked, the password is changed, and a tablespace quota is increased:

```
SQLPLUS> ALTER USER "username"  IDENTIFIED BY "newpwd" QUOTA UNLIMITED
ON TOOLS ACCOUNT UNLOCK;
```

You've now created a user and it's time to grant them some privileges. Let's see how you do this in the next section.

CRITICAL SKILL 5.10

Manage Privileges for Database Users

Creating a user in Oracle has accomplished the first part of user setup, which is authentication. You have a user ID and password and have authorized this user to use an Oracle database. Once the user logs in, however, they will not be able to do very much because they will not have privileges that allow them to access any objects. This leads you to the second step of setting up a user: authorization. In order to authorize a user to perform their tasks, you need to grant access.

Grant Authority

You now need to give permission to the user to do things in Oracle. Actions such as accessing a table, executing a procedure, or running a utility require you to "grant" the authority to that user. When you perform a grant, you can specify four things:

- The user that is being granted the authority.

- The object that is being granted. Examples of these are a table, procedure, or role.

- The type of access being granted, such as select, insert, update, or delete on a table, or execute on a procedure, function, or package.

- Whether this user has authority to then grant the same authority to other users. By default, they do not, but this can be added by using the With Grant option.

Here are two examples that grant a user "NEWUSER" access to a table and then to a package:

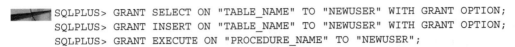

```
SQLPLUS> GRANT SELECT ON "TABLE_NAME" TO "NEWUSER" WITH GRANT OPTION;
SQLPLUS> GRANT INSERT ON "TABLE_NAME" TO "NEWUSER" WITH GRANT OPTION;
SQLPLUS> GRANT EXECUTE ON "PROCEDURE_NAME" TO "NEWUSER";
```

Types of Grants

Two types of grants can be given to a user: system privileges and object privileges.

- System privileges are predefined Oracle privileges granting authority to overall system objects: for example, using ANY object or the ability to execute types of statements rather than relating to an individual object or schema. CREATE TABLESPACE, CREATE SESSION, ALTER SYSTEM, and the ability to back up any table are just a few examples of some system-level privileges that can be granted to a user. There are over 150 different system privileges, which you can view by looking at the DBA_SYS_PRIVS view.

- Object privileges are a lower-level authority where a named object is granted to a user. So, the ability to perform an operation on a particular table, or to execute an individual function, package, or procedure is an object privilege, as opposed to the ability to execute any procedure or select any table, which is a system-level privilege.

Take Away Authority

What is given can be taken away. In order to take privileges away from a user, you use the REVOKE command; the syntax is very similar to the syntax you use when issuing a grant. Here are two examples of a REVOKE operation:

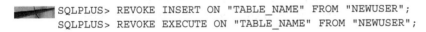

```
SQLPLUS> REVOKE INSERT ON "TABLE_NAME" FROM "NEWUSER";
SQLPLUS> REVOKE EXECUTE ON "TABLE_NAME" FROM "NEWUSER";
```

Roles

When you think of the number of privileges that need to be managed in situations where you have thousands of database objects as well as thousands of users, you quickly realize that it would be nice to organize the privileges into groups that can be easily managed. This is where roles come into play.

A "role" is used to group privileges into a predefined group that can be granted to users. So, rather than granting object and system privileges individually to every user in your system, you can grant them to a role, which in turn is granted to the user. With the amount of system privileges that can be granted as well as several thousand objects that could be in a schema, using roles makes it at least a little easier to manage grants and permissions.

Oracle-Defined Roles

Some special roles are created by Oracle through the install process or by running Oracle-supplied scripts. DBA, CONNECT, RESOURCE, IMP_FULL_DATABASE, and SELECT_CATALOG_ROLE are some examples of roles that are supplied by Oracle and should not be changed.

Create and Grant a Role

Roles are created using the CREATE ROLE statement in the same manner as creating users. You can also revoke privileges from roles and drop roles when they are no longer needed. Roles can also be granted to other roles. You can see an example of this next where the Oracle role CONNECT is granted to the newly created role TESTROLE, along with a system and object privilege:

```
SQLPLUS> CREATE ROLE "TESTROLE";
SQLPLUS> GRANT CONNECT TO "TESTROLE";
SQLPLUS> GRANT EXECUTE ANY PROCEDURE TO "TESTROLE";
SQLPLUS> GRANT SELECT ON "table_name" TO "TESTROLE";
```

The new role can then be granted to a user as shown here, where TESTROLE is granted to user TESTUSER:

```
SQLPLUS> GRANT "TESTROLE" to "TESTUSER";
```

The TESTROLE is then dropped because it is no longer required:

```
DROP ROLE "TESTROLE";
```

Now that you've created users and roles, you can fine-tune your management of these by implementing some user policies through *profiles,* which you will explore next.

Profiles

A profile can be used to implement the management for strong passwords as well as establish limits in resources for a user. When you created the user NEWUSER earlier, a password was supplied along with the DEFAULT profile. With Oracle 12c, using this DEFAULT profile, the passwords will be set to expire, requiring users to eventually change their passwords. The good news is that passwords by default are case-sensitive and there are no limits placed on any system resources. You can create new profiles to implement your corporate password policies in Oracle. For example, you can specify the number of days after which a user must change his or her password. You can also establish a rule where a password cannot be reused within a certain period of time and must contain a certain number of changes. A function can be used to ensure that a complex password is created by the user. For example, you may require that a password be more than eight characters long, use alpha-numeric, and special characters, and that it does not repeat a character more than twice. This can all be implemented in a function. An account can be locked after a specified number of login attempts and can remain locked for the number of days defined in the profile.

System limits for a user can also be implemented by a profile. These include limiting system resources such as those for CPU, connect, and idle time as well as the number of sessions employed by the user, limits on reads, and the SGA used. You should note, however, that the Database Resource Manager is the preferred way to limit resources and that you should use profiles to manage passwords.

The following is an example of the creation of a new profile that will lock an account after three failed login attempts and will keep the account locked indefinitely. The password needs to be changed every 60 days and the new password will be verified by your custom function COMPLEX_PASSWORD. The old password cannot be reused for 120 days:

```
SQLPLUS> CREATE PROFILE "NEWPOLICY"
FAILED_LOGIN_ATTEMPTS 3
PASSWORD_LOCK_TIME UNLIMITED
PASSWORD_LIFE_TIME 60
PASSWORD_REUSE_TIME 120
PASSWORD_VERIFY_FUNCTION COMPLEX_PASSWORD;
```

Now, let's add this profile to user NEWUSER:

```
SQLPLUS> ALTER USER NEWUSER PROFILE NEWPOLICY;
```

The profile can be used for system resources, too:

```
SQLPLUS> CREATE PROFILE LOW_RESOURCE_PROFILE   LIMIT

SESSIONS PER USER      UNLIMITED

CPU PER SESSION               2

CPU PER CALL               3000

CONNECT TIME                 45;

SQLPLUS> ALTER USER BACKUP_USER LOG_RESOURCE_PROFILE;
```

Tie It All Together

As you have seen in this chapter, there is a great deal that a DBA needs to be aware of to properly manage a database. The good news is that you will have tools such as SQL Developer, OEM Express, and OEM 12c Cloud Control to help you. Do your best to keep your environment as simple as you possibly can! You will be glad that you did as your overall database environment continues to grow.

Project 5-1 Create Essential Objects

This project will walk you through the creation of the essential storage and schema objects after a database has been created, which in this project will be called ora12c. You will create a new tablespace called NEW_TS and will then add a user NEW_USER who will be given a quota for this tablespace in order to be able to create objects in the tablespace. You will then create a role called NEW_ROLE and grant privileges to it. Afterward, you'll grant this role to the new user. A table and index will be created on this tablespace by the new user. Last, you will resize the UNDO tablespace to make it larger. You will see how to do this in OEM, and the generated SQL will also be shown to you so you can do this in SQL*Plus.

Step by Step

1. You have been asked to create a new user named NEW_USER who will need to create objects in a new tablespace called NEW_TS that should be sized at 5MB. Your first step is to create the tablespace. In OEM Express for ora12c, log in as user SYSTEM, choose Storage from the menu, and then choose Tablespaces and click Create. Enter the new tablespace name, and at the next arrow, enter the data file name and all properties, including the size. Make this a locally managed tablespace, 5MB in size, with uniform extents as autoallocate. If you choose the Show SQL button, you will see the generated SQL. It should look something like the following. You can either apply the change in OEM Express or you can copy and paste the generated SQL and run it in SQL*Plus:

```
CREATE TABLESPACE "NEW_TS"
DATAFILE '/u01/oradata/ora12c/NEW_TS1.ora' SIZE 5M
LOGGING DEFAULT NOCOMPRESS ONLINE
EXTENT MANAGEMENT LOCAL AUTOALLOCATE
SEGMENT SPACE MANAGEMENT AUTO;
```

(continued)

2. Now you will create NEW_USER. As with the preceding tablespace creation, you can use an existing user as a model. In OEM Express, go to Security and then to Users, highlight an existing user, choose Create Like to model an existing user, and enter a new username and password. Walk through the wizard to create the new user, and you should see the permissions and defaults there for the existing user that is being mimicked. The user should now have a password of new_password, which will be unlocked. Set the default tablespace to NEW_TS:

```
CREATE USER "NEW_USER"  PROFILE "DEFAULT" IDENTIFIED
BY "new_password" PASSWORD EXPIRE DEFAULT TABLESPACE "NEW_TS"
TEMPORARY TABLESPACE "TEMP" QUOTA UNLIMITED  ON "TEMP";
```

3. Create a role called NEW_ROLE. In OEM Express, go to Security and choose Role. Select Create and enter the role name:

```
CREATE ROLE "NEW_ROLE"  NOT IDENTIFIED;
```

4. Grant the CREATE TABLE system privilege, the OLAP_USER role, and the object privilege SELECT on table SQLPLUS_PRODUCT_PROFILE to NEW_ROLE. In OEM, go to Role and choose NEW_ROLE. Edit Privileges and Roles to grant roles, and switch tabs to objects to choose the objects listed for grants here. Click the Apply button to make the changes. The generated SQL will look like the three grants listed next:

```
GRANT CREATE TABLE TO "NEW_ROLE";
GRANT SELECT ON  "SYSTEM"."SQLPLUS_PRODUCT_PROFILE"
TO "NEW_ROLE";
GRANT "OLAP_USER" TO "NEW_ROLE";
```

5. Grant NEW_ROLE and connect to NEW_USER. Also, give NEW_USER an unlimited quota on NEW_TS to allow for objects to be created in the tablespace. In OEM Express, navigate to Users and choose NEW_USER. Once there, choose the Privileges and Role tab and select NEW_ROLE, and then select the down arrow. Click the Apply button to make the change:

```
GRANT "NEW_ROLE" TO "NEW_USER";
ALTER USER "NEW_USER" DEFAULT ROLE  ALL;
ALTER USER "NEW_USER"  QUOTA UNLIMITED ON "NEW_TS";
```

6. You will now log into the database as NEW_USER and can use SQL Developer with the NEW_USER account. Once in SQL Developer, you will create a table called NEW_TABLE with columns col01 as number(15) and col02 as varchar2(30). In SQL Developer, in the toolbar, select Object and

under that choose Create, and then choose Table. Make sure the table is created in NEW_TS. Follow the screens to add col01 and col02. You will then create a primary key called NEW_TABLE_PK using col01. Follow the screens and choose the options you would like. We recommend that you name any keys and constraints rather than relying on system defaults. Choose Finish and you have created a new table with a primary key!

```
CREATE TABLE "NEW_USER"."NEW_TABLE"
("COL01" NUMBER(15) NOT NULL,
 "COL02" VARCHAR2(30) NOT NULL,
CONSTRAINT "NEW_TABLE_PK" PRIMARY KEY("COL01"),
CONSTRAINT "NEW_TABLE_U1" UNIQUE("COL01"))
TABLESPACE "NEW_TS";
```

7. You now have one last task: resizing the UNDO tablespace to add 100MB to it. Log into OEM Express as the user System and navigate to Storage, and then choose Tablespaces, and choose the data file under the undo tablespace. Enter the new size and click Apply. It's as easy as that. The SQL to increase this from 50MB to 150MB is shown here:

```
ALTER DATABASE DATAFILE '/u01/oradata/ORA11g/UNDOTBS01.DBF'
RESIZE  150M;
```

Project Summary

This project has taken you through the basic steps of creating an environment for a new user, including using roles and granting privileges. You've seen how to manage users as well as space and have even created objects. Armed with these capabilities, you are now on your way to being a productive DBA. Congratulations!

☑ Chapter 5 Mastery Check

1. What is the benefit of a role?

2. Should a table that is in tens or hundreds of extents be reorganized?

3. What is the preferred method for collecting object statistics?

4. What is a segment?

5. What is an extent?

6. Name two reasons for implementing an index.

7. How can you place a database in maintenance mode without first shutting it down?

8. How can you limit the resources that a particular user can consume, and how does this work?

9. When managing UNDO segments, what are the things that you need to think about?

10. What is likely to happen if you turn on the AUTOEXTEND property for UNDO and temporary tablespaces with a MAXSIZE set to UNLIMITED?

11. What is special about the SYS user account, and how does it differ from SYSTEM?

12. What are temporary tablespaces used for?

13. What are the two aspects of security that are covered in Oracle's implementation?

14. Name and describe the types of privileges that can be granted to a user.

15. How would you implement your corporate password policy in Oracle?

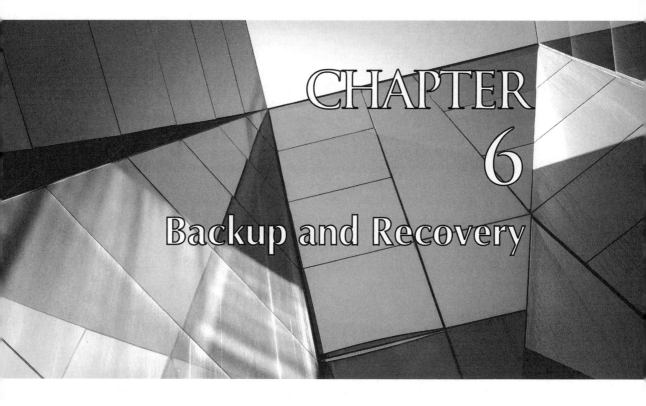

CHAPTER
6
Backup and Recovery

CRITICAL SKILLS

Whenever you take an exam, you normally carry an extra pen or pencil just in case. Why do you do that? Because the exams are very critical for you, and you don't want to take risk, and you want to ensure that after doing so much work in preparation, you don't end up failing the exam just because of that broken pen or pencil.

We know that this is an information age and information is the blood flowing across the veins of an organization and without it we cannot survive. What if someday you log in to your bank account online and see that yesterday's deposit is not shown? What if the customer service department of your bank tells you that it had a database crash and it doesn't have an extra copy of the data so that deposit of yours is lost? Can you imagine that sort of conversation ever happening? People can get upset about a missing tweet about their cat let alone a missing bank transaction. It is a fact of life that bad things happen. Databases crash, disks corrupt, data gets deleted, tsunamis drown data centers, and many other unexpected things occur. Information that is critical has to be backed up and should be placed at a different location from its original so that if something bad happens, information can be obtained or restored from the copy.

Information is stored in databases, and every database system provides some means of backup and recovery. Oracle's answer to that is RMAN, which stands for Recovery Manager. There are many options to back up and perform recovery in Oracle database, but RMAN is the one that is recommended and should be used.

In 1997, RMAN was released with Oracle 8.0, and now that 12*c* is here, RMAN is the most mature and easy way to back up and recover the Oracle databases. You don't have to install it. If you have installed the Oracle database, it is already there, ready to be used.

Understand RMAN

Recovery Manager (RMAN) is the tool for backup and recovery of Oracle databases. RMAN is client software that connects to a target database and performs backups or recovery on it. RMAN always stores data about itself and its operations in the database control files as well as a special schema in another database. The best practice is to use the schema for storing the metadata of RMAN, which is called a recovery catalog.

RMAN is a command line–based tool and a GUI option embedded in Oracle Enterprise Manager as well as grid/cloud control. It is the most efficient way to back up and recover any Oracle database. It is tightly integrated with the server, providing features such as block-level corruption detection during backup and restore activities. It has self-optimizing features, including multiplexing of backup channels and sophisticated compression of backupset pieces.

RMAN Metadata

By default, the RMAN metadata is stored in the database control files. RMAN also offers a recovery catalog feature, which is simply another database used in addition to the control files to store metadata backup. Many DBAs prefer using the catalog approach as it offers an opportunity to store metadata about a handful of Oracle databases and leads to easy consolidation of backup information. The catalog is optional and many adopters prefer using this approach for redundancy and manageability. Figure 6-1 illustrates the main components of an RMAN implementation, including

- **The target database**   The repository being backed up.

- **The control files**   A standard component of any Oracle database implementation.

- **The catalog database**   The optional secondary database storage location for RMAN metadata.

- **Media manager**   Provides an interface to third-party storage technology whose usage is not directly bundled with the RMAN technology.

- **Flash Recovery Area (FRA)**   One can store RMAN backupset pieces once this Oracle-managed area is defined in the system parameter file.

- **Traditional storage**   Disk backup location(s) where RMAN backupset pieces are written.

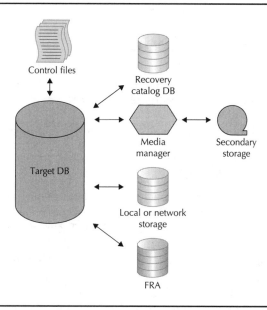

FIGURE 6-1.   *RMAN architecture*

See Reasons to Use RMAN

RMAN makes it very easy to implement the simple and advanced backup strategies. With RMAN, you can automate the backup tasks. RMAN can delete unneeded and obsolete backup files automatically. RMAN can compress the backups allowing you to save storage. RMAN provides you with comprehensive reporting regarding your backups. If you are using the Automatic Storage Management (ASM) feature, then RMAN is the best tool to handle the files. You can test your backups with RMAN. You can even check whether your backups are recoverable without actually recovering the backups. RMAN also checks for any block corruption while backing up, and the list of benefits goes on. In addition to what has already been discussed, RMAN is the obvious choice for backing up the 12*c* database for the following reasons:

- Automated management of backups once instructions have been registered with the RMAN engine as to how they should be retained, declared obsolete, and aged out of the repository

- Ability to store and run user-defined scripts in the recovery catalog database

- Comprehensive reporting capabilities

- Enterprise-wide management of and consistent implementation of corporate-wide standards through cloud control and Enterprise Manager

Understand Storage Media

The two main targets used for RMAN backups are disk and tape. These have been the location of all backups for decades. There are tradeoffs to using one or the other media. The primary advantages of each are as follows:

- Disk access is quicker than tape from a backup and recovery perspective.

- Disk space is not unlimited and that is the main reason why many organizations depend more on tape.

- Tape backups are much cheaper to store and the media more portable. While many state-of-the-art disks are portable, there's nothing like tape with its dense media and sophisticated robotic mechanisms. The media managers for backing up directly to tape with RMAN are numerous and also expensive. The media management layer (MML) software works with RMAN and the vendor's hardware to allow backups to sequential media devices such as tape drives. A media manager handles loading, unloading, and labeling of sequential media such as tapes. You must purchase and install media manager software to use RMAN with sequential media devices.

When RMAN is instructed to send backups to tape, it uses third-party software. The same is true when RMAN reads data back from the backed-up files for restoration purposes. RMAN can take advantage of a special storage location defined within the database called the *Flash Recovery Area* (FRA). FRA is a location on the disk where Oracle can be instructed to place files related to the backup and recovery. Out of the box, RMAN easily interacts with FRA, which can hold an assortment of players in the database technology layer. RMAN's integration with FRA is seamless for the following reasons:

- By default, it backs up all of the files that hold the information available in Oracle Database 12*c*—referred to as *full backups*

- It can perform incremental backups containing only portions of the database data files that contain changed information since the most recent successful full backup—referred to as *incremental backups*

- It backs up all the components of the database infrastructure, including

  - The control files that contain metadata about the database and are being continually updated while the database runs

  - The archived redo logs, which are painstakingly organized and stored by Oracle to be used for recovery

  - The system parameter file, which is read by Oracle as the database starts and defines a majority of its runtime environment

RMAN is automatically aware of FRA once set up by the Database Machine Administrator (DMA). It always knows what has been backed up, and what hasn't been.

NOTE
FRA is not mandatory for using RMAN for your backup and recovery, although seasoned DMAS tend to use it because of its turnkey integration with RMAN and other Oracle tools.

The following two items are set in the system parameter file to define the characteristics of FRA:

- DB_FILE_RECOVERY_DEST specifies the location of the Flash Recovery Area on the disk.

- DB_FILE_RECOVERY_DEST_SIZE specifies the size of the Flash Recovery Area.

Let's now have a look at the primary tasks that are performed using the power of RMAN.

CRITICAL SKILL 6.4

Examine RMAN Components

Once you get started with RMAN and become familiar with its three main concepts and the tasks it can perform, you are ready to move onto more advanced concepts. The three concepts are

- **Backup** Making another copy of data in an organized format on disk or tape

- **Restore** Getting that copy of data back into a location where the database can be partially or completely rebuilt

- **Recovery** Applying transaction information stored in the archived redo logs

Figure 6-2 illustrates the three components. Let's take a more detailed look at these components of RMAN.

Backup

You want to back up your database? Simply issue the following command:

```
backup database;
```

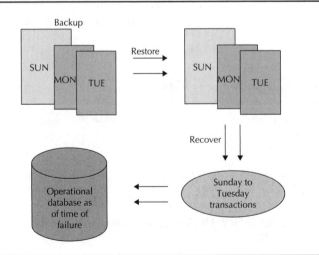

FIGURE 6-2.   *Relationship between backup/restore/recovery*

Yes, it's that easy. Likewise, you can back up your data files, tablespaces, control files, archived logs, and so on. Backing up a database means that RMAN copies your database into a file or set of files and stores the data in those files in its own proprietary format.

Restore

Now if something bad has happened and you want your backup back, first you need to ask RMAN to place the backup back to a location, and then RMAN reads the backup, extracts the actual data out of its proprietary format, and places it at that location. This is called *restore of a backup*.

Recovery

Now after restore of that backup, RMAN applies that restored data to the database so that missing or corrupted data is replaced with the good data from the backup you restored. This application of restored data to the database is called recovery.

CRITICAL SKILL 6.5
Invoke RMAN

In order to perform online backups of an Oracle database, it must be running with media recovery enabled. All of the databases one manages are usually running in this mode, also referred to as *archivelog mode.* The database must be open to perform these online backups. When a database is created using Oracle's database configuration assistant (DBCA), the recovery options dialog allows you to specify *Enable archiving,* which sets the stage for online backups.

RMAN is a binary that normally resides in a location under where the Oracle Database 12c software has been installed. It is started from the operating system command prompt, using the same command regardless of whether you are running on Linux or Windows:

```
# I'm on Linux so …
$ rman
:: I'm on Windows so …
C:\Oracle\Backup> rman
```

Then you come to the RMAN prompt, as shown in the next listing:

```
Recovery Manager: Release 12.1.0.1 - Production on Sat Sep 8 10:22:57
2015
Copyright (c) 1982, 2012, Oracle and/or its affiliates.  All rights
reserved.
RMAN>
```

Now at the RMAN prompt, you are just about ready to issue RMAN commands to back up, restore, or recover. Before you do that, you need to connect to the database where you want to perform those operations, and you do that by issuing the following command:

```
Recovery Manager: Release 12.1.0.1.0 - Production on Sat Sep 8 11:52:36
2017
Copyright (c) 1982, 2012, Oracle and/or its affiliates.  All rights
reserved.
RMAN> connect target

connected to target database: OBEG12C (DBID=2791683606)
RMAN>
```

TARGET specifies the database where you want to perform operations such as backup, restore, or recover. Notice that RMAN displays the DBID of the database connected to and that this piece of information is crucial to all database backups.

NOTE
A handful of operating system and database privileges must be in place to work with RMAN. They must be set up prior to performing any activity with RMAN.

You can also start RMAN while connecting with the database you want to back up, restore, or recover by mentioning the TARGET keyword:

```
$ rman target /
```

TARGET / specifies that you are connecting with highest privileges to the database you want to perform a backup, restore, or recover operation, or you might just want to get some information about the backups. As mentioned before, a plethora of errors could be thrown if the appropriate set of privileges has not been established before invoking RMAN. In order to perform some work, you have to connect to a target database. From day one, you will more than likely receive feedback from RMAN when issuing a command that it does not understand. All error stacks from RMAN contain the 00569 text, as shown next:

```
RMAN-00571: ===========================================================
RMAN-00569: =============== ERROR MESSAGE STACK FOLLOWS ===============
RMAN-00571: ===========================================================
RMAN-00558: error encountered while parsing input commands
RMAN-01009: syntax error: found "identifier": expecting one of:
"advise, allocate, alter, backup,@, catalog, change, configure,
```

```
connect, convert,
...
...
RMAN-01008: the bad identifier was: liid
RMAN-01007: at line 1 column 1 file: standard input
```

Ask the Expert

Q: Is RMAN capable of compressing RMAN backupset pieces as they are written?

A: Native compression arrived with Oracle Database 10*g*. As one codes the backup command, compression is triggered by including *as compressed backupset*.

Q: Are there any stipulations on the running mode of a database to be backed up using RMAN while open?

A: The database must have media recovery enabled; this is often referred to as ARCHIVELOG mode.

Q: Can RMAN be used to build a database if the backup was written on one operating system (for example, Windows) and the new repository on another (for example, Linux)?

A: Under certain circumstances—yes. Those circumstances are well documented in the Oracle documentation.

Q: Some earlier versions of RMAN had more than two levels of backups—why the change such that one can use only levels 0 and 1?

A: The reasons are more than likely numerous, but over the years, it became obvious that most organizations were using only 0 and 1.

Q: Can a database be backed up if it does not have media recovery enabled?

A: Yes, but it cannot be open when being backed up. Not being able to have a database open when RMAN backs it up is one of many shortcomings of not enabling media recovery.

Learn RMAN Commands

RMAN is a tool waiting for your instructions. The majority of RMAN commands have parameters and they end with a semicolon. There are some commands that don't require a semicolon, such as CONNECT. If you enter a command that is supposed to be terminated by a semicolon but leave it out, RMAN will not hesitate to let you know that you have done something wrong. You may interactively type the RMAN commands at the prompt, as in the following:

```
RMAN> backup database plus archivelog;
```

The preceding command can also be written in multiple lines. Note that the line numbers are placed there by RMAN and cannot be typed:

```
RMAN> backup database
2> plus
3> archivelog
4> ;
```

You may give those instructions or commands to RMAN either by typing interactively at its prompt or by putting commands in a file and running them all. For example, suppose your daily task is to back up the database and archivelogs, and you interactively type the following two commands daily at the RMAN prompt:

```
RMAN> backup database;
RMAN> backup archivelog all;
```

Why not just write these commands in a file and then run that file from the RMAN prompt? When you do that, you call that file a command file, and you run a command file like the following from an operating system command prompt:

```
$ rman target / @mycommandfile
```

Or you can run that command file from an RMAN prompt:

```
RMAN> @mycommandfile
```

After the command finishes, RMAN doesn't exit from the prompt; you may exit from the RMAN prompt by issuing the following:

```
RMAN> exit
```

The next listing shows our first database backup performed with RMAN. Later in this chapter, we present and discuss backup and recovery commands in more detail.

```
oracle@localhost.localdomain-->(obeg12c)
/home/oracle> rman
Recovery Manager: Release 12.1.0.1.0 - Production on Sat Sep 8 12:16:18
2016
Copyright (c) 1982, 2012, Oracle and/or its affiliates.  All rights
reserved.

RMAN> connect target /
connected to target database: OBEG12C (DBID=2791683606)

RMAN> backup database;

Starting backup at 08-SEP-12
using target database control file instead of recovery catalog
allocated channel: ORA_DISK_1
channel ORA_DISK_1: SID=35 device type=DISK
channel ORA_DISK_1: starting full datafile backup set
channel ORA_DISK_1: specifying datafile(s) in backup set
input datafile file number=00001
name=/home/oracle/app/oracle/oradata/obeg12c/system01.dbf
input datafile file number=00002
name=/home/oracle/app/oracle/oradata/obeg12c/sysaux01.dbf
input datafile file number=00003
name=/home/oracle/app/oracle/oradata/obeg12c/undotbs01.dbf
input datafile file number=00004
name=/home/oracle/app/oracle/oradata/obeg12c/users01.dbf
channel ORA_DISK_1: starting piece 1 at 08-SEP-12
channel ORA_DISK_1: finished piece 1 at 08-SEP-12
piece
handle=/home/oracle/app/oracle/flash_recovery_area/OBEG12C/backupset/20
12_09_08/o1_mf_nnndf_TAG20120908T121628_84pvtwqp_.bkp
tag=TAG20120908T121628 comment=NONE
channel ORA_DISK_1: backup set complete, elapsed time: 00:00:15
channel ORA_DISK_1: starting full datafile backup set
channel ORA_DISK_1: specifying datafile(s) in backup set
including current control file in backup set
including current SPFILE in backup set
channel ORA_DISK_1: starting piece 1 at 08-SEP-12
channel ORA_DISK_1: finished piece 1 at 08-SEP-12
piece
handle=/home/oracle/app/oracle/flash_recovery_area/OBEG12C/backupset/20
12_09_08/o1_mf_ncsnf_TAG20120908T121628_84pvvdwf_.bkp
tag=TAG20120908T121628 comment=NONE
channel ORA_DISK_1: backup set complete, elapsed time: 00:00:01
Finished backup at 08-SEP-12
```

```
RMAN> backup archivelog all;

Starting backup at 08-SEP-12
current log archived
using channel ORA_DISK_1
channel ORA_DISK_1: starting archived log backup set
channel ORA_DISK_1: specifying archived log(s) in backup set
input archived log thread=1 sequence=2 RECID=1 STAMP=793455450
channel ORA_DISK_1: starting piece 1 at 08-SEP-12
channel ORA_DISK_1: finished piece 1 at 08-SEP-12
piece
handle=/home/oracle/app/oracle/flash_recovery_area/OBEG12C/backupset/20
12_09_08/o1_mf_annnn_TAG20120908T121730_84pvwtcr_.bkp
tag=TAG20120908T121730 comment=NONE
channel ORA_DISK_1: backup set complete, elapsed time: 00:00:01
Finished backup at 08-SEP-12
RMAN>
```

Notice where RMAN placed the backupset pieces, as shown in the previous listing—flash_recovery_area/OBEG12C/backupset/2016_09_08. This is one of many advantages of using FRA for backups. See how Oracle organizes by the date the backup was taken; it's a nice feature. Remember Chapter 1's claim about how a database is self-describing. What could be more true?

On an RMAN prompt, you can also group many RMAN commands and run them together. You can group multiple commands by putting them in a block called a RUN block. For example:

```
run
{
backup database;
backup archivelog all;
}
```

RMAN runs all the commands in the RUN block in sequence, and if one command fails, remaining commands are not executed. As you descend further into RMAN land, you will encounter situations that mandate using a RUN block as well as others, which for some reason must be outside a RUN block. One secret to learning new software can be summed up by the familiar adage: *Don't bite off more than you can chew.* An RMAN-centric takeoff to that is: *Do not forget to restore everything you have backed up on a regular basis.*

In previous releases of RMAN, there were many situations where one needed to leave RMAN and enter some commands in sqlplus. In Oracle Database 12*c*, you can now issue many useful SQL commands at the RMAN prompt.

Progress Check

1. What item of punctuation terminates close to all RMAN commands?

2. After invoking RMAN and viewing the prompt displayed, what must one do before being able to back up the database?

3. Where does RMAN always store information about the backups it has completed?

4. What is the Flash Recovery Area (FRA) and what does RMAN use it for?

5. What item of punctuation is used in RMAN to invoke a command file or script?

6. When RMAN encounters an error in a series of commands in a RUN block, what does it do?

CRITICAL SKILL 6.7

Review RMAN Channels

Although RMAN is tightly integrated with the Oracle database, it's still a separate executable, and you run it from the operating system command prompt. Remember that RMAN doesn't reside in the database; rather, it's a binary outside of Oracle database, although it stores its metadata (data about data) in the database. RMAN's residency outside of a database enables you to back up, restore, or recover the database, even when it's not open.

Progress Check Answers

1. The semicolon terminates all RMAN commands.

2. One must connect to the database to be backed up, commonly referred to as the TARGET database.

3. RMAN always stores backup information in the database control file(s) and the recovery catalog if instructed.

4. The Flash Recovery Area is a location reserved for RMAN backups and information required to assist maintenance of database consistency. It is also used to flashback a database to a previous point in time.

5. A script is invoked at the RMAN prompt using the @ sign.

6. When encountering an error, RMAN throws a number of errors beginning with the text RMAN; the error stack always includes an RMAN-00569 error message.

Because RMAN resides outside, it needs a pathway to communicate with the database in order to perform backups, restores, and recoveries. This pathway is called a *channel*. A channel enables RMAN to facilitate data transfer between database and media. You can have single or multiple channels from RMAN, and each channel corresponds to a server process at the database server, which performs the backup, restore, or recovery processes from disk or tape to your database.

By default, RMAN already has a preconfigured channel to disk, but you may also configure the channel manually to disk or tape device. You can set automatic channel allocation by configuring the channel in RMAN so that you don't have to specify the channel every time you run the RMAN commands at the RMAN prompt, as follows:

```
RMAN> configure channel device type disk format '/u01/%u';
```

Now, if you back up your database from RMAN, the backup will go to the location /u01 and %u will ensure that your backup files have unique names. There are many RMAN format mask parameters that can be specified when a channel is allocated. The most common and therefore important are found in Table 6-1.

If you want to manually allocate your channel, you can do so in the RUN blocks as follows:

```
run
{
 allocate channel mychannel device type disk format '/u01/%u';
 backup database plus archivelog;
}
```

Format String	Meaning
%u	Ensures uniqueness among backupset piece names; if not specified, once RMAN attempts to use a name of an existing piece, it aborts. Believe us when we say that, as strange as it seems, this will happen.
%d	The uppercase name of the database being backed up appears at the start of the filename for each backupset piece.
%t	The date the backup pieces were written in the format YYYYMMDD.
%I	Includes the DBID of the database being backed up in each backupset piece name.

TABLE 6-1. *The Four Most Important RMAN Piece Format Masks*

CRITICAL SKILL 6.8

Examine RMAN Configuration

RMAN is very flexible and you can configure it according to your own requirements. The tool enables you to make permanent settings for your backup and recovery operations. For example, you can set a default channel and default formats of the backup files, and you can specify how long a backup should be retained and whether a control file should be backed up automatically with other backup jobs.

Ask the Expert

Q: What standard keywords are used when allocating a tape channel?

A: With disk, we discussed specifying *type disk* as the channel allocation is defined, and with tape, one uses TYPE 'SBT_TAPE' alongside a handful of other mandatory tape environment specifications.

Q: How free form are the rules for entering commands at the RMAN prompt?

A: RMAN is very flexible with command formatting as long as the syntax of each command is correct and the appropriate punctuation is included where required.

Q: Do syntactically incorrect commands passed to RMAN do any harm to the database?

A: Because RMAN parses the command text received before performing any activity, damage to the database is not possible. With that said, passing (mistakenly) a SHUTDOWN command at the RMAN prompt would pass the syntax checking and close an operational database.

Q: Has Oracle introduced any further security enhancements to RMAN to further ensure that unauthorized access to the database is restricted?

A: Oracle Database 12*c* introduces a new database role called SYSBACKUP. This role is not as powerful as the familiar SYSDBA and can be used to permit the running of RMAN backups without giving out the omnipotent SYSDBA role.

You can obtain a partial set of configurable RMAN settings, as shown in the next listing:

```
RMAN> show all;
RMAN configuration parameters for database with db_unique_name OBEG12C
are:
CONFIGURE RETENTION POLICY TO REDUNDANCY 1; # default
CONFIGURE BACKUP OPTIMIZATION OFF; # default
CONFIGURE DEFAULT DEVICE TYPE TO DISK; # default
CONFIGURE CONTROLFILE AUTOBACKUP OFF; # default
CONFIGURE CONTROLFILE AUTOBACKUP FORMAT FOR DEVICE TYPE DISK TO '%F'; #
default
CONFIGURE DEVICE TYPE DISK PARALLELISM 1 BACKUP TYPE TO BACKUPSET; #
default
CONFIGURE DATAFILE BACKUP COPIES FOR DEVICE TYPE DISK TO 1; # default
CONFIGURE ARCHIVELOG BACKUP COPIES FOR DEVICE TYPE DISK TO 1; # default
CONFIGURE MAXSETSIZE TO UNLIMITED; # default
CONFIGURE ENCRYPTION FOR DATABASE OFF; # default
CONFIGURE ENCRYPTION ALGORITHM 'AES128'; # default
CONFIGURE COMPRESSION ALGORITHM 'BASIC' AS OF RELEASE 'DEFAULT'
OPTIMIZE FOR LOAD TRUE ; # default
CONFIGURE ARCHIVELOG DELETION POLICY TO NONE; # default
CONFIGURE SNAPSHOT CONTROLFILE NAME TO
'/home/oracle/app/oracle/product/12.1.0/dbhome_1/dbs/snapcf_obeg12c.f';
# default
```

A configurable item can be changed with the appropriate command as shown next; after the change is a snippet from the output of SHOW ALL, indicating what has just changed:

```
RMAN> CONFIGURE CONTROLFILE AUTOBACKUP ON;
new RMAN configuration parameters:
CONFIGURE CONTROLFILE AUTOBACKUP ON;
new RMAN configuration parameters are successfully stored
...
...
CONFIGURE CONTROLFILE AUTOBACKUP ON;
```

The RMAN SHOW command is used to view the details of any configuration item, as illustrated in the next few examples:

```
RMAN> show retention policy;

RMAN configuration parameters for database with db_unique name OBEG12C
are:
CONFIGURE RETENTION POLICY to RECOVERY WINDOW OF 14 DAYS;

RMAN> show device type;
```

```
RMAN configuration parameters for database with db_unique name OBEG12C
are:
CONFIGURE DEVICE TYPE DISK PARALLELISM 1 BACKUP TYPE TO BACKUPSET; #
default

RMAN> show maxsetsize;
RMAN configuration parameters for database with db_unique name OBEG12C
are:
CONFIGURE MAXSETSIZE TO UNLIMITED; # default
```

CRITICAL SKILL 6.9

Explore Backup Commands

In an Oracle database, RMAN can take the backup of the following:

- Database
- Tablespace
- Datafile
- Server parameter file
- Archived redo log
- Control file

RMAN backs up these items in one or two backupsets; you can configure how many files a backupset can contain.

Database

After invoking RMAN from the operating system prompt, take a full database backup by issuing the following command at the RMAN prompt:

```
RMAN> backup database;
```

The preceding command will back up all the datafiles, control files, and server parameter files in your database. Because no channel is specified, RMAN will use a default channel to back up the database.

Tablespace

Once in RMAN, the heart of this activity resembles the following:

```
RMAN> backup tablespace system;
```

You can take a backup of multiple tablespaces at the same time. For example, the following command takes a backup of three tablespaces: SYSTEM, USERS, and TBS1.

```
RMAN> backup tablespace system, users, tbs1;
```

Datafile

If you know the unique file ID for one or more database files, they can be backed up as follows:

```
RMAN> backup datafile 2,3,4;
```

The preceding command backs up data files numbered from 2 to 4. You can get the number of data files from the FILE_ID column of the DBA_DATA_FILES view from the database.

Control File

Manually, you initiate a control file backup by issuing the following command:

```
RMAN> backup current controlfile;
```

If you manually back up the control file and you have also configured autobackup of the control file, RMAN will make two copies of your control file; you can never have too many backups of your control file.

Server Parameter File

With every backup, the server parameter file is automatically backed up, and you can also manually back it up by issuing the following command at the RMAN prompt:

```
RMAN> backup spfile;
```

Archived Redo Logs

You can back up the archived redo logs by issuing the following command at the RMAN prompt:

```
RMAN> backup archivelog all;
```

If you want to delete archived logs after backing them up to make more space on the disk, you may issue the following command:

```
RMAN> backup archivelog all delete all input;
```

This very brief discussion of some backup commands will hopefully whet your appetite for this extremely robust, friendly, and easy-to-use tool called RMAN.

CRITICAL SKILL 6.10

Conduct Incremental Backups

The data in the databases always grows, and as the backup is a copy of the data, it grows too. As the size of the backup grows, it takes more space on the disk and it takes more time to back up. When the database becomes large, you still want to back it up faster to avoid any risk of losing any data.

In your database, the majority of your data doesn't change daily. Rather, only some of it changes daily or maybe weekly, and some new data comes in with the time. So you likely have a huge amount of data that doesn't change, and so there is no need to back it up daily. What you can do here is start by taking a full backup of the database one day, and then take the backup of only that data that has changed or is new, and do that daily. This is called an incremental approach to backup. The first backup is called a *level 0* backup and then the subsequent backups are called *level 1* backups. A level 0 backup of a database can be taken with the following command:

```
RMAN> backup incremental level = 0 database;
```

A level 1 backup of the database can be taken with the following command:

```
RMAN> backup incremental level = 1 database;
```

One of the most common approaches to writing RMAN backups over a work week is shown in Figure 6-3 where the size of each rectangle reflects the amount of data written to each backup.

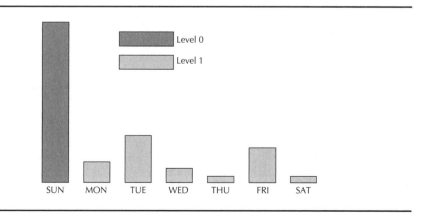

FIGURE 6-3. *A week's worth of RMAN backup levels*

This is where the power of incremental backups comes into play because

- Consistent backups are written every day, with Monday to Saturday's backups taking less time to complete and occupying less precious storage.

- A recovery activity on a Tuesday can be satisfied by overwriting database blocks that were backed up on the previous Sunday and days up to and including when the disaster occurred. In other words Sunday + Monday + Tuesday = required recovery.

CRITICAL SKILL 6.11

List Backups

You can view the information about backups and copies in RMAN with the help of the LIST command. For example, in order to view the information about the backup of a database, use the following:

```
RMAN> list backup of database;
```

To view information about the backups, use this:

```
RMAN> list backup;
```

There is an inherent "nuisance" with the way RMAN displays dates in the LIST BACKUP command with all its options. The default display format with Oracle Database 12*c* is DD-MON-YY. Did we not learn anything going from the twentieth to the twenty-first century? Picture the following snippet from a LIST BACKUP command:

```
List of Backups
===============
Key     TY LV S Device Type Completion Time  Tag
------- -- -- - ----------- ---------------- ---
1       B  F  A DISK        08-SEP-12        TAG20120908T121628
2       B  F  A DISK        08-SEP-12        TAG20120908T121628
3       B  A  A DISK        08-SEP-12        TAG20120908T121730
4       B  A  A DISK        08-SEP-12        TAG20120908T131229
5       B  F  A DISK        08-SEP-12        TAG20120908T131230
6       B  A  A DISK        08-SEP-12        TAG20120908T155502
7       B  F  A DISK        08-SEP-12        TAG20120908T155503
8       B  A  A DISK        08-SEP-12        TAG20120908T155528
9       B  F  A DISK        08-SEP-12        TAG20120908T155530
```

See the problem here? The completion time for each backupset piece is expressed as a date with no timestamp. In Windows, this can be fixed by setting an environment variable, as shown here:

```
# export nls_date_format='dd-mon-yyyy hh24:mi:ss'
C:\Oracle> set nls_date_format='dd-mon-yyyy hh24:mi:ss'
```

Once this is done, the completion times in the preceding listing would change to something more useful, as in the following:

```
Completion Time
-------------------
08-SEP-2012 12:16:42
08-SEP-2012 12:16:44
08-SEP-2012 12:17:30
08-SEP-2012 13:12:29
08-SEP-2012 13:12:30
08-SEP-2012 15:55:02
08-SEP-2012 15:55:22
08-SEP-2012 15:55:29
08-SEP-2012 15:55:30
```

This highlights one of the many outstanding features of working with RMAN and many other tools that are delivered with Oracle Database 12c—they are highly configurable when the information they display by default is not usable.

CRITICAL SKILL 6.12

See RMAN Metadata

When you take backup or make any configuration setting or perform an operation with RMAN, RMAN needs to store that information somewhere for future use—this is called *RMAN metadata*. This metadata gets stored either in the control file or in a database schema.

When the metadata of RMAN is stored in a schema in a database, it is called a *recovery catalog*. The recovery catalog commonly resides in a separate, dedicated database. You can have one recovery catalog for many target databases; that way, you can have a centralized repository containing backup and recovery information for your all databases. It makes the reporting of backup information very easy, manageable, and fast.

The recovery catalog's metadata about the RMAN operation includes data about

- Backupsets
- Image copies

- Archived redo

- Structure of database-like tablespaces and their corresponding data files

- Details of permanent configuration settings of RMAN

If you want to create a recovery catalog, once the preliminary requirements for setting up the infrastructure to support it have been met, use the following command at the RMAN prompt:

```
RMAN> create catalog;
```

You can specify the tablespace name for the catalog in the CREATE CATALOG command, as shown here:

```
RMAN> create catalog tablespace rc_tbs;
```

If you want to store the metadata of your RMAN operations on your target database in the recovery catalog, first you need to register the target database. If you don't do that, you cannot use the recovery catalog. Registering a database in a recovery catalog is simple, as shown next.

1. Ensure the database that will house the catalog exists and is running.

2. Ensure you can connect to the recovery catalog database using the Oracle Net standard convention (for example, *@rcat*).

3. A recovery catalog has been created.

4. Connect to the target database and the recovery catalog, as shown in the next listing, and register the database.

   ```
   oracle@localhost.localdomain-->(obeg12c)
   /home/oracle> rman target / catalog rman/rman@rcat
   Recovery Manager: Release 12.1.0.1.0 - Production on Sat Feb 30
   16:25:47 2016
   Copyright (c) 1982, 2009, Oracle and/or its affiliates.  All
   rights reserved.

   connected to target database: OBEG12C (DBID=2791683606)
   connected to recovery catalog database

   RMAN> register database;
   database registered in recovery catalog
   starting full resync of recovery catalog
   full resync complete
   ```

In the preceding command, you are connecting to a target database where you need to perform the RMAN operations such as backup. In addition, you are telling RMAN to use recovery catalog in an existing *RMAN* schema whose password is also *RMAN*. The last piece in the connection scheme uses the network handle RCAT, which has been defined to connect remotely to the database where the catalog resides. We recommend that you use a recovery catalog in the production databases.

Progress Check

1. When a database schema is set up to house RMAN metadata, what must be created before that schema can be used to store details about backup and recovery activity?

2. What environment variable can be set in the operating system to instruct RMAN to display a timestamp in its date fields shown as part of its backup listings?

3. What new secure role was created with Oracle Database 12*c* related to backups and why?

4. What is the difference between a full and an incremental backup?

5. What is the syntax used in RMAN to back up the database control files?

6. What RMAN command is used to display existing configuration information?

Progress Check Answers

1. The recovery catalog must be created using the CREATE CATALOG command.

2. NLS_DATE_FORMAT is used to instruct RMAN to display dates in a format that differs from Oracle's default.

3. The SYSBACKUP role was created to further increase security opportunities when working with RMAN.

4. A full backup writes all database information to a backupset, whereas an incremental backup only copies new or changed information.

5. The code BACKUP CURRENT CONTROLFILE is used in RMAN to back up a control file.

6. The SHOW ALL command will display existing configuration settings in RMAN.

CRITICAL SKILL **6.13**

Use RMAN Restore

As we noted earlier, when you create backups with RMAN, they get created in one or more backupsets; these backupsets are in proprietary format. In order to use them again for recovery, first you need to extract them from this proprietary format. This process is called *restore*.

You use the RESTORE command of RMAN to restore the backup. For example, in order to restore the backup of a database, use the following command at the RMAN prompt:

```
RMAN> restore database;
```

One or more tablespaces can be restored using the following commands:

```
RMAN> sql 'alter tablespace sysaux offline';

sql statement: alter tablespace sysaux offline
starting full resync of recovery catalog
full resync complete

RMAN> restore tablespace sysaux;
Starting restore at 08-SEP-2012 16:31:39
using channel ORA_DISK_1

channel ORA_DISK_1: starting datafile backup set restore
channel ORA_DISK_1: specifying datafile(s) to restore from backup set
channel ORA_DISK_1: restoring datafile 00002 to
/home/oracle/app/oracle/oradata/obeg12c/sysaux01.dbf
channel ORA_DISK_1: reading from backup piece
/home/oracle/app/oracle/flash_recovery_area/OBEG12C/backupset/2012_09_0
8/o1_mf_nnndf_TAG20120908T163016_84qbprpx_.bkp
channel ORA_DISK_1: piece
handle=/home/oracle/app/oracle/flash_recovery_area/OBEG12C/backupset/20
12_09_08/o1_mf_nnndf_TAG20120908T163016_84qbprpx_.bkp
tag=TAG20120908T163016
channel ORA_DISK_1: restored backup piece 1channel ORA_DISK_1: restore
complete, elapsed time: 00:00:07
Finished restore at 08-SEP-2012 16:31:47

RMAN> recover datafile 2;
Starting recover at 08-SEP-2012 16:34:45
using channel ORA_DISK_1starting media recovery
media recovery complete, elapsed time: 00:00:00
Finished recover at 08-SEP-2012 16:34:45
```

```
RMAN> sql 'alter tablespace sysaux online';
sql statement: alter tablespace sysaux online
starting full resync of recovery catalog
full resync complete
RMAN>
```

CRITICAL SKILL 6.14

Understand RMAN Recover

The *R* in RMAN stands for recovery, and it is said that recovery is one of the most important skill sets a DBA can have, mandatory or succeeding in the role as a DBA or DMA. RMAN makes it very easy to recover the files once they've been restored. For recovery, RMAN applies the data from the restored backup to the database where it is missing or corrupted. You can recover a database, or tablespace, or a data file. In order to recover a database, for example, use the following command at the RMAN prompt:

`RMAN> recover database;`

CRITICAL SKILL 6.15

Learn About Backup Retention

Backups are very important, but they have a shelf life, too. You cannot just keep taking backups and retain all of them forever. You need to decide how long you would like to retain your backups before you can safely remove them in order to make space for more backups. Storage on a disk or tape device is always limited, and you have to come up with some retention policy.

RMAN helps you implement the retention policy for the backups in a very easy, automatic, and efficient way. You can either specify your retention policy in terms of time, or you can define it in terms of number of backup copies. In other words, you can say that you want to retain 30 days of backup, or you can decide that you want to retain 2 copies of backup. In this case, the backups older than 30 days or the oldest third copy of the backup and above will be termed obsolete. You can use the following command to specify the backup retention policy in RMAN in terms of time:

`RMAN> configure retention policy to recovery window of 30 days;`

Now after making the preceding persistent configuration, any backups older than 30 days will be considered obsolete. You can use the following command to specify the backup retention policy in RMAN in terms of number of copies:

`RMAN> configure retention policy to redundancy 2;`

Now after making the preceding persistent configuration, the oldest third copy of the backup will be considered obsolete. You can also opt to have no retention policy at all in your RMAN configuration by using the following command:

```
RMAN> configure retention policy to none;
```

After setting the retention policy, you can run the following command to delete the backups that are obsolete:

```
RMAN> delete obsolete;
```

You can also use the following command to see which backups are obsolete:

```
RMAN> report obsolete;
```

Another term used in RMAN is *expired backups*. When RMAN is unable to find any backed-up file, it flags that file as *expired* in its repository. It is important to differentiate between expired and obsolete backups:

- Expired backups are those that are not found by RMAN.

- Obsolete backups are those that are no longer required by RMAN for recovery.

CRITICAL SKILL 6.16

Check Syntax

If you are confused about the syntax of the RMAN commands and want to verify it, you can leverage RMAN to assist. One easy way is to put your commands in a text file and then ask RMAN to check the file using the following command with the RMAN utility:

```
$ rman CHECKSYNTAX @/u01/mycommandfile.cmd
```

CRITICAL SKILL 6.17

Recover a Table

If you just want to recover a table or partition of a table from the backup, you can do it easily with RMAN. In order to recover a table, your database must be open and have media recovery enabled. You need to have the backup of the table accessible to the restore and recovery activities.

If the table you are recovering already exists in the database, RMAN doesn't re-create it; it just adds the rows from the backup to the existing table. Following is an example where the table BAR, owned by the user FOO, is recovered to some previous point in time. After the recovery, the table is renamed NEW_BAR.

```
RMAN> recover table foo.bar
    2>until time 'to_char('10/12/2016 11:33:00',
    3> 'mm/dd/yyyy hh24:mi:ss')'
    4> auxiliary destination '/u01/tabrecover'
    5> remap table foo.bar:new_bar;
```

CRITICAL SKILL 6.18

Pull It All Together

That's been quite a ride into the wide and wonderful world of RMAN. Before moving on to the next event in your journey into Oracle Database 12c, let's have a look at a few scripts that will take advantage of what you have read so far.

Backup Script

The following script groups together RMAN commands in a RUN block to take a full backup of a database and its archivelogs. It assumes that you have configured the control file autobackup on in the RMAN configuration settings, and the backup retention policy is 14 days. The numbers beside each line in this case were put there by RMAN:

```
RMAN> run
    2> {
    3>    allocate channel d1 type disk format
    4>            '/u01/RMAN_full_%U.bkp';
    5>    backup as compressed backupset database
    6>           plus archivelog;
    7>    crosscheck all;
    8>    delete noprompt obsolete;
    9>    release channel d1;
   10> }
```

Table 6-2 uses the line numbers from the listing to discuss this script.

Line	Notes
1	Start of the RUN block.
2	The punctuation that defines the start of the RUN block.
3	Allocates a channel, a pathway to the disk location for the backup.
4	Describes the location and format to be used as backupset pieces are written.
5–6	A full backup of the database is created, and it will include the archivelogs, too. The COMPRESSED keyword is used here, which means that RMAN will automatically compress the backup, which will lessen the size of the backup. During recovery, RMAN doesn't need to uncompress it in order to apply it to the database.
7	The CROSSCHECK command is used to check whether the backups mentioned in the repository of RMAN still exist where expected. Those not found are marked as expired.
8	After running CROSSCHECK, the script tells RMAN to delete the backups, which are out of the retention policy and are not required for recovery now.
9	Then the channel at the end of the script is released.
10	The end of RUN block punctuation.

TABLE 6-2.   *RMAN Backup Script Discussion Points*

Restore and Recovery Script

The following is a simple script that can be used to restore then recover the database files using RMAN:

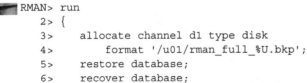

```
RMAN> run
  2> {
  3>    allocate channel d1 type disk
  4>        format '/u01/rman_full_%U.bkp';
  5>    restore database;
  6>    recover database;
  7>    release channel d1;
  8> }
```

Table 6-3 discusses this script, again using the line numbers from the listing.

Line	Notes
1	Start of the RUN block.
2	The punctuation that defines the start of the RUN block.
3	Allocates a channel, a pathway to the disk for the ensuing restore and recovery activities.
4	Describes the location and format of the backupset pieces that will be read to facilitate the exercise.
5	Restores the database, and after this command all the data files and tablespaces will be created.
6	Now data will be applied from the backupset to the database.
7	Explicitly releases the channel at the end of the script.
8	Punctuation to terminate the RUN block.

TABLE 6-3. *RMAN Restore/Recovery Script Discussion Points*

☑ Chapter 6 Mastery Check

1. What are the three tasks performed by RMAN?

2. What format command does one use to ensure all the backupset pieces receive a unique name?

3. Where does RMAN always store its metadata?

4. What is the difference between expired and obsolete backups?

5. Why is it a good idea to use scripts when continually using RMAN over a wide assortment of corporate databases?

6. What are the two main advantages of using a recovery catalog with RMAN?

7. What is the difference between a recovery window and redundancy?

8. What is the RMAN error message number common to all error situations?

9. When invoking RMAN from the command line, what convention is used to connect to the database to be backed up?

10. What is the difference between restore and recovery?

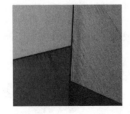

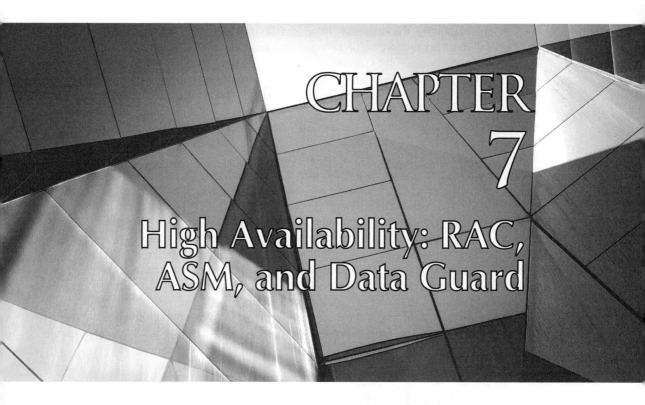

CHAPTER
7

High Availability: RAC,
ASM, and Data Guard

CRITICAL SKILLS

High availability, the capability to access the databases and applications anytime, is critical for some companies. Database outages can be very expensive and result in significant losses depending on the amount of time the database is unavailable. Even maintenance must be done with minimum downtime. Reducing planned (or even unplanned) downtime is a goal of database systems, especially in environments that require accessibility 24x7. Oracle 12*c* continues to offer high availability features such as Real Application Clusters (RAC), Automatic Storage Management (ASM), and Active Data Guard. 12*c* has also added Transaction Guard to enable application continuity.

In architecting database environments, the combinations of RAC and Data Guard will provide fast provisioning of new instance nodes for capacity, instance failover, and even disaster recovery to an offsite standby server. In planning the configurations and combinations, you must look at cost-effective ways to provide the business with the availability that it requires. Examining the features and how to implement them will assist you in providing a plan for a reliable, scalable, and stable environment that can handle the loss of a piece of hardware or be recoverable in the event of an unplanned circumstance. Let's also not forget the need to maintain the databases in Oracle 12*c*. With the rolling patches working by patching one node of a cluster and then continuing to the next node so that at least one node is available while patching, even the planned maintenance window now becomes smaller.

CRITICAL SKILL 7.1

Define High Availability

What does high availability mean to the business? What is the level of risk tolerance? How much data loss is acceptable? Are there current issues with backups or reporting? These are all questions that need to be asked to start mapping out the components that are needed. You may decide that absolutely no data loss can be tolerated or, alternatively, that it is fine if the application is down for a day or two.

Also, it helps to look at what kind of outages can happen and then build in fault tolerance for these situations. Examples of unplanned outages are hardware failures, such as disk or server failures; human error, such as dropping a data file or making a bad change; and network and site failures. Then, add on to these examples the planned outages needed for applying patches, database changes and migrations, and application changes that might include table and database object changes and upgrades. Look for the areas in the system with single points of failure and then match up solutions to start to eliminate those areas.

This chapter just touches on a couple of areas necessary for building a highly available environment: Real Application Clusters, Automatic Storage Management,

Data Guard, and Transaction Guard. Transaction Guard is the newest tool from these components being introduced with Oracle Database 12c. Understanding these components, plus researching other Oracle options such as Flashback Query, Transaction and Database, Flash Recovery Area, Data Recovery Advisor, and Secure Backups, will assist in synching the environment with the business needs in the area of availability. The goal of these options is to achieve Maximum Availability Architecture (MAA), and it is important to understand the options available and what they can provide.

Depending on application and the business needs, if there are planned outages for maintenance to allow for downtime to patch the environment, rolling patches might not be as much of a concern. Instead, testing application changes as well as the patches might be possible via Flashback technologies or a production-like server. If the business doesn't allow for downtime or a regular maintenance window, and you know each minute down will cost the company a serious amount of money, you can use a combination of components for the solution: rolling patches, prevention of outages from hardware failures, having failover servers through clusters, and Data Guard.

Working with the business teams and having some understanding of different options available for architecting a solution that meets budget restrictions and business needs will take some discussions and planning. Policies can also be defined to manage the server pools and allow for flexibility in the highly available architecture.

Working with the application team enables you to take advantage of the application continuity and the use of the logical transaction identifier (LTXID). Using the globally unique identifier will allow a transaction to be submitted only once. If there was a failure of the database during a transaction, the LTXID would be used to recover the transaction, and the application can be coded to handle the transactions if it is to be resubmitted based on the states.

The rest of this chapter will give you an understanding of some of these components and basic information on what it takes to implement them.

CRITICAL SKILL 7.2

Understand Real Application Clusters

Oracle Real Application Clusters (RAC) provides a database environment that is highly available as well as scalable. If a server in the cluster fails, the database instance will continue to run on the remaining servers or nodes in the cluster. With Oracle Clusterware, implementing a new cluster node is made simple. RAC provides possibilities for scaling applications further than the resources of a single server, which means that the environment can start with what is currently needed and then servers can be added as necessary. Oracle 9*i* introduced the Oracle Real Application Clusters; with each subsequent release, management and implementation of RAC have become more straightforward, with new features providing a stable environment and performance improvements. Oracle 12*c* brings additional enhancements to the RAC environment, and even more ways to provide application continuity.

In Oracle 11*g*, Oracle introduced rolling patches for the RAC environment. Previously, it was possible to provide ways to minimize downtime by failing over to another node for patching, but it would still require an outage to finish patching all of the nodes in a cluster. Now with Oracle 12*c,* the patches can be applied, allowing other servers to continue working even with the non-patched version. They get applied to the Oracle Grid Infrastructure Home, and can then be pushed out to the other nodes. Reducing any outages, planned or unplanned, in companies with 24x7 operations is key. The Oracle Clusterware is the piece that helps in setting up new servers and can clone an existing ORACLE_HOME and database instances. Also, it can convert a single-node Oracle database into an RAC environment with multiple nodes.

The RAC environment consists of one or more server nodes; of course, a single server cluster doesn't provide high availability because there is nowhere to fail over to. The servers or nodes are connected through a private network, also referred to as an *interconnect.* The nodes share the same set of disks, and if one node fails, the other nodes in a cluster take over.

A typical RAC environment has a set of disks that are shared by all servers; each server has at least two network ports: one for outside connections and one for the *interconnect* (the private network between nodes and a cluster manager). The shared disk cannot just be a simple filesystem because it needs to be cluster-aware, which is the reason for Oracle Clusterware. RAC still supports third-party cluster managers, but the Oracle Clusterware provides the hooks for the new features for provisioning or deployment of new nodes and the rolling patches. The Oracle Clusterware is also necessary for Automatic Storage Management (ASM), which will be discussed in the latter part of this chapter.

The shared disk for the clusterware comprises two components: a voting disk for recording disk membership and an Oracle Cluster Registry (OCR), which contains the cluster configurations. The voting disk needs to be shared and can be raw devices, Oracle Cluster File System files, ASM, or NTFS partitions. The Oracle Clusterware is the key piece that allows all of the servers to operate together.

Without the interconnect, the servers do not have a way to talk to each other; without the clustered disk, they have no way to have another node to access the same information. Figure 7-1 shows a basic setup with these key components. Next, we will look at how to set up and install these pieces of the RAC environment.

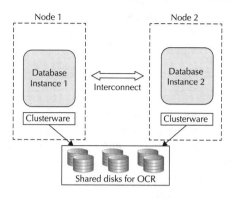

FIGURE 7-1. *RAC components*

Install RAC

Before runInstaller or setup.exe is even executed, a checklist of pre-installation steps needs to be completed. These vary from network setup to making sure the proper disk is in place. Also, before the database is even installed on one of the nodes for RAC, the Clusterware needs to be present. Several of these steps need to be done only once to set up the backbone of the RAC environment no matter how many nodes are being installed. Then tools for cloning the configuration can be used for deployment of new nodes in the cluster.

Each server needs to be set up with the necessary kernel parameters and system parameters that are required for the operating system. (Please refer back to Chapter 2 for more details on installing Oracle.) Just as there were steps that needed to be completed for that install, network addresses and the shared disks need to be configured before Clusterware is installed.

Configurations for network addresses and connections are different from configurations for a standalone database. Three different IP addresses are needed: the virtual network, the private network (interconnect), and the normal or public network. The hosts need a non-domain name listed for each node in the /etc/hosts files on the nodes as well as the IP addresses. That is, each host will have at least three listings in the /etc/hosts files, and each one will have its own unique IP address and alias or name for the host.

```
cat /etc/hosts
#eth0 - Public Network
mmrac1.domain1.com          mmrac1
```

```
mmrac2.domain1.com            mmrac2
#eth1 - Private/Interconnect Network
10.0.0.1   mmrac1priv.domain1.com   mmrac1priv
10.0.0.2   mmrac2priv.domain1.com   mmrac2priv
#VIPs - Virtual Network
192.168.10.104   mmrac1vip.domain1.com     mmrac1vip
192.168.10.05    mmrac2vip.domain1.com     mmrac2vip
```

The public and private networks need to be configured on the same adapter for all of the nodes. So from the example host file, all of the nodes in the cluster must have *eth0* set to the public network and *eth1* to the private. These nodes should be tested and reachable by pinging them. The interconnect network should be reserved for traffic between the nodes only, and it is even recommended that it have its own physically separate network. (This means with hardware setup there should have been at least two network adapters installed.) This will certainly help with the performance of the cache fusion, which is the memory sharing of the buffer caches between the nodes.

The shared disk needs to be available to be able to record the configuration about the cluster being installed. This disk will house the Oracle Cluster Registry and the cluster membership.

Multiple voting disks should be available to the Oracle Cluster; if not added at installation, disks can be added, backed up, and restored if necessary. There is a command-line interface, cluster administrator (CRSCTL), to perform tasks and get status information for the cluster environment. To add disks, the following must be run as root; the path is the fully qualified name for the disk (for example, /dev/oraasm/disk1) that is being added:

```
crsctl add votedisk css path -force
```

Verify by pulling a current list of voting disks:

```
crsctl query css votedisk
```

To back up voting disks in Linux/Unix, run the following:

```
##Generic names:
dd if=voting_disk_name of=backup_file_name
##Same command with example names
dd if=votedisk of=/orabackup/votedisk/votedisk_bkup
```

In Windows, use the following:

```
ocopy voting_disk_name backup_file_name
```

To restore voting disks in Linux/Unix, run the following:

```
dd if=backup_file_name of=voting_disk_name
```

In Windows, use the following:

```
ocopy backup_file_name voting_disk_name
```

With all of these different pieces needed before RAC can even be installed, the importance of verifying and checking the configurations is extremely high. When installing the clusterware, it is critical that the initial configuration of the virtual and private networks is set up properly. Verifying the network, disk, operating system, and hardware prerequisites is the first step for installation. The clusterware will not install properly if any of these requirements is missing. The option to install the Real Application Cluster when installing the Oracle software will not be available if the clusterware is not installed or installed correctly.

The Cluster Verification Utility (CVU) assists in this area and should be run before you attempt to install the clusterware. It will verify the hardware and operating system prerequisites as well as the network configurations. From the software install directory, run the following:

```
./runcluvfy.sh stage -pre crsinst -n mmrac1, mmrac2
```

Unknown outputs could mean that the user doesn't have the privileges it needs to run the check, or a node is unavailable or having resource errors. Running CLUVFY checks after clusterware is installed verifies the install and other prerequisites before the Oracle database install. Failures should be addressed here before attempting the database install; otherwise, you may find yourself uninstalling and reinstalling many more times than necessary.

NOTE
When setting up OS logins for the installs of Oracle software, it might be wise to plan to have different OS logins for Clusterware and ASM. ASM and Clusterware need to be set up in different Oracle Homes from the instance and can have separate owners of these directories where the software is installed. This is a best practice for security. Oracle 12c ASM can now be on separate servers from the Oracle database, and access to the different servers can also provide a way to give separate permissions. You can create users such as CRSADMIN, ASMADMIN, and ORACLE on the needed servers.

Now that the requirements are in place, the installation of the Clusterware is ready to go; by using the Oracle installer, the option should be available to install clusterware. If the installation of clusterware does not come up, then go back through and run the Cluster Verification Utility and fix any issues first. Figure 7-2 shows the network information that was configured for the three network addresses as well as the name of the cluster being defined.

After your Clusterware is successfully installed, it's time to install Oracle Database because the framework has already been completed on the nodes. From the first node in the cluster, run the Oracle installer (*runInstaller* on Linux/Unix, *setup.exe* on Windows). Install the Enterprise Edition, which follows along the same path as a single instance, except for the Cluster installation choices (see Figure 7-3) after the location of the install information. We recommend that you just do a software install without creating the database so that the software install can first be verified. Then, you can use the database configuration assistance to create the database on the nodes of the cluster.

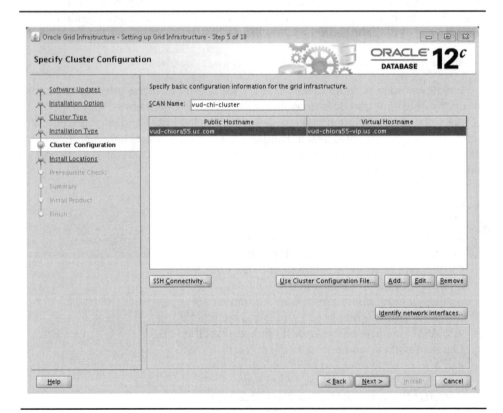

FIGURE 7-2. *Clusterware install*

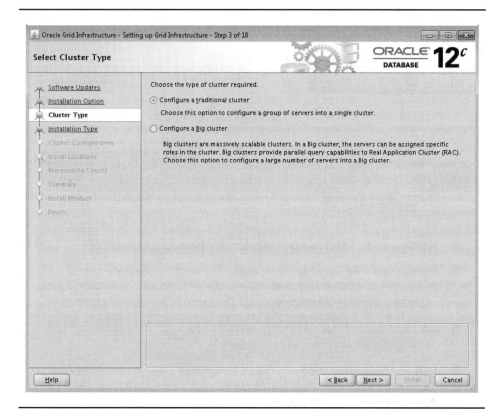

FIGURE 7-3. *RAC install*

Progress Check ⏱

1. How does RAC provide high availability?

2. What does the clusterware use the shared disks for?

3. What is the Cluster Verification Utility?

4. What is the private network used for in the RAC environment?

5. What is a logical transaction identifier?

Test RAC

RAC environments should first be created for testing and proving concepts for how the failover works for different applications. The RAC test environments should continue to be available for testing for production systems because different workloads and failover can't be tested against a single node. After the installs of the Oracle Clusterware and database nodes, it's useful to test several different scenarios of failover in order to verify the install as well as to determine how the application fails over.

Create a test list and establish the pieces of the application that need to be part of that testing. Testing should include hardware, interconnect, disk, and operating system failures. Simulations of most of these failures are possible in the environment. Here is an example test list:

- **Interconnect** Disconnect network cable from network adapter.

- **Transaction failover when node fails** Connect to one node, run the transaction, and then shut down the node; try with selects, inserts, updates, and deletes.

- **Backups and restores** Perform an RMAN backup of the database and verify that the database can be restored.

- **Loss of a data file or disk** Delete a data file or simulate losing access to the storage. This will test how the system will react, and the backup can be used to restore the database.

- **Test load balancing of transactions** Verify that the services are valid and are allowing for workload balancing.

Progress Check Answers

1. RAC provides high availability through failover to another node when there are hardware issues with one of the nodes.

2. The clusterware uses the shared disks for the Oracle Cluster Registry and the voting disk.

3. The Cluster Verification Utility is the utility you run to verify the environment before running the clusterware install.

4. The private network is used for the interconnect, which allows the nodes to talk to each other directly and does a health check of the nodes.

5. A logical transaction identifier (LTXID) provides a unique ID for a transaction to be able to guarantee that it is committed only once. It can be used to provide continuity in the applications on failover, and it uses the LTXID to recover the transaction.

Workload Manager

Using RAC databases on the back end of applications doesn't necessarily mean that the application is RAC aware. The application as a whole may not fail over, even though the database is failing over current transactions and connections. There might be a small outage when one of the nodes needs to fail over. However, with server calls about the failover, these events can be used to trigger automated processes for reconnecting or restarting application pieces. In previous releases, these are the Fast Application Notification events and can be used for failover and for workload balancing. Now in Oracle 12c, these events are coming from Transaction Guard, which handles the transactions on failover, including providing the application the needed information to know the state of the transaction and how it needs to be handled.

In earlier RAC releases, having different pieces such as reporting tables or materialized views of the application connect to different nodes helped with load balancing in some ways. Oracle Clusterware and the Load Balancing Advisor distribute the workload across the RAC environment more effectively. Along with better workload distribution, Oracle 12c RAC environments provide simplified ways to provision new nodes. You can create policy-managed databases around the workloads, and use the nodes in the cluster for off-loading workloads such as backups and maintenance, a high demand period for an application, or a timezone type of activity based on region. Server pools allow for different sized hardware to be used and added as demand is needed in the RAC environment. Categories are assigned to each of the servers so that they can be used according to the different server pools. A minimum number of servers can be required for the pool, and servers can be moved from one pool to another. These resources remain transparent to the applications, and the application connects via a service to the available server pools. The services are designed to be integrated with several areas of the database, and not just CPU resources.

What is even better about the server pools is that there is a way to do "what if" scenarios to assess the impact of downtime on different nodes, validate policies, and plan for nodes being added, moved, or removed. This is done through the cluster administrator (CRCTL) command or in a DBA service (SRVCTL) command with the parameter of EVAL.

ASM

As mentioned with the RAC environment, Automatic Storage Management (ASM) is both the file and disk manager for the Oracle database files. Now you might be thinking that this seems like a more advanced topic, and possibly too detailed for a beginner's guide. However, ASM is an important component in a highly available database environment and for addressing performance issues and management of

Ask the Expert

Q: Is tuning an RAC environment different from tuning single instances?

A: When tuning the RAC environment, the beginning steps are the same as with a single instance. The next step is to look at interconnect performance and issues. The tools available to tune single instances are RAC aware, such as Automatic Workload Repository (AWR) reports, which detail the information collected about performance statistics, waits, and long running SQL statements, along with other details about how the database resources are being used. Oracle Enterprise Manager also provides good insight into issues, enabling you to see things at a cluster level. The dictionary views are available at the node level as well as at the global level, so for RAC environments, look for the V$ and GV$ views.

Oracle files. Even after years of working with applications and databases, there is always I/O contention, and reading and writing to disk is a main part of what a database does. So, database administrators end up understanding more about disks, mirroring, and striping than they might really want to know. Debating different RAID strategies and optimizing I/O may seem like intermediate topics, but even some of these areas are handled by ASM and have simplified the management of the Oracle disk and file needs.

Previous to Oracle 12*c*, ASM shared storage connectivity, Global Lock Manager had intense communication during node failure, and there was instance overhead on each node. Now 12*c* Flex ASM provides a more stable environment that is a set of clusters to provide the storage to ASM clients. The ASM clients can use network connectivity to access the storage, and if an ASM instance fails, the other nodes in the ASM cluster take over and allow all of the databases to continue to access the ASM cluster. There is no longer the need to have an ASM instance on every database node.

There are several more in-depth discussions and topics revolving around ASM, but this chapter provides only a general introduction as well as the basic configuration and information about how to get started with ASM.

With this new flexible architecture, there are more reasons to have an ASM cluster supporting the databases. As you can see, there is even more stability in providing highly available systems. The database data files are more easily managed and are more centralized in the ASM cluster. In large databases, the number of data files for an instance can grow out of control; even a tablespace for a large environment can become unmanageable. Then, any disk migrations or moving of tablespaces becomes a very difficult task and leaves areas of vulnerabilities open due to the sheer number of data files. ASM manages the files using disk groups, and disks are added to the disk groups even while the database is open and running and the ASM instance is being accessed.

CRITICAL SKILL 7.5

Set Up the ASM Instance

The ASM instance can now be set up as a local ASM instance on the database server or as an ASM cluster. An ASM instance can manage the following files for all of the instances on each cluster node: control files, data files, tempfiles, spfiles, redo logs, archive logs, RMAN backups, Data Pump dumpsets, and Flashback logs. The database does not need to be set up as an RAC database to use ASM. In fact, ASM can be used for a single database install.

There are a few alternative ways to set up ASM for the environment, and the next couple of figures will demonstrate the options. Depending on the configuration, ASM can be more fault tolerant, provide a quicker failover, and support various database and application environment configurations. In previous releases, when allocating the disks to ASM, there was still a risk of a non-Oracle process overwriting something on that disk. The current version of ASM rejects non-Oracle I/O and protects the disks from being overwritten.

Starting with Figure 7-4, you'll see the different options to use ASM. The first option is a database instance with an ASM instance. One ASM instance can manage the files for more than one database instance on that server. Each of the databases for that ASM instance on that server has access to all of the disk groups, which are the available disks that have been allocated by creating groups.

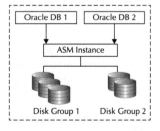

FIGURE 7-4. *ASM instance standalone*

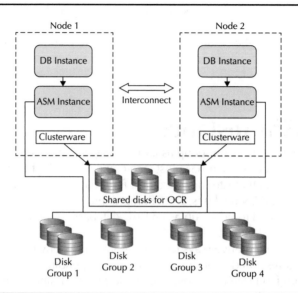

FIGURE 7-5. *ASM instance RAC*

As you can see in Figure 7-5, the difference with ASM instances in the RAC environment is that they are also instances that are available for failover; this means that RAC components need to be available to manage the failover. An ASM instance is still created on each node, but the instances manage the disk groups and files across all of the nodes. The ASM instances manage the client files and ship the data or client information to the database server.

Figure 7-6 does show the option to have the database server directly connect to the ASM cluster. Here, the ASM instance is no longer on the database server and through ASM Listeners and network connections access is available to ASM. The ASM Listeners are registered as remote listeners and can load balance across the ASM clusters.

There is another option to have an I/O Server that can deliver the file data and export the disk groups as a service to the database servers. This is an indirect connection from the database server to the ASM cluster through the I/O Server instance, as shown in Figure 7-7.

Any of the architectures provide dictionary tables to manage and get information about the ASM instance and the clients. For example, V$ASM_CLIENT provides the

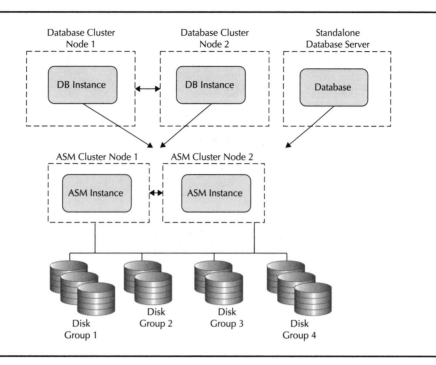

FIGURE 7-6. *ASM cluster*

information about the database clients that are using that ASM instance. You can use the V$ASM_CLIENT and the ALTER SYSTEM command to relocate a client to another node gracefully to prepare for maintenance. Also, the ASM instance is still a small database instance because it is mostly composed of the memory structures and not physical data. The ASM instance provides the framework for managing disk groups, which contain several physical disks and can be from different disk formats such as a raw disk partition, LUNS (hardware RAID), LVM (redundant functionality), or NFS (can load balance over NFS systems and doesn't depend on the OS to support NFS). However, the advantage of ASM is that it uses raw devices that bypass any OS buffering.

The ASM instance can be created on installation of the grid software or by using the database configuration assistant (DBCA). The name of the instance normally starts with +ASM, and then the Oracle Cluster Synchronization Server (CSS) must be configured. This service is added with the localconfig script, which will add the

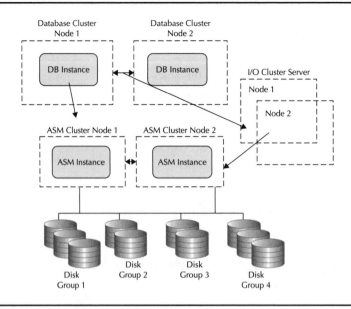

FIGURE 7-7. *I/O Server with ASM cluster*

OCR repository that is necessary for ASM. Also, there is a new security role to log in as administrator of the ASM instance, SYSASM. The OS group of OSASM goes along with this new role.

To get started, the grid infrastructure needs to be installed, as shown in Figure 7-8. If you want to create a database using ASM, the ASM instance needs to be created first. However, you can also migrate an existing database to ASM, allowing the instance to be created for that migration as well.

Commands can be used to add disks and create disk groups for the ASM instance. The ASM Configuration Assistant (ASMCA) is also available to add disk groups and volumes for the filesystem. Figure 7-9 shows the ASMCA, which can stop and start an ASM instance, and Figure 7-10 shows the creation of disk groups using ASMCA. This is an easy-to-manage ASM instance and a clustered filesystem.

In order for the ASM instance to discover the available disks, an initialization parameter is used: ASM_DISKSTRING. Other parameters include ASM_DISKGROUPS, which specifies which files are managed by ASM, and ASM_POWER_LIMIT, which

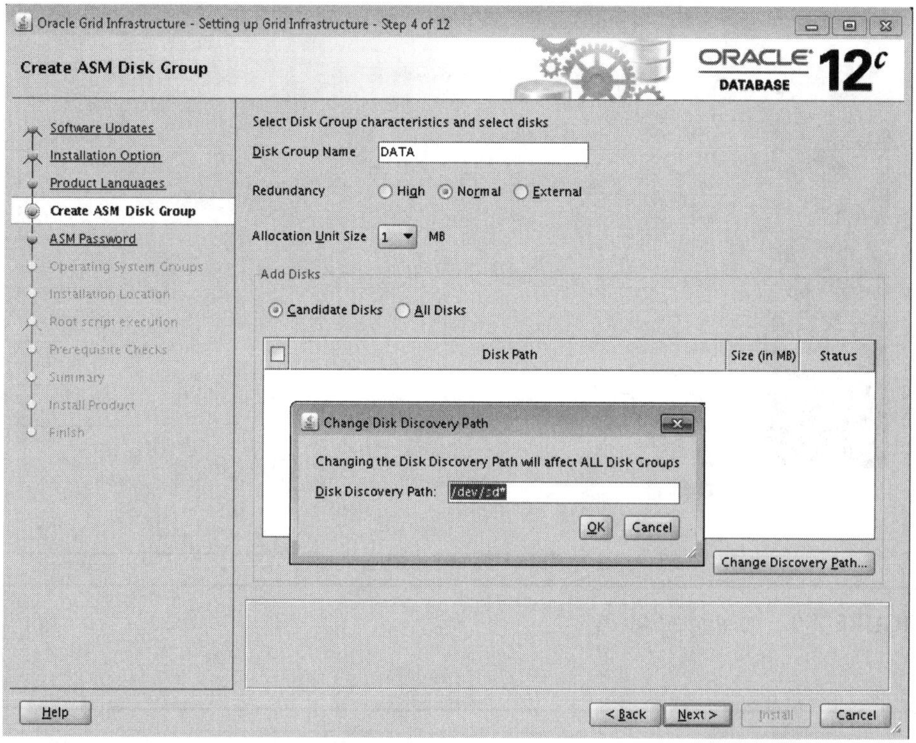

FIGURE 7-8. *Configuring ASM infrastructure*

is the default value for disk rebalancing. INSTANCE_TYPE is set to indicate that the instance is an ASM instance and not a database:

```
Parameters:
ASM_DISKGROUPS = CONTROLFILE, DATAFILE, LOGFILE
ASM_DISKSTRING = /dev/rdsk/*
ASM_POWER_LIMIT = 0   /* 0 to 11 0 disables and 11 to enable
rebalancing more quickly */
INSTANCE_TYPE = ASM
```

Disk groups can be created during instance creation. After the instance is created, sqlplus is used to start up ASM. SRVCTL is a good way to manage the ASM cluster, and CRSCTL can also assist with status information about the ASM instance.

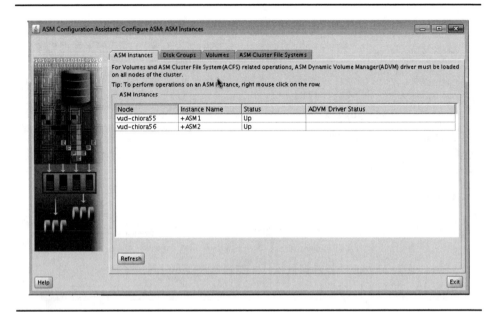

FIGURE 7-9. *Using ASMCA*

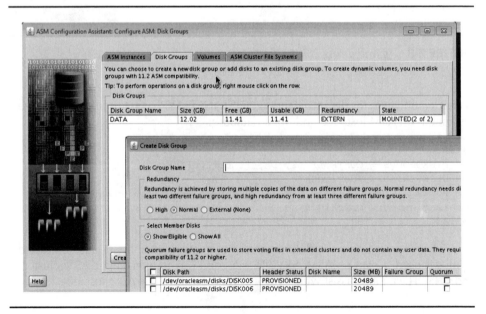

FIGURE 7-10. *Creating a new disk group using ASMCA*

Project 7-1 Install ASMLib

For Linux, there is an option for using raw devices or ASMLib to manage the available disks for Automatic Storage Management. ASMLib is a tool that will need to be installed as a Linux operating system package.

Step by Step

1. After installing the packages as the root user, the Linux software, and the Oracle software, the following packages are needed for the ASMLib:

```
# rpm -Uvh oracleasm-support-2.0.1.-1.i386.rpm
# rpm -Uvh oracleasmlib-2.0.1.-1.i386.rpm
# rpm -Uvh oracleasm-2.6.9-34.ELsmp-2.0.1-1.i686.rpm
```

2. Verify that the package is installed:

```
#  rpm -q oracleasm*
```

3. The previous step installed the ASMLib software. Now, to configure, run the following:

```
# /etc/init.d/oracleasm configure
```

4. With the ASMLib software installed, the available partitions can be used to create ASM disks:

```
# /etc/init.d/oracleasm createdisk VOL1 /dev/disk1
# /etc/init.d/oracleasm createdisk VOL2 /dev/disk2
```

5. To view the disks that were just created from the OS command line:

```
# /etc/init.d/oracleasm listdisks
VOL1
VOL2
```

Project Summary

This project has taken you through the steps to install the package needed for the ASMLib utility as well as demonstrated some of the tasks that can be completed using this command-line utility. Having ASMLib configured will be useful for managing ASM disks and files.

Create ASM Disk Groups

Starting up the ASM instance is very similar to starting up a database instance. Instead of connecting as SYSDBA, SYASM should be used:

```
ORACLE_SID=+ASM
SQLPLUS /NOLOG
SQL> connect SYS as SYSASM
Enter password: sys_password
Connected to an idle instance.
SQL> STARTUP
ASM instance started
```

Shutdown is also similar to shutting down database instances, but the IMMEDIATE clause checks for databases that are still connected to the ASM instance and returns an error if this is the case. Any databases connected to the ASM instance during a shutdown abort will also abort:

```
SQL> SHUTDOWN NORMAL\IMMEDIATE\ABORT
```

The redundancy type for a DISKGROUP is specified when the group is created and cannot be changed. However, new groups can be created with different redundancy types and then migrated to. There are three types of redundancy: EXTERNAL, NORMAL, and HIGH. With EXTERNAL, ASM is not providing any redundancy and is assuming that an outside source such as the storage array is providing fault tolerance. NORMAL requires two groups for failover and will handle the failure of one group. HIGH redundancy needs three groups, and it will handle the failure of two of the three groups. The NORMAL and HIGH redundancies also eliminate the single point of failure for the ASM disk. A small number of disk groups can normally be used even for a large database.

Project 7-2   Create Disk Groups

The next steps will give the commands for creating disk groups with external redundancy or normal redundancy. Once the groups are created, they are available to create tablespaces.

Step by Step

1. Create disk groups by using the following:

```
SQL> create diskgroup DGEXT1 external redundancy disk '/dev/rdsk1/disk1';
SQL> create diskgroup DGNORM1 normal redundancy
FAILGROUP controller1 DISK
'/dev/rdsk/disk1' name disk1,
'/dev/rdsk/disk2' name disk2
FAILGROUP controller2 DISK
'/dev/rdsk/disk3' name disk3,
'/dev/rdsk/disk4' name disk4;
```

2. Now that you've created the disk groups, validate them by looking at the views that give you information about disks and disk groups:

   ☐ **V$ASM_DISKS**   Available disks reflect values in the parameter ASM_DISKSTRING:

   ```
   select * from v$asm_disk;
   ```

   ☐ **V$ASM_DISKGROUPS**   Available disk groups and details on redundancy type:

   ```
   SQL> select name, state from v$asm_diskgroup;
        NAME                STATE
        ------------------- -------------------
        DGEXT1              MOUNTED
        DGNORM1             MOUNTED
   ```

3. You can add disks to the disk groups as needed to grow space for the databases:

```
alter DISKGROUP DGNORM1 add DISK
'/dev/rdsk/disk5' name disk5,
'/dev/rdsk/disk6' name disk6;
```

4. After ASM is started and disk groups are created, using the available disk space is as simple as saying CREATE TABLESPACE TS_DATA1 and giving the size of the data file, but there is no need to include the actual data file name if allowing Oracle to name and manage the file:

```
SQL> create tablespace DATATBS1 datafile size 1024M;
```

(continued)

Project Summary

This project walked you through how to create and alter disk groups. After the creation of the disk groups, steps were taken to verify that the disk groups were created or altered as expected.

Progress Check

1. What is a typical name for an ASM instance?

2. What does ASM stand for?

3. What are the three types of redundancy for disk groups?

4. What is the initialization parameter for ASM to discover the available disks?

5. Does the ASM instance need to be on the same server as the database?

CRITICAL SKILL 7.7

Use ASMCMD and ASMLib

Managing ASM instances can be done through Oracle Enterprise Manager, as well as the command line in sqlplus and ASMCMD, which is the ASM command-line utility. ASMCMD has commands to copy files, back up and restore metadata, and list and remap ASM files.

The following is a list of a few commands for the ASMCMD to copy, back up, and restore:

- **cp** Copies files between ASM disk groups and copies files from disk groups to the operating system. For example:

```
ASMCMD >cp +DISKGRP1/MMDB.CTF1 /backups
```

Progress Check Answers

1. A typical name for an ASM instance is +ASM.

2. ASM stands for Automatic Storage Management.

3. NORMAL, HIGH, and EXTERNAL are the three types of redundancy for disk groups.

4. ASM_DISKSTRING is the initialization parameter for ASM to discover the available disks.

5. No, it can still be created that way and have the ASM instance and database instance on the same server, but another option is to create an ASM cluster for storage. The ASM instance is not required to be on the database server in 12*c*.

- **lsdsk**   Lists disk information, which is good for creating a list of disks an ASM instance uses

- **md_backup**   Creates a backup file containing the metadata for one or more disk groups to enable you to re-create the disk groups in the future

- **md_restore**   Restores a disk group using the backup from md_backup

- **remap**   Recovers bad blocks on a disk by moving a good copy to a different location on disk

There are other ASMCMD commands to move around the ASM disk and file systems; this is not a complete list, and you will start to see that these are similar to Linux/Unix commands:

- **cd**   Changes the directory

- **du**   Displays the total disk space

- **exit**   Exits out of the ASMCMD command line

- **find**   Lists occurrences for the specified name

- **ls**   Lists the contents of the ASM directory (when logging into ASM, it starts in the /root directory)

- **mkdir**   Creates ASM directories

- **pwd**   Displays the path of the current directory

- **lsct**   Lists information about current ASM clients

CRITICAL SKILL 7.8

Convert an Existing Database to ASM

Migrating an instance from regular storage to ASM is actually a simple task, but only if the ASM instance has already been created. Using Oracle Enterprise Manager is probably the most straightforward way to do this.

Start by opening up Oracle Enterprise Manager and choosing the option to migrate to ASM. The screen shown in the following illustration is what comes up after you select to migrate to ASM. Migration requires you to first choose the files to be migrated, which, of course, include database files, but can also include recovery type files, such as archive logs and backup and control file copies. If not chosen, the log files and control files will remain on the current disk.

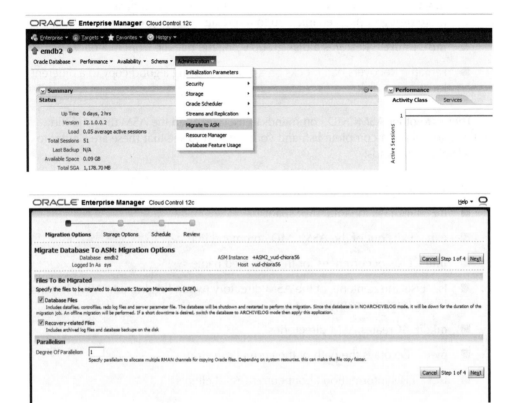

The next screen has options for choosing the disk groups that this database should migrate to.

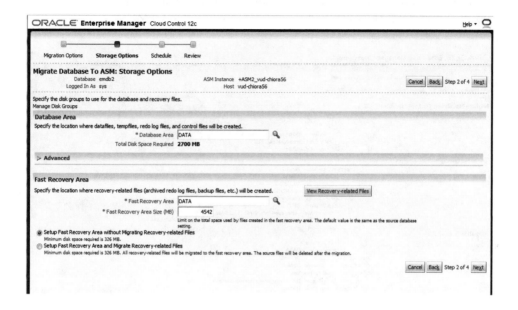

The job can be scheduled to run as needed with the settings in the following screen. This does require some downtime of the database to run the migration.

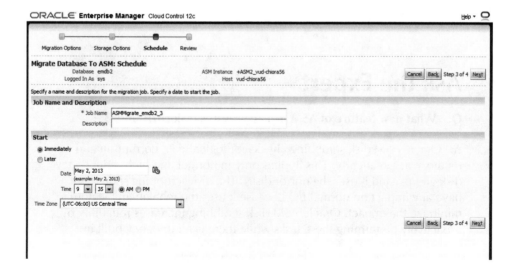

The next step summarizes the selections, and then the final step is to submit the job, as shown next. The migration job can be monitored in OEM.

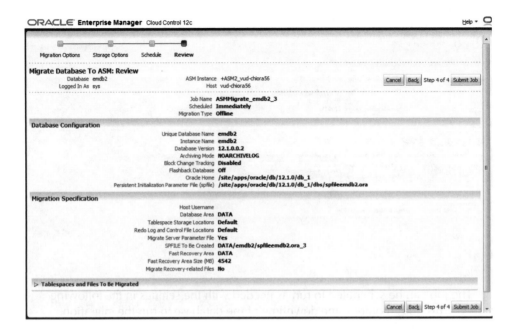

Ask the Expert

Q: What new feature of ASM in 12*c* prevents disk corruption?

A: Oracle ASM disk scrubbing checks for logical data corruption and repairs it automatically. This applies only in normal and high redundancy disk groups, and it uses the mirror disks. The disk scrubbing should not have any impact on normal I/O because it uses the rebalancing feature to minimize the impact. Oracle ASM disk scrubbing increases reliability by proactively performing these tasks while there is redundancy built in.

CRITICAL SKILL 7.9

Understand Data Guard

Providing highly available, recoverable, and secure stable environments requires a multifaceted approach. We have already discussed RAC and ASM; the Oracle Data Guard environment offers an additional piece to this architecture. Cluster servers normally reside in the same data center because of the requirements for the interconnect between nodes of the cluster and clusters share disk requirements. Because of this, there is the potential for failure of this environment. Also, what about restores and disaster recovery sites? Data Guard can provide solutions in this area, as well as help offload some of the intense resource consumers such as hot backups, exports, and reporting. The standby server can be an active server that can be used to offload reporting and backups, as well as continue to operate in its standard role for failover and to provide a disaster recovery server. With Data Guard 12*c*, there is a Far Sync capability to allow for synchronizing the standby databases even if the servers are separated by miles and miles. The Far Sync option provides better performance, smaller footprint for the standby, and the ability to failover without data loss. Using Data Guard, one or more standby servers could be at different locations to allow for failover to a different site. So, for high availability, Data Guard provides solutions on both fronts of failover and recovery.

Data Guard has been available in some form since Oracle 8*i*; however, since 11*g* the secondary database can recover while it is open for reading. Even better, with 12*c*, there are changes to global temporary tables that don't generate redo. DML queries can be executed on standby because of writes to the global tables. This also means that ad hoc queries (ones that probably haven't been tuned and are resource hogs), reports, backups, and exports can be off loaded to this system. Being able to use the failover hardware for useful business purposes makes it a cost-effective part of a disaster recovery plan.

The Data Guard manager provides a practical way to manage the primary and secondary servers. It can allow for manual failover, set up the automatic failover, and place the secondary server in snapshot mode. The snapshot mode actually puts the database in read and write mode so that testing can be done against a current set of production data. More on this snapshot mode in a little bit, but first let's walk through some of the architecture and setup for Data Guard.

CRITICAL SKILL 7.10

Explain Data Guard Protection Modes

The different modes of setup for Data Guard allow for different configurations that are adaptive and that are dependent on available hardware, processes, and ultimately business needs.

The modes for the Data Guard configuration include maximum protection, maximum availability, and maximum performance. The Data Guard configuration can also have more than one standby database. Having multiple standby databases is even recommended in modes like maximum protection in order to make sure at least one standby is available.

Maximum protection is designed for zero data loss, while the redo transport is synchronous. Synchronous transport means that you're applying the database transactions at the same time on the primary and secondary database servers. The primary waits for a response telling it that the transaction has been applied to the standby database before it commits the transaction. Having two standbys or even a RAC setup on the secondary site is recommended in this situation because if the standby fails, the primary will be halted in this mode.

Maximum availability also has the goal of zero data loss (again, with the redo transport being synchronous). The difference is that if the standby fails or if there is a connectivity issue, it will allow the primary to continue and the standby to fall slightly behind. It is not as critical to have more than one standby for this mode because of the fault tolerance.

Maximum performance has the possibility of minimal data loss, but performance is the concern on the primary because the redo transport is done asynchronously, and it doesn't have to check back with the primary before the primary does a commit. So, if transport is a concern for slowing down the primary database and the performance risk is higher than any data loss, the maximum performance mode will allow for that.

NOTE
It can be especially hard with discussions regarding costs and business expectations to come to an agreement on which mode to use. It is probably simplest to set the protection mode; the ability to use the standby server in very practical ways should help defray concerns. To set the protection mode for the database, issue the following statement:

```
ALTER DATABASE SET STANDBY DATABASE TO MAXIMIZE
(PROTECTION | AVAILABILITY | PERFORMANCE);
```

The Oracle Database 12*c* now allows for confirmation that the transaction has been received even if still in memory with the NOAFFIRM attribute. FASTSYNC doesn't wait for the actual write because if the system has slower disk or I/O contention, it will be able to receive the information the transport executed.

FASTSYNC allows the primary database to perform as expected in a maximum available configuration and not be dependent on I/O performance of the standby database.

As discussed earlier, each mode has different services that take care of the transport and application:

- **Transport Services** are the pieces that handle the synchronous and asynchronous transport. These services move the log or transactions to available standby servers and verify that they are being applied to these servers. Synchronous transports validate that transactions have been applied on both primary and standby servers before committing the transactions. The asynchronous transport will validate that transactions have been sent, but transactions will be committed on the primary even if not completed on the standby.

- **Apply Services** take care of the SQL Apply or the Redo Apply. Apply Services take the SQL statements or redo logs and control how they're applied to the standby databases. SQL Apply takes the redo and transforms it into SQL statements. After running the SQL statements on primary and standby databases, the standby matches the primary database and can be used as a logical standby database. Redo logs are used for keeping the physical standby database consistent with the primary database. Redo information is applied to the standby databases by Redo Apply and controlled by the Apply Services.

- **Role Management Service** enables you to switch from standby to primary. This is used either for a planned switchover or for the failover due to an outage of one of the servers.

Figure 7-11 shows a configuration of the Data Guard environment and how the primary and standby servers do not even need to be in the same location. The servers can be in the same data center, down the street, or cities apart from each other, depending on the purpose and need. Having the servers in a different city provides high availability even in the event of a disaster in the location of the primary database. Also in Figure 7-11, notice the options that are available for the standby server to use, such as reporting, system testing, or even running backups, to take this type of load off of the primary server.

With Redo Apply, the standby database can be opened for read-only queries. The recovery on the standby is canceled and the database is then opened. If you're using the Active Data Guard option, the Redo Apply can be started again to allow

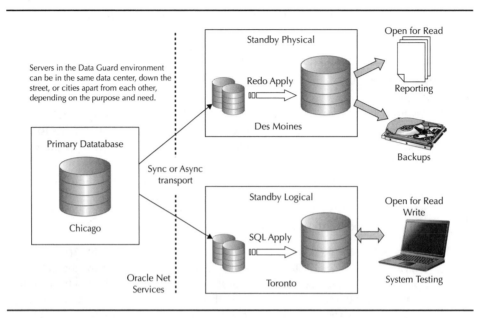

FIGURE 7-11. *Data Guard configuration*

the standby to have real-time data while having the database open. This can be done in sqlplus on the standby database:

```
SQLPLUS> ALTER DATABASE RECOVER MANAGED STANDBY DATABASE CANCEL;
SQLPLUS> ALTER DATABASE OPEN READ ONLY; /*And then to start applying
the redo again:*/
SQLPLUS> ALTER DATABASE RECOVER MANAGED STANDBY DATABASE
USING CURRENT LOGFILE DISCONNECT;
/* The database is still open for read-only queries and reporting as
the logs are being applied. */
```

You can also use the standby database as a snapshot database that can be updated and used for testing. During this time, no logs are applied. After testing, the snapshot database is converted back to a standby database by using a restore point with a flashback database:

```
Create Snapshot:
SQLPLUS> ALTER DATABASE CONVERT TO SNAPSHOT STANDBY;
Convert back to Standby:
SQLPLUS> ALTER DATABASE CONVERT TO PHYSICAL STANDBY DATABASE;
```

When using a snapshot database with SQL Apply, stopping the apply of the SQL statements is not necessary because the standby is kept synchronized by having the same SQL applied on both the primary and the standby. So, while the standby is still being synchronized, it is also available for queries, running reports, or backups. The commands shown here for setting up the standby for read access are not necessary, but are done during the initial setup to show that SQL Apply is being used:

```
SQLPLUS> ALTER DATABASE START LOGICAL STANDBY APPLY IMMEDIATE;
```

Progress Check

1. What service handles the failover from primary to standby?

2. What protection mode will cause the primary to wait on new transactions if it is not able to apply logs to at least one of the standbys?

3. How many protection modes are there?

Create a Physical Standby Server

All of the databases, whether physical or logical, must be created as a physical standby first. The tools used to create the standby are RMAN, Data Guard Broker, or Oracle Grid Control. Steps must be completed on both primary and standby servers. However, the steps on the primary database need to be done only once, no matter how many standby servers are being created. Once again, separation of duties and responsibilities can come into play with the user who manages the Data Guard environment. The administration role for Data Guard is SYSDG and can be used with the Data Guard Broker to manage the standby databases. Next, let's take a look at actually creating a physical standby server; RMAN provides a simple command for creating the standby database and backing up the database at the same time.

Progress Check Answers

1. The Role Management Service handles the failover from primary to standby.

2. Maximum protection mode causes the primary to wait on new transactions if it is not able to apply logs to at least one of the standbys.

3. There are three protection modes: maximum protection, maximum availability, and maximum performance.

Project 7-3   Create a Physical Standby Server

This project will step through creating a standby database on a different server than the primary database. There are steps to be followed on both the primary and standby database server. We recommend only using a development environment to work through this project because of the parameter changes to the primary database.

Step by Step

1. Complete the following steps on the primary server:

   ```
   SQLPLUS>select FORCE_LOGGING from v$database;
        SQLPLUS>alter database force logging;
        -- forces all changes to be logged even if nologging
        might be set on an object
   ```

2. Configure the redo transport authentication; use a remote login password file.

3. Add standby logfiles to the primary server. The logs on the standby server need to be the same size or larger than on the primary server in order for the primary redo to be applied to the standby redo logs.

   ```
   SQLPLUS> alter database add standby logfile
   '/u/u02/oraarch/DG02' size 50M;
   ```

4. Set initialization parameters on the primary server:

   ```
   DB_NAME = DG01
   DB_UNIQUE_NAME=DG01 ## (Doesn't change even if the standby becomes
   the primary)
   CONTROL_FILES
   LOG_ARCHIVE_CONFIG='dg_config=(DG01,DG02)'
   LOG_ARCHIVE_DEST_1='LOCATION=/u01/oraarch/DG01'  ## local archive directory
   LOG_ARCHIVE_DEST_2='service=DG01 ASYNC
   VALID_FOR=(ONLINE_LOGFILE,PRIMARY_ROLE) db_unique_name=DG01' ## sets the
   type of transport and used for physical standby
   REMOTE_LOGIN_PASSWORDFILE = Exclusive
   LOG_ARCHIVE_DEST_STATE_1 = ENABLE
   LOG_ARCHIVE_DEST_STATE_2 = ENABLE
   ```

   The parameters that are set on the primary server control how the redo will be transmitted to the standby server. The LOG_ARCHIVE_DEST_1 would be set for the primary server's archive log location even if there was not a standby server. Additional locations can be set by adding a number in place of the n for LOG_ARCHIVE_DEST_n.

5. Put the primary server in ARCHIVELOG MODE. If the database is not already in ARCHIVELOG MODE, then it will need to be restarted after issuing an ALTER DATABASE command.

    ```
    SQLPLUS> alter database archivelog;
    ```

6. The network configurations for the standby database need to be configured on both the primary and secondary servers. In configuring a service name, use the UNIQUE_DB name for the standby server. After setting up the listener and service on both servers, verify that the password file has been copied over and the directories for ADUMP, BDUMP, Flashback, and so on have been created.

7. To create the standby database over the network on the standby server, start up the standby database in NOMOUNT mode:

    ```
    SQLPLUS> startup nomount;
    ```

8. On the primary server, issue the RMAN command and connect as sysdba:

    ```
    RMAN> connect auxiliary sys/passwordDG02
    RMAN> run {
    allocate channel disk1 type disk;
    allocate auxiliary channel stby type disk;
    duplicate target database for standby from active database
    spfile
    parameter_value_convert 'DG01','DG02'
    set db_unique_name='DG02'
    set db_file_name_convert='/dg01/','/dg02/'
    set log_file_name_convert='/dg01/','/dg02/'
    set control_files='/u01/app/oradata/controlfiles/dg02.ctl'
    set log_archive_max_processes='5'
    set fal_client='dg02'  ## FAL (fetch archive log) client and is used if
    roles are switched
    set fal_server='dg01'
    set standby_file_management='AUTO'
    set log_archive_config='dg_config=(dg01,dg02)'
    set log_archive_dest_1='service=dg01 ASYNC
    valid_for=(ONLINE_LOGFILE,PRIMARY_ROLE) db_unique_name=DG01'
    ;}
    ```

9. Log in to the primary server and switch the logfile:

    ```
    SQLPLUS>alter system switch logfile;
    ```

10. Start the recovery process on the standby server:

    ```
    SQLPLUS> alter database recover managed standby database
    using current logfile disconnect;
    ```

(continued)

11. Primary and standby servers have been created and now should be verified. To verify that the logs are being applied on the standby, queries can be executed on the standby and primary servers.

```
--on standby
SQLPLUS> select sequence#, first_time, next_time
from v$archived_log
order by sequence#;
--on primary server
SQLPLUS> alter system switch logfile;
--on standby
SQLPLUS> select sequence#, first_time, next_time
from v$archived_log
order by sequence#;
--You should see that the next log sequence was applied
```

Project Summary

In this project, primary and standby databases were created. The configuration of the parameters and startup of the instances all need to be completed before the recovery process on the standby server starts. Following these steps should give you a good idea what it takes to create a standby server.

To manage the Data Guard system, you can use the Data Guard Broker (DGMGRL for command line) or Oracle Enterprise Manager Grid Control. In order to use the Data Guard Broker, the parameter DG_BROKER_START needs to be set to TRUE and the LISTENER needs to have the databases with broker services added. DGMRGL is the command to invoke the broker. For Oracle Grid Control, once the database targets are added to the grid, Data Guard management is possible. These tools provide a way to fail over the database to the standby and back again to primary. They hold the configurations and allow modifications as well as managing and monitoring the Data Guard environment.

Tie It All Together

High availability is an important topic for database systems. In designing an architecture that is highly available, an effort needs to be made to remove all single points of failure in business-critical applications systems. Business continuity can be looked at from the application and database level with the enhancements to high availability in the Oracle 12*c* environment. There are several components of Oracle 12*c* database, which, either standing alone or in combination, provide highly available solutions. Oracle Real Application Clusters (RAC), implemented together with Data Guard, provides a very fast failover system with the capabilities of an off-site standby database for disaster recovery. Automatic Storage Management (ASM) offers several advancements for managing the database files and disks in order to provide a stable environment that can minimize maintenance windows and downtime. Planning with your business and reviewing these as well as other database features should assist you in developing and implementing a well-architected, highly available database system.

☑ Chapter 7 Mastery Check

1. Which component is not part of an RAC environment?

   A. Interconnect

   B. Clusterware

   C. DGMGRL

   D. OCR

2. True or false: The Cluster Verification Utility is run after the RAC database is created to verify that the interconnect is running properly.

3. In an RAC environment, OCR stands for

   A. Oracle Cluster Registry

   B. Oracle Connection Repository

   C. Oracle Clusterware Record

   D. Oracle Cluster Recovery

4. When using ASM, does the database server need an ASM instance too?

5. What is the command-line interface that can be used to copy, back up, and list the files in ASM directories?

6. True or false: ASM redundancy types are EXTERNAL, HIGH, and LOW.

7. When SHUTDOWN ABORT is used to shut down the ASM instance, what happens to the database instances connecting to that ASM instance? What happens when the ASM instance is in an ASM cluster?

8. What is the administrator's login role on the ASM instance? What is the administrator's login role for Data Guard?

9. What does the following sqlplus command do? Does it run against the primary or standby server?

```
SQLPLUS> alter database recover managed standby database using current
logfile disconnect;
```

10. True or false: Asynchronous transport of redo logs means that the redo is being written to the primary and standby locations at the same time.

11. Which of the following is not a characteristic of the Data Guard protection mode of maximum protection?

    A. Synchronous transport

    B. Zero data loss

    C. Standby fails, primary is halted

    D. Performance is the biggest concern

12. Which tools can be used to manage the Data Guard environment?

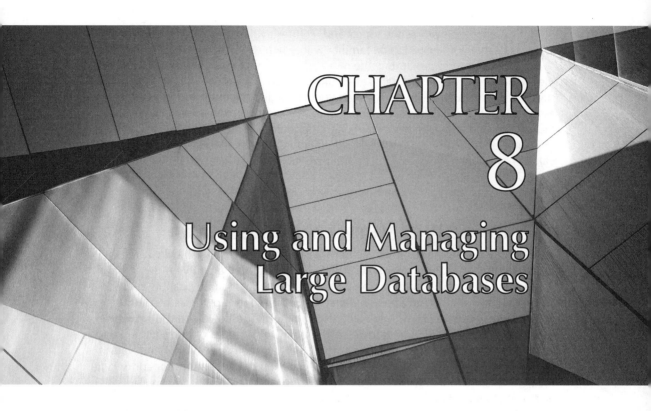

CHAPTER
8

Using and Managing
Large Databases

CRITICAL SKILLS

8.1 Learn to Identify a Very Large
Database

8.2 How and Why to Use Data
Partitioning

8.3 Compress Your Data

8.4 Use Parallel Processing to Improve
Performance

8.5 Use Materialized Views

8.6 Use SQL Aggregate and Analysis
Functions

8.7 Create SQL Models

This chapter explores the topics and features available in Oracle Database 12*c* that you'll need to be familiar with when working with large databases. These features are among the more advanced that you will encounter, but they're necessary because databases continue to grow larger and larger. When you start working with Oracle, you will find yourself facing the trials and tribulations associated with large databases sooner rather than later. The quicker you understand the features and know where and when to use them, the more effective you will be. Of course, these features are not just valuable for large databases; they provide value to everyone who is looking to optimize their Oracle database environment.

CRITICAL SKILL 8.1
Learn to Identify a Very Large Database

Let's start by describing what we mean by a very large database (VLDB). *Large* is a relative term that changes over time. What was considered large five or ten years ago is small by today's standards, and what is large today will be peanuts a few years from now. How many people remember buying a computer with 20MB of storage and wondering how they could ever fill it up? Today, personal computers may come with more than a terabyte of storage; with the types of information you store, you know that you will fill these storage systems to capacity sooner or later. Each release of Oracle has included new features and enhancements for addressing the need to store more and more data. For example, Oracle8*i* was released in 1999 and could handle databases with *terabytes* (1024 gigabytes) of data. In 2001, Oracle9*i* was released and could deal with up to 500 *petabytes* (1024 terabytes). Oracle Database 11*g* offered support for *exabyte* (1024 petabytes) databases. Now there are databases with exabytes, and starting to approach the zettabyte (1024 exabytes) range. Hardware is also playing a part in allowing the databases to increase to these sizes. Oracle is producing new high-performance hardware and software in the Exa-Machines—Exadata, Exalogic, and Exalytics, with more to come. The Exa-Machines will provide speed improvements and large amounts of storage as the importance of large databases continues to expand and evolve over time. You'll see more on Exadata in the next chapter.

The most obvious examples of large database implementations are data warehouses and decision support systems. These environments usually have tables with millions or billions of rows or wide tables with large numbers of columns and many rows. There are also many OLTP systems that are very large and can benefit from the features you are about to explore. Because you have many topics to get through, let's jump right in and start with data partitioning.

NOTE
Many of the topics discussed in this chapter could take an entire book to cover completely. Because this is an introductory book, specifics for some topics have been omitted. Real-world experiences and additional reading will build on the material presented here.

CRITICAL SKILL 8.2

How and Why to Use Data Partitioning

As user communities require more and more detailed information to remain competitive, it has fallen to database designers and administrators to help ensure that the information is managed effectively and can be retrieved for analysis efficiently. In this section, we discuss partitioning data and the reasons why it is so important when working with large databases. Afterward, you'll follow the steps required to make it all work.

Why Use Data Partitioning

Let's start by defining *data partitioning*. In its simplest form, it is a way of breaking up or subsetting data into smaller units that can be managed and accessed separately. It has been around for a long time, both as a design technique and as a technology. Let's look at some of the issues that gave rise to the need for partitioning and the solutions to these issues.

Tables containing very large numbers of rows have always posed problems and challenges for DBAs, application developers, and end users alike. For the DBA, the problems are centered on the maintenance and manageability of the underlying data files that contain the data for these tables. For the application developers and end users, the issues are query performance and data availability.

To mitigate these issues, the standard database design technique was to create physically separate tables, identical in structure (for example, columns), but each containing a subset of the total data (this design technique will be referred to as *non-partitioned* here). These tables could be referred to directly or through a series of views. This technique solved some of the problems, but still meant maintenance for the DBA with regard to creating new tables and/or views as new subsets of data were acquired. In addition, if access to the entire dataset was required, a view was needed to join all subsets together.

Figure 8-1 illustrates a non-partitioned design. In this sample, separate tables with identical structures have been created to hold monthly sales information for 2005. Views have also been defined to group the monthly information into quarters using a union query. The quarterly views themselves are then grouped together into a view that represents the entire year. The same structures would be created for each year of data. In order to obtain data for a particular month or quarter, an end user would have to know which table or view to use.

Similar to the technique illustrated in Figure 8-1, the partitioning technology offered by Oracle Database 12*c* is a method of breaking up large amounts of data into smaller, more manageable chunks, with each of the partitions having their own unique name and their own storage definitions. But, like the non-partitioned technique, it is transparent to the end user, offering improved performance and reduced maintenance. Figure 8-2 illustrates the same SALES table, but implemented using Oracle Database 12*c*'s partitioning option. From the end user's perspective, there is only one table called SALES and all that is required to access data from the correct partition is a date (or a month and year).

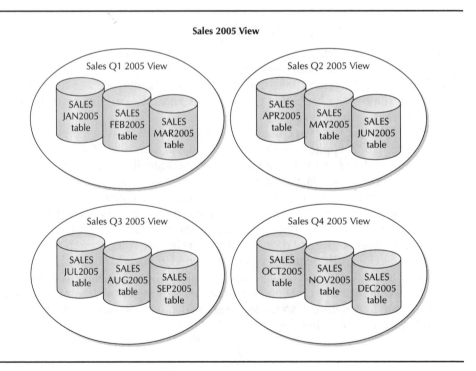

FIGURE 8-1. *Partitioning using physically separate tables (non-partitioned)*

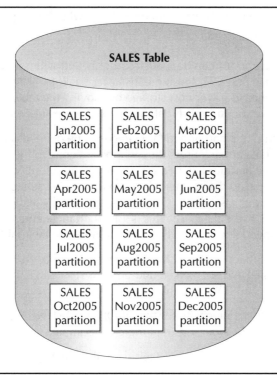

FIGURE 8-2.   *Partitioning using Oracle 12c partitioning*

Oracle partitioning was first introduced in Oracle 8, is only available with the Enterprise Edition, and is an additional option to the core database license. As previously suggested, it is one database option that is a must-have for anyone with a large volume of data that needs to be quickly retrievable or with a need for speedy data archiving. Many improvements have been made since then, and Oracle Database 12*c* contains all of the latest features and enhancements to maintain the objects. The remainder of this section discusses these features in more detail.

Manageability

When administering large databases, DBAs are required to determine the most efficient and effective ways to configure the underlying data files that support the tables in the database. The decisions made at this time will affect your data accessibility and availability as well as backup and recovery.

Some of the benefits for database manageability when using partitioned tables include the following:

- Historical partitions can be made read-only and will not need to be backed up more than once. This also means faster backups. With partitions, you can move data to lower-cost storage by moving the tablespace, sending it to an archive via an export (datapump), or some other method.

- The structure of a partitioned table needs to be defined only once. As new subsets of data are acquired, they will be assigned to the correct partition, based on the partitioning method chosen. In addition, with Oracle 12c you have the ability to define intervals that allow you to define only the partitions that you need. It also allows Oracle to automatically add partitions based on data arriving in the database. This is an important feature for DBAs, who currently spend time manually adding partitions to their tables.

- Moving a partition can now be an online operation, and the global indexes are maintained and not marked unusable. ALTER TABLE…MOVE PARTITION allows DDL and DML to continue to run uninterrupted on the partition.

- Global index maintenance for the DROP and TRUNCATE PARTITION happens asynchronously so that there is no impact to the index availability.

- Individual tablespaces and/or their data files can be taken offline for maintenance or archiving without affecting access to other subsets of data. For example, assuming data for a table is partitioned by month (later in this chapter, you learn about the different types of partitioning) and only 13 months of data is to be kept online at any one time, the earliest month is archived and dropped from the table when a new month is acquired. This is accomplished using the command ALTER TABLE abc DROP PARTITION xyz and does not affect access to the remaining 12 months of data.

- Other commands that would normally apply at the table level can also be applied to a particular partition of the table. These include but are not limited to DELETE, INSERT, SELECT, TRUNCATE, and UPDATE. TRUNCATE and EXCHANGE PARTITION operations allow for cascading data maintenance for related tables. You should review the *Oracle Database VLDB and Partitioning Guide* for a complete list of the commands that are available with partitions and subpartitions.

Performance

One of the main reasons for partitioning a table is to improve I/O response time when selecting data from the table. Having a table's data partitioned into subsets can yield much faster query results when you are looking for data that is contained within one subset of the total. Let's look at an illustrative example.

Assume the SALES table contains 100 million records representing daily sales revenue for the years 2008 to 2010 inclusive. You want to know what the total revenue is for February 2010. Your query might look something like this:

```
select sum(amount_sold)
from sales
where time_id between to_date('2008-02-01', 'YYYY-MM-DD')
  and to_date('2010-02-28', 'YYYY-MM-DD');
```

With a non-partitioned table design, all 100 million rows would need to be scanned to determine if they belong to the date criteria. With a partitioned table design based on monthly partitions, with about 2.8 million rows for each month, only those rows in the February 2012 partition (and therefore only about 2.8 million rows) would be scanned. The process of eliminating data not belonging to the subset defined by the query criteria is referred to as *partition pruning.*

With the basic concepts of partitioning and an understanding of why you use it under your belt, you can now learn about the finer details of how to implement partitioning.

Ask the Expert

Q: Can you use the analyze table command to gather statistics on partitioned tables?

A: No, at least not correctly. The supplied DBMS_STATS package should be used to gather statistics on partitioned tables instead. The analyze table command does not gather all required statistics for partitioned tables (in particular, global statistics). In addition, the analyze command will eventually be phased out (for all types of table and indexes), and only those statistics gathered by the DBMS_STATS package will be used by the cost-based optimizer. Oracle Database 12c provides an enhancement for using resources with DBMS_STATS. Using the parameter CONCURRENT set to TRUE, the statistics will be gathered on multiple partitions from separate statistics gathering jobs for each partition. Depending on the system resources and how many available jobs are in the queue, more jobs will be executed. Being able to run these jobs concurrently can reduce the time it takes to gather the statistics.

Implement Data Partitioning

Implementing data partitioning in Oracle Database 12*c* is a process that requires careful planning to ensure success. You will need to understand your database environment, hardware, structures, and data before you can make the appropriate decisions. The next few sections will outline the steps you will take when partitioning. Let's start by looking at the characteristics of the candidate table.

Analyze the Candidate Table

The first step in the partitioning process is to analyze and understand the candidate table, its environment, and its uses. Following are some criteria to consider.

Table Structure and Data Contents   You will need to look at the attributes that are available and the distribution of the data within each attribute. You must consider currently available data as well as projected future data. The distribution of data over each attribute is important because you want to ensure that the resulting data subsets are evenly distributed across the defined partitions.

Consider a table called PHONE_USAGE that contains detailed mobile phone call records with over 300 million records per month. It has many attributes, including the toll type (toll_type_cd) and the date of call (call_date). Table 8-1 shows a sample row count for a month by toll_type_cd. As you can see, using this attribute would probably not be an ideal choice for creating subsets because the distribution is heavily skewed toward LOCAL calls.

Table 8-2 looks at the distribution of the same data by the day of the week (for example, Sunday to Saturday based on call_date).

You can see that the day of the week provides a relatively even distribution that is more suitable for partitioning. Having a relatively equal data distribution of your data across the partitions will result in better performance during queries, as processing can be spread equally across the partitions. When a table is skewed to one partition, this can result in a very large data set within your table, which would defeat the purpose of partitioning the table in the first place.

toll_type_cd	Record Count (Sample Month)
INTNL	27,296,802
CONTNL	52,227,998
LOCAL	189,554,584
NRTH AMRCA	36,367,841

TABLE 8-1.   *Toll Type and Record Counts*

Day of the Week (Based on call_date)	Record Count (Sample Month)
SUN	41,635,356
MON	44,235,019
TUE	42,875,502
WED	43,235,721
THU	43,922,997
FRI	45,005,293
SAT	44,537,337

TABLE 8-2. *Counts Based on Day of the Week*

To access the data, you will need to know what the most common data selection criteria are. This is perhaps the most important part of the analysis because, as stated earlier, query performance is the most noticeable gain of data partitioning. In order for this to be realized, your data subsets need to be defined according to the most common selection criteria so that unnecessary partitions can be pruned from the result set. The selection criteria will be determined largely by your user community and can be determined using historical query patterns (if available) or consulting business requirements.

Referring to the SALES table example, your analysis of query patterns for a three-month period (averaging 400 queries per month) yields the results shown in Table 8-3.

Attribute	Times Used in Query Selection Criteria (Average/Month)
prod_id	33
cust_id	40
time_id	355
channel_id	55
promo_id	298
quantity_sold	25
amount_sold	20

TABLE 8-3. *Query Counts Based on Data Attributes*

The analysis tells you that time_id and promo_id are both frequently used as query predicates. You could use this information along with the corresponding row distribution to determine which attribute would result in the better partitioning strategy.

Identify the Partition Key

Once you understand the characteristics of your candidate table, the next step in the partitioning process is to select the attribute(s) of the candidate table that will define the partition subsets and how the subsets will be defined. The selected attributes will form the *partition key*. Only one set of attributes can be chosen to partition the data. This is an important decision because it will affect the manageability and usability of the table.

The results of your analysis of the candidate table should provide you with a good idea of the attributes to use. The best attributes will be those that satisfy the most criteria. Keep in mind, however, that the adage "you can satisfy some of the criteria some of the time, but you can't satisfy all of the criteria all of the time" applies here. Despite your best efforts and planning, there will still be situations when the table will be treated as if it were non-partitioned. Take, for example, a perfectly valid query submitted by the user community that does not include the attributes of the partition key as part of the selection criteria or groups by the partition key, this would result in the query missing the core indexes and will impact performance by reading across all partitions. In this case, data from the entire table (that is, all partitions) would be scanned in order to satisfy the request.

Select the Type of Partitioning

After you have selected the partition key, the next step in the partitioning process is to decide which type of partitioning you want to implement on the candidate table. Partitioning options provide seven ways to partition data:

- Range partitioning
- List partitioning
- Hash partitioning
- Composite partitioning
- Reference partitioning
- Virtual column-based partitioning
- Interval partitioning

The type of partitioning you choose will depend on the results of your analysis of the candidate table. The most common type of partitioning is range partitioning so we cover it in detail. Let's look at the characteristics of each type of partitioning.

Range partitioning has been around the longest of all partitioning types and is the type implemented most often. In most cases, the ranges are based on some date column, such as quarters, months, or, in the case of very large data volumes, days. (Assuming you have a time component, theoretically, you can go down to any level of time—hours, minutes, and so on. However, there are implications to defining this many partitions.) The ranges selected will again be based on the results of your analysis of the table, using dates, numeric values, or character values. Following is an example based on the SALES table you saw earlier in the chapter.

NOTE
The partitioning examples presented in this chapter do not address all of the command options available. They are meant to give you a taste of what is available.

To create your SALES table as non-partitioned, you would use the standard create table statement, as shown in this listing:

```
create table sales (
    prod_id          number           not null,
    cust_id          number           not null,
    time_id          date             not null,
    channel_id       number           not null,
    promo_id         number           not null,
    quantity_sold    number (10,2)    not null,
    amount_sold      number (10,2)    not null)
tablespace example_tblspc_1;
```

Based on the analysis of the usage patterns and row distribution, you have decided that the optimal partition strategy for this table is based on sales month. You will now redefine the SALES table using time_id as your partition key to create monthly partitions for January 2012 to December 2015, inclusive. Creation of data partitions is accomplished using extensions of the create table statement. The following listing shows the creation of the table with range partitions. Explanations of the important lines are given in Table 8-4.

```
1 create table sales (
2     prod_id          number           not null,
3     cust_id          number           not null,
4     time_id          date             not null,
5     channel_id       number           not null,
6     promo_id         number           not null,
7     quantity_sold    number (10,2)    not null,
8     amount_sold      number (10,2)    not null)
```

```
 9  storage (initial 65536  minextents 1 maxextents 2147483645)
10 partition by range (time_id)
11 (partition sales_201201 values less than
12                        (to_date('2012-02-01','YYYY-MM-DD'))
13                        tablespace sales_ts_201201,
14  partition sales_201202 values less than
15                        (to_date('2012-03-01','YYYY-MM-DD'))
16                        tablespace sales_ts_201202,
17  partition sales_201203 values less than
18                        (to_date('2012-04-01','YYYY-MM-DD'))
19                        tablespace sales_ts_201203,
...
113  partition sales_201411 values less than
114                        (to_date('2014-12-01','YYYY-MM-DD'))
115                        tablespace sales_ts_201411,
116  partition sales_201412 values less than
117                        (to_date('2015-01-01','YYYY-MM-DD'))
118                        tablespace sales_ts_201412,
119  partition sales_max values less than (MAXVALUE)
120                        tablespace sales_ts_max);
```

Lines	Important Points
9	This defines the default table-level storage parameters that will apply to all partitions. It is possible to override these defaults at the partition level in favor of specific parameters required for a particular partition.
10	This defines the type of partitioning (for example, range) and the partition key (for instance, time_id).
11–118	Define each partition based on the values of time_id (repetitive lines for April 2012 to October 2014 omitted for brevity's sake). For each partition, the upper boundary of the partition key value is specified (as defined by the function's LESS THAN clause), as well as the name of the tablespace where the subset is to be stored. Values must be specified in ascending order and cannot overlap. It is good practice to give meaningful names to both the partitions and tablespaces.
119–120	Records that exceed the defined criteria will be placed into the final catchall partition, which uses the literal MAXVALUE. The MAXVALUE literal can be defined for the highest partition. It represents a virtual infinite value that sorts higher than any other possible value for the partitioning key, including the NULL value.

TABLE 8-4. *Explanation of Range Partitioning Syntax*

NOTE
Lines 11 to 13 define the first partition to hold data where time_id is less than February 1, 2012. The intention in this example is that this first partition will only hold data for January 2012 (our data analysis tells us that there is no data before this date). However, if there happens to be data prior to January 2012, it will also be placed in this partition and may skew the row distribution by placing many more rows than intended in this partition.

That completes the discussion on range partitioning. Let's now have a look at list and hash partitioning.

There may be cases when, after your analysis of a candidate table, you decide that range partitioning is not the best fit for your table. Another way to subset your data is to use *list partitioning,* where you group a set of discrete partition key values. By using this type of partitioning, you can control the placement of the records in specified partitions, thereby allowing you to group related records together that may not otherwise have a relationship.

As an example, assume you have an INS_COVERAGE table that contains insurance coverage. Your analysis of this table and its usage leads you to decide that you should partition, based on the attribute COV_TYPE_CD, into the buckets shown in Table 8-5.

COV_TYPE_CD	Grouping
TERM 65	Life
UL	Life
ADB	Life
COLA	GIB
GPO	GIB
WP	Disability
DIS	Disability

TABLE 8-5. *Insurance Coverage Groupings*

The syntax of the CREATE TABLE statement is similar to that for range partitioning. Table 8-6 provides an explanation.

```
1 create table ins_coverage (
 2  plan_id         number      not null,
 3  cust_id         number      not null,
 4  time_id         date        not null,
 5  dist_channel_id number      not null,
 6  cov_type_cd  varchar2(50)  not null,
 7  cov_amt  number (10,2) not null,
 8  prem_amt  number (10,2) not null)
 9  storage (initial 65536  minextents 1 maxextents 2147483645)
10 partition by list (cov_type_cd)
11  (partition cov_life values ('TERM 65', 'UL', 'ADB')
12                  tablespace cov_life_ts,
13  partition cov_gib values ('COLA', 'GIB')
14                  tablespace cov_gib_ts,
15  partition cov_dis values ('WP', 'DIS')
16                  tablespace cov_dis_ts,
17  partition cov_inv values ('MF')
18                  tablespace cov_inv_ts
19  partition cov_other values(default));
```

TIP
If you discover missing partition key values that need to be added to existing partition definitions after the table has been created, you can issue an ALTER TABLE abc MODIFY PARTITION xyz ADD VALUES ('value1', ...).

Lines	Important Points
10	Defines the type of partitioning (for example, list) and the partition key (cov_type_cd, for instance). Note that with list partitioning, only one attribute from the table can be chosen as the partition key. In other words, multicolumn partition keys are not permitted.
11–18	Defines each partition based on the groups of values of cov_type_cd.

TABLE 8-6. *Explanation of List Partitioning Syntax*

If you determine from your table analysis that neither range nor list partitioning is appropriate for your table, but you still want to reap the benefits offered by partitioning, there is a third partitioning option called *hash partitioning*. With hash partitioning, you define up to 16 partition key attributes as well as the number of partitions you want to spread the data across. As long as each partition is on its own physical device and most of the queries use the partition key as a predicate, you should see performance gains. Hash partitioning is useful if the distribution of data is unknown or unpredictable.

The following listing is an example of hash partitioning. Table 8-7 explains the important lines:

```
1 create table sub_activations (
2   sub_id          number  not null,
3   dist_channel_id number  not null,
4   act_date        date    not null,
5   deact_date      date    not null,
6   sales_rep_id    number  not null)

7 partition by hash (sub_id)
8 partitions 4
9 store in (subact_ts1, subact_ts2, subact_ts3, subact_ts4);
```

It is beyond the scope of this book to discuss the hashing algorithm used by Oracle Database. However, it is based on the number of attributes in the partition key and the number of partitions selected.

Another method of partitioning is a combination of two of the previous types. Combining two types of partitioning is called *composite partitioning*. There are a few basic combinations: range with hash, range with range, and range with list and others. Using composite partitioning allows you to take advantage of the features of either hash or list partitioning within the higher groupings of ranges.

Lines	Important Points
7	Defines the type of partitioning (for instance, hash) and the partition key (for example, sub_id)
8	Specifies the number of partitions over which to spread the data
9	Specifies the tablespaces into which the partitions will be placed

TABLE 8-7. *Explanation of Hash Partitioning Syntax*

A good example of where this type of partitioning is used is the PHONE_USAGE table you saw in your candidate table analysis. In this case, you have a table that is being loaded with 300 million records per month. You could choose to implement range partitioning by month and then subdivide the monthly partitions into four hash partitions. The following listing shows the SQL syntax that accomplishes this, and Table 8-8 provides the explanation of the important lines:

```
1 create table phone_usage
 2 (sub_id          number,
 3  call_date       date,
 4  call_type_id    number,
 5  called_location      varchar2(50),
 6  service_carrier_id   number)
 7 storage (initial 65536?  minextents 1 maxextents 2147483645)
 8 partition by range (call_date)
 9 subpartition by hash(sub_id)
10 subpartition template(
11  subpartition sub1 tablespace ph_usg_ts1,
12  subpartition sub2 tablespace ph_usg_ts2,
13  subpartition sub3 tablespace ph_usg_ts3,
14  subpartition sub4 tablespace ph_usg_ts4)
```

Lines	Important Points
8	Defines the higher-level partitioning type (for example, range) and its partition key (for instance, call_date).
9	Specifies the secondary partitioning type (in this case, hash) and its partition key (here, sub_id).
10–14	Specifies a template that will be used to define the tablespace names for each subpartition, as well as the tablespace names. The name of each subpartition will be composed of the higher-level partition name concatenated with an underscore, then the subpartition name specified in the template. For example, data for January 2012 will be placed in tablespace ph_usg_ts1 and divided into four subpartitions called PHONEUSG_201201_SUB1, PHONEUSG_201201_SUB2, PHONEUSG_201201_SUB3, and PHONEUSG_201201_SUB4.
15–27	Specifies the ranges for the higher-level partition based on the call_date partition key.

TABLE 8-8. *Explanation of Composite Partitioning Syntax*

```
15 (partition phoneusg_201201 values less than
16                       (to_date('2012-02-01','YYYY-MM-DD')),
17  partition phoneusg_201202 values less than
18                       (to_date('2012-03-01','YYYY-MM-DD')),
19  partition phoneusg_201203 values less than
20                       (to_date('2012-04-01','YYYY-MM-DD')),
21  partition phoneusg_201204 values less than
22                       (to_date('2012-05-01','YYYY-MM-DD')),
23  partition phoneusg_201205 values less than
24                       (to_date('2012-06-01','YYYY-MM-DD')),
25  partition phoneusg_201206 values less than
26                       (to_date('2012-07-01','YYYY-MM-DD')),
27  partition phoneusg_max values less than (maxvalue));
```

Reference partitioning is one of the latest methods that Oracle has provided you for partitioning your data. The method used by reference partitioning allows you to partition data based upon referential constraints. As previously discussed, referential integrity (RI) in a database allows data to be correct and to be consistent. The idea is that you would not have any order line items without an order. RI is implemented to ensure data is correct, complete, and consistent. This leads you to the challenge of partitioning data in a productive manner, such that you may have consistent partitioning between parent and child tables. So, if you partition ORDERS by date range, you want the ORDER_ITEMS to follow the same method. Before its introduction in Oracle 11*g*, you could achieve this in a manual way, which may include adding additional attributes to child records (ORDER_ITEMS) to allow you to provide the same partition keys. With reference partitioning, you can now equi-partition parent and child tables without the need to duplicate keys. In addition, partition maintenance tasks will cascade from parent to child to reduce errors or omissions in the two tables.

Ask the Expert

Q: **If the partition key of record in a partitioned table is updated and the new value means that the data belongs to a different partition, does Oracle Database automatically move the record to the appropriate partition?**

A: Yes, but the table must have the ENABLE ROW MOVEMENT option before the update is made. This option is invoked as either part of the CREATE TABLE statement or using an ALTER TABLE statement. Otherwise, the UPDATE statement will generate an Oracle error.

Let's look at an example of how you could set up a reference partitioned table. First, you should define the parent table:

```
CREATE TABLE orders
     ( order_id        NUMBER(12),
       order_date      DATE,
       order_meth      VARCHAR2(8),
       customer_id     NUMBER(6),
       order_status    NUMBER(2),
       order_tot       NUMBER(8,2),
       sales_rep_id    NUMBER(6),
       campaign_id     NUMBER(6),
       CONSTRAINT orders_pk PRIMARY KEY(order_id)
     )
PARTITION BY RANGE(order_date)
     ( PARTITION Q1_2012 VALUES
                      LESS THAN (TO_DATE('01-APR-2012','DD-MON-YYYY')),
       PARTITION Q2_2012 VALUES
                      LESS THAN (TO_DATE('01-JUL-2012','DD-MON-YYYY')),
       PARTITION Q3_2012 VALUES
                      LESS THAN (TO_DATE('01-OCT-2012','DD-MON-YYYY')),
       PARTITION Q4_2012 VALUES
                      LESS THAN (TO_DATE('01-JAN-2013','DD-MON-YYYY')),
       PARTITION UNCLASSIFIED_ORDER VALUES (DEFAULT)   )
/
```

Now that you have the parent ORDERS table defined, you should take the time to notice that you defined a primary key constraint within the table definition. This is a requirement for the next step. Oracle reference partitioning depends solely on the definition of this integrity between entities, so consider this when deciding to utilize this method of partitioning. Now you can move on to the child table definition. In this case, you will define the table and then reference back to the parent table so that the partitioning is now based upon the parent's partitioning methods, ultimately leveraging the database's defined referential integrity:

```
CREATE TABLE order_items
     ( order_id      NUMBER(12)   NOT NULL,
       line_item_id  NUMBER(3)    NOT NULL,
       product_id    NUMBER(6)    NOT NULL,
       unit_price    NUMBER(8,2),
       quantity      NUMBER(8),
       CONSTRAINT order_items_fk
       FOREIGN KEY(order_id) REFERENCES orders(order_id)
     )
  PARTITION BY REFERENCE(order_items_fk)
/
```

As can see in the previous listing, this is a powerful method for partitioning data in a manner that logically follows the way that you store and read your data in a parent-child type relationship. Although you define only one partitioning method, this will reduce your workload because it really defines the method used by two or more tables, ultimately reducing the maintenance of your database. This method should be considered in operational and more relationship-oriented data sets.

Virtual columns are columns that are defined in metadata and are provided with the ability to create in-table derivations. This is valuable to many applications. To extend the virtual column idea to partitioning is the next logical extension of this functionality. Since Oracle Database 11*g*, Oracle has provided *virtual column-based partitioning.* By implementing this method of partitioning, you can use value derivations.

Before we discuss this method, we need to discuss the concept of the *INTERVAL* clause. The INTERVAL clause is used by Oracle to calculate the range of partitions. In our example, we will use a one-month interval, but this range can be set to other values. It should also be noted that in version 12*c* that Oracle has added the combination of INTERVAL and REF partitioning to extend it even further than simple INTERVAL partitioning. Let's now look at an example of how a table is partitioned using the basic INTERVAL method:

```
CREATE TABLE sales
   ( prod_id       NUMBER(6) NOT NULL
   , cust_id       NUMBER NOT NULL
   , time_id       DATE NOT NULL
   , channel_id    CHAR(1) NOT NULL
   , promo_id      NUMBER(6) NOT NULL
   , quantity_sold NUMBER(3) NOT NULL
   , amount_sold   NUMBER(10,2) NOT NULL
   , total_amount AS (quantity_sold * amount_sold)
   )
PARTITION BY RANGE (time_id) INTERVAL (NUMTOYMINTERVAL(1,'MONTH'))
SUBPARTITION BY RANGE (total_amount)
SUBPARTITION TEMPLATE
   ( SUBPARTITION p_small VALUES LESS THAN (1000)
   , SUBPARTITION p_medium VALUES LESS THAN (5000)
   , SUBPARTITION p_large VALUES LESS THAN (10000)
   , SUBPARTITION p_extreme VALUES LESS THAN (MAXVALUE)
   )
 (PARTITION sales_before_2007 VALUES LESS THAN
         (TO_DATE('01-JAN-2007','dd-MON-yyyy'))
ENABLE ROW MOVEMENT
PARALLEL NOLOGGING;
```

The previous example provides you with a few partitioning features. The first is the use of the virtual column partitioning. As you can see, the virtual column *total amount* is the column that will be used in the subpartitions. Subpartitions are used in secondary partitioning. This is known as *composite partitioning,* or the combining of two types of partitioning providing two layers of partitioned data. In this example, you are combining columns using the partitioning methods of range and date or range and the virtual column to give you some guidance on how to partition data correctly. The power of virtual columns is focused on providing complete control over how and where data is stored to optimize performance.

Define the Partitioned Indexing Strategy

Okay, so now you have decided how you are going to partition your data. To really get the most out of partitioning, you will need to look at some indexing strategies. There are two types of indexes applicable to partitioned tables: local and global. Let's take a brief look at each.

Local partitioned indexes are indexes that are partitioned in the exact same manner as the data in their associated table—that is, they have a direct one-to-one relationship with the data partitions and use the same partition key. This association is illustrated in Figure 8-3; as you can see, each partition has its own associated "local" index. This drawing is based on Figure 8-2, which you saw at the beginning of the chapter. It shows how the data and indexes for each monthly subset are related and then joins using the partitions with the local index.

Because of this relationship, the following points apply to local indexes:

- You cannot explicitly add or drop a partition to/from a local index. The index automatically adds or drops index partitions when related data partitions are added or dropped. Consider Figure 8-3: If you dropped the data partition for January 2005, the corresponding index partition would automatically be dropped as well. Likewise, if you added a new data partition for January 2012, a new index partition would automatically be created.

- One of the advantages of partitioning data is to allow access to other subsets while maintenance is being carried out on another partition. Because local index partitions are in line with the data partitions, this advantage still exists.

- Local partitioned indexes require less maintenance than global indexes, as you will see later in this chapter.

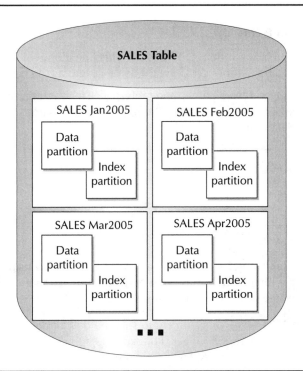

FIGURE 8-3. *Local partitioned indexes*

The SQL syntax for creating a local index is presented in the next listing, which refers to the SALES table you created earlier in the chapter. Using RANGE partitioning we can now add a local index. Table 8-9 contains an explanation of the syntax:

```
 1 create index sales_idx_l1 on sales (time_id)
 2 local
 3 (partition sales_idx_200501  tablespace sales_ts_idx_200501,
 4  partition sales_idx_200502  tablespace sales_ts_idx_200502,
 5  partition sales_idx_200503  tablespace sales_ts_idx_200503,
...
37  partition sales_idx_200711  tablespace sales_ts_idx_200711,
38  partition sales_idx_200712  tablespace sales_ts_idx_200712,
39  partition sales_idx_max  tablespace sales_ts_idx_max);
```

Lines	Important Points
2	Specifies that the index is to be local. This line alone tells you that the index is to be partitioned along the same ranges as the data.
3–39	Defines the partition names and tablespaces for each partition. These lines are optional, but without them, the partition names will be assigned by the database.

TABLE 8-9. *Syntax Highlights*

Ask the Expert

Q: After a table and its local indexes have been defined using range partitioning with a default maxvalue partition, how can you add more partitions as new subsets of data are received?

A: Use an ALTER TABLE statement to split the default data partitions, adding your new partition ranges. For example, to add a data partition for January 2008 data in the SALES table in the previous listing, issue the following command:

```
alter table sales
split partition sales_max at
(to_date('2008-02-01','YYYY-MM-DD'))
into (partition sales_200801 tablespace sales_ts_200801,
      partition sales_max tablespace sales_ts_max);
```

This ALTER TABLE command will split the default index partition for sales_idx_l1. However, it will use the data partition names (for example, sales_200801) and tablespaces (sales_ts_200801, for instance); remember in the local index example you explicitly specified the partition names and tablespaces for the index. Therefore, the partition names and tablespaces will need to be adjusted using ALTER INDEX commands, as follows:

```
alter index sales_idx_l1
rename partition sales_200801 to sales_idx_200801;

alter index sales_idx_l1
rebuild partition sales_idx_200801 tablespace
sales_ts_idx_200801;

alter index sales_idx_l1
rebuild partition sales_idx_max tablespace sales_ts_idx_max;
```

Some other points about local partitioned indexes:

- They can be unique, but only if the data partition key is part of the index key attributes.

- Bitmap indexes on partitioned tables must be local.

- Subpartitioned indexes are always local.

- They are best suited for data warehouses and decision support systems.

- Local unique indexes also work well in OLTP environments.

Global partitioned indexes are indexes that are not directly associated with the data partitions. Instead, their partitions are defined independently, with the partition key sometimes different from the data partition key. This association is illustrated in Figure 8-4. (This figure is again based on Figure 8-2, shown at the beginning of the chapter.) It shows that the data is partitioned by monthly ranges, with a global index partitioned by product.

One advantage of global indexes is that if partition pruning cannot occur for the data partitions because of the predicates of a query, index partition pruning may still be possible with the global partition index. Global partitioned indexes are available as either range-based or hash-based. When using range-based global indexes, you must specify a default partition with maxvalue. Let's look at an example for creating a global partitioned index and then discuss how it would be used.

Referring again to the PHONE_USAGE table you created earlier in the chapter, you should now create a global index on the call_type_id. The following listing is the SQL for this, with the explanation presented in Table 8-10:

```
 1 create index phone_usg_idx_g1 on phone_usage (call_type_id)
 2 global
 3 partition by range (call_type_id)
 4 (partition ph_usg_idx_g1 values less than (2)
 5                 tablespace ph_usg_ts_idx_1,
 6  partition ph_usg_idx_g2 values less than (3)
 7                 tablespace ph_usg_ts_idx_2,
 8  partition ph_usg_idx_g3 values less than (4)
 9                 tablespace ph_usg_ts_idx_3,
10  partition ph_usg_idx_g4 values less than (5)
11                 tablespace ph_usg_ts_idx_4,
12  partition ph_usg_idx_gmax values less than (maxvalue)
13                 tablespace ph_usg_ts_idx_max);
```

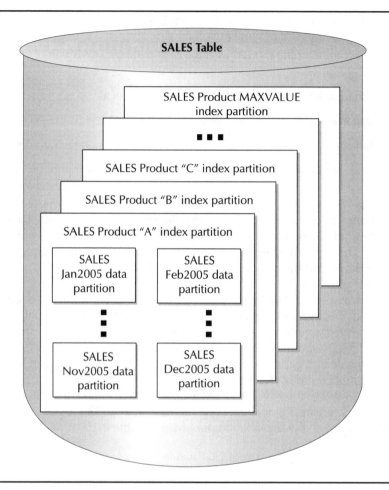

FIGURE 8-4. *Global partitioned indexes*

Now, assume the following query is executed against the PHONE_USAGE table:

```
select count(*)
from phone_usage
where call_type_id = 3;
```

Without the global index you just defined, no partition pruning would occur because the query predicate does not refer to the data partition key call_date. But, with the global index, only the index entries from the partition ph_usg_idx_g3

Lines	Important Points
2	Specifies that the index is to be global
3	Defines the type of partitioning (here, range) for this index and the partition key (call_type_id, in this case)
4–13	Defines the partition names and tablespaces for each partition

TABLE 8-10. *Explanation for Global Partitioned Index Syntax*

would be scanned and therefore only data records related to those entries would be used in the result set.

Some other points on global partitioned indexes:

- Before 12*c,* globally partitioned indexes required more maintenance than local indexes, especially when you drop data partitions, because the indexes would become invalid and required rebuilding before they are available for use. Now the indexes are maintained at the same time as the DROP or TRUNCATE PARTITION command and no longer become invalid.

- They can be unique.

- They cannot be bitmap indexes.

- They are best suited for OLTP systems for direct access to specific records.

- Partial indexes are now available in 12*c.* These are indexes on a subset of the partitions of a table, which provides more flexibility for the globally partitioned indexes.

In your travels through the world of partitioning, you will hear the terms *prefixed* and *nonprefixed* partition indexes. These terms apply to both local and global indexes. An index is prefixed when the leftmost column of the index key is the same as the leftmost column of the index partition key. If the columns are not the same, the index is non-prefixed. That's all well and good, but what effect does it have?

It is a matter of performance: Non-prefixed indexes cost more, from a query perspective, than prefixed indexes. When a query is submitted against a partitioned table and the predicate(s) of the query include(s) the index keys of a prefixed index, pruning of the index partition can occur. If the same index is non-prefixed instead, all index partitions may need to be scanned. (Scanning of all index partitions will depend on the predicate in the query and the type of index: global or local. If the data partition key is included as a predicate and the index is local, then the index partitions to be scanned will be based on pruned data partitions.)

Project 8-1 Create a Range-Partitioned Table and a Local-Partitioned Index

Data and index partitioning are an important part in maintaining large databases. We have discussed the reasons for partitioning and shown the steps to implement it. In this project, you will create a range-partitioned table and a related local-partitioned index.

Step by Step

1. Create two tablespaces, called inv_ts_2007q1 and inv_2007q2, using the following SQL statements. These will be used to store data partitions:

```
create tablespace inv_ts_2007q1
    datafile 'inv_ts_2007q1_1.dat' size 10m;

create tablespace inv_ts_2007q2
    datafile 'inv_ts_2007q2_1.dat' size 10m;
```

2. Create two tablespaces, called inv_idx_ts_2007q1 and inv_idx_2007q2, using the following SQL statements. These will be used to store index partitions:

```
create tablespace inv_idx_ts_2007q1
    datafile 'inv_idx_ts_2007q1_f1.dat' size 10m;

create tablespace inv_idx_ts_2007q2
    datafile 'inv_idx_ts_2007q2_f1.dat' size 10m;
```

3. Create a partitioned table called INVOICE with column names and types based on the following information:

   a. Define the table with the columns identified in Table 8-11.

   b. Use order_date as the partition key and then subset the data into the first and second calendar quarters 2007.

Column Name	Data Type
invoice_id	NUMBER
customer_id	NUMBER
order_date	DATE
ship_date	DATE

TABLE 8-11. *INVOICE Table Columns*

c. Define the table with the data partitions and tablespaces identified in Table 8-12.

d. Use the enable row movement option:

```
create table invoice (
  invoice_id  number,
  customer_id  number,
  order_date  date,
  ship_date  date)
partition by range (order_date)
 (partition INV_2007Q1 values less than

(to_date(2007-04-01','YYYY-MM-DD'))
                         tablespace inv_ts_2007Q1,
  partition INV_2007Q2 values less than

(to_date('2007-07-01','YYYY-MM-DD'))
                         tablespace inv_ts_2007Q2,
  partition inv_max values less than (maxvalue)
                         tablespace inv_ts_max)
  enable row movement;
```

4. Create a local partitioned index called inv_order_dt_idx on call_date using the following listing as well as the index partitions and tablespaces identified in Table 8-12.

```
create index inv_order_dt_idx on invoice(order_date)
local
 (partition inv_idx_2007q1  tablespace inv_idx_ts_2007q1,
  partition inv_idx_2007q2  tablespace inv_idx_ts_2007q2,
  partition inv_idx_max  tablespace inv_idx_ts_max);
```

	Partition Name	**Tablespace Name**	**Upper Range Limit**
Data Partitions	INV_2007Q1	INV_TS_2007Q1	Apr 1, 2007
	INV_2007Q2	INV_TS_2007Q2	July 1, 2007
	INV_MAX	INV_TS_MAX	MAXVALUE
Index Partitions	INV_IDX_2007Q1	INV_IDX_TS_2007Q1	Apr 1, 2007
	INV_IDX_2007Q2	INV_IDX_TS_2007Q2	July 1, 2007
	INV_IDX_MAX	INV_IDX_TS_MAX	MAXVALUE

TABLE 8-12.   *INVOICE Table Data and Index Partitions*

(continued)

Project Summary

The steps in this project reinforce some of the more common scenarios you will encounter: range-based partitioning and prefixed local partitioned indexes. Separate tablespaces were used for data and indexes, quarterly partitions were defined, a local index was defined, and the enable row movement was used to allow the database to automatically redistribute rows to their related partitions in the event of an update to the partition key.

Well, you have certainly covered a lot in this section. Having the background information on these topics will serve you well when maintaining and tuning large databases. Before you move on to the next section, let's take a quick progress check to make sure it all sank in.

Progress Check

1. List at least three DML commands that can be applied to partitions as well as tables.

2. What does partition pruning mean?

3. How many table attributes can be used to define the partition key in list partitioning?

4. Which type of partitioning is most commonly used with a date-based partition key?

5. Which partitioning types cannot be combined together for composite partitioning?

6. How many partition keys can be defined for a partitioned table?

7. Which type of partitioned index has a one-to-one relationship between the data and index partitions?

8. What is meant by a prefixed partitioned index?

Progress Check Answers

1. The following DML commands can be applied to partitions as well as tables: delete, insert, select, truncate, and update.

2. Partition pruning is the process of eliminating data not belonging to the subset defined by the criteria of a query.

3. Only one table attribute can be used to define the partition key in list partitioning.

4. Range partitioning is most commonly used with a date-based partition key.

5. List and hash partitioning cannot be combined for composite partitioning.

6. Only one partition key may be defined.

CRITICAL SKILL 8.3

Compress Your Data

As you load more and more data into your database, performance and storage maintenance can quickly become concerns. Usually at the start of an implementation of a database, data volumes are estimated and projected a year or two ahead. However, oftentimes these estimates turn out to be on the low side and you find yourself scrambling for more space in order to load new data. In addition to the partitioning abilities discussed in the previous section, there is the ability to compress your data and indexes to further address the concerns of performance and maintenance.

Compression can be performed at the data or index levels. The tablespace can also be set up for compression, which means the objects in the tablespace will be compressed depending on the method. In this section, you learn about the options available and the impact these options have on your database.

Data Compression

With *data compression,* duplicate values in a database block are removed, leaving only a reference to the removed value, which is placed at the beginning of the block. All of the information required to rebuild the data in a block is contained within the block.

By compressing data, the physical disk space required is reduced; disk I/O and memory usage are also reduced, thereby improving performance. However, there are some cases when data compression is not appropriate. The following should be considered when looking at whether or not to compress data:

- Does the table exist in an OLTP or data warehousing environment? Data compression is best suited for data that is updated infrequently or, better yet, is read-only. Because most data in a data warehouse is considered read-only, data compression is more compatible with this type of environment.

- Does the table have many foreign keys? Foreign keys result in a lot of duplicate values in data. Tables with these structures are ideal candidates for data compression.

- How will data be loaded into the table? The loading method will determine the compression method. With basic compression, data is only compressed during bulk loading (for example, SQL*Loader), even when compression is enabled. To compress data when using a standard INSERT INTO statement, OLTP compression should be used.

Compression can be specified for various data-related objects using the CREATE or ALTER object commands. Table 8-13 identifies these objects and their first-level

Object Type	Compression Property Inheritance Parent
Table	Tablespace
Materialized View	Tablespace
Partition	Table

TABLE 8-13. *Compression Property Inheritance*

parent object, from which default compression properties are inherited if not specified for the base object. For example, if no compression property is specified for a table, it will inherit the property from its tablespace. The same applies to a data partition—if not specified at the partition level, the default property from the table will be used.

The following listing demonstrates the creation of a table with compression enabled. Line 7 contains the keyword COMPRESS to tell Oracle that data compression is to be enabled:

```
1 create table commission (
2  sales_rep_id     number,
3  prod_id          number,
4  comm_date        date,
5  comm_amt         number(10,2))
6 tablespace comm_ts
7 compress;
```

Ask the Expert

Q: Can existing data in a table be compressed and uncompressed?

A: Yes. There are two methods. The first is to use an alter table statement such as

```
alter table sales move compress;
```

To uncompress:

```
alter table sales move nocompress;
```

The second method is to use the utilities contained in the dbms_redefinition package.

COMPRESS in the previous code can be exchanged for different compression methods. COMPRESS FOR OLTP, COMPRESS FOR QUERY, and COMPRESS FOR ARCHIVE will compress data for both direct-path and DML, such as inserts and updates. The difference is in the level of compression, and with a higher level of compression, the CPU consumption will also be higher.

Because compression can be enabled or disabled at different points in an object's lifetime (say, by using an alter command), and because the compression action occurs only on new data being loaded, it is possible for an object to contain both compressed and uncompressed data at the same time.

Index Key Compression

Index key compression works in a similar manner to data compression in that duplicated values are removed from the index entries. It's a little more complicated, however, because it has more restrictions and considerations than data compression, partly due to the way indexes are structured. Because the details of these structures are beyond the scope of this book, you will focus on the benefits of, and the mechanisms for, defining index compression.

Compressing indexes offers the same benefits as data compression—that is, reduced storage and improved (usually) performance. However, performance may suffer during index scans as the burden on the CPU is increased in order to rebuild the key values. One restriction we should mention is that index compression cannot be used on a unique index that has only one attribute.

Enabling index compression is done using the create index statement. If you need to compress or uncompress an existing index, you must drop the index first and then re-create it with or without the compression option enabled. The following listing illustrates the syntax for creating a compressed index. Table 8-14 provides an explanation of the syntax.

```
1 create index comm_sr_prod_idx
2 on commission (sales_rep_id, prod_id)
3 compress 1;
```

Using data and index compression can provide substantial benefits in the areas of storage and performance.

Automatic Data Optimization

Compression, partitioning, and archiving are all part of managing the data and Information Lifecycle Management (ILM). With VLDB, it is important to manage the underlying data such that it allows what is most important to be accessed most efficiently first while still having older and not as frequently accessed data available. Different levels of compression are good for this to set older data at a high level,

Lines	Important Points
1–2	This specifies that the index is to be created on columns sales_rep_id and prod_id.
3	This specifies that the index is to be compressed, with the number of prefixing (leading) columns to compress. In this case, you used a value of 1 to indicate that duplicate values of the first column, sales_rep_id, are to be removed.

TABLE 8-14.   *Explanation of Index Compression Syntax*

where frequently accessed data might not be compressed or at a lower level. Managing this level of ILM might be a difficult process if there wasn't some way to automate it.

In Oracle 12*c*, the Automatic Data Optimization (ADO) manages ILM by providing a way to specify policies at the table and row level. These policies can be set up to compress data at different levels of compression and to move data to different tiers of storage within the database.

The PL/SQL procedure, EXECUTE_ILM, provides a way to enforce the ADO policies immediately and outside of any scheduled optimization policies. Along with the procedures, there are tables to verify the policies and results of the ILM executes. The following example provides a high-level look at this:

```
-- Enable tracking for the activity statistics
> alter table emp_ilm2 ilm enable activity tracking segment access;
Table altered.
-- Add policy for ILM compression
>alter table emp_ilm2 ilm add emp_ilm2_com_pol compress for OLTP
segment after 15 days of no modification;
Table altered.
--View the policy added in the DBA_ILMDATAMOVEMENTPOLICIES
 select policy_name, action_type, compression_level, condition_type,
condition_days
from dba_ilmdatamovementpolicies
order by policy_name;
POLICY_NAME  ACTION_TYPE   COMPRESSION_LEVEL  CONDITION_TYPE
CONDITION_DAYS
-----------  -----------   -----------------  --------------
--------------
EMP_ILM2_POL COMPRESSION   OLTP               LAST MODIFICATION TIME    15
--Execute immediately a policy using DBMS_ILM.EXECUTE_ILM
declare
v_executionid number;
>begin
```

```
dbms_ilm.execute_ILM (ilm_scope => dbms_ilm.scope_database,
execution_mode => dbms_ilm.ilm_execution_offiline,
execution_id => v_executionid);
end;
```

With this very brief example, we hope you realize that these policies can help automate the management of the data and information. Oracle Database 12c features for ILM to manage compression and archiving are extremely helpful in VLDB environments. And this will help with I/O and accessing the data efficiencies. In the next section, you see how to improve query performance using parallel processing options.

CRITICAL SKILL 8.4

Use Parallel Processing to Improve Performance

Improving performance (and by this we usually mean query performance) is always a hot item with database administrators and users. One of the best and easiest ways to boost performance is to take advantage of the parallel processing option offered by Oracle Database 12c (Enterprise Edition only).

Using normal (that is, serial) processing, the data involved in a single request (for example, user query) is handled by one database process. Using *parallel processing*, the request is broken down into multiple units to be worked on by multiple database processes. Each process looks at only a portion of the total data for the request. Serial and parallel processing are illustrated in Figures 8-5 and 8-6, respectively.

Parallel processing can help improve performance in situations where large amounts of data need to be examined or processed, such as scanning large tables, joining large tables, creating large indexes, and scanning partitioned indexes. In order to realize the benefits of parallel processing, your database environment should not already be running at, or near, capacity. Parallel processing requires

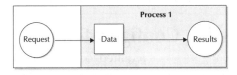

FIGURE 8-5.   *Oracle serial processing*

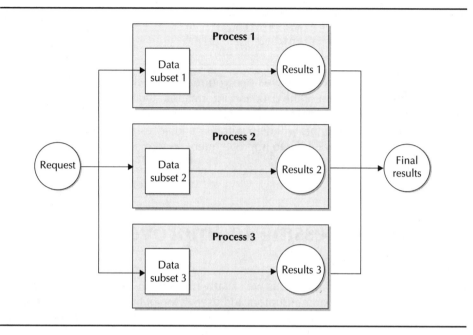

FIGURE 8-6. *Oracle parallel processing*

more processing, memory, and I/O resources than serial processing. Before implementing parallel processing, you may need to add hardware resources. Let's forge ahead by looking at the components involved in parallel processing.

Parallel Processing Database Components

The parallel processing components are the *parallel execution coordinator* and the *parallel execution servers*. The parallel execution coordinator is responsible for breaking down the request into as many processes as specified by the request. Each process is passed to a parallel execution server for execution during which only a portion of the total data is worked on. The coordinator then assembles the results from each server and presents the complete results to the requester.

Parallel Processing Configuration

Generally, not much configuration is required for the database to perform parallel processing. There are, however, a number of configuration options that are required and will affect the effectiveness of parallelism.

To begin with, parallel processing is enabled by default for DDL (for example, create and alter) and query (for example, select) commands, but disabled for DML (say, insert, update, delete and merge) commands. If you wish to execute a DML command in parallel mode, you must first issue the following command for the session in which the command is to be executed:

```
alter session enable parallel dml;
```

Parallel processing can also be disabled for queries, DML, and DDL:

```
alter session disable parallel ddl;
```

It can also be forced with a degree of parallelism:

```
alter session force parallel ddl parallel 5;
```

Several database initialization parameters affect parallel processing. When an Oracle instance starts, the parameters in the initialization file are used to define or specify the settings for the instance. Table 8-15 identifies the initialization parameters that affect parallel processing. In many cases, the default values will provide adequate results for your large database. Specifics of your own environment will influence your decisions on the best values to use.

As you can see from Table 8-15, there are dependencies between parameters. Modifying one may necessitate modifying others. If you modify any of the parallel processing parameters, you may also have to modify the following database/instance parameters:

- INSTANCE GROUPS
- PROCESSES
- SESSIONS
- TRANSACTIONS

Invoke Parallel Execution

Parallel execution can be applied to tables, views, and materialized views. If all necessary configurations have been made, there are several ways to invoke parallel execution. The first way is during table creation (including materialized views), using the parallel clause. If the table is being created using the results of a subquery, the loading of the table will be parallelized. In addition, by default, all queries that

Parameter	Default Setting	Comment
PARALLEL_ADAPTIVE_MULTI_USER	True	When set to True, this enables an adaptive algorithm designed to improve performance in multiuser environments that use parallel processing.
PARALLEL_AUTOMATIC_TUNING	False	No longer used. Exists for backward compatibility only.
PARALLEL_EXECUTION_MESSAGE_SIZE	Installation Dependent	Specifies the byte size of messages for parallel processing.
PARALLEL_INSTANCE_GROUP	Installation Dependent	This is used in Real Application Cluster environments to restrict parallel query operations to a limited number of database instances.
PARALLEL_MAX_SERVERS	Number of CPUs available to the database instance	Specifies maximum number of parallel processes for the database instance.
PARALLEL_MIN_PERCENT	0	Specifies minimum percentage of parallel processes required for parallel processing. Value is a percentage of PARALLEL_MAX_SERVERS.
PARALLEL_MIN_SERVERS	0	Specifies minimum number of parallel processes for the database instance. Cannot be greater than the value of PARALLEL_MAX_SERVERS.
PARALLEL_THREADS_PER_CPU	Usually set to 2, depending on operating system	Specifies the number of parallel processes per CPU.

TABLE 8-15. *Initialization Parameters Affecting Parallel Processing*

are executed against the table will be parallelized to the same extent. The next listing shows an example of specifying the parallel option for a table creation:

```
1 create table commission (
2  sales_rep_id    number,
3  prod_id         number,
4  comm_date       date,
5  comm_amt        number(10,2))
6 tablespace comm_ts
7 parallel;
```

The important line here is Line 7, specifying the parallel clause. This line could also have included an integer to specify the *degree of parallelism*—that is, the number of processes that are to be used to execute the parallel process. As the degree of parallelism is omitted in this example, the number of processes used will be calculated as the number of CPUs × the value of the PARALLEL_THREADS_PER_CPU initialization parameter. The degree of parallelism for a table or materialized view can be changed using an alter statement.

Parallel processing can also be invoked when the parallel hint is used in a select statement. This hint will override any default parallel processing options specified during table creation. The following listing illustrates the use of the parallel hint. Line 1 contains the parallel hint, specifying the table to be parallelized (commission) and the degree of parallelism (4):

```
1 select /*+ parallel (commission, 4) */
2  prod_id, sum(comm_amt), count(*)
3 from commission
4 group by prod_id;
```

In some cases, Oracle Database 12c will alter how, or if, parallel processing is executed. Examples of these include the following:

- Parallel processing will be disabled for DML commands (for example, insert, update, delete, and merge) on tables with triggers or referential integrity constraints.

- If a table has a bitmap index, DML commands are always executed using serial processing if the table is non-partitioned. If the table is partitioned, parallel processing will occur, but Oracle will limit the degree of parallelism to the number of partitions affected by the command.

Parallel processing can have a significant positive impact on performance. Impacts on performance are even greater when you combine range- or hash-based partitioning with parallel processing. With this configuration, each parallel process can act on a particular partition. For example, if you had a table partitioned by month, the parallel execution coordinator could divide the work up according to those partitions. This way, partitioning and parallelism work together to provide results even faster.

CRITICAL SKILL 8.5

Use Materialized Views

So far, you have reviewed several features and techniques that you can use to improve performance in large databases. In this section, we discuss another feature of the Oracle Database that you can include in your arsenal: materialized views.

Originally called snapshots, *materialized views* were introduced in Oracle8*i* and are only available in the Enterprise Edition. Like a regular view, the data in a materialized view results from a query. However, the results of a regular view are transitory—they are lost once the query is complete and, if needed again, the query must be re-executed. In contrast, the results from a materialized view are kept and physically stored in a database object that resembles a table. This feature means that the underlying query only needs to be executed once and then the results are available to all who need them.

Oracle Database 12*c* allows for synchronous refreshes of the materialized views when configured to use a refresh method besides manual or on-demand. It utilizes partitioning and dependencies between the objects to minimize the time it takes to refresh and maintain the data as close to the underlying tables as possible.

From a database perspective, materialized views are treated like tables:

- You can perform most DML and query commands such as insert, delete, update, and select.

- They can be partitioned.

- They can be compressed.

- They can be parallelized.

- You can create indexes on them.

Materialized views are different in other ways and have some interesting features associated with them. Before we talk about those, let's look at some ways to use materialized views.

Uses for Materialized Views

Materialized views are used as a performance-enhancing technique. In this section, you learn about the following uses of these views, as they are applicable to the topic of large databases.

- Performing data summarization (for example, sums and averages)

- Prejoining tables

- Performing CPU-intensive calculations

- Replicating and distributing data

In large databases, particularly data warehousing environments, there is always a need to summarize, join, perform calculations, or do all three operations at once on large numbers of records for the purposes of reporting and analysis. To improve performance in the past, a combination of views and physical tables were usually implemented that contained the results of these operations. The summary tables would require some type of extraction, transformation, and load (ETL) process to populate and refresh them. In addition to the base tables containing the detailed data, the users would need to know which combinations of the views and/or summary tables to use. These structures are illustrated in Figure 8-7.

Using materialized views has several advantages over more traditional methods. These include the following:

■   Materialized views have a built-in data refresh process, which can provide an automatic update or repopulation of a materialized view without any programming on the part of the DBA.

■   As mentioned earlier, the data in materialized views can be partitioned, using the same techniques that apply to tables.

■   Materialized views are transparent to the users. This is probably the most attractive feature of using materialized views. We expand more on this in the next section when we discuss automatic query rewriting.

Figure 8-8 illustrates summarization using materialized views.

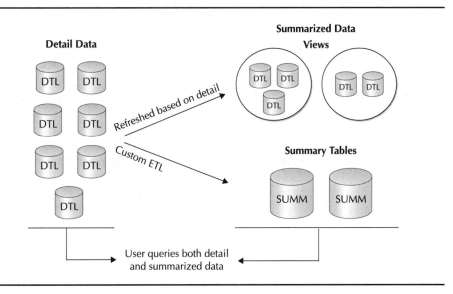

FIGURE 8-7.   *Summarization using views and summary tables*

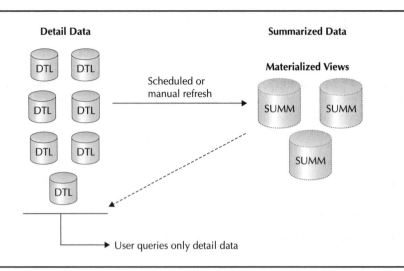

FIGURE 8-8. *Summarization using materialized views*

Query Rewrite

Earlier, you learned that one of the benefits of using materialized views was that they are transparent to the users. But what exactly does that mean and how can they be used if the users can't see them? In fact, because materialized views are so much like tables, you can give the users access to materialized views, although generally this is not done.

Instead, as indicated in Figure 8-8, the users always query the tables with the detail data—they don't usually query the materialized views directly because the query optimizer in Oracle Database 12c knows about the materialized views and their relationships to the detail tables and can rewrite the query on-the-fly to access the materialized views instead. This results in huge performance gains without the user having to do anything special—just query the detail data. There is a maintenance benefit of this feature for the user as well: The queries do not have to change to point to different summary tables, as is the case with the more traditional summarization approach.

In order for the query to be rewritten, the structure of the materialized view must satisfy the criteria of the query. The following two listings demonstrate the query rewrite process. Let's assume you need to summarize the COMMISSION table you saw in the data compression section using the following query:

```
select prod_id, to_char(comm_date, 'YYYY-MM'), count(*), sum(comm_amt)
from commission
group by prod_id, to_char(comm_date, 'YYYY-MM');
```

Assume further that a materialized view (called comm_prod_mv) exists that contains summarized commission data by sales_rep_id, prod_id and comm_date (full date). In this case, the query would be automatically rewritten as follows:

```
select prod_id, to_char(comm_date, 'YYYY-MM'), count(*), sum(comm_amt)
from comm_prod_mv
group by prod_id, to_char(comm_date, 'YYYY-MM');
```

By rewriting the query to use the materialized view instead, a large amount of data-crunching has been saved and the results will return much more quickly. Now turn your attention to determining what materialized views should be created.

When to Create Materialized Views

At this point, you may be asking yourself: "How do I determine what materialized views to create and at what level of summarization?" Oracle Database 12c has some utilities to help. These utilities are collectively called the SQL Tuning Advisor and will recommend materialized views based on historical queries, or based on theoretical scenarios. They can be run from the Oracle Enterprise Manager (OEM) Grid Control, or by calling the dbms_advisor package.

Create Materialized Views

Materialized views are created using a create materialized view statement, which is similar to a create table statement. This can be performed using SQL Developer, SQL*Plus, or OEM. The following listing shows a simple example of how to create the comm_prod_mv materialized view mentioned earlier, and Table 8-16 provides an explanation of the syntax:

```
1 create materialized view comm_prod_mv
2    tablespace comm_prod_mv_ts
3    refresh complete  next sysdate + 7
4    enable query rewrite
5 as select sales_rep_id, prod_id, comm_date, count(*), sum(comm_amt)
6    from commission
7    group by sales_rep_id, prod_id, comm_date;
```

Lines	Important Points
2–3	Specifies the tablespace and storage parameters.
4	Specifies how and when to refresh the data. In this case, the materialized view will be populated immediately and be completely refreshed every seven days thereafter.
5	Specifies that query rewrite is to be enabled.
6–8	Specifies the query that will act as the source of the data.

TABLE 8-16.   *Explanation of Materialized View Creation Syntax*

CRITICAL SKILL 8.6

Use SQL Aggregate and Analysis Functions

Once your database has been loaded with data, your users or applications will, of course, want to use that data to run queries, perform analysis, produce reports, extract data, and so forth. Having large sets of data is only valuable to the business if it can be aggregated and reported on in an efficient manner. Oracle Database 12c provides many sophisticated aggregation and analysis functions that can help ease the pain sometimes associated with analyzing data in large databases.

Aggregation Functions

Oracle Database provides extensions to the standard SQL group by clause of the select statement that generate other totals as part of the result set that previously required multiple queries, nested subqueries, or importing into spreadsheet type applications. These extensions are rollup and cube.

rollup

The rollup extension generates subtotals for attributes specified in the group by clause, plus another row representing the grand total. The following example of the rollup extension uses the SALES table:

```
select c.cust_gender gender,
       b.channel_class channel_class,
       to_char(a.time_id, 'yyyy-mm') month,
       count(*) unit_count,
       sum(a.amount_sold) amount_sold
```

```
from sales a, channels b, customers c
where a.channel_id = b.channel_id
and   a.cust_id = c.cust_id
and   to_char(a.time_id, 'yyyy-mm') between '2001-01' and '2001-02'
group by rollup(c.cust_gender,
               b.channel_class,
               to_char(a.time_id, 'yyyy-mm'));
```

GENDER	CHANNEL_CLASS	MONTH	UNIT_COUNT	AMOUNT_SOLD
F	Direct	2001-01	4001	387000.9
F	Direct	2001-02	3208	365860.13
F	Direct		7209	752861.03
F	Others	2001-01	2486	242615.9
F	Others	2001-02	2056	229633.52
F	Others		4542	472249.42
F	Indirect	2001-01	1053	138395.21
F	Indirect	2001-02	1470	189425.88
F	Indirect		2523	327821.09
F			14274	1552931.54
M	Direct	2001-01	7038	719146.28
M	Direct	2001-02	6180	641192.61
M	Direct		13218	1360338.89
M	Others	2001-01	4310	414603.03
M	Others	2001-02	3751	391792.61
M	Others		8061	806395.64
M	Indirect	2001-01	1851	211947.81
M	Indirect	2001-02	2520	285219.79
M	Indirect		4371	497167.6
M			25650	2663902.13
			39924	4216833.67

In the results, you can see that counts and sums of amount_sold are returned at the following levels:

- By GENDER, CHANNEL_CLASS, and MONTH
- Subtotals by CHANNEL_CLASS within GENDER
- Subtotals by GENDER
- Grand total

cube

The cube extension takes rollup a step further by generating subtotals for each combination of the group by attributes, totals by attribute, and the grand total. The following example of the cube extension uses the same query you used for rollup:

```
select c.cust_gender gender,
       b.channel_class channel_class,
       to_char(a.time_id, 'yyyy-mm') month,
       count(*) unit_count,
       sum(a.amount_sold) amount_sold
from sales a, channels b, customers c
where a.channel_id = b.channel_id
and    a.cust_id = c.cust_id
and    to_char(a.time_id, 'yyyy-mm') between '2001-01' and '2001-02'
group by cube(c.cust_gender,
                 b.channel_class,
                 to_char(a.time_id, 'yyyy-mm'));
```

GENDER	CHANNEL_CLASS	MONTH	UNIT_COUNT	AMOUNT_SOLD
			39924	4216833.67
		2001-01	20739	2113709.13
		2001-02	19185	2103124.54
	Direct		20427	2113199.92
	Direct	2001-01	11039	1106147.18
	Direct	2001-02	9388	1007052.74
	Others		12603	1278645.06
	Others	2001-01	6796	657218.93
	Others	2001-02	5807	621426.13
	Indirect		6894	824988.69
	Indirect	2001-01	2904	350343.02
	Indirect	2001-02	3990	474645.67
F			14274	1552931.54
F		2001-01	7540	768012.01
F		2001-02	6734	784919.53
F	Direct		7209	752861.03
F	Direct	2001-01	4001	387000.9
F	Direct	2001-02	3208	365860.13
F	Others		4542	472249.42
F	Others	2001-01	2486	242615.9
F	Others	2001-02	2056	229633.52
F	Indirect		2523	327821.09
F	Indirect	2001-01	1053	138395.21
F	Indirect	2001-02	1470	189425.88
M			25650	2663902.13
M		2001-01	13199	1345697.12

M		2001-02	12451	1318205.01
M	Direct		13218	1360338.89
M	Direct	2001-01	7038	719146.28
M	Direct	2001-02	6180	641192.61
M	Others		8061	806395.64
M	Others	2001-01	4310	414603.03
M	Others	2001-02	3751	391792.61
M	Indirect		4371	497167.6
M	Indirect	2001-01	1851	211947.81
M	Indirect	2001-02	2520	285219.79

In the results, you can see that counts and sums of amount_sold are returned at the following levels:

- By GENDER, CHANNEL_CLASS, and MONTH

- Subtotals by MONTH within CHANNEL_CLASS

- Subtotals by MONTH within GENDER

- Subtotals by CHANNEL_CLASS within GENDER

- Subtotals by MONTH

- Subtotals by CHANNEL_CLASS

- Subtotals by GENDER

- Grand total

Analytic Functions

Oracle Database 11c provides a number of ranking and statistical functions that previously would have required some pretty heavy SQL to perform or an extract to a third-party application. In this section, you look at the available analysis functions and examine examples of their use where appropriate.

NOTE
Some of the functions in this section are based on complex statistical calculations. Don't be worried if you are unfamiliar with these concepts. It is more important for you to know that these functions exist than it is to understand the theory behind them.

Ranking Functions

Ranking functions provide the capability to rank a row of a query result relative to the other rows in the result set. Common examples of uses for these functions include identifying the top ten selling products for a period, or classifying or grouping a salesperson's commissions into one of four buckets. The ranking functions included in Oracle Database are

- RANK
- DENSE_RANK
- CUME_DIST
- PERCENT_RANK
- NTILE
- ROW_NUMBER

The simplest ranking functions are RANK and DENSE_RANK. These functions are very similar and determine the ordinal position of each row within the query result set. The difference between these two functions is that rank will leave a gap in the sequence when there is a tie for position, whereas dense_rank does not leave a gap. The results of the following listing illustrate the difference between the two:

```
select prod_id,
       sum(quantity_sold),
       rank () over (order by sum(quantity_sold) desc) as rank,
       dense_rank () over (order by sum(quantity_sold) desc) as
dense_rank
from sales
where to_char(time_id, 'yyyy-mm') = '2001-06'
group by prod_id;
   PROD_ID SUM(QUANTITY_SOLD)       RANK DENSE_RANK
---------- ------------------ ---------- ----------
        24                762          1          1
        30                627          2          2
       147                578          3          3
        33                552          4          4
        40                550          5          5
       133                550          5          5
        48                541          7          6
       120                538          8          7
        23                535          9          8
       119                512         10          9
       124                503         11         10
       140                484         12         11
```

148	472	13	12
139	464	14	13
123	459	15	14
131	447	16	15
25	420	17	16
135	415	18	17
137	407	19	18
146	401	20	19

As you can see, the ordinal position 6 does not exist as a value for RANK, but it does for DENSE_RANK. If, from this result set, you wanted to see the top ten listings for prod_id, you would use the original query as a subquery, as in the following listing:

```
select * from
   (select prod_id,
          sum(quantity_sold),
          rank () over (order by sum(quantity_sold) desc) as rank,
          dense_rank () over (order by sum(quantity_sold) desc) as
dense_rank
    from sales
    where to_char(time_id, 'yyyy-mm') = '2001-06'
    group by prod_id)
where rank < 11;
```

To see the bottom ten prod_ids, use the same query, but change the order by option from descending (DESC) to ascending (ASC). The next two functions, cume_dist and percent_rank, are statistical in nature but still part of the family of ranking functions, so the important feature is that these functions properly handle ties in the rankings.

The CUME_DIST function calculates the cumulative distribution of a value in a group of values. Because this is not a statistics beginner's guide, we will not attempt to provide the theoretical background on cumulative distribution. However, we can offer these points:

- The range of values returned by cume_dist is always between 0 and 1.

- The value returned by cume_dist is always the same in the case of tie values in the group.

- The formula for cumulative distribution is

      # of rows with values <= value of row being evaluated /
      # of rows being evaluated

Consider the query we used when discussing rank; the following listing calculates the cumulative distribution for quantity_sold. The results immediately follow the listing.

```
select prod_id,
    sum(quantity_sold),
    cume_dist () over (order by sum(quantity_sold) asc) as cume_dist
from sales
where to_char(time_id, 'yyyy-mm') = '2001-06'
group by prod_id
order by sum(quantity_sold) desc;
   PROD_ID SUM(QUANTITY_SOLD)   CUME_DIST
---------- ------------------ ----------
        24                762          1
        30                627 .985915493
       147                578 .971830986
        33                552 .957746479
        40                550 .943661972
       133                550 .943661972
        48                541 .915492958
       120                538 .901408451
        23                535 .887323944
       119                512 .873239437
       124                503  .85915493
       140                484 .845070423
       148                472 .830985915
       139                464 .816901408
       123                459 .802816901
       131                447 .788732394
        25                420 .774647887
       135                415  .76056338
       137                407 .746478873
       146                401 .732394366
```

The percent_rank function is similar to the cume_dist function, but calculates a percentage ranking of a value relative to its group. Again, without getting into the theory, we can make some points about percent_rank:

- The range of values returned by the function is always between 0 and 1.

- The row with a rank of 1 will have a percent rank of 0.

- The formula for calculating percent rank is

  rank of row within its group – 1 /
  # of rows in the group – 1

The next listing and its results use the base query you have been using in this section to demonstrate the PERCENT_RANK function:

```
select prod_id,
    sum(quantity_sold),
    rank () over (order by sum(quantity_sold) desc) as rank,
percent_rank ()
over (order by sum(quantity_sold) asc) as percent_rank
from sales
where to_char(time_id, 'yyyy-mm') = '2001-06'
group by prod_id
order by sum(quantity_sold) desc;
```

PROD_ID	SUM(QUANTITY_SOLD)	RANK	PERCENT_RANK
24	762	1	1
30	627	2	.985714286
147	578	3	.971428571
33	552	4	.957142857
40	550	5	.928571429
133	550	5	.928571429
48	541	7	.914285714
120	538	8	.9
23	535	9	.885714286
119	512	10	.871428571
124	503	11	.857142857
140	484	12	.842857143
148	472	13	.828571429
139	464	14	.814285714
123	459	15	.8
131	447	16	.785714286
25	420	17	.771428571
135	415	18	.757142857
137	407	19	.742857143
146	401	20	.728571429

The ntile function divides a result set into a number of buckets specified at query time by the user, and then assigns each row in the result set a bucket number. The most common numbers of buckets used are 3 (tertiles), 4 (quartiles), and 10 (deciles). Each bucket will have the same number of rows, except in the case when the number of rows does not divide evenly by the number of buckets. In this case, each of the leftover rows will be assigned to buckets with the lowest bucket numbers until all leftover rows are assigned. For example, if four buckets were specified and the number of rows in the result set was 98, buckets 1 and 2 would have 25 rows each, and buckets 3 and 4 would have 24 rows each.

Let's look at an example. Using your base query of amount_sold in the SALES table, you want to look at amount_sold by product subcategory and rank the amounts into four buckets. Here's the SQL:

```
select b.prod_subcategory,
       sum(a.quantity_sold),
       ntile(4) over (ORDER BY SUM(a.quantity_sold) desc) as quartile
from sales a, products b
where a.prod_id = b.prod_id
and to_char(a.time_id, 'yyyy-mm') = '2001-06'
group by b.prod_subcategory;
```

As you can see in the following results, the number of product subcategories was not evenly divisible by the number of buckets specified (in this case, 4). Therefore, six subcategories were assigned to the first quartile (bucket 1) and five subcategories were assigned to the second, third, and fourth quartiles.

PROD_SUBCATEGORY	COUNT(*)	SUM(A.QUANTITY_SOLD)	QUARTILE
Accessories	3230	3230	1
Y Box Games	2572	2572	1
Recordable CDs	2278	2278	1
Camera Batteries	2192	2192	1
Recordable DVD Discs	2115	2115	1
Documentation	1931	1931	1
Modems/Fax	1314	1314	2
CD-ROM	1076	1076	2
Y Box Accessories	1050	1050	2
Printer Supplies	956	956	2
Memory	748	748	2
Camera Media	664	664	3
Home Audio	370	370	3
Game Consoles	352	352	3
Operating Systems	343	343	3
Bulk Pack Diskettes	270	270	3
Portable PCs	215	215	4
Desktop PCs	214	214	4
Camcorders	196	196	4
Monitors	178	178	4
Cameras	173	173	4

The ROW_NUMBER function is a simple one that assigns a unique number to each row in a result set. The numbers are sequential, starting at 1, and are based on the order by clause of the query.

You will again use your SALES table query as an example. Using the query from your ntile example and adding a new column using row_count, you get the following:

```
select b.prod_subcategory,
       sum(a.quantity_sold),
       ntile(4) over (ORDER BY SUM(a.quantity_sold) desc) as quartile,
       row_number () over (order by sum(quantity_sold) desc) as
rownumber
       from sales a, products b
where a.prod_id = b.prod_id
and to_char(a.time_id, 'yyyy-mm') = '2001-06'
group by b.prod_subcategory;
```

In the following results, each row is assigned a number, depending on its position defined by the order by clause. As you can see, the ROWNUMBER is simply the row position in the list without any intelligence, whereas quartile is a calculated field and could have repeating values:

PROD_SUBCATEGORY	SUM(A.QUANTITY_SOLD)	QUARTILE	ROWNUMBER
Accessories	3230	1	1
Y Box Games	2572	1	2
Recordable CDs	2278	1	3
Camera Batteries	2192	1	4
Recordable DVD Discs	2115	1	5
Documentation	1931	1	6
Modems/Fax	1314	2	7
CD-ROM	1076	2	8
Y Box Accessories	1050	2	9
Printer Supplies	956	2	10
Memory	748	2	11
Camera Media	664	3	12
Home Audio	370	3	13
Game Consoles	352	3	14
Operating Systems	343	3	15
Bulk Pack Diskettes	270	3	16
Portable PCs	215	4	17
Desktop PCs	214	4	18
Camcorders	196	4	19
Monitors	178	4	20
Cameras	173	4	21

Windowing Functions

Before you get into the details, you need to learn a couple of terms: analytic partitioning and analytic window:

■ *Analytic partitioning* is the division of the results of an analytic function into groups within which the analytic function operates. This is accomplished using the partition by clause of the analytic function. Do not confuse this partitioning with data partitioning discussed earlier in this chapter. Analytic partitioning can be used with any of the analytic functions we have discussed so far.

■ An *analytic window* is a subset of an analytic partition in which the values of each row depend on the values of other rows in the window. There are two types of windows: physical and logical. A physical window is defined by a specified number of rows. A logical window is defined by the order by values.

Windowing functions can only be used in the select and order by clauses. They can be used to calculate the following:

■ Moving sum

■ Moving average

■ Moving min/max

■ Cumulative sum

■ Statistical functions

Now look at an example of a moving sum function. The following shows the listing and results for calculating the moving sum from the SALES table by product category for a six-month period:

```
select b.prod_category,
       to_char(a.time_id, 'yyyy-mm'),
       sum(a.quantity_sold),
       sum(sum(a.quantity_sold)) over (partition by b.prod_category
                                 order by to_char(a.time_id, 'yyyy-mm')
                                 rows unbounded preceding) as cume_sum
from sales a, products b
where a.prod_id = b.prod_id
and b.prod_category_id between 202 and 204
and to_char(a.time_id, 'yyyy-mm') between '2001-01' and '2001-06'
```

```
group by b.prod_category, to_char(a.time_id, 'yyyy-mm')
order by b.prod_category, to_char(a.time_id, 'yyyy-mm');
PROD_CATEGORY                    TO_CHAR SUM(A.QUANTITY_SOLD)   CUME_SUM
------------------------------   ------- --------------------   ----------
Hardware                         2001-01                  281          281
Hardware                         2001-02                  306          587
Hardware                         2001-03                  442         1029
Hardware                         2001-04                  439         1468
Hardware                         2001-05                  413         1881
Hardware                         2001-06                  429         2310
Peripherals and Accessories      2001-01                 5439         5439
Peripherals and Accessories      2001-02                 5984        11423
Peripherals and Accessories      2001-03                 5104        16527
Peripherals and Accessories      2001-04                 5619        22146
Peripherals and Accessories      2001-05                 4955        27101
Peripherals and Accessories      2001-06                 5486        32587
Photo                            2001-01                 2802         2802
Photo                            2001-02                 2220         5022
Photo                            2001-03                 2982         8004
Photo                            2001-04                 2824        10828
Photo                            2001-05                 2359        13187
Photo                            2001-06                 3225        16412
```

As you can see in the results, the moving sum is contained within each product category and resets when a new product category starts. In the past, windowing analysis used to require third-party products such as spreadsheet applications. Having the capabilities to perform these functions right in the database can streamline analysis and report generation efforts.

Other Functions

Many other functions are included with Oracle Database 12c that can be used to analyze data in large databases. While we will not be going into any detail for these, they are listed here for completeness:

- Statistical functions, including the following:
  - Linear regression functions
  - Descriptive statistics functions
  - Hypothetical testing and crosstab statistics functions (containing a new PL/SQL package called dbms_statistics)
- first/last functions
- lag/lead functions

- Reporting aggregate functions

- Inverse percentile functions

- Hypothetical rank and distribution functions

As stated earlier, database administrators do not have to know the theory behind the functions provided by Oracle Database 12c or even how to use the results. However, you should be able to let your users know what capabilities are available. Knowing this, your users will be able to take advantage of these functions and construct efficient queries. In the next section, you learn about a new feature in Oracle Database 12c—SQL models.

Create SQL Models

One of the more powerful data analysis features introduced in Oracle Database 12c is *SQL models.* SQL models allow a user to create multidimensional arrays from query results. Formulas, both simple and complex, can then be applied to the arrays to generate results in which the user is interested. SQL models allow inter-row calculations to be applied without doing expensive self-joins.

SQL models are similar to other multidimensional structures used in business intelligence applications. However, because they are part of the database, they can take advantage of Oracle Database's built-in features of scalability, manageability, security, and so on. In addition, when using SQL models, there is no need to transfer large amounts of data to external business intelligence applications.

A SQL model is defined by the model extension of the select statement. Columns of a query result are classified into one of three groups:

- **Partitioning** This is the same as the analytic partitioning defined in the "Windowing Functions" section.

- **Dimensions** These are the attributes used to describe or fully qualify a measure within a partition. Examples could include product, sales rep ID, and phone call type.

- **Measures** These are the numeric (usually) values to which calculations are applied. Examples could include quantity sold, commission amount, and call duration.

One of the main applications of SQL models is projecting or forecasting measures based on existing measures. Let's look at an example of the model clause to illustrate. The listing and its results show an aggregate query using the SALES table:

```
select c.channel_desc, p.prod_category, t.calendar_year year,
       sum(s.quantity_sold) quantity_sold
from sales s, products p, channels c, times t
where s.prod_id = p.prod_id
and    s.channel_id = c.channel_id
and    s.time_id = t.time_id
and    c.channel_desc = 'Direct Sales'
group by c.channel_desc, p.prod_category, t.calendar_year
order by c.channel_desc, p.prod_category, t.calendar_year;
CHANNEL_DESC       PROD_CATEGORY                        YEAR QUANTITY_SOLD
----------------   ----------------------------------   ------ -------------
Direct Sales       Electronics                          1998          7758
Direct Sales       Electronics                          1999         15007
...
Direct Sales       Hardware                             2000          1970
Direct Sales       Hardware                             2001          2399
Direct Sales       Peripherals and Accessories          1998         44258
...
Direct Sales       Software/Other                       2000         64483
Direct Sales       Software/Other                       2001         49146
```

In the results, you can see the historical aggregate quantity_sold for each year by product category for the Direct Sales channel. You can use the model clause to project the quantity_sold. In the following listing, you'll project values for 2002 for the product category Hardware in the channel. The quantity_sold will be based on the previous year's value (2001), plus 10 percent. Table 8-17 explains the syntax of the listing.

```
 1 select channel_desc, prod_category, year, quantity_sold
 2 from
 3  (select c.channel_desc, p.prod_category, t.calendar_year year,
 4          sum(s.quantity_sold) quantity_sold
 5  from sales s, products p, channels c, times t
 6  where s.prod_id = p.prod_id
 7  and    s.channel_id = c.channel_id
 8  and    s.time_id = t.time_id
 9  group by c.channel_desc, p.prod_category, t.calendar_year) sales
10 where channel_desc = 'Direct Sales'
11 model
12    partition by (channel_desc)
13    dimension by (prod_category, year)
14    measures (quantity_sold)
```

```
15    rules (quantity_sold['Hardware', 2002]
16    = quantity_sold['Hardware', 2001] * 1.10)
17 order by channel_desc, prod_category, year;
```

Following are the results of the previous query. Notice that a new row has been added for Hardware in 2002. Its quantity_sold is 2638.9, which is the previous year's value (2399) plus 10 percent.

```
CHANNEL_DESC      PROD_CATEGORY                        YEAR QUANTITY_SOLD
----------------  -----------------------------------  ----- -------------
Direct Sales      Electronics                          1998          7758
Direct Sales      Electronics                          1999         15007
...
Direct Sales      Hardware                             2000          1970
Direct Sales      Hardware                             2001          2399
Direct Sales      Hardware                             2002        2638.9
Direct Sales      Peripherals and Accessories          1998         44258
...
Direct Sales      Software/Other                       2000         64483
Direct Sales      Software/Other                       2001         49146
```

Lines	Important Points
3–9	Defines an in-line select that will be the source for the query. It is basically the same query you started with before the model clause.
10	Specifies that you are only going to look at Direct Sales channels.
11	Specifies the model clause.
12	Specifies the partition by clause (in this case, channel_desc).
13	Specifies the dimension by clause (here, prod_category and year). These elements will fully qualify the measure within the channel_desc partition.
14	Specifies the measures clause (quantity_sold).
15–16	Specifies the rules clause—that is, calculations you want to perform on the measure. In this example, we are referring to a specific cell of quantity_sold, described by the dimensions prod_category (Hardware) and year (2002).

TABLE 8-17. *Explanation of Model Clause Syntax*

The model clause has many variations and allows for very powerful calculations. We want to point out some of the characteristics and/or features you should be aware of. Supported functionalities include the following:

- Looping (for example, FOR loops)

- Recursive calculations

- Regression calculations

- Nested cell references

- Dimension wildcards and ranges

- The model clause does not update any base table, although in theory, you could create a table or materialized view from the results of the query using the model clause.

Restrictions include the following:

- The rules clause cannot include any analytic SQL or windowing functions.

- A maximum of 20,000 rules may be specified. This may seem like plenty, but a FOR loop is expanded into many single-cell rules at execution time.

Project 8-2   Use Analytic SQL Functions and Models

Once all the database structures have been put in place and data has been loaded, the users will want to analyze this data which has been placed in the database. Knowing what functions are available is important, and so is their use as well, at least to some extent. So, this project walks you through a more complex analytical example that includes using the lag function and creating a SQL model.

Step by Step

1. Create a view of the SALES table using the following listing. (The SALES table should have been created during your Oracle installation process.) This view will calculate the percentage change (called percent_chng) of quantity_sold from one year to the next using the lag function, summarized by prod_category, channel_desc, and calendar_year.

```
create or replace view sales_trends
as
select p.prod_category, c.channel_desc, t.calendar_year year,
       sum(s.quantity_sold) quantity_sold,
       round((sum(s.quantity_sold)
```

(continued)

```
                  lag(sum(s.quantity_sold),1)
                     over (partition by p.prod_category,
    c.channel_desc
                        order by t.calendar_year)) /
                  lag(sum(s.quantity_sold),1)
                     over (partition by p.prod_category,
    c.channel_desc
                        order by t.calendar_year) *
                  100 ,2) as percent_chng
    from sales s, products p, channels c, times t
    where s.prod_id = p.prod_id
    and   s.channel_id = c.channel_id
    and   s.time_id = t.time_id
    group by p.prod_category, c.channel_desc, t.calendar_year;
```

2. Select from the sales_trends view using the following listing. Notice that quantity_sold and percent_chng reset after each channel_desc. This is a result of the lag function's partition by clauses in the view definition.

```
    select prod_category, channel_desc, year, quantity_sold,
    percent_chng
    from sales_trends
    where prod_category = 'Electronics'
    order by prod_category, channel_desc, year;
```

3. Select from the sales_trends view using the following listing, which contains a model clause. In this query, you are projecting quantity_sold and percent_chng according to the following rules:

   a. Filter the prod_category to select only Electronics.

   b. Project for years 2002 to 2006 inclusive.

   c. The projected quantity_sold is calculated as the previous year's value plus the average percent_chng over the previous three years.

   d. The projected percent_chng is the average percent_chng over the previous three years:

```
    select prod_category, channel_desc, year, quantity_sold,
    percent_chng
    from sales_trends
    where prod_category = 'Electronics'
    model
       partition by (prod_category, channel_desc)
       dimension by (year)
       measures (quantity_sold, percent_chng)
```

```
rules (
   percent_chng[for year from 2002 to 2006 increment 1] =
      round(avg(percent_chng)[year between currentv()-3 and
                                       currentv()-1], 2),
   quantity_sold[for year from 2002 to 2006 increment 1] =
      round(quantity_sold[currentv()-1] *
         (1 + (round(avg(percent_chng)[year between
currentv()-3 and
currentv()-1] ,2) / 100))))
   order by prod_category, channel_desc, year;
```

4. Notice the projected values for 2002 to 2006 for each channel_desc.

Project Summary

The steps in this project build on the discussions you've had on Oracle Database's analytic capabilities. You used the lag function to calculate percentage change and used the model clause of the select statement to project sales five years into the future based on past trends. By going to the next level of examples, you can start to appreciate the significance of these functions and how they can be used.

Oracle Database 12*c*'s analytic functions provide powerful and efficient analysis capabilities that would otherwise require complex SQL and/or third-party tools. All of these functions are part of the core database—ready and waiting to be exploited by your users.

So, now you have come to the end of your exploration of large database features. We've presented a great deal of material in this chapter, and you have really only seen the tip of the iceberg! However, you can feel confident that with this background information, you are primed to tackle almost any large database environment out there.

☑ Chapter 8 Mastery Check

1. What data population methods can be used on a compressed table that results in the data being compressed?

2. What are the three basic types of partitioning?

3. _____ partitioned indexes are defined independently of the data partitions, and _____ partitioned indexes have a one-to-one relationship with the data partitions.

4. Explain the functions of the parallel execution coordinator in parallel processing.

5. For which of the following SQL commands is parallel processing *not* enabled by default?

   A. SELECT

   B. INSERT

   C. CREATE

   D. ALTER

6. What is meant by "degree of parallelism"?

7. What analytic feature can be used to forecast values based on existing measures?

8. What two methods can be used to run the SQL Tuning Advisor utilities for materialized views?

9. _____ partitioning allows you to control the placement of records in specified partitions based on sets of partition key values.

10. What analytic function would you use to assign each row from a query to one of five buckets?

11. What are the two types of windows that can be used in analytic functions?

12. The _____ automatically collects workload and performance statistics used for database self-management activities.

13. When creating partitioned tables, what option should you use to ensure that rows are redistributed to their correct partition if their partition key is updated?

14. List the ways in which parallel processing can be invoked.

CHAPTER
9

Oracle's Engineered Systems:
From the Database Appliance
to Exadata

CRITICAL SKILLS

On September 24, 2008, Oracle's chairman, Larry Ellison, introduced the first of what would become a major focus for Oracle: engineered systems of hardware and software components. Since that time, the engineered system family has proliferated, benefiting from Oracle's acquisition of Sun Microsystems. The systems all continue to have several characteristics in common:

- **Bundled hardware and software**   All engineered systems consist of hardware and software components that are designed and sold as a single unit.

- **Unique software functionality**   Engineered systems include software functionality, typically centered on performance or manageability, which is exclusively available with the engineered system. Examples include storage offload, hybrid columnar compression, and the Oracle Appliance Manager.

- **Single point of support**   Engineered systems are supported as single units through Oracle's worldwide support organization, avoiding situations where software and hardware vendors blame each other for problems.

- **Standardized configuration**   Engineered systems are available in a limited number of configurations. Therefore, the same configurations used by Oracle development and quality assurance are used in the field, and issues and solutions encountered by one user can be quickly reproduced and distributed to the entire user base.

- **Simplified management**   Engineered systems are built to reduce management effort. It starts with pre-assembled and installed hardware and software, and also includes central monitoring and administrative functionality through Oracle Enterprise Manager.

- **Commodity hardware**   Engineered systems are built from non-proprietary, industry-standard hardware. By using well-known hardware components, they can leverage the reliability of well-tested and widely used components, and regularly upgrade hardware as faster components become available.

Although Oracle's engineered system family spans middleware, storage, in-memory analytics, and much more, this chapter focuses on two engineered systems specifically focused on Oracle Database: Oracle Database Appliance and Oracle Exadata.

CRITICAL SKILL 9.1

Understand Oracle Database Appliance

The first of the systems we will discuss is Oracle Database Appliance (ODA), which is an Oracle-engineered system designed to make it easy to build out and manage a two-node RAC cluster. The design is based around two independent, Linux-based servers that are connected to a set of shared storage devices. The result is that the two server nodes can run in a fault-tolerant cluster configuration in a pre-integrated, self-contained system. Failed drives can be replaced while the machine is running, and an entire failed server node can be replaced while the other stays running. ODA optionally supports Oracle Virtual Machine by allowing rapid and repeatable application deployments through templates, and simplifying consolidation of multiple applications onto a single ODA environment.

Shared storage consists of a combination of hard drives and flash drives. Unlike Exadata, which we discuss later in the chapter, the flash drives are not a flash cache, but instead used for redo logs. The storage is provided through one, or optionally two, storage shelves, each of which holds a combination of hard drives and flash drives, and connected through the industry-standard SCSI Attached Storage (SAS) bus. Beyond the storage shelves, it is possible to add external storage like an Oracle ZFS storage appliance. CPU and memory capacity are fixed, although it is possible to run the database on a subset of the CPU cores to save licensing costs. This can be decided upon once you have the machine and configure it to your needs.

CRITICAL SKILL 9.2

Manage Oracle Database Appliance

Database management operations are similar to any other Oracle database. One addition in the database appliance is a built-in validation tool that can be used to validate both software and hardware configuration, as well as benchmarking disk I/O throughput.

To run all validation tests, you can issue the following command in the ODA:

```
/opt/oracle/oak/bin/oakcli validate -a
```

This command will print a series of color-coded response lines indicating successes, warnings, failures, and informational messages, and noting where work is required to resolve validation issues.

Initial Configuration

The initial Oracle Database Appliance configuration offers similar configuration options as Oracle RAC, but has a front end that centralizes the gathering of this information in one place. This Java-based configurator, seen in Figure 9-1, can even be used before your database appliance has been delivered, as it only requires a Java-capable computer. The configuration tool can be downloaded from the Oracle technology network at www.oracle.com/technetwork/server-storage/engineered-systems/database-appliance/.

The configurator will ask you a number of questions about the initial system configuration, including the following:

- The system name to use.

- Deployment type: RAC, RAC one node, or Enterprise edition (non-RAC). See Chapter 7 for more information about Oracle RAC.

- Passwords.

- IP addresses and hostnames for the various network interfaces.

- Database parameters, including name and expected size.

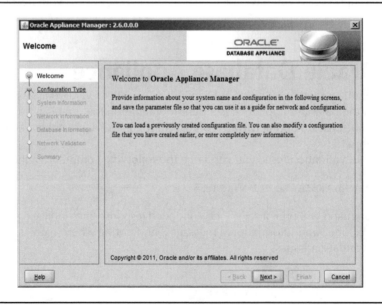

FIGURE 9-1. *The Oracle Appliance Manager configurator*

Once this information has been collected, an optional network validation will be run to make sure that IP addresses and DNS entries are properly configured. This test must be run on a machine in the same physical network as the ODA is to be installed.

And finally, the resulting configuration file is displayed and can be saved to a file for automated deployment on the database appliance itself (once initial network configuration and end-user bundle installation are complete) using the OAKCLI command:

```
cd /opt/oracle/oak/bin
./oakcli deploy -conf /tmp/name_of_package_file
```

CRITICAL SKILL 9.3

Learn about Exadata's Main Components

Another type of engineered system is Oracle's Exadata series of machines, which has been originally designed from the ground up to provide "extreme" performance and scalability for large data-warehousing, transaction-processing, and database consolidation workloads. This capability is delivered through a series of components, carefully chosen to integrate well together. Figure 9-2 shows the relationship between these components.

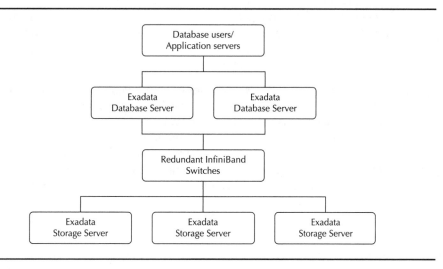

FIGURE 9-2. *Major Exadata components*

Let's look at how these components work together to provide the best possible performance:

- **Database servers**   Database servers are the components that will be most familiar to Oracle DBAs. They are enterprise-class servers that run Oracle Grid Infrastructure, Automatic Storage Management, and database software. The database instances run on database servers and receive connections from database users.

- **Storage servers**   Exadata storage servers (also known as storage cells) are a component only found in Oracle-engineered systems. Like database servers, they run enterprise-class server hardware. But they also contain a large collection of hard drives that store actual database data, and flash-memory cards that provide low-latency data caching. Storage servers do not run database software, but instead run Exadata Storage Server Software, a set of software programs that manage I/O requests coming from database servers and asking for data to be returned to the user or process.

- **InfiniBand networking**   Exadata's internal networking is built on InfiniBand, which is a protocol designed for high-performance computing environments to deliver low-latency communications and extensive scalability. The InfiniBand infrastructure consists of InfiniBand interface cards in database and storage servers connected via fiber-optic cables to a set of InfiniBand switches. The switches are configured to allow the Exadata machine to continue running in case of a switch failure, and to permit multiple Exadata racks to be connected together into one large cluster. If you have other InfiniBand-capable equipment such as an Exalogic system, it can be connected directly to the InfiniBand switches for high-speed communication with the Exadata database machine.

- **Management components**   A series of components is provided to allow hardware to be managed remotely, which is important when the Exadata database machine is located in a far-away datacenter facility. Components include integrated lights-out management (ILOM) controllers inside database and storage servers, a management-specific network switch, and network-accessible power distribution units. These components are designed to allow data access even when other components are inaccessible.

These components are bundled together in balanced configurations, intended to ensure that the processing capacity of each component is used efficiently while still maintaining high availability, so that any single component can fail while the overall system continues running. Configurations range from an eighth-rack up to a full rack with a full eight database servers and fourteen storage servers. Even larger configurations are possible by interconnecting multiple racks. It is also possible to add individual storage servers to an existing Exadata configuration, although care should be taken to ensure that the additional storage I/O volumes do not overwhelm the capacity of the database servers to process it.

CRITICAL SKILL 9.4

Understand Exadata Storage

To understand Exadata's performance, it's helpful to look at traditional enterprise storage. Traditional storage is dominated by large storage area networks (SANs) and network attached storage (NAS) devices. These storage architectures help to share and manage storage among multiple client devices, but their main building blocks are large banks of rotating hard drives and solid-state storage devices. These drives use the same underlying technology as storage in personal computers, although they're built to handle the higher speeds and usage volumes that enterprise workloads demand.

These disks are connected to storage heads, which are themselves computers that handle the "smarts" of the storage. They spread data across multiple disks and duplicate data across disks to handle the failure of individual drives using various types of RAID (redundant array of independent disk) storage technology. Storage heads process data access requests from client devices (such as database servers), pass them on to individual drives, and assemble the result, passing it back to the client device. Storage heads are, therefore, able to present large arrays of drives as large logical drives, hiding the complexity from client devices.

As storage demands increase, it's relatively simple to add more disk drives. But because the storage heads handle requests for multiple disk drives, it's much more difficult to add processing capacity. Similarly, the links between storage heads and database servers need upgrading as data volumes increase.

Exadata is architected very differently from traditional storage: Because there is no central storage head, system capacity can be expanded by simply adding more database and storage servers. Because it's a switched network configuration, the InfiniBand network increases aggregate network capacity as servers are added.

Exadata Storage Concepts

Exadata storage servers each contain a set of disk drives that form permanent storage. The actual disk storage is organized into a hierarchy of disk types, as described in Figure 9-3.

Each grid disk corresponds to an ASM disk on the database server. The PATH column in V$ASM_DISK lists the storage server IP address and grid disk name. This example lists paths of the grid disks in diskgroup DATA_EXA1:

```
select path from v$asm_disk where group_number in
(select group_number from v$asm_diskgroup where name = 'DATA_EXA1');
PATH
-------------------------------------------------------------------------
o/192.168.10.5/DATA_EXA1_CD_11_exa1cel01
...
```

On storage servers, disk objects can be viewed and manipulated through CELLCLI commands or with Oracle Enterprise Manager (see Critical Skill 9.9 for more information on managing Exadata with Oracle Enterprise Manager).

Each of the CELLCLI listing commands has similar syntax:

```
CellCLI> list griddisk DATA_EXA1_CD_11_exa1cel01 attributes celldisk
         CD_11_exa1cel01
CellCLI> list celldisk CD_11_exa1cel01 attributes lun,deviceName,status
         0_11    /dev/sdl        normal
CellCLI> list lun 0_11 attributes physicalDrives, status
         20:11   normal
```

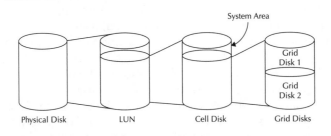

FIGURE 9-3. *Exadata storage layout*

The DETAIL keyword returns a full list of object attributes and values:

```
CellCLI> list physicaldisk 20:11 detail
         name:                  20:11
         deviceId:              8
...
```

Additionally, grid disks can take advantage of hot and cold disk placement to take advantage of a unique property of rotating magnetic disks at constant angular velocity: Outer tracks are physically bigger and can store more data, allowing higher transfer volumes per disk rotation than inner tracks. This type of layout is commonly used to place database contents on faster outer tracks, and the less performance-intensive fast recovery area on slower outer tracks. And because frequently used database data is spread over a smaller part of the disk, less time is wasted moving disk heads between tracks.

Hot/cold placement is simply configured by creating the "hot" grid disks first. They will be automatically placed on the fastest part of the disk, and remaining diskgroups on progressively slower parts.

Progress Check ⏱

1. What's the difference between Oracle Database Appliance and Oracle Exadata?

2. How is Oracle Database Appliance configured?

3. What's the difference between an Exadata database server and a storage server?

4. How is technical support handled with an Oracle-engineered system?

5. What is InfiniBand?

6. What part of a disk is faster: inner or outer tracks?

7. Why is traditional storage hard to scale?

Accelerate Large Queries with Storage Offload

Storage offload is a key performance optimization found only in Exadata. The Exadata storage server software understands Oracle database file layouts, so you can use smart scans to perform part of the work database servers normally do. By doing data processing closer to the storage, Exadata storage servers reduce the amount of data transferred to database servers and database-server processing power. Storage offload operations include the following:

- Predicate filtering, acting on the WHERE clause of SQL statements to exclude rows that do not match the query results

- Column projection, returning only the columns required by the query

- Bloom filter offloading, where the storage software assists in performing bloom filter-based table joins

Smart Scan in Action

To get the most benefits from smart scan, you need a large table. In this example, we'll use a large join from Oracle's built-in DBA_SOURCE view to give us lots of rows to select from. From this row source, we'll create a table with 1 million rows almost 8KB in size, for a table near 8GB in total bytes. We will be disabling compression and the flash cache, as these will be covered in future examples.

Progress Check Answers

1. Oracle Database Appliance focuses on simplicity for relatively small workloads, whereas Oracle Exadata focuses on performance and scalability for large enterprise workloads.

2. Initial configuration of Oracle Database Appliance is simplified by the graphical Oracle Appliance Manager tool, with command-line configuration done through OAKCLI.

3. Database servers run Oracle database software and receive connections from database users. Storage servers run Oracle Storage Server Software and receive connections from database servers.

4. Oracle's engineered systems feature a single point of contact for all support issues.

5. InfiniBand is a low-latency, highly scalable communication protocol.

6. Since outer tracks store more data than inner tracks, higher data volumes can be transferred per rotation than inner tracks, resulting in higher transfer throughput.

7. Traditional storage relies on a central storage head that is difficult and expensive to add I/O capacity to.

We will also disable in-memory parallel query by setting PARALLEL_DEGREE_POLICY to MANUAL because it can cause Oracle to attempt to cache the table in the buffer cache, affecting physical I/O statistics. These examples are designed to be run from a user other than the built-in SYS user. Feel free to create a new user just for these examples. (See Chapter 5 for more information about creating users.)

```
alter session set parallel_degree_policy='manual';
create table big_table
    nocompress storage (cell_flash_cache none) parallel 8
    as select rownum as num, lpad(rownum,7500) as filler
    from dba_source s1, dba_source s2
    where rownum <= 1*1000*1000;
```

And now we count the rows:

```
select count(*) from big_table;
```

At this point, we will retrieve two of the statistical counters that the Oracle database maintains for our session: the total bytes read from storage, and the total returned to the database servers via smart scan:

```
col name format a60
select name,value/1000000 from v$mystat m, v$statname n
where m.statistic#=n.statistic#
and (name like 'cell physical%predicate offload'
or name like 'cell physical%smart scan');
NAME                                                         VALUE/1000000
------------------------------------------------------------ -------------
cell physical IO bytes eligible for predicate offload          8192.37683
cell physical IO interconnect bytes returned by smart scan      129.783976
```

This table has three columns: NUM, which is a simple number a few bytes in size, and two filler columns resulting in rows nearly 7 kilobytes in size. The 7KB row size ensures that each 8KB data block (using the default size) holds a single row. To count the rows, we only need the first column, and Exadata's column filters indeed return us the first row only. It means that of 8192 million bytes of data, the database servers had to process only 129 million, a 98.5 percent reduction.

To look at predicate filtering, we'll build on the last example. But instead of counting *all* the rows in the table, we're going to count only those rows with a row number ending in the digit 8. This can be accomplished by using the SQL modulus operator.

Reconnect to SQL*Plus to reset the V$MYSTAT counters:

```
connect
alter session set parallel_degree_policy='MANUAL';
```

Confirm that the MOD() function is offloadable:

```
select distinct offloadable from v$sqlfn_metadata where name = 'MOD';
```

We now run the same COUNT(*) query as before, but add a SQL WHERE clause with the MOD() function:

```
select count(*) from big_table where mod(num,10) = 8;
```

The count should return 100000, as we're selecting 10 percent of the table:

```
select name,value/1000000 from v$mystat m, v$statname n
where m.statistic#=n.statistic#
and (name like 'cell physical%predicate offload'
or name like 'cell physical%smart scan');
NAME                                                        VALUE/1000000
----------------------------------------------------------- -------------
cell physical IO bytes eligible for predicate offload          8192.37683
cell physical IO interconnect bytes returned by smart scan       14.425384
```

So instead of returning 129MB of data from the storage servers to database servers, transfer volume has dropped to 14MB through row predicate filtering.

Why Smart Scans May Not Happen

A commonly asked question is: "Why doesn't my query use smart scan?" Under the hood, the Oracle software makes a number of checks designed to make sure that the smart scans can return correct results and give a performance advantage. Common reasons why storage operations aren't offloaded include the following:

- The operation wasn't a full table scan or an index fast full scan.
- The table is too small to offload efficiently.
- There are no WHERE clause predicates to filter on.
- Lack of a parallel query prevents direct path reads from happening.
- Consistent read is required due to in-flight object modifications.
- Operations on LOB or hash cluster objects.

CRITICAL SKILL 9.6

Understand Storage Indexes

Storage indexes build on the smart scan functionality by dividing the physical table data into storage regions and tracking the highest and lowest values for each storage region. When a SELECT query is run on the table, the smart scan code can compare the saved high and low values with the where clause from the SQL, and if the WHERE clause excludes all the rows of the storage region, it can avoid reading the rows entirely.

Unlike row and column projections, storage indexes have an additional advantage in that they actually avoid disk I/O entirely, as opposed to simply reducing data transfers to database servers.

Because storage indexes are based on physical regions on disk, they depend on the on-disk data having some sort of physical order. Fortunately, many real-world data sets have this ordering naturally, especially based on the timestamp of the data load. Table 9-1 shows an example of how storage indexes might be laid out for BIG_TABLE if each storage region contained 100 rows.

Num	Filler	Storage index for Num
1	7000 spaces	min = 1 max = 99
2	7000 spaces	
...	...	
100	7000 spaces	
101	7000 spaces	min = 101 max = 200
102	7000 spaces	
...	...	
200	7000 spaces	
901	7000 spaces	min = 901 max = 1000
902	7000 spaces	
...	...	
1000	7000 spaces	

TABLE 9-1. *A Potential Storage Index Layout for big_table*

Storage Indexes in Action

Again here we build on the previous example, but we look only at values of NUM over 900,000. Because all the rows with these row numbers are physically located at the end of the table, we can use storage indexes to help us. There's no special action required to create storage indexes. They were already created when we selected the first count from BIG_TABLE.

```
connect
alter session set parallel_degree_policy='MANUAL';
select count(*) from big_table where mod(num,10) = 8 and num >
900*1000;
```

The count should return 10000 because we're selecting 10 percent of the last 100,000 rows of the table:

```
select name,value/1000000 from v$mystat m, v$statname n
where m.statistic#=n.statistic#
and (name like 'cell physical%predicate offload'
or name like 'cell physical%smart scan');
NAME                                                            VALUE/1000000
--------------------------------------------------------------- -------------
cell physical IO bytes eligible for predicate offload             8192.37683
cell physical IO interconnect bytes returned by smart scan             2.745
```

The data volume returned to storage servers has dropped again, from 14MB to 2.5MB.

CRITICAL SKILL 9.7

Use the Exadata Flash Cache

The Exadata flash cache makes use of flash memory to speed up access to commonly used data. Flash-based solid-state storage has latency times and I/O operation rates much higher than rotating storage, improving performance particularly in transaction-processing applications. The flash cache is stored on flash-memory cards on storage servers. The storage server software manages the flash cache and can recognize different types of I/O requests so that non-repeatable data access like RMAN backup I/O does not flush database blocks from the cache. It also prioritizes frequently accessed block types such as redo logs, control files, and index root blocks.

Note that the Exadata flash cache works completely differently from the similarly named database smart flash cache.

Database administrators can control which objects are cached by using the CELL_FLASH_CACHE property of database objects. Available values are

- **none**   Exclude the object from the flash cache entirely.

- **default**   Give the object a normal priority for caching.

- **keep**   Give the object a higher priority for caching. Note that setting CELL_FLASH_CACHE KEEP for an object does not guarantee that it will be cached, just that it is given a higher priority

Trying Out the Flash Cache

When we created BIG_TABLE, we intentionally set CELL_FLASH_CACHE to none to prevent the flash cache from being used. Now we'll turn it on and see the difference.

First we reconnect to the database server:

```
connect
alter session set parallel_degree_policy='manual';
```

Make the table eligible for caching and count the rows:

```
alter table big_table storage (cell_flash_cache keep);
select count(*) from big_table;
```

Because flash cache statistics are counted by read request rather than bytes retrieved, we will use request-level statistics:

```
select name,value from v$mystat m, v$statname n
where m.statistic#=n.statistic#
and (name like 'physical read IO requests'
or name like 'cell flash cache read hits');
NAME                                                            VALUE
-------------------------------------------------------------- ----------
physical read IO requests                                        8024
cell flash cache read hits                                       8024
```

As the table isn't yet cached, none of the reads came from the cache. But now that we read the table from disk, it will be in cache for the next run. We will reconnect and re-run the query after the change:

```
connect
alter session set parallel_degree_policy='manual';
select count(*) from big_table;
select name,value from v$mystat m, v$statname n
where m.statistic#=n.statistic#
and (name like 'physical read IO requests'
Lor name like 'cell flash cache read hits');
NAME                                                           VALUE
-------------------------------------------------------- ----------
physical read IO requests                                       8024
cell flash cache read hits                                      8024
```

The entire table read came off flash, and we didn't need to access the hard drives at all. Note that the flash cache is considered a physical device, so statistics such as physical read IO requests include requests fulfilled by the flash cache.

And depending on the state of the cache, you may notice that less than 100 percent of the table was cached.

Save Storage Space with Hybrid Columnar Compression

Hybrid columnar compression (HCC) changes the way row data is stored to obtain dramatically better compression ratios, often 10x or more. Rather than storing a series of rows inside a data block, HCC operates on an aggregate group of data blocks called a *compression unit*. Within the compression unit, HCC-compressed data contains the data for each column. And because most data tables tend to repeat the same column values, HCC saves space by storing each value once. By reducing storage space, HCC also reduces disk I/O requirements and uses less cache memory, too.

Figures 9-4 and 9-5 illustrate the difference between uncompressed and HCC-compressed data blocks.

Although HCC was first introduced in Exadata, it is available on certain other Oracle storage technologies. As of this writing, they include Oracle's family of ZFS storage appliances and Oracle's Pillar Axiom SAN storage.

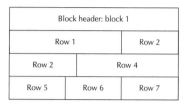

FIGURE 9-4. *Data block without HCC*

HCC has four possible levels: QUERY LOW, QUERY HIGH, ARCHIVE LOW, and ARCHIVE HIGH. These levels provide increased levels of compression, but have an increasingly higher CPU-usage overhead.

Columnar compression has some disadvantages compared to row storage. One disadvantage is CPU usage overhead for compressing and decompressing row data. Another is that DML locks affect entire compression units rather than individual rows. Also, data changes must be done using direct path operations. Examples of direct path operations include

- CREATE TABLE AS SELECT
- INSERT /*+APPEND*/ … SELECT …
- ALTER TABLE MOVE
- SQL*Loader direct path

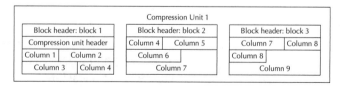

FIGURE 9-5. *Data block with HCC*

This list is relatively short; any operation that sends a single row at a time to the database server cannot be used to generate compression units. That means that data created by any of the following row-by-row operations do *not* utilize HCC compression:

- INSERT without an /*+APPEND*/ hint and SELECT clause
- UPDATE
- DELETE
- SQL*Loader conventional path

What happens when data is loaded by row-by-row operations into an HCC-compressed table? To maintain compatibility with existing applications, HCC transparently reverts to row-based storage. A common mistake is to configure tables with HCC, but not to get HCC compression levels because data was loaded or modified in an incompatible way.

Hybrid Columnar Compression in Action

Remember BIG_TABLE? Let's see how well it compresses. We'll compress it with the query high compression level, which generally provides a good trade-off between compression ratio and performance overhead. We'll use CREATE TABLE AS SELECT, which is compatible with HCC compression.

```
create table big_table_hcc
  compress for query high
  as select * from big_table;
col segment_name format a20
select segment_name, trunc(bytes/1024/1024) as size_in_megs
  from user_segments where segment_name like 'BIG_TABLE%';
SEGMENT_NAME          SIZE_IN_MEGS
-------------------- ------------
BIG_TABLE                    7850
BIG_TABLE_HCC                  13
```

Not bad: From 7.8GB to 13MB, a compression ratio of over 500. Granted, our data is very compressible, as we repeated the same 7000 spaces in each row.

Now let's try clearing out BIG_TABLE_HCC with a truncate statement and loading it using an insert statement without an /*+APPEND*/ hint, which results in a row-by-row insert that's not compatible with HCC storage:

```
truncate table big_table_hcc;
insert into big_table_hcc
  select * from big_table;
```

```
commit;
select segment_name, trunc(bytes/1024/1024) as size_in_megs
  from user_segments where segment_name like 'BIG_TABLE%';
SEGMENT_NAME            SIZE_IN_MEGS
-------------------     ------------
BIG_TABLE                       7850
BIG_TABLE_HCC                   7887
```

You will probably notice that while this command completed successfully, it took quite a bit longer than the CREATE TABLE AS SELECT command. And if you look at the resulting object, it's even larger than the original, uncompressed table.

Using DBMS_COMPRESSION to Estimate Compression

DBMS_COMPRESSION is a PL/SQL package supplied with the Oracle database, and can be used to estimate compression levels without actually compressing an object. It also allows compression ratios from HCC compression to be estimated on any Oracle database, even those that would not normally support HCC.

To avoid needing another 8+ gigabytes of temporary storage for DBMS_COMPRESSION to run, we'll create a smaller dataset. HCC_TEST has one million rows like BIG_TABLE, but instead of 7000 spaces, it uses the actual PL/SQL source code from the DBA_SOURCE data dictionary view.

```
create table hcc_test
  as select rownum as num, s1.text as filler
  from dba_source s1, dba_source s2
  where rownum <= 1*1000*1000;
```

We'll then call the DBMS_COMPRESSION PL/SQL package. It has many arguments that require a long piece of PL/SQL to call.

```
set serveroutput on
declare
  v_blkcnt_cmp pls_integer;
  v_blkcnt_uncmp pls_integer;
  v_row_cmp pls_integer;
  v_row_uncmp pls_integer;
  v_cmp_ratio number;
  v_comptype_str varchar2(60);
begin
  dbms_compression.get_compression_ratio (
    scratchtbsname => 'USERS',
    ownname => user,
```

```
    objname => 'HCC_TEST',
    subobjname => null,
    comptype => dbms_compression.comp_for_query_high,
    blkcnt_cmp => v_blkcnt_cmp,
    blkcnt_uncmp => v_blkcnt_uncmp,
    row_cmp => v_row_cmp,
    row_uncmp => v_row_uncmp,
    cmp_ratio => v_cmp_ratio,
    comptype_str => v_comptype_str);
 dbms_output.put_line('Compression type: ' || v_comptype_str);
 dbms_output.put_line('Estimated compression ratio: ' || v_cmp_ratio);
 dbms_output.put_line('Blocks before compression: ' || v_blkcnt_uncmp);
 dbms_output.put_line('Blocks after compression: ' || v_blkcnt_cmp);
end;
/
Compression Advisor self-check validation successful. select count(*)
on both
Uncompressed and EHCC Compressed format = 1000000 rows
Compression type: "Compress For Query High"
Estimated compression ratio: 267.6
Blocks before compression: 8564
Blocks after compression: 32
```

While not quite as good as BIG_TABLE_HCC in the previous section, this table compresses pretty well, too, at an estimated compression ratio of 267.9. Most data sets aren't quite this repetitive, however; try it out on your own tables to see how much storage you can save.

CRITICAL SKILL 9.9

Enable Database Consolidation with I/O Resource Management

In addition to being designed for high performance, Exadata has been designed with database consolidation in mind. In particular, Exadata's I/O Resource Management (IORM) capability allows I/O requests to be prioritized in a similar way to the database resource manager (DBRM). See Chapter 5 for more about the DBRM. These priorities can be applied to individual resource consumer groups, but also to entire pluggable or standalone databases. IORM can be configured using Oracle Enterprise Manager or via the command line. IORM can be activated through a single command using DCLI and CELLCLI:

```
dcli -g cell_group cellcli -e 'alter iormplan active;'
```

Once IORM is enabled, existing database CPU-usage priorities from DBRM plans will automatically apply to I/O capacity, too. IORM plans can also support multiple databases; the next project will show you how to set one up.

Project 9-1 Create an Interdatabase IORM Plan

IORM plans aren't limited to a single database like DBRM. They can also be used to prioritize critical databases in a multidatabase environment, which is particularly useful when consolidating multiple databases onto an Exadata environment. Table 9-2 shows our desired resource plan: We'll guarantee 75 percent of I/O bandwidth to the DBM database and give it exclusive use of the flash cache.

Step by Step

1. Create a script file containing CELLCLI commands to run on each storage server. These commands will create an interdatabase resource plan with two levels: 75 percent priority allocation to database DBM, and allowing other databases to use what's left over. Then we enable I/O resource management.

```
cat > iormplan.scl <<-EOF
alter iormplan dbplan=((name=dbm, level=1, allocation=75,
flashCache=on), -
(name=other,level=2,allocation=100, flashCache=off))
alter iormplan active
EOF
```

2. Use DCLI's -f option to transfer this script to each storage server:

```
dcli -g cell_group -l celladmin -f iormplan.scl
```

	DBM	Others
I/O priority level 1	75	
I/O priority level 2		100
Flash cache enabled	Yes	No

TABLE 9-2. *Sample I/O Resource Management Plan*

(continued)

3. Using DCLI, run the script with CELLCLI on each storage server:

```
dcli -g cell_group -l celladmin "cellcli < iormplan.scl"
```

DCLI will output the result of the script on each storage server, prepended with the name of the storage server the output came from. We'll talk more about DCLI on the next page. If IORM was already enabled when you ran the script, you will see a warning that it's already on.

Project Summary

This project has taken you through the steps of defining an IORM plan script, transferring it to each storage server, and actually running it. You've learned how to use scripts to automate the process of running the commands and how to use DCLI to run it on all storage servers at once.

CRITICAL SKILL 9.10

Perform Common Exadata Management Tasks

Exadata databases are managed very much like any other Oracle database. That being said, administrative tasks specific to storage servers have their own management tools: the command-line CELLCLI, and the Exadata plugin for Oracle Enterprise Manager.

User Accounts on Exadata Storage Servers

Exadata storage servers have a fixed set of operating system accounts for user logins. They are

- **celladmin** User for routine management tasks
- **cellmonitor** User for read-only monitoring like Oracle Enterprise Manager's monitoring agent DCLI
- **root** The super-user, able to perform privileged tasks on the system like startup and shutdown

Using DCLI to Retrieve Metrics from the Storage Server

Because storage servers don't communicate with each other directly, configuration changes must be made to each server. Oracle supplies a tool, DCLI, to run a command on all servers at once.

Log into the first database server as oracle, and look for the group files in the oracle user's home directory. These are created at installation time and pre-populated with lists of database and storage servers.

```
cd /home/oracle
ls *group
cat cell_group
```

Look up the name of the metric. In this case, we are looking at flash cache bytes used. We use the first storage server name returned by the previous command.

```
dcli -c exa1cel01 -l celladmin "cellcli -e list metricdefinition
fc_by_used detail"
exa1cel01: name:              FC_BY_USED
exa1cel01: description:       "Number of megabytes used on
FlashCache"
exa1cel01: metricType:        Instantaneous
exa1cel01: objectType:        FLASHCACHE
exa1cel01: unit:              MB
```

Using the identified group file, we run DCLI with a command. In this case, we retrieve metric values from each storage server.

```
dcli -g cell_group -l celladmin "cellcli -e list metriccurrent
fc_by_used"
exa1cel01: FC_BY_USED    FLASHCACHE    105,864 MB
exa1cel02: FC_BY_USED    FLASHCACHE    105,916 MB
exa1cel03: FC_BY_USED    FLASHCACHE    106,296 MB
exa1cel04: FC_BY_USED    FLASHCACHE    105,906 MB
exa1cel05: FC_BY_USED    FLASHCACHE    106,014 MB
exa1cel06: FC_BY_USED    FLASHCACHE    106,045 MB
exa1cel07: FC_BY_USED    FLASHCACHE    106,202 MB
```

Flash cache is quite well balanced, with a bit over 100GB used on each storage server.

Using EXACHK to Validate Exadata Configurations

Because Exadata database machines have a limited number of configurations, it's possible to automatically identify configurations that do not match Oracle's recommendations. Oracle supplies a tool called EXACHK that validates the current configuration and presents a report with a compliance score and recommendations for configuration changes.

EXACHK is available from the *My Oracle Support* web site using document ID 1070954.1 *Oracle Exadata Database Machine exachk or HealthCheck*. To run a full set of checks, passwords for the root user on database and storage servers are required, although a more limited set of checks can be run from the oracle user. To run exachk

- Download the latest version to your local machine. Note that EXACHK is updated frequently, and it's important to run the latest version.

- Extract the .zip file.

- Read the instructions in the .zip file, as they can change between versions.

- Identify the hostname of an Exadata database server.

- Install a secure copy client on your local machine if you don't have one already; common tools include command-line PSCP from the PuTTY program or graphical WinSCP. Use this tool to transfer EXACHK.ZIP to the database server you identified.

```
scp exachk.zip oracle10.10.0.40:
oracle10.10.0.40's password:
exachk.zip                | 1827 kB | 152.3 kB/s | ETA: 00:00:00
| 100%
```

- Connect to the same Exadata database server hostname using SSH, and create a directory for EXACHK:

```
ssh oracleexa1db01
mkdir -p exachk
cd exachk
```

- Unpack the archive, and run EXACHK itself:

```
unzip ../exachk.zip
./exachk
```

- Select the databases to run the check on, and enter passwords when prompted.

- Once complete, EXACHK will list the location of a detailed HTML report file.

- Use SCP or a similar file transfer tool to send this .html file to your local machine, and view it in a web browser.

CRITICAL SKILL 9.11

Manage Exadata with Oracle Enterprise Manager

Oracle Enterprise Manager Cloud Control has an Exadata plugin that allows the state of the various Exadata components to be examined. These components include storage servers, InfiniBand switches, the management switch, and power distribution units.

All Exadata systems can be viewed by selecting Targets on the top menu bar, and then Exadata. Then click on the database machine you would like to administer. A DB Machine screen comes up, showing a schematic of the Exadata database machine's rack configuration, as shown in Figure 9-6.

On the Target Navigation pane on the left side of the screen, the various Exadata components are listed: database servers, ILOM management cards in the database servers, the Cisco management switch, storage servers (labeled "Exadata Grid"), and the InfiniBand network.

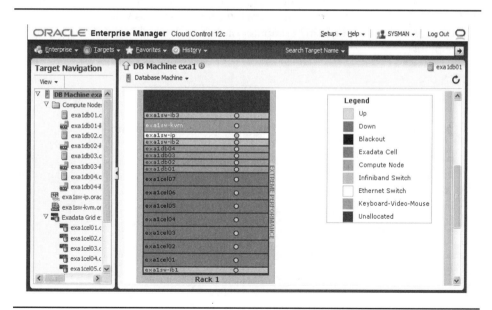

FIGURE 9-6.   *The Exadata Database Machine screen in Oracle Enterprise Manager Cloud Control*

Wrapping Up

You've now learned about two of Oracle's engineered systems: the Oracle Database Appliance and Oracle Exadata. These machines have been designed and engineered to make the implementation and deployment easier, and they can be an important part of your overall Oracle database solution. Each machine has a place in your Oracle infrastructure and can help you achieve performance that far exceeds that of your standard Oracle database deployment. You've seen a brief overview of the Oracle Database Appliance and its simplified configuration capabilities, which allow you to rapidly deploy a fully working clustered database, whereas Exadata provides you with the capability to manage large volumes of data very effectively while still benefiting from Oracle's own engineering. Exadata's main components have been explained, and you've learned how to use Exadata features such as smart scans, the flash cache, hybrid columnar compression, and I/O resource management. This, together with your newfound skills in the Oracle database and the functionality contained within it, can help you meet needs you may encounter in today's growing world of data.

The ability to install, manage, and optimize is one that will serve you well in today's world where data is thought of as an asset. These assets must be protected and effectively utilized. By using your newfound skills, you now have a database that you can learn on your home computer or deploy for the biggest data consumers on the planet.

☑ Chapter 9 Mastery Check

1. Which is not a component of an Exadata database machine?

   A. Storage server

   B. Database server

   C. Network server

   D. InfiniBand switch

2. What is a smart scan?

3. Which tool performs tasks on multiple servers at once?

   A. CELLCLI

   B. OAKCLI

   C. DCLI

   D. SSH

4. Which is not a user on an Exadata storage server?

   A. oracle

   B. celladmin

   C. cellmonitor

   D. root

5. What is hot/cold storage placement? Give an example of where it might be used.

6. What type of object does an ASM disk correspond to on an Exadata storage server?

7. What tool would you use to guarantee disk bandwidth for a critical application?

8. Where can one find the EXACHK software?

9. Which Exadata feature is most beneficial for latency-intensive transaction-processing applications?

   A. Storage index

   B. Predicate filtering

   C. Hybrid columnar compression

   D. Flash cache

10. Which operation will give a lower compression ratio with hybrid columnar compression?

    A. CREATE TABLE AS SELECT

    B. INSERT /*+APPEND */ ... SELECT ...

    C. SQL*Loader conventional path

    D. ALTER TABLE MOVE

11. What's an ILOM controller and when is it useful?

12. How do you prevent a table from being cached in the flash cache?

13. How can you check if smart scans are happening?

14. Which operation is automatically deprioritized from flash caching?

   A. Controlfile I/O

   B. ALTER TABLE MOVE

   C. Tables with hybrid columnar compression

   D. RMAN backup I/O

15. What CELLCLI command would you use to find the LUNs associated with cell disk CD_11_exa1cel01?

16. Which level of hybrid columnar compression would you use for data that is almost never accessed?

APPENDIX

Mastery Check Answers

Chapter 1: The Database: The Foundations of 12*c*

1. **How many megabytes are there in a gigabyte?**

   1024 megabytes

2. **Why are storage factors in the computer industry expressed as a factor of 2 and not the more common 10?**

   Computers all run on the binary numbering system with a base of 2; thus, everything is expressed in units of storage that are powers of 2.

3. **Which comes first—the table or the view?**

   A table is defined, and then a subset of its columns can be logically associated with a view; thus, the table comes first.

4. **What is the three-fold challenge presented to modern database management technologies?**

   The challenge is a combination of getting the data into the database efficiently, allowing for quick discovery of that data as required, and getting the data out of the database for application interaction in a timely fashion.

5. **If two users are looking at the same data and one session starts modifying the data, when does the other session see the changes, if ever?**

   The other session sees the changed data if the session that performed an edit saves its work. If the changed data is not saved, the second session continues to see the original state of the data.

6. **What is the maximum number of characters that can be stored in a varchar2 field in the database?**

   32,000 bytes

7. **What form of structured data is most common in full motion video—semi-structured or unstructured? Why?**

   Video is unstructured data because the representation of the information has no pre-defined format and similar pieces of the same video clip can be represented internally in different ways.

8. **What is a data anomaly? Give an example to illustrate your definition.**

   If a personnel record holds the state code KP, which doesn't actually exist as a state code, that is referred to as a data anomaly.

9. **What is the biggest number that can be stored in a field defined as *number (6,3)*?**

   999.999

10. **Can a view contain 13 columns when the table it is built on contains 23?**

    Yes, that is the power of a view—it can contain a subset of the table columns upon which it is built.

11. **Can a PDB be plugged into more than one CDB?**

    A PDB can be plugged into only one CDB at a time.

Chapter 2: Installing Oracle

1. **How much disk space is needed for installing Oracle software on Linux?**

   The software requires between 3.5 and 5GB just for the binaries. You also need to add space for your data needs.

2. **What users and groups are used for installing the Oracle software?**

   The user that is needed is the oracle user. The groups that are needed include oinstall and dba.

3. **True or false: Installing Oracle software will automatically install an Oracle database.**

   False. This is an option, but it is not automatic.

4. **What are the prerequisites for installing Oracle software?**

   You need to review OS requirements, hardware requirements (1GB RAM), disk space, kernel parameters, and needed OS packages before installing the Oracle software and database.

5. **What is the Oracle home directory? Can there be more than one?**

   The Oracle home directory is where the Oracle software is installed. Yes, there can be a different Oracle Home for each version of the Oracle software or different options that are installed in each Oracle Home.

6. **Besides the database, what are some of the other products that are installed by default?**

   SQL Developer, Database Vault, Configuration Manager, Application Express, and Warehouse Builder are installed during the standard installation of the Oracle database.

7. **What is a container database?**

   A container database is a physical database that has one or more pluggable databases. It has one root container that has the metadata to manage the pluggable databases.

8. **What is the tool for creating a database after the Oracle software install?**

   The tool that is provided to create a database is named the database configuration assistant (DBCA).

9. **What tool can be used for managing pluggable databases?**

   The database configuration assistant (DBCA) is used to create pluggable databases, and SQL Developer can be used to manage pluggable databases.

10. **Which scripts need to be run by root (system administrator) after the install of the software?**

    The scripts that need to be run after installing the Oracle software on Linux or Unix are root.sh and orainstRoot.sh.

Chapter 3: SQL: Accessing and Retrieving Data

1. **DDL and DML translate to _____ and _____, respectively.**

   DDL and DML translate to <u>Data Definition Language</u> and <u>Data Manipulation Language</u>, respectively.

2. **Which of the following descriptions is true about insert statements?**

   A. Insert statements must always have a WHERE clause.

   B. Insert statements can never have a WHERE clause.

   C. Insert statements can optionally include a WHERE clause.

   B. Insert statements can never have a WHERE clause. Every insert will create a row, providing it doesn't violate any constraints.

3. **In addition to the two mandatory keywords required to retrieve data from the database, there are three optional keywords. Name them.**

The optional parts of a select statement are the where clause, the order by clause, and the group by clause.

4. **Write a SQL statement to select the customer last name, city, state, and amount sold for the customer represented by customer ID 100895.**

Possible solutions include any of the Oracle and ANSI join options. The following SQL statement joins the CUSTOMERS and SALES tables using a simple Oracle join:

```
SQL> select cust_last_name, cust_city, cust_state_province,
2   amount_sold
3   from   customers c, sales s
4   where c.cust_id = s.cust_id
5   and c.cust_id = 100895;
```

5. **Retrieve a list of all product categories, subcategories, names, and list prices where the list price is greater than $100 while displaying the results for the product category all in uppercase.**

The following statement returns a list of all product categories, subcategories, and names for products with list prices greater than $100. The product categories are also all output in uppercase.

```
SQL> select UPPER(prod_category),
2   prod_subcategory,
3   prod_name,
4   prod_list_price
5   from products
6   where prod_list_price > 100;
```

6. **Rewrite the query from the previous question and round the amount sold so that there are no cents in the display of the list prices.**

The following SQL statement alters the previous answer to return the list price without cents:

```
SQL> select UPPER(prod_category),
2   prod_subcategory,
3   prod_name,
4   round(prod_list_price,0)
5   from products
6   where prod_list_price > 100;
```

7. **Retrieve a list of all customer IDs and last names where the customer has more than 200 entries in the SALES table in SH schema.**

   The list of all customer IDs and last names for customers that had more than 200 sales is returned by the following SQL statement:

   ```
   SQL> select c.cust_id, cust_last_name, count(*)
   2   from customers c, sales s
   3   where c.cust_id = s.cust_id
   4   group by c.cust_id, cust_last_name
   5   having count(*) > 200;
   ```

8. **Display the product name of all products that have the lowest list price.**

   To display all the product names that have the lowest list price, you would use the following SQL statement:

   ```
   SQL> select prod_name
   2   from products
   3   where prod_list_price = (select min(prod_list_price)
   4                                      from products);
   ```

9. **Create a view that contains all products in the Electronics category.**

   The DDL to create a view with only Electronics products could be created this way:

   ```
   SQL> create view electronics_products
   2   as
   3   select prod_name
   4   from products
   5   where prod_category = 'Electronics';
   ```

10. **Sequences provide _____ generated integers.**

    Sequences provide <u>sequentially</u> generated integers. In previous releases without this valuable object, sequentially generated numbers could only be produced programmatically. In 12c, IDENTITY columns can now be used.

11. **This referential integrity constraint defines the relationship between two tables. Name it.**

    A foreign key is the referential integrity constraint that relates two tables to each other.

12. **Check constraints enable users to define and enforce rules for:**

    A. One or more tables

    B. No more than one column

C. One or more columns

D. Only one table

C. Check constraints enable users to define and enforce rules individually for one or more columns within the table.

13. **Deferred constraints are not checked until the _____ statement is executed.**

    Deferred constraints are not checked until the <u>commit keyword</u> statement is executed.

Chapter 4: Programming in the Database

1. **Where is PL/SQL executed?**

   PL/SQL is executed within the database, just as a SQL statement is.

2. **Which types of PL/SQL statements would you use to increase the price values by 15 percent for items with more than 1500 in stock and by 20 percent for items with fewer than 500 in stock?**

   A. A cursor FOR loop

   B. An IF/THEN/ELSE command

   C. An INSERT statement

   D. An UPDATE statement

   A, B, and D. The FOR loop would be used to loop through all of the items in the database, and then by using the IF/THEN/ELSE command, you can process information based on specific conditions such as the count of items in stock. Finally, you will need to UPDATE the record in the database to increase or decrease the prices.

3. **What is the FETCH command used for?**

   The FETCH command is used to load data into the memory structures from data that has been defined in a cursor definition.

4. **What will the following command do?**

   ```
   V_PRICE_TOLERANCE := 500;
   ```

   This command will set the program variable to an initial value of 500. This is normally done in the DECLARE section of your PL/SQL program.

5. **What is wrong with this function definition?**

```
CREATE OR REPLACE FUNCTION raise_price
(original_price IN NUMBER)
RETURN number
IS
BEGIN
RETURN (original_price * 1.25);
END lower_price;
```

The parameter has been defined only as an IN parameter, but if we want to return the updated value, then we need to change the definition to (original_price IN OUT NUMBER).

6. **What is the advantage of using the %TYPE attribute when defining PL/SQL variables?**

By using the %TYPE attribute, you do not have to be concerned if a column's definition ever changes. By using %TYPE, Oracle will verify that the types are correct. If some change has occurred, then the program will be recompiled using the new field definitions.

7. **What values are returned from the SQLCODE and SQLERRM functions?**

The SQLCODE returns the latest code of the error that has been encountered, while SQLERRM returns the error message associated with the code.

8. **A COMMIT command that is issued in a PL/SQL program will commit what?**

The COMMIT command will result in all of the work and changes to be committed to the database. In a PL/SQL program, this means that everything up to the processing of the COMMIT statement will be committed, not simply the current rows, but all rows.

Chapter 5: The Database Administrator

1. **What is the benefit of a role?**

A role is used to group privileges together so that the group (called a role) can be granted to an Oracle user. Beyond the management savings, think about the savings that are achieved in the catalog. If you give the same 2000 grants to 1000 users, you would have 6,000,000 grants stored in the database. If the grants were put into a single role, however, there would be only 3000 grants. An extreme example perhaps, but it illustrates the point.

2. Should a table that is in tens or hundreds of extents be reorganized?

No. Do not reorganize (reorg) tables unless you need to. The tables' extents are a contiguous set of blocks and if these are large enough, having many extents will not impact performance. You need to reorg a table only when it has a large number of chained rows.

3. What is the preferred method for collecting object statistics?

In Oracle Database 12*c*, use an automatic statistics collection whenever possible. Setting the Oracle Database 12*c* initialization parameter STATISTICS_LEVEL to typical (the default) allows Oracle to automatically update statistics as a background task. In pre–Oracle Database 10*g* releases, the DBMS_STATS package should be run manually.

4. What is a segment?

Each segment is a single instance of a table, partition, cluster, index, temporary segment, or undo segment. A segment is broken down further into extents.

5. What is an extent?

An extent is a collection of contiguous data blocks that all belong to the same segment. One or more extents can exist for a single segment. New extents can be added to the segment as long as space allows.

6. Name two reasons for implementing an index.

Indexes are optional objects built on tables to improve performance and/or to help implement integrity constraints such as primary keys and uniqueness.

7. How can you place a database in maintenance mode without first shutting it down?

SYS and SYSTEM users can query the database without stopping the database and performing a subsequent startup restrict using the command ALTER SESSION QUIESCE RESTRICT when the Database Resource Manager option has been set up. The activities of other users continue until they become inactive.

8. How can you limit the resources that a particular user can consume, and how does this work?

You can use the profile feature to do some of this, but profiles are now being used more to manage password policies than system resources. The preferred approach is to use the DATABASE_RESOURCE_MANAGER package to limit system resources such as CPU, parallelism, undo pool space, execution time limits, and the number of sessions that can be active for a group.

A resource plan schedule can be used to schedule when groups will be enabled and disabled. Group switching can move a user to another group once a specified threshold has been met.

9. **When managing UNDO segments, what are the things that you need to think about?**

You need to first determine the length of time that undo will need to be retained for. Once you have decided this, you'll need to calculate the UNDO tablespace size based on system activity.

10. **What is likely to happen if you turn on the AUTOEXTEND property for UNDO and temporary tablespaces with a MAXSIZE set to UNLIMITED?**

They will continue to grow until they eventually use up all of the space in the directory. It depends on the activity of the database. Making sure these are sized properly can potentially cause an error in a query that needs an unexpected amount of TEMP or UNDO, but will prevent the disk space from being filled up and causing other issues.

11. **What is special about the SYS user account, and how does it differ from SYSTEM?**

The SYS account is used as the schema to store the Oracle catalog. This has the DBA role as well as the SYSDBA privilege. The SYSTEM account also has the DBA role but not the SYSDBA privilege.

12. **What are temporary tablespaces used for?**

Temporary tablespaces store internal data used by Oracle when queries are running. Sort operations make use of the temporary tablespace if there is not enough room in the SGA to perform the sort operation. Data in temporary tablespaces is transient and not persistent. As soon as a transaction has completed, the data in the temporary tablespace can no longer be used. It can be thought of as a scratch pad area for Oracle.

13. **What are the two aspects of security that are covered in Oracle's implementation?**

Two key security aspects that must be implemented are authentication and authorization. Creating a distinct user in Oracle accomplishes authentication in that users must be authenticated when they enter the database and we must know who they are. Once in the database, they still need to be authorized to access objects and resources. This is accomplished by granting privileges to the user.

14. **Name and describe the types of privileges that can be granted to a user.**

Two types of privileges can be given to a user: system and object. System privileges are used to give authority to overall system objects rather than individual ones. The capability to perform a CREATE TABLESPACE is an example of this. Object privileges are a lower-level authority where a named object is granted to a user. Granting select permissions on an individual table is an example of an object privilege.

15. **How would you implement your corporate password policy in Oracle?**

A profile can be used to implement a password management policy as well as to limit resources for a user. You can specify the number of days after which a user must change their password. You can also establish a policy where a password cannot be used again before a specified number of days has elapsed, and/or the new password must differ from the old one by a certain number of changes. A function can also be used to ensure that the user will create a complex password.

Chapter 6: Backup and Recovery

1. **What are the three tasks performed by RMAN?**

Backup, restore, and recovery.

2. **What format command does one use to ensure all the backupset pieces receive a unique name?**

One includes the %U format mask in a persistent or one-time configuration to ensure backupset pieces receive unique names.

3. **Where does RMAN always store its metadata?**

In the database control file.

4. **What is the difference between expired and obsolete backups?**

An expired backupset piece is one that can no longer be retrieved from storage media, as it has been deleted. An obsolete backupset piece is one that is no longer required for recovery based on the retention period defined for the database backups.

5. **Why is it a good idea to use scripts when continually using RMAN over a wide assortment of corporate databases?**

   Scripting provides consistency between environments and reduces the possibility of "surprises" during recovery. Scripting allows unified enforcement of corporate standards.

6. **What are the two main advantages of using a recovery catalog with RMAN?**

   The recovery catalog database is a second copy of the backup metadata and can also be used for query purposes, as the metadata stored in the catalog is sitting in standard database tables.

7. **What is the difference between a recovery window and redundancy?**

   A recovery window is a number of days after which a backupset is declared obsolete. Redundancy refers to the number of distinct backupsets retained for potential recovery requirements.

8. **What is the RMAN error message number common to all error situations?**

   RMAN-00569

9. **When invoking RMAN from the command line, what convention is used to connect to the database to be backed up?**

   The database being backed up is referred to as the *target* database when rman is invoked.

10. **What is the difference between restore and recovery?**

    Restore is the act of copying backupset pieces from storage media into their locations in the database directory hierarchy. Recovery is bringing restored database files to a point in time later than when they may have been successfully backed up.

Chapter 7: High Availability: RAC, ASM, and Data Guard

1. **Which component is not part of an RAC environment?**

   A. Interconnect

   B. Clusterware

    C. DGMGRL

    D. OCR

    C. DGMGRL is the command for accessing the Data Guard Broker.

2. **True or false: The Cluster Verification Utility is run after the RAC database is created to verify that the interconnect is running properly.**

    False. The Explanation Cluster Verification Utility is run before the install of the Clusterware. This verifies that the environment is configured to have Clusterware installed.

3. **In an RAC environment, OCR stands for**

    A. Oracle Cluster Registry

    B. Oracle Connection Repository

    C. Oracle Clusterware Record

    D. Oracle Cluster Recovery

    A. Oracle Cluster Registry

4. **When using ASM, does the database server need an ASM instance, too?**

    No, the ASM instance is not required to be on the same server as the database server. It can be created in an ASM cluster.

5. **What is the command-line interface that can be used to copy, back up, and list the files in ASM directories?**

    ASMCMD

6. **True or false: ASM redundancy types are EXTERNAL, HIGH, and LOW.**

    False. The ASM redundancy types are EXTERNAL, HIGH, and NORMAL.

7. **When SHUTDOWN ABORT is used to shut down the ASM instance, what happens to the database instances connecting to that ASM instance? What happens when the ASM instance is in an ASM cluster?**

    If they are on the same server supporting the database, they will also SHUTDOWN ABORT. If the ASM instance is in an ASM cluster, that node will just failover to another node and ASM and the database should continue to be available.

8. **What is the administrator's login role on the ASM instance? What is the administrator's login role for Data Guard?**

   SYSASM is the administrator's login role for the ASM instance; SYSDG is the administrator's login role for Data Guard.

9. **What does the following sqlplus command do? Does it run against the primary or standby server?**

   ```
       SQLPLUS> alter database recover managed standby database
   using current
       logfile disconnect;
   ```

   The command is run on the standby database and starts the log apply services, which in this case is real-time apply.

10. **True or false: Asynchronous transport of redo logs means that the redo is being written to the primary and standby locations at the same time.**

    False. That is true for synchronous transport.

11. **Which of the following is not a characteristic of the Data Guard Protection mode of maximum protection?**

    A. Synchronous transport

    B. Zero data loss

    C. Standby fails, primary is halted

    D. Performance is the biggest concern

    D. The biggest concern is the data and changes.

12. **Which tools can be used to manage the Data Guard environment?**

    OEM Grid Control or DGMGRL (Data Guard Broker).

Chapter 8: Using and Managing Large Databases

1. **What data population methods can be used on a compressed table that result in the data being compressed?**

   For data to be compressed, you must either bulk load it into the table or issue an alter table statement to compress existing data.

2. **What are the three basic types of partitioning?**

   RANGE, HASH, and LIST.

3. _____ **partitioned indexes are defined independently of the data partitions, and** _____ **partitioned indexes have a one-to-one relationship with the data partitions.**

   <u>Global</u> partitioned indexes are defined independently of data partitions, and <u>local</u> partitioned indexes have a one-to-one relationship with the data partitions.

4. **Explain the functions of the parallel execution coordinator in parallel processing.**

   The parallel execution coordinator is responsible for breaking down a request into as many processes as specified by the request. After the processes are complete, it then assembles all of the results and presents the complete data set to the requester.

5. **For which of the following SQL commands is parallel processing *not* enabled by default?**

   A. SELECT

   B. INSERT

   C. CREATE

   D. ALTER

   B. Parallel processing is not enabled by default for INSERT.

6. **What is meant by "degree of parallelism"?**

   "Degree of parallelism" refers to the number of processes that are to be used to execute a parallel process.

7. **What analytic feature can be used to forecast values based on existing measures?**

   The SQL model clause in a select statement can be used to forecast values based on existing measures.

8. **What two methods can be used to run the SQLTuning Advisor utilities for materialized views?**

   OEM or dbms_advisor package can be used to run the SQLTuning Advisor utilities for materialized views.

9. _____ partitioning allows you to control the placement of records in specified partitions based on sets of partition key values.

List partitioning allows you to control the placement of records in specified partitions based on sets of partition key values.

10. **What analytic function would you use to assign each row from a query to one of five buckets?**

ntile is used to assign each row from a query to one of five buckets.

11. **What are the two types of windows that can be used in analytic functions?**

Physical and logical windows are the two types of windows that can be used in analytic functions.

12. **The _____ automatically collects workload and performance statistics used for database self-management activities.**

The Automatic Workload Repository automatically collects workload and performance statistics used for database self-management activities.

13. **When creating partitioned tables, what option should you use to ensure that rows are redistributed to their correct partition if their partition key is updated?**

Use enable row movement in the create table or alter table statements to ensure that rows are redistributed to their correct partition if their partition key is updated.

14. **List the ways in which parallel processing can be invoked.**

Parallel processing can be invoked based on the parallelism specified for the table or object at the time of its creation, or by providing the parallel hint in a select query.

Chapter 9: Oracle's Engineered Systems: From the Database Appliance to Exadata

1. **Which is not a component of an Exadata database machine?**

    A. Storage server

    B. Database server

C. Network server

D. InfiniBand switch

C. Exadata systems consist of database servers, storage servers, InfiniBand networking, and management components.

2. **What is a smart scan?**

A smart scan can offload processing that database servers would normally do to storage servers, improving the performance of the overall system.

3. **Which tool performs tasks on multiple servers at once?**

A. CELLCLI

B. OAKCLI

C. DCLI

D. SSH

C. DCLI allows simultaneous execution of a command on multiple machines, such as Exadata storage servers.

4. **Which is not a user on an Exadata storage server?**

A. oracle

B. celladmin

C. cellmonitor

D. root

A. Exadata storage servers have a fixed set of user accounts, including root, celladmin, and cellmonitor. The oracle user exists only on database servers.

5. **What is hot/cold storage placement? Give an example of where it might be used.**

Hot/cold storage placement allows performance-intensive data to be placed on the faster outer tracks of a disk. This type of layout is often used to place database files on "hot" storage and the fast recovery area on "cold" storage.

6. **What type of object does an ASM disk correspond to on an Exadata storage server?**

ASM disks on database servers correspond to griddisks on Exadata storage servers.

7. **What tool would you use to guarantee disk bandwidth for a critical application?**

   Disk I/O prioritization and bandwidth guarantees are done by the I/O Resource Manager (IORM).

8. **Where can one find the EXACHK software?**

   EXACHK software is frequently updated, so it should be downloaded from My Oracle Support, where the most recent version is always identified.

9. **Which Exadata feature is most beneficial for latency-intensive transaction-processing applications?**

   A. Storage index

   B. Predicate filtering

   C. Hybrid columnar compression

   D. Flash cache

   D. Unlike other Exadata features, the Exadata flash cache is particularly beneficial for transaction-processing applications.

10. **Which operation will give a lower compression ratio with hybrid columnar compression?**

    A. CREATE TABLE AS SELECT

    B. INSERT /*+APPEND */ ... SELECT ...

    C. SQL*Loader conventional path

    D. ALTER TABLE MOVE

    C. As a non-direct-path operation, conventional path loads will not achieve the same levels of compression as direct path operations.

11. **What's an ILOM controller and when is it useful?**

    The ILOM, or Integrated Lights-out Management controller, allows database and storage servers to be reached even when powered off, hung, or otherwise inaccessible.

12. **How do you prevent a table from being cached in the flash cache?**

    The CELL_FLASH_CACHE NONE attribute prevents an object from being cached in the Exadata flash cache.

13. How can you check if smart scans are happening?

Smart scans can be monitored by looking at session statistics, examining a session's wait events, or looking at storage server metrics.

14. Which operation is automatically deprioritized from flash caching?

 A. Controlfile I/O

 B. ALTER TABLE MOVE

 C. Tables with hybrid columnar compression

 D. RMAN backup I/O

D. Because RMAN backup traffic is less likely to be re-read from the cache than other database operations, it is automatically deprioritized by the flash cache algorithm.

15. What CELLCLI command would you use to find the LUNs associated with cell disk CD_11_exa1cel01?

The command LIST LUN WHERE CELLDISK="CD_11_EXA1CEL01" will list LUNs associated with CELLDISK CD_11_EXA1CEL01.

16. Which level of hybrid columnar compression would you use for data that is almost never accessed?

The ARCHIVE HIGH compression level provides the highest level of compression (and highest processing overhead). It's designed for data that's accessed very infrequently.

Index

D

Can I copy Java
code to an HTML
extension?

I want to improve
the performance of
my application...

Is the app
customizable?

I coded it
this way...

Here's where you
can find the
latest release.

How does
restricted task
reassignment
work?

Just watch the
live webcast on
virtualization.

The best way to migrate
Oracle E-Business
Application Suite Tier
servers to Linux is...

Where can I find
technical articles on
logging in Java ME?

Oracle Technology Network. It's code for sharing expertise.

Come to the best place to collaborate with other IT professionals.

Oracle Technology Network is the world's largest community of developers, administrators, and architects using industry-standard technologies with Oracle products.

Sign up for a free membership and you'll have access to:

- Discussion forums and hands-on labs
- Free downloadable software and sample code
- Product documentation
- Member-contributed content

Take advantage of our global network of knowledge.

JOIN TODAY ▷ Go to: oracle.com/technetwork